C0-AUJ-385

THE BANKRUPTCY AND WORKOUT MARKET DIRECTORY AND SOURCE BOOK

A. David Silver

HarperBusiness
A Division of HarperCollins*Publishers*

Acknowledgments

"ME AND BOBBY MCGEE" by Kris Kristofferson and Fred Foster
© 1969 TEMI COMBINE INC.
All Rights Controlled by COMBINE MUSIC CORP. and Administered by
    EMI BLACKWOOD MUSIC INC.
All Rights Reserved. International Copyright Secured. Used by Permission.

Copyright © 1991 by A. David Silver. All rights reserved. No part of this
publication may be reproduced, stored in a retrieval system, or transmitted in
any form or by any means, electronic, mechanical, photocopy, recording, or
otherwise, without the prior written consent of the publisher.

International Standard Book Number: 0-88730-478-8

Library of Congress Catalog Card Number: 90-23960

Printed in the United States of America

Library of Congress Cataloging-in-Publication Data

Silver, A. David (Aaron David), 1941–
    The bankruptcy and workout market directory and source book / A.
David Silver.
        p.   cm.
    Includes bibliographical references.
    ISBN 0-88730-478-8 : $54.95
    1. Bankruptcy—United States.   2. Corporate reorganizations—
United States.   3. Corporate reorganizations—United States—
Directories.   I. Title.
KF1524.S56   1991
346.73′ 078—dc20
[347.30678]
                                                                           90-23960
                                                                           CIP

91 92 93 94 PS/HC 9 8 7 6 5 4 3 2 1

LIBRARY
ALMA COLLEGE
ALMA, MICHIGAN

Sylvia Werner Silver

OTHER BOOKS BY A. DAVID SILVER

Upfront Financing

The Entrepreneurial Life

Successful Entrepreneurship

Who's Who in Venture Capital, 3 eds.

Venture Capital

Entrepreneurial Megabucks

The Silver Prescription

Upfront Financing: Revised

When the Bottom Drops

Your First Book of Wealth

The Inside Raider

The Middle-Market Leveraged Financing
Directory and Source Book

The Middle-Market Business Acquisition
Directory and Source Book

CONTENTS

Preface   vii

CHAPTER 1
Introduction   1

CHAPTER 2
The Emergence of the Workout Consultant   9

CHAPTER 3
The Primary Causes of Business Failures   41

CHAPTER 4
Crisis Management Strategies   55

CHAPTER 5
Workout Consultants' Views of Troubled Companies   87

CHAPTER 6
How to Select a Workout Consultant   99

CHAPTER 7
How the Workout Consultant Operates   111

CHAPTER 8
The Redirect and Grow Plan   125

CHAPTER 9
A Bankruptcy Primer   135

Directory of Workout Consultants   143

Directory of Debtor-Advocate Bankruptcy Lawyers   311

PREFACE

America is learning about troubled companies as a result of Donald Trump's financial difficulties and the bankruptcy filings of Federated Department Stores, Allied Stores, B. Altman, Bonwit Teller, Revco Drugstores, Cuisinarts, Tracor, and others. New words and phrases are entering the business lexicon, including "fraudulent conveyance," "a Bobby McGee condition," "cram down provision," "standstill agreements," "free cash flow," and "vulture capitalists."

But these words and phrases mean practically nothing, except to a few professionals who say to their upset clients, "I'll buy some time for you with a standstill agreement, then I'll help you find some free cash flow. We'll make a fair offer to the creditors but also show them a low ball offer from a vulture capitalist. They should take the first offer because of your Bobby McGee condition. But if not we can file a Chapter 11 and push through a plan similar to our first offer, maybe worse, and, if we need to, use a cram down provision." This sounds like gibberish to you if you have never captained your company through a crisis; but these concepts are very important in the process of working out and rehabilitating a crisis-riven company.

The special words and phrases of entrepreneurship became part of our vocabulary in the 1970s. You remember: "skunk works," "burn rate," "price/revenue multiple," "non-rev IPO," and "AWSSUD," or "another work station start-up deal." Turn the calendar to the 1980s and you'll remember that we learned the special vocabulary of leveraged buyouts: "air ball," "junk bond," "asset-based loans," "mezzanine lender," and "LBO-IPO flip."

Just when we thought new stages in the wealth creation process were pretty well understood, along came the Age of the Workout. Out goes the old curriculum and in comes the new. What may surprise you is that the workout and turnaround of a troubled company is a *process*: one that can be learned, that has stages, that produces winners among the serious students and losers among the poor students.

Another thing that may surprise you is that crises can be *springboards for success*. Wealth is made in hard times and lost at the top of the cycle. As you slim down a broad and unwieldy troubled company, locked up cash can begin to flow, weak employees will leave, and questions you have never dreamed of asking your creditors ("Can we pay you out over time?") and your customers ("We'd like you to pay us in advance of shipment. Is that acceptable to you?") you ask because you must, and you are not surprised when they accept.

I have enjoyed the workout consulting business for many years for the same reasons that I like renovating old houses. There is an inexplicable satisfaction in preserving the given-up-for-dead and an explicable joy in having it appreciate in value. If your company is in trouble, you need this book very badly, as badly as you need a flashlight when your car blows a tire in the middle of the night on a dark stretch of road. It shows you how to steer your company through very troubled times and which professionals to hire as company doctors. As you get into the book I think you will find yourself agreeing that the workout process can be as stimulating and rewarding as the other stages through which you have guided your company.

It takes a pretty smart publishing house to see the need for a book on the workout and rehabilitation process, at an early stage of the phenomenon. Although my publishers are located in a Manhattan office tower, they know surfing talk: you can't catch a wave that has already begun to break. For their perspicacity, those of you who run troubled companies can thank the financiers and editors at HarperCollins who have presented you with this gift of a flashlight: Mark Greenberg, Martha Jewett, Lee Watson, and Barbara Wilkinson. They know what the market needs.

While we're thanking people who want to help you rehabilitate your company, please help me with a round of applause for my literary agent, Jeff Herman, and for my staff, Dorothy E. Moore, Carolyn L. Williams, and Julianne Romero. Also I had to learn the workout craft in order to write about it, and my patient tutors were James C. Jacobsen, Arnold M. Quittner, William Y. Tauscher, Roger E. Main, Stephen R. Davis, and other folks.

For supplemental reading on the subject, which is constantly evolving, you might want to join the Turnaround Management Association based in Durham, North Carolina, in order to read its newsletters and attend its seminars. Two of my earlier books by HarperCollins, *The Middle-Market Leveraged Financing Directory and Source Book* and *The Middle-Market Business Acquisition Directory and Source Book*, are very good sources of financing for troubled companies and for buying companies that can provide free cash flow. Yet another HarperCollins book of mine, *The Inside Raider*, will show you dozens of ways to find cash inside your company, which you will have to generate in order to negotiate an acceptable plan of reorganization.

My wife and children were extraordinarily patient with me in giving birth to *The Bankruptcy and Workout Market Directory and Source Book*, and I am grateful to them for their generosity of spirit.

A. David Silver

CHAPTER 1

Introduction

Man plans. God laughs.

—German proverb

The notion that inefficient companies should die is essential to capitalism. But should the owner or the manager of a poorly run company concede defeat? American bankruptcy laws permit owners or managers to make that decision. Their choices are three: informal reorganization; formal reorganization (Chapter 11); or liquidation (Chapter 7). The owner's or manager's choices are influenced by several factors.

The ability of the owner or manager to handle the stress of a crisis is an important consideration. Also, to come out of Chapter 11 or avoid Chapter 7 filing, owners or managers must recognize the existence of therapists to troubled companies, known as *workout consultants* or *workout managers*, who can guide the company through a reorganization and rehabilitation. Further the troubled company's capitalization structure, particularly the relation of its secured to unsecured debt, can predispose the owner or manager to one of the three options. The ability of the troubled company to raise cash to fund a reorganization plan is important in the rehabilitation process. And, finally, if the company's crisis has been caused by exogenous variables ostensibly beyond management's control, such as the collapse of a key customer, severe industry downturn, massive product liability litigation, or the failure of an important supplier, the only logical choice may be a Chapter 11 filing.

Many owners and managers of troubled companies immediately seek protection under Chapter 11 of the bankruptcy act. And, because of the unusual abundance of troubled companies today, bankruptcy specialists are the most highly sought after lawyers in their profession. Courses on the workout and turnaround process are among the most popular at the nation's 200 business schools. As Exhibit 1.1 indicates, bankruptcies in the United States are on the rise and most accountants and lawyers who make a living as watchdogs to bankrupt companies are expecting corporate bankruptcies to go platinum in the 1990s.

Exhibit 1.1   Bankruptcy Petitions Filed in the United States 1980–1989

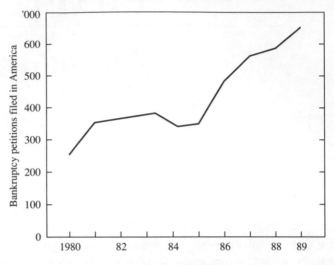

The average annual increase in filings from 1985 to 1989 was approximately 14 percent, after being fairly flat in the five previous years. Bankruptcy court statisticians expect 735,000 filings in 1990, up from 658,000 in 1989. The court is projecting increases of 10 percent in 1991 and again in 1992.

One reason owners and managers of troubled companies are quick to select the Chapter 11 option is that they are generally permitted to remain in control of the company. This encourages some managers to make a career of taking companies into and out of bankruptcy so as to set aside contracts or to wear down creditors or plaintiffs. Cynics accused Frank Lorenzo, who used to run Texas Air Corporation, of this tactic.

But most owners and managers of distressed companies are not considering such machinations. They are looking for a cure for the disease that has struck their companies, and Chapter 11 is the palliative most frequently recommended by the first person the distressed owner or manager telephones: the lawyer.

In Chapter 11, the court provides the debtor corporation with legal protection from its creditors while it reorganizes its business and negotiates a consensual settlement with its creditors. When the U.S. bankruptcy laws were revised in 1978, the authors acknowledged that liquidation was not the only solution and that in fact, because the liquidation option, or Chapter 7, wipes out all debts, it is ultimately not good for the credit markets. The Chapter 11 option, when described to the distressed owner or manager, acts as a script that foretells what is likely to happen in court.

Some lawyers are reticent to tell their troubled clients about the informal reorganization option because it does not fill their time sheets. *But the informal reorganization is an extremely valid option.* Many owners and managers of troubled companies do not know much about it. That is why I have written this book. My point of view, sharpened by nearly 20 years in the workout and turnaround field, can be summarized as follows:

1. Most troubled companies can restructure their operations outside of formal bankruptcy proceedings.

2. A troubled company needs its *distress* and its *operations* managed simultaneously, and this is best done with the aid of an experienced workout consultant.

3. One of the critical steps in turning around a distressed company is to attract new financing, and bankruptcy lawyers are not raisers of capital. Workout consultants frequently are.

4. The savings in legal fees and time of an informal reorganization can be as much as 60 to 70 percent of the total costs of the rehabilitation process.

5. In other countries, where there are few lawyers per capita, such as Japan, most workouts and turnarounds of distressed companies are done outside of the courts.

THE BENEFITS OF AN INFORMAL REORGANIZATION

Although most distressed owners and managers wait too long to call for help and thereby move closer to either the Chapter 11 or the liquidation option, in most cases a workout consultant can diagnose the problems rapidly, lower the level of distress inside the company, which often impedes positive movement, obtain a standstill agreement from creditors, develop a workable recapitalization plan that is acceptable to all creditors, locate new sources of financing and implement a redirect and grow plan, and accomplish these tasks in six to nine months.

The bankruptcy lawyer can monitor the troubled company through bankruptcy court, develop an acceptable recapitalization plan, and present it to the court and to the creditors; but there his or her duties end. *In Chapter 11, a plan of reorganization is approved if two thirds of the creditors (measured by dollar amount) and a majority of the creditors (measured by number) vote for it.* No bankruptcy attorney, at the beginning of a case, can guarantee that he or she can achieve the two thirds and 51 percent votes. However, a workout consultant, at the beginning of an assignment, *can* guarantee that in substantially less time and at a significantly lower cost to the distressed client, he or she can develop a recapitalization plan and identify sources of refinancing that can be submitted to creditors for an informal vote and still provide the owner or manager of the troubled company with the option of filing for protection.

THE BASEBALL ANALOGY

Stated another way the manager of a crisis-riven company is like a baseball manager whose team is down 5 to 2 in the bottom of the ninth with two men on base. With two outs and only one at bat left, the manager would choose the bankruptcy lawyer to pinch hit. But if there is only one out and two at bats remaining, the manager would choose the workout consultant.

But how does the owner or manager of the troubled company know how many at bats are left? There is always one: a bankruptcy petition. But to find out if there are two, the owner or manager needs to call in a workout consultant to perform a *diagnosis*.

THE MEDICAL ANALOGY

When a person is ill, he or she visits a physician, who performs a series of tests to diagnose the illness in order to recommend a treatment. When a company is ill, the owner or manager generally visits a lawyer who recommends a formal reorganization under Chapter 11, during which the patient is monitored for several months or even years. At least, that is the scenario in the United States.

In Japan, on the other hand, there are significantly fewer lawyers per capita, and practically all corporate restructurings are performed outside of formal bankruptcy proceedings. The decline in bankruptcy filings in Japan, as shown in Exhibit 1.2, is as steep as the rise of filings in the United States.

Exhibit 1.2   Number of Bankruptcy Cases in Japan 1983–1989

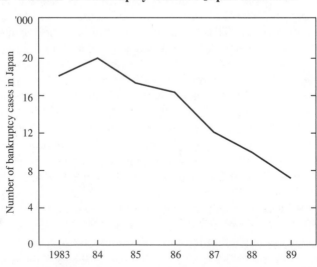

THE BARBEQUE ANALOGY

The distressed owner or manager of a severely troubled company is like the speaker in T.S. Eliot's poem *Ash Wednesday* who laments:

> Although I do not hope to turn again
> Although I do not hope
> Although I do not hope to turn
>
> Wavering between the profit and the loss
> In this brief transit where the dreams cross*

Harvey Miller, head of the Bankruptcy Department of Weil, Gotschal & Manges, arguably the most highly regarded bankruptcy law firm in the country, says, "The person who cannot pay his debts used to be drawn and quartered. The stigma of bankruptcy still remains with us to an extent." Faced with the curse of liquidation, the stigma of failure, and the feeling of helplessness—of not knowing where to turn for help—the troubled manager is ineluctably drawn toward the bankruptcy lawyer's office, where eventually he or she will feel like a skewered and basted pig turning over and over on a barbeque spit as the creditors line up for the main course.

But, if you would not visit a radiological oncologist and request chemotherapy to treat an undetermined disease, why would you call on a bankruptcy lawyer to treat a severe liquidity crisis before its degree of life threateningness has been diagnosed? The answer is *lack of information*.

WORKOUT CONSULTANTS ARE UNKNOWN

In the yellow pages of history, there has been a blank space of 911 numbers for the owner or manager of a distressed company to call. There are many more lawyers (every company has one) than there are workout consultants; thus they have monopolized the distress category for themselves. So far, that is. Condition red is flashing in the American economy. A situation has arisen in which there are more corporate patients than bankruptcy attorneys to service them without running into conflicts of interest, and the *n*th troubled company will have to hire a workout consultant. This troubled company's manager will emerge from the depths of financial despair and tell of his or her satisfaction to the *n*th plus one troubled manager, who will tell the *n*th plus two and so on until the process of reorganization *outside of the courts* is as well understood as the process of entrepreneurship or any other stage in the life of a company.

To illuminate the systematic process of corporate rehabilitation outside of Chapters 11 or 7, I have written this sourcebook.

---

* *Modern American and British Poetry,* edited by Louis Untermeyer (New York: Harcourt Brace and Company, 1955), p. 226.

CRISIS AS A SPRINGBOARD FOR SUCCESS

Vincent Van Gogh was perhaps the most unsuccessful painter while he lived of any artist about whom critical works have been written. He sold perhaps two paintings out of 900, yet during some periods of his life, particularly at Arles where he was becoming progressively mad as the furies drove him to despair, he was his most productive and some critics say at the peak of his artistic ability.

Theo, his brother, sent Vincent money each month for his few necessities, plus news of the Paris art scene and news of possible interest in Vincent's paintings. Theo's letters were answered by Vincent, and fortunately they were collected and saved. Today, these letters are considered to be among the most vibrant literature of the 19th century.

Since I am entrepreneurial by nature, one of my favorite passages is the following:

> You do not know how paralyzing that staring of a blank canvas is; it says to the painter, *You can't do anything.* The canvas stares at you like an idiot, and it hypnotizes some painters, so that they themselves become idiots. Many painters are afraid of the blank canvas, but the blank canvas is afraid of the really passionate painter who is daring—and who has once and for all broken the spell of 'you cannot'. . . . *

How like the painter facing the blank canvas is the owner or manager who stares into blankness as his or her office rings with a cacophony of creditors demanding money, customers shouting for product, the controller pleading that credit is being shut off, process servers shuffling through the waiting room with lawsuits to be served, and the production manager begging for materials to complete the work in process. It's enough to despair about.

Distress must be contained before a rehabilitation plan can be established and a redirect and grow plan installed. The ability of a company to manage its crisis will depend upon its *crisis-meeting resources.* If it is incapable of dealing with a crisis with its internal management resources, then the distressed company will have all the more reason to hire a workout consultant who will be able to demonstrate the fundamental axiom about business crises:

> All great fortunes were made in hard times and, if subsequently lost, they were wasted in good times.

Crises are motivators. The proper response to crises are threefold: (1) take the impact head-on, (2) recoil from it, and (3) begin implementing so-

---

* *Van Gogh: A Self Portrait*, edited by W. H. Auden (Greenwich, CT: New York Graphic Society, 1961), p. 222.

lutions. When a company does not respond properly, solutions do not fill the blank canvas, and the company becomes disorganized and begins to disintegrate. Here are the steps necessary for responding to a crisis effectively:

1. *Perception*. Further the correct perception of the situation by seeking new information and by keeping the problem in front of you.
2. *Nomination*. Manage the effects on personnel by giving names to the crisis-provokers and rewards to the problem-solvers.
3. *Delegation*. Develop procedures for seeking and using help inside and outside the company and give tasks to these helpers.

It is virtually impossible for the owner or manager of a troubled company to respond properly to the crisis if he or she feels *victimized*. A "woe is me" attitude is paralyzing. If this happens, the workout consultant takes on the added responsibility of surrogate management in order to put the circuit breakers into place. Once that is done, the craft of working through the company's symptoms of failure and implementing a successful therapy can begin.

Many of today's most successful companies and entrepreneurs were once stretched on the rack and tortured with the hot coals of creditors burned into their ribs. General Motors, J.I. Case, Sam Walton, Toys 'R' Us, Frederick E. Smith and his Federal Express Corp., and The Great Atlantic & Pacific Tea Co. are some shining examples. The great family fortunes tied to the success of General Motors are not those of its founders, but rather those of its managers who took the company through a difficult period of time in the early 20th century and received common stock purchase warrants for guaranteeing bank loans to finance GM's redirect and grow plan.

In chapter 4, you will be presented with crisis management strategies to implement while waiting for the workout consultant to arrive.

REHABILITATION

America is an incredibly credit-intensive society. Advertisements for credit cards and loans tell us that debt is synonymous with enjoying the good life. We make projections about our future cash flow—projections that are estimates supported by guesses. They frequently do not materialize, and, if we have borrowed too much money in light of the projections, we or our companies can quickly fall into a financial crisis.

The rampant use of debt has influenced the evolution of bankruptcy laws. At the turn of the century and until the post-war era, creditors stood almost no chance of getting their money back from a bankrupt borrower. But creditors have influenced the modification of bankruptcy laws, from punishment of the debtor to rehabilitation, for it is through rehabilitation that creditors can hope to get some of their money back.

This evolution is critical to an understanding of the strategy of reorganizing outside of bankruptcy court. It says, in effect: "Any company can run out of cash. If the debtor has a credible plan to repay its creditors, it has captured their attention."

MY OBJECTIVE IN WRITING THIS SOURCE BOOK

The torrid pace of business failures in the absence of guidelines for surviving them calls for directories of workout consultants and bankruptcy lawyers who represent debtors. The directories at the end of this book do not merely provide names, addresses, and telephone numbers but also industry experience, client references, and fee structures. The Directory of Workout Consultants attempts to be as inclusive as possible, recognizing that circumstances can change between the time a directory is assembled and the time it finds its way into bookstores.

The Directory of Bankruptcy Lawyers is not all inclusive. It includes firms recommended by the workout consultants for their expertise in representing debtors and from other sources such as personal contacts, seminars, and published material (properly cited where appropriate).

My objective in writing this source book is to train the owner or manager of a company in crisis to think and act like a workout consultant, if he or she cannot afford to hire one, and to learn how they think and act if affordability is not a problem. The failure of a business may not be fatal. It may mean that the business has grown too fat, has too much debt, or has lost its focus, and a new business plan must be crafted and implemented. This takes *time* and the presence of a company doctor on the scene. The workout consultant is the physician to crisis-torn companies and my intent is to show you how to find these healers, how to hire them, what they will do for you, and how to monitor their performance.

I make the assumption from the outset that your company is or soon may be in crisis. You may be feeling desperate and alone, but I can assure you that after you have read a few pages of the *Bankruptcy and Workout Source Book*, your spirits will improve dramatically. If I succeed in my objectives, this book will sit alongside the collection of your other most cherished business guidebooks.

CHAPTER 2

The Emergence of the Workout Consultant

Freedom's just another word for nothing left to lose.

—Kris Kristofferson

The word "bankruptcy" is derived from *banca rotta*, Italian for broken bench. It was customary that when a medieval trader was unable to pay his creditors his trading bench was broken. Today, the means for dealing with failed businesses are less direct but considerably more complicated. Once you understand what might happen to your company in both Chapter 11 and Chapter 7, you will be prepared to choose between either of them or an informal reorganization.

THE BOBBY McGEE CONDITION

In the Kris Kristofferson song "Me and Bobby McGee," the singer describes the condition of a perfect candidate to remain out of bankruptcy: "Freedom's just another word for nothing left to lose." If all of a company's assets are pledged to secured creditors, then should the unsecured creditors try to force the company into Chapter 7—a liquidation for the benefit of creditors— they will receive nothing—zero. Thus, the debtor company has "freedom." Freedom to avoid liquidation and to choose a reorganization plan, either informally or formally in Chapter 11.

Workout consultants can usually do their best work when a company is in the Bobby McGee condition because the unsecured creditors are boxed out from forcing a debtor company into liquidation. This is not to say that they will believe the owner or manager who says to them, "If you force us into Chapter 7 there will be no money to pay you. But, if you give us time to work ourselves out of our trouble and come up with a plan, we will be able to pay you some of what we owe you."

Unsecured creditors are more likely to accept this statement from the company's workout consultant or bankruptcy lawyer, if the Chapter 11 option is selected, because the company's credibility with its creditors may have suffered as the company slid behind in payments.

INVOLUNTARY BANKRUPTCY

The Bobby McGee condition can be used to explain to unsecured creditors that they will receive nothing or very little in the way of cash or assets if the company is forced into Chapter 7, but, if the unsecured creditors are sufficiently angry, they may force the company into *involuntary bankruptcy*, whether or not they anticipate receiving any value for their claims. Because most people act rationally, an involuntary bankruptcy is more likely to occur when there exist some unsecured assets to be auctioned in order to raise cash for paying unsecured creditors. The combination of (a) a procrastinating debtor who has stretched the rubber band of credibility with his creditors to the breaking point or (b) the existence of, or the belief by the creditors that, unsecured assets can be liquidated to pay them 15 to 25 percent of the amount of their note or account payable is usually enough to force an involuntary bankruptcy on the debtor.

Some degree of *cooperation* among creditors is required to effect an involuntary bankruptcy. If the debtor corporation has 12 or more creditors, then any three of them who are owed $5,000 or more in the aggregate can petition the bankruptcy court to force a company into Chapter 7. If the debtor has fewer than 12 creditors, then one creditor who is owed at least $5,000 can force a company into Chapter 7.

It takes at least three creditors whose debts aggregate at least $5,000 to force a partnership into Chapter 7 if there are more than 12 creditors, and it takes one creditor who is owed at least $5,000 if there are fewer than 12 creditors.

In Chapter 7, the court appoints a trustee to sell the assets and apply the resulting cash to pay creditors. The trustee is insensitive to the debtor's pleas to seek higher prices by holding onto the assets for a while longer. The trustee has an incentive to convert assets to cash quickly: he or she receives a fee for services equal to a percentage of the cash realized through auction or otherwise. The fee is the same among the 286 bankruptcy court jurisdictions throughout the country: approximately 3 percent of the amounts raised through foreclosure and sale. Thus, a liquidation that realizes $2 million in cash for the benefit of creditors will result in a fee of $60,000 for the trustee. You can see that an attempt to persuade the trustee to wait for six months to realize perhaps another $200,000 probably will not be successful.

THE COMPLEXITIES OF BANKRUPTCY
CREATED THE WORKOUT CONSULTANT

Alas, the longer a company waits to hire a workout consultant or bankruptcy lawyer, the more desperate the situation becomes and the angrier become the unsecured creditors. Additionally, if the owner of the company has personally guaranteed obligations to certain unsecured creditors, he or she is facing an almost certain Chapter 11 filing or Chapter 13 filing (a filing for individuals with less than $1 million of assets), although the company may be rehabilitated informally, in order to stay the seizure of his or her personal assets. There are a baker's dozen intricacies that demand the diagnosis of a workout consultant at the onset of a crisis. By asking you a day's worth of questions, the workout consultant can provide you with a probability analysis of what is likely to happen to your company in bankruptcy court.

The first two questions he or she will ask will probably relate to the length of time the company has been in crisis—that is, has not paid its bills on time—and the existence of *personal guarantees* to creditors. Let's examine the importance of these factors, as well as the other 11. Exhibit 2.1 lists all 13 factors that the workout consultant will evaluate in his or her diagnosis.

Time

In questionnaires filled out and returned to me by the nation's leading workout consultants, procrastination ranked first or second among almost all respondents as the principal justification for the services of a workout consultant. As workout consultant William Gano of Delta Management in Memphis said, "When a company gets into trouble its management either ignores the

---

Exhibit 2.1   Factors that Justify the Existence of Workout Consultants

1. Time
2. The personal exposure of the owner or manager
3. Choosing the best bankruptcy lawyer
4. The existence of free cash flow
5. The crisis-readiness of the management team
6. The characteristics of the bankruptcy judges in your jurisdiction
7. The reputations of the creditors with debtor companies
8. The capitalization of the company
9. The prospects for raising capital
10. The likelihood that a trustee will be appointed to run the company
11. The prospects for selling the company
12. The courage of the owner or manager
13. The economic validity of the business

---

signals, tries to fight its way out by getting creditor cooperation over and over again, or uses ineffective workout strategies, all of which consume time and usually make a bad situation worse."

If a workout consultant is called in at the first sign of trouble, most companies can have their problems diagnosed and remedial strategies implemented within four to six weeks. If a workout consultant is called in after five law suits have been filed and most creditors have been stiff-armed for 120 days, it will require more than a Homeric effort to save the company, which is probably as dead as Nineveh and Tyre.

Jack Welch, the highly regarded CEO of General Electric Company, maintains a permanent crew of workout consultants on staff to visit each division of the company to attempt to slash expenses and introduce efficiencies. General Electric is certainly not in a crisis, but Welch does not intend to be caught by surprise.

A creditor that is normally and customarily paid within 45 days may permit one 45-day extension, with a plausible explanation. But if he or she receives another alibi at the end of 90 days, then another at the end of 120 days, the good will of the creditor will have been exhausted and his or her willingness to extend additional credit will have evaporated. A request for an additional shipment will probably result in a demand for payment of the outstanding balance, or a substantial portion of it, with the requested shipment to be paid on a C.O.D. basis. If that cannot be achieved, then the creditor will adopt a cathartine attitude toward the debtor and he or she will try to sink his or her claws into the deceptive carrion debtor's derriere.

There are some highly effective crisis management strategies that I have described in a previous book* and which are elaborated on in chapter 4, but most owners and managers are unfamiliar with them. Consequently, workout consultants or bankruptcy lawyers are generally called upon too late to do their most effective work. The longer the owner or manager of a crisis-riven company waits to call in the doctor, the longer it will take the workout consultant to save the company, if indeed he or she is able to, and the greater the expense, since the workout consultant generally works on an hourly basis.

Personal Exposure of the Owner or Manager

Nothing so obfuscates the terrain of troubled companies as the personal guarantees of the owners and managers. It is one thing for a company's existence to be at risk but quite another for its owner or manager to place his or her assets—home, cars, furnishings, securities—in jeopardy. The validity of the workout consultant is heightened dramatically in this situation because

---

*A. David Silver, *The Business Bible for Survival* (Rocklin, CA: Prima Publishing Co., 1989).

it requires the skill of an experienced crisis consultant to both protect the owner's or manager's assets and save the company from extinction.

The reason for the existence of personal guarantees in the first place is that the company was unable to obtain sufficient credit without additional collateral, or a backstop for the company's collateral. The optimism of owners or managers leads them to believe that their company's cash flow will improve and that their personal guarantees will never be called upon. Moreover, creditors generally have a time—and experience-tested—guarantee form that they submit to owners and managers for signature, which is frequently signed without the benefit of a legal review by the signer. It is frequently an inflexible document that permits the creditor to demand payment from the guarantor if it is not paid by the primary obligor.

Although owners or managers may cry in their pillows at night as they contemplate the imminent auction of the household goods on the front lawn, the workout consultant is not frightened. He or she can usually find a loophole in the language of the personal guarantee, a condition in the state's laws pertaining to when a guarantee can be called, or financial logic to persuade the guaranteed creditors to think twice before forcing the company and the guarantor into involuntary bankruptcy. And because they are not frightened by creditor drum-beating, workout consultants can work methodically and carefully on this thorny area.

My own method in assisting managers of troubled companies who have personal guarantees outstanding involves the following steps:

1. Read the signed personal guarantee carefully to look for steps that the creditor must take before demanding payment from the guarantor. This may include selling off the assets that secure the debt in a "commercially reasonable" manner. To permit the creditor to take back its goods, sell them at auction and then determine if there is a balance owing from the guarantor; this may obviate a bankruptcy proceeding because it favors one creditor over the others. (See chapter 9 for details.)

2. Review the state's laws, particularly recent case law, with the company's counsel to see how the judges have been reacting to creditors who hastily go after a personal guarantor. The laws may set up several hurdles for the creditor to jump before it can take the guarantor into court and demand payment. These may include establishing the exact amount owing, for example.

3. Review the invoices submitted by the creditor to the company and the correspondence, with the intent of finding a *service* feature to the relationship or a series of goods returned as a result of defects. If I am fortunate enough to find inconsistencies in the vendor's service record, shipping history, or product quality, then perhaps I can persuade the creditor that it will not prevail if it sues the guarantor.

4. With the results of my diagnosis carefully assembled, I telephone the creditor and ask permission for a visit. At the meeting I present my case for patience while an informal reorganization plan is set in place. I promise to communicate regularly and honestly, and I attempt to convert an enemy into an ally and to win a cheerleader for an informal reorganization.

The preceeding steps do not always prevent the creditor posse from capturing the guarantor, throwing a rope over the limb of the tallest tree, tying a noose onto the end of it, and inviting the guarantor to put his neck into it. But there are many steps between organizing the posse and the eventual hanging, and the personal guarantor needs the modern equivalent of the Lone Ranger to save his neck.

Choosing the Best Bankruptcy Lawyer

Lawyers are in business to make money. Make no mistake about it. Like other professionals who sell their intellects by the hour, lawyers have 2,500 hours per year to fill with paying clients. Therefore, when a distressed owner or manager calls his or her company's counsel to recommend a bankruptcy lawyer, chances are the lawyer will recommend a friend who is most likely to reciprocate. That's fine for the lawyers, but the troubled owner or manager may not be well served.

In the bankruptcy field there are lawyers who specialize in representing creditors and those who specialize in advocating on behalf of debtors. Because some lawyers do not turn down potential clients who can pay for their services and who do not present a conflict of interest, some lawyers skilled in representing creditors are not likely to turn down a debtor client. The complexities of the Federal Bankruptcy Code and the ebb and flow of case law modifying it mandates that the debtor hire a *debtor-experienced* bankruptcy lawyer. The distinction is important.

There are exceptions. If the debtor is incorporated in a jurisdiction where the skills of one bankruptcy lawyer tower over those of all others, notwithstanding that the superior lawyer has built his or her reputation representing debtors, it may be critical that you act precipitously so that he or she not be hired to represent one of your creditors. The stature of this particular lawyer will very likely place him or her at the head of the creditor's committee and he or she will become the debtor's bête noir.

Workout consultants know many of their region's bankruptcy lawyers, and, because of their experience in negotiating with them and in reviewing their pleadings and motions, the workout consultants can judge the abilities of various bankruptcy lawyers. And if they are assisting a client in an unfamiliar jurisdiction, the workout consultant can ask others of his ilk to recommend the best debtor-experienced bankruptcy lawyers in the region.

Workout consultants can also help with bankruptcy judges. Some judges are more pro-debtor than others. Workout consultants have a copy of the racing form of judges, and if they do not have the most up-to-date information, they can ask their friends among the bankruptcy lawyers to provide them with the latest data.

I asked the nation's leading workout consultants to name the best debtor-advocate bankruptcy lawyers with whom they have worked. Exhibit 2.2 provides the results of their votes. The law firms are ranked according to number of votes received. For a more complete listing of debtor-experienced bankruptcy lawyers, see the directory at the end of the book.

The Existence of Free Cash Flow

The owner or manager of the seriously troubled company is frequently too paralyzed with fear or shame to look for sources of cash to meet the company's obligations. Workout consultants, when they come into a troubled company, divide the liabilities into three major categories: bullets, criticals, and occasionals. The terminology varies among workout specialists, but the categories are the same, viz:

- Bullets: Those obligations that if not paid will probably put the company out of business suddenly and unequivocally.
- Criticals: Those obligations that are critical to the company's operations but for which timely payment is not a live or die situation.
- Occasionals: Those obligations that should receive at least partial payment some of the time in order to let them know they haven't been forgotten.

Exhibit 2.2   The Country's Best Debtor-Advocate Bankruptcy Lawyers

	Firm Name	Home Office
1.	Weil Gotschal & Manges	New York
2.	Stroock & Stroock & Lavan	New York
3.	Stutman Triester & Glatt	Los Angeles
4.	Winston & Strawn	Chicago
5.	Latham & Watkins	New York
6.	Murphy Weir & Butler	Los Angeles
7.	Levin Weintraub Crames & Edelman*	New York
8.	Jones Day Reavis & Pogue	Cleveland
9.	Skadden Arps Meagher Slate & Flomm	New York
10.	Steinfeld Maley & Kay	Houston

* Recently merged with Kaye, Scholer, Herman, Hays & Handler, a
  firm 25 times its size.

There may be variations within these categories, and there may be additional categories depending upon the depth of the crisis at the time the doctor is called in. For example, if the workout consultant is called in after the owner or manager has been sued by a handful of creditors and they have been awarded judgments by the court and the sheriff is seizing assets, then there is very little the workout specialist can do except assist the company in filing for protection under Chapter 11 and in developing a plan of reorganization to help the client springboard out of it.

But, if the workout consultant is called in sooner, there is usually ample time to categorize the liabilities, contact the creditors, and diagnose their degree of animus or consanguinity and set up payment schedules for the bullets and the criticals. To do this successfully requires creating cash flow statement projections on a weekly basis and reviewing and modifying them as frequently as needed. The cash flow statement projection is the troubled company's road map out of the swamp.

After examining the categories of liabilities, the workout specialist will meet with senior management and report the need for a specific dollar amount of cash every week, another amount every other week, and yet another amount every month and every two months. What he or she is seeking is *free cash flow*—not cash flow required for payroll, raw materials, and operating expenses, nor cash flow destined for the company's operations, but over and above that, cash flow to pay the bullets and the criticals. If the company's senior management replies that they don't know where it will come from or that it's not there, the workout consultant will probe more deeply until he or she locates sources of overhead that can be slashed until he finds cash.

The situation could be so desperate that the workout consultant cannot find all the cash needed to help the company dodge the bullets, in which case a Chapter 11 filing is prepared. But most workout consultants who have had sufficient experience can generate free cash flow. Exhibit 2.3 lists some of the places that they look first.

The workout consultant attempts to find cash and to do so quickly. In this respect, he is like the corporate raider who takes over a company with mountains of borrowed money and immediately and single-mindedly ferrets out cash to repay the debt. I wrote about the expense slashing strategies of raiders in my book *The Inside Raider.**

Many owners and managers in crisis are frozen with fear that they will lose their company as it now exists, and they cannot react objectively to what needs to be done. The workout consultant focuses on cash first and begins trying to free it up in the most logical place: corporate overhead.

---

*A. David Silver, *The Inside Raider* (New York: Harper & Row, 1990).

Exhibit 2.3   Expenses Workout Consultants Slash First

1. Facilities costs, including buildings and warehouses, equipment, airplanes, trucks, vans, cars, and other fixed assets.
2. Communications costs, including postage, couriers, telephone, facsimile, and electronic mail.
3. Travel costs, including airplanes, rental cars, hotels, restaurants, and customer entertainment expenses.
4. Employee health insurance expenses, generally considered the largest overhead expense and the fastest rising.
5. Legal expenses, including an examination of the company's outside law firms, the services they render, and the cost of these services.
6. Audit and accounting expenses, including an analysis of the services that may be brought in-house.
7. Advertising expenses: a review of their importance to product sales and the effectiveness of lower cost alternative forms of creating product awareness such as direct response marketing and public relations.
8. Borrowing costs, including an examination of all loan agreements, trade credit, letters of credit, employee credit cards, and bank charges.
9. Employee costs: Can the company be managed with fewer employees?
10. Peripheral division expenses in relation to the company's mission. The workout consultant's task is to save the core, if at all possible, which may require selling off peripheral divisions.

The Crisis Readiness of the Management Team

Many management teams are not battle-scarred. They have not taken their company through the roller coaster ride of a crisis. They are unfamiliar with the early warning signals of crises, or they selectively choose not to listen to them. Many management teams are expansion oriented, trying to push the company or their division of the company above the previous year's level.

When a crisis develops, there is a downward slump in the organization. Work is done with less enthusiasm. Conflicts within the organization are expressed or converted into tensions. Relations become strained. Eventually the company might begin to disintegrate. When the workout consultant intercedes and begins to create order, things improve. New routines are put into effect and members of the company reach new agreements about how the goals are to be reached. Middle managers begin to rally around the workout consultant when they begin to observe the systematic method by which he or she utilizes the dynamics of the company to generate new sources of cash and calm the troubled creditor waters.

Students of dysfunctional companies have identified how the company can successfully adjust to its crisis. The stages of adjusting to a crisis in a company are set forth in Exhibit 2.4.

Exhibit 2.4   The Stages by which a Company Adjusts to a Crisis

1. Attempts to deny the problem.
2. Attempts to eliminate the problem.
3. Disorganization.
4. Attempts to reorganize in spite of the problem.
5. Efforts to escape the problem: key personnel resign when the owner or CEO fails to recognize the many stressor signals as a full-blown crisis.
6. Reorganization of the CEO's authority: a workout consultant or bankruptcy lawyer takes over many responsibilities in order to manage the distress and the operations.
7. Reorganization of the entire company with a stronger cash position and capital base.

The adjustment to crisis looks like a roller coaster in profile. Naturally, a company cannot go through a bumpy, roller coaster ride without some personal shocks. Weaker companies lose members at the earlier stages through either shock, disbelief, numbness, or mourning. Well-integrated and adaptable companies, particularly those that identify the crisis for what it is at an early stage and call in a company doctor, take the roller coaster ride in stride. They are invulnerable to it and rise to a higher level of homeostasis after the crisis is past.

The roller coaster ride of a company in crisis is shown in Exhibit 2.5.

A company that experiences drastic demoralization on the downhill ride was probably poorly organized and had a dubious economic validity that precluded universal loyalty to its stated mission in the first place. When the workout consultant finally arrives, he or she may find that the company should get out of its business entirely in order to be saved. Many workout consultants have been heard to say to the managers of a seriously troubled and demoralized company, "You're not in the widgets business anymore. Forget it. You're in the survival business."

We will review crisis management strategies in depth in chapter 4 to provide you with the necessary steps to take while awaiting the arrival of the workout consultant.

The Characteristics of the Bankruptcy Judges in Your Jurisdiction

The backdrop that justifies the existence of workout consultants is provided by the obfuscated rules set forth in the Federal Bankruptcy Act of 1978 and the case law that has arisen since then. There is a considerable amount of confusion and uncertainty about what is likely or unlikely to happen to a company that files for protection under Chapter 11 of the Bankruptcy Act.

Exhibit 2.5   The Roller Coaster Ride of a Company in Crisis

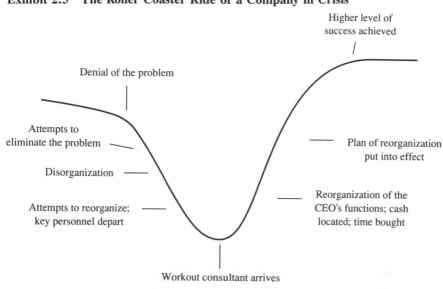

Higher level of
success achieved

Denial of the problem

Attempts to
eliminate the problem

Disorganization

Attempts to reorganize;
key personnel depart

Plan of reorganization
put into effect

Reorganization of the
CEO's functions; cash
located; time bought

Workout consultant arrives

When I became involved for the first time as a workout consultant in 1975, I searched the libraries and bookstores for books dealing with the *process* of workouts and turnarounds. Regrettably, there was nothing.

I did find a military strategies book, *The Art of War*, by Sun Tzu, written nearly 2,500 years ago and first brought to the attention of the Western world by a Jesuit missionary to Peking, Father J. J. M. Arniot, who published the book in Paris in 1772. *The Art of War* may have been studied by Robert E. Lee because his military strategies mirror those of Sun Tzu. Lee's Confederate Army, you may recall, was outnumbered over 10 to 1 in nearly all of its battles with the Union Army, yet it won most of its battles for four years. *The Art of War* has had a profound influence on Japanese and Chinese military thought. It is the source of Mao Tse-Tung's strategic theories and of the tactical doctrine of the Chinese armies.

When a company is in crisis, it is at war. It is a war of survival. *The Art of War* formulates a rational basis for the planning and conduct of military operations. The principal of *The Art of War* is that battles are won without loss of life only by realizing that the primary battlefield is in the mind of the opposing commander.*

The bankruptcy judge who may decide the fate of your company, if it files for protection under Chapter 11, is neither your *de facto* enemy

---

*Sun Tzu, *The Art of War* (circa 500 B.C.), translated by Samuel P. Griffith (Oxford: Oxford University Press, 1963).

nor your opposing military commander. But he or she has the power to counteract and oppose your actions. So bankruptcy judges can be viewed as opposing military commanders to the extent that they may hear motions by your creditors to place your company in Chapter 7 liquidation.

Accordingly, knowing how the bankruptcy judges think is an important factor in your turnaround strategy. The workout consultants whom you interview should be aware of the predilections of the bankruptcy judges toward creditors or debtors. If they don't, then you should certainly ask the bankruptcy lawyers whom you interview to tell you which judges are pro-debtor and your chances of reorganizing if you file a petition in their court.

As Sun Tzu wrote: "A skilled general must be master of the complementary arts of simulation and dissimulation. . . . His primary target is the mind of the opposing commander."* To survive your crisis, you must get inside the minds of your opponents. This applies to the company's most important and outspoken creditors as well.

The Reputations of the Creditors with Debtor Companies

Not only is it possible but it should also be your constant goal to use a crisis to pole-vault to a higher level of achievement. Crises are meant to be springboards for success. Never enter a period of uncertainty or crisis by fearing for your survival; rather, plan to come out of it better off than when you entered it. The Chinese word for crisis, "Wei-Ji," is made up of two characters. The first means danger; the second, opportunity. *Fortunes are made in hard times and lost in good times.* Or, as Nietzche put it, "You must be a chaos to give birth to a rising star."

Remember this, yours is not the first company to fall on hard times. Nor will it be the last. Some industries have very high rates of failure. John Maynard Keynes noticed that companies with the highest failure rates add value to products in vertical industries.† The reason is that they are dependent upon supply and demand forces that affect the companies' suppliers and customers. Distribution companies, consequently, are prime candidates for failure.

The pharmaceutical and health and beauty aids (HBA) industry has witnessed so many bankruptcies that its credit association has a small auditorium on Lexington Avenue in New York City, where its credit managers may be addressed by debtors. In 1978, I stepped onto that stage with William Y. Tauscher, 29, and his chief financial officer, Richard H. Bard, 33, when they took over the management of the $80 million (revenues) Lag Drug

---

*Ibid., p. 41

†John M. Keynes, *The General Theory* (London: Harbinger Books, 1935).

Company, a Chicago pharmaceutical and HBA distributor, only to find it hopelessly insolvent. Tauscher and Bard put Lag Drug into Chapter 11 and they were immediately "invited" by the company's creditors to ascend the stage and explain their plans to get the creditors paid. It was the first time that any of the three of us had spoken to an audience of hostile adversaries.

There were over thirty credit managers in the audience, who were on average over 20 years older than Tauscher, Bard, and me and who were owed between $200,000 and $5 million. Merck's credit manager was there, as was Clairol's, Pfizer's, Upjohn's, RJR/Nabisco's, American Tobacco's, and more. We feared the worst.

Later on, I will tell you the plan that Tauscher, Bard, and I conceived and implemented for Lag Drug Company because it was both unique and successful. It may have been the first leveraged buyout of a cash flow positive company by a company in Chapter 11. Today, the successor to Lag Drug, FoxMeyer Corporation, is the second largest pharmaceutical and HBA distributor in the country, with sales of over $3.5 billion per year.

The three of us were very young and very inexperienced; but the Federal Bankruptcy Act was very young and very inexperienced as well. The creditors did not understand the options open to them and Tauscher, Bard, and I did not know the limits of our ability to leverage the creditors. So we stretched them to the maximum.

That isn't possible today. There are many more business failures, and the credit managers have much more experience with a multitude of debtors and have heard every kind of story from debtor "stages" in many industries. The lap top PC goes to creditor meetings these days, and it can quickly compute the creditor categories, the amounts owing each, and the ability of cash flow to service debt. Moreover, the creditors know each other well in many instances. They hire workout consultants and creditor-advocate bankruptcy lawyers to represent them in the larger situations. They know the bankruptcy lawyers very well, and they frequently hire the "best in the business" to keep the debtor from hiring them.

But the best workout consultants know the minds of the creditors very well. They know how the creditors and their advisors are likely to react to different proposals, how patient they will be before a plan of reorganization is proposed, how they are likely to react to various plans submitted to them, and what may be going on inside their minds.

Naive debtors will not be considered charming and innocent by creditor committees today. They will be tossed into Chapter 7 and their companies liquidated unless they approach their workout problems in a business-like and professional manner. A debtor who is fearless to the point of facing down a roomful of angry creditors without a workout consultant riding shotgun is going to be in for a big surprise. The creditors want someone in the crisis-riven company who understands them, who speaks their language, who has worked with them before.

The Capitalization of the Company

The archetypical financially troubled company is one with too much debt in relation to its equity. We know that many companies such as Tracor, Campeau, and Hooker are in bankruptcy proceedings because they were aggressive junk bond borrowers and buyers of companies at premium prices. The corporate raiders who took over these companies with massive amounts of 16 percent to 18 percent interest rate junk bonds could not generate cash quickly enough via spin-offs and asset sales.

Akin to soldiers who died for a cause they did not understand and for a war they were not trained for, the junk bond raiders who borrowed too much money are like the row after row of Confederate dead in Allen Tate's majestic poem:

> Row after row with strict impunity
> The headstones yield their names to the element
> The wind whirs without recollection;
> In the riven troughs the splayed leaves
> Pile up, of nature the casual sacrament
> To the seasonal eternity of death,
> Then driven by the fierce scrutiny
> Of heaven to their business in the vast breath,
> They sough the rumor of morality.*

But it is not always excessive debt that leads to business failures. After all, financial service companies, leasing companies, commercial banks, and trading companies operate successfully with debt to equity ratios of 10 to 1 and more. When they stick to their core businesses, they succeed handsomely. However, when they reach for risky loans or leases or when they go on an acquisition tear as did Bank of New England in the late 1980s, excessive leverage will put them in Tate's Confederate graveyard in a heartbeat.

Leverage cuts both ways. When a business is growing and generating new channels of cash flow, leverage is a fulcrum that raises the company to new heights. But when adverse circumstances strike the company, debt cannot be serviced and leverage becomes the bête noir that takes the blame for the company's failure.

Leverage is a double-edged sword. A company can get into trouble by not borrowing to finance growth and having competitors take bites out of market share. On the other hand, a company can get into serious trouble faster by borrowing.

---

*Allen Tate, "Ode to the Confederate Dead," in *Modern American & Modern British Poetry,* editied by Louis Untermeyer (New York: Harcourt, Brace and Co., 1955), p. 321.

Because interest payments on borrowed money are deductible from income taxes and dividends on preferred and common stock are not, many owners and managers prefer to finance their companies' growth with borrowed money rather than the sale of stock. If they do so too aggressively and circumstances clobber their carefully sculpted cash flow projections, it is practically inevitable that in their plans of reorganization they will issue common or preferred stock to creditors as a means of confirming a plan of reorganization. What goes around comes around, as the saying goes. Businesses are pendulums. If they swing too far out on the debt curve, they are likely to be forced to swing back in the other direction and sell equity in their companies at a later date and at distress prices.

Workout consultants have a broad grasp of the optimum capitalization structures in a variety of industries. They can apply certain quick tests to determine if a company is over-leveraged for its industry. The most frequently used ratios are shown in Exhibit 2.6.

"I can go in and do an analysis on a troubled company's capitalization," says Diane M. Freaney, a Delaware Valley workout consultant. "That analysis will usually tell me how much time I have to try and turn the company around." For example, if a company's ratio of cash to current liabilities is less than .1 and if its ability to service debt ratio is less than 1.0, the company is not only severely over-leveraged but it is on the edge of the diving board overhanging an unfilled swimming pool.

On the other hand, if a company's total debt to net worth ratio is in excess of 5 to 1 but its ability to service debt ratio is slightly over 1.0, it is certainly over-leveraged, but it is not sitting on a ticking time bomb. This company may need a *recapitalization*—that is, the replacement of some of its short-term debt with longer term debt or preferred stock.

An overly-leveraged capitalization is generally a predictive factor of bankruptcy in one class of industries, while other financial ratios which we will discuss are indicators of significant bankruptcy potential in certain other industries.

Short-term illiquidity and excessive total debt/total assets and total debt/net worth ratios can be deadly in the mining, paper processing, chemical pro-

---

Exhibit 2.6   Ratios that Measure Leverage

Overall leverage	Total debt/total assets
Short-term liquidity	Short-term debt/total debt
Cash position	Cash/current liabilities
Banker's view of leverage	Total debt/net worth
Ability to service debt	Annual interest + principal payment/cash flow

---

cessing, retail, wholesale distribution, construction, and service industries. These industries are subject to outside forces, such as sudden changes in demand or supply, that can make excessive leverage particularly punitive.

Notwithstanding the selectivity of leverage in killing certain companies faster than others, workout consultants realize at some point in their assignments they will probably have to recapitalize the company, and this means raising capital.

The Prospects for Raising Capital

The workout consultant is in many respects like a radiological oncologist. He has a medical degree and can treat a variety of illnesses, but his specialty is saving the terminally ill cancer victim, with every available palliative, including radiation, chemotherapy, hyperthermia, lasers, herbology, pleasant thoughts, and anything that works.

Workout consultants did not obtain a post-graduate degree in their field because the specialization is only now being taught. They previously did something else, and, because of their circumstances, they were asked to fix a troubled company, probably succeeded at it, and began looking for a next assignment in the boneyard. The workout consultants in the directory at the end of this book come from the manufacturing and service industries, management consulting, executive search, accounting, commercial banking, and investment banking. Some are better at making changes in management; perhaps their background is in executive search. Others are better at creating a new marketing plan; their background may be in management or management consulting. However, the workout consultants that can probably do the best job at raising capital may have once been investment bankers. You will see in the directory a number of investment banks with workout divisions.

At some time during the roller coaster ride, the troubled company will have to raise capital. It will have to replace losses, or raise capital to retire indebtedness, or fund a new marketing plan. Many workout consultants are capable of raising capital for troubled companies, but if not they probably know an investment banker who can do the job.

The prospects for raising capital are derivative of the company's ability to provide appropriate answers to the five questions that all investors or lenders ask when they are presented with a financing proposal:

1. How much can I make?
2. How much can I lose?
3. How do I get my money back?
4. Who else is in the deal?
5. Who says this management team is good?

These important questions are not trivial. They are the five single most important issues that an investor in a "concept" seeks answers to. The concept that you are offering them is that you can turn red ink into black using their money. The idea is biblical: you conceptually claim to be able to manage the investor's capital more successfully than the investor, notwithstanding prior sins of the company that trashed early investors' capital. Thus, in selling a concept the management team must provide answers to tough questions in these five key areas:

1. Performance
2. Protection from loss
3. Liquidification
4. Historical track record
5. Endorsement

Although it is not impossible for the people who ran the company into the ground to raise the capital to turn it around, it is useful for the stockholders to replace the senior manager with a workout manager in order that the one who claims he or she can deliver black ink isn't the one who produced the red ink.

Raising capital for anything requires writing a business plan and carefully rendering 36-month cash flow and operating statement projections that provide the text in the business plan with its credibility.

How Much Can I Make?   The essence of the business plan lies in the answer to this question. The investor is interested in knowing how much money the manager projects that the investor will make in three to five years on the investment. In financial terms, this is known as a rate of return on investment, or ROI.

Most high-risk investors have a target ROI of 45-60 percent compounded per annum over a three- to five-year period. For boneyard investment opportunities, or risky deals, the target is closer to 60 percent. For less risky deals, the target is closer to 45 percent. Investors convert the ROI percentage to four to five turns on their money in three years or approximately 10 turns on their money in five years. They assume that the company will achieve a public market for its common stock within three to five years or sell out for cash or stock, thus producing the return. These rates of return may strike you as overly ambitious, pie-in-the-sky, unrealistic, and as false targets thrown at naive managers to make them shelve their business plans and search for cash elsewhere. Not true. If an investor can achieve these ROIs in 3 or 4 investments out of 10, he or she is way ahead of market yields. By picking companies with favorable product niches in huge markets and with good people, you can peddle even those that do not make it to large corporations at prices in excess of the investor's cost.

The first section of the business plan that investors read is the three- to five-year operating statement projections. They look at the third year's projected earnings and multiply by an appropriate price/earnings ratio for similar companies, say 10.0 to 12.0 times. Then they multiply the amount they are being asked to invest by 4 or 5 and divide the resulting number by the first sum to determine the required percentage ownership. If it is too high, then the projections are too low, and the deal will be turned down. If the required ownership level is too low, they will ask if there is pricing flexibility and a willingness to negotiate, before they go forward.

Operating statement projections are known as hockey sticks because most of them take the shape of a hockey stick. The company's earnings are at the base of the hockey stick, but if it receives venture capital, they will move up to the handle.

In the hockey stick in Exhibit 2.7, the company projects third-year Net Profits After Taxes (npat) of $2 million or a market value at that time of $24 million using a p/e of 12. The investor multiplies $1.5 million by 5 and divides the resulting value $7.5 million by $24 million to see how much ownership his or her $1.5 million should purchase—about 31 percent in this case. If the business plan offers an ownership percentage of about that amount, the investor will read the business plan in more depth. The valuation formula once again is as follows:

$$\frac{\text{Investment} \times \text{4 or 5}}{\text{third year npat} \times \text{10 or 12}} = \begin{array}{l}\text{Ownership level necessary}\\\text{to achieve target ROI}\end{array}$$

Referring to Exhibit 2.7, the valuation formula translates as follows:

$$\frac{\$1,500,000 \times 5}{\$2,000,000 \times 12} = \frac{\$7,500,000}{\$24,000,000} = 31.25\%$$

There are two red flags in this formula that could result in a quick turndown, and they have to do with proportionality. If, in the case of the above example, the company claimed that it could achieve the $2 million earnings level with a small amount of capital, say $150,000, the deal would sound too unrealistic and too optimistic. It would not appear reasonable to the investor that a fairly dramatic surge in earnings would result from so minuscule an investment: the steeper the earnings ramp, the greater the fuel requirement at the base. "Why surely you would not want to give this investment opportunity to a perfect stranger," would be the investor's initial reaction. Or, "What's wrong with this deal that so little investment can create $24 million in market value in three years?"

Earnings in the third year are multiplied by 10 or 12 to determine the company's market value. The investor's capital is multiplied by 4 or 5, and

Exhibit 2.7   The Hockey Stick

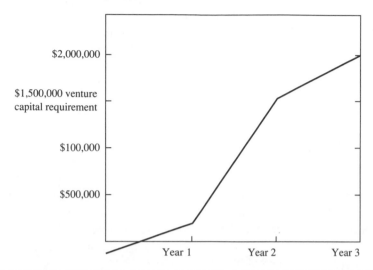

the first sum is divided into the second to determine the investor's required ownership position. If indeed the investor asks for that ownership position (the manager may initially offer less), he or she will make four to five times the investment, a 45–60 percent compound annual ROI (before capital gains taxes) if the projections are met.

On the other hand, assume that the $24 million of market value required an initial investment of $6 million to achieve $2 million in third year earnings. Four times $6 million equals $24 million, and the investor would have to buy all of the company to justify the investment. Or, the projections should perhaps be extended a few more years, at which point they may begin to grow more vertically and create a more attractive rate of return in the fifth year. There are a number of deals that require years of laying pipe before the oil is pumped. MCI Communications took three rounds of financing; Federal Express, which raised $96 million on its first round, needed two more massive financings before it began to generate income. By the time of its third round, Federal was on death's doorstep and did a down and dirty financing at approximately one tenth the price per share of its second-round financing. The investor might also look behind the $6 million to see if some portion of it might be done with debt to reduce the equity investment and increase the return on investment.

Boneyard investors are extraordinarily busy people for whom time is unusually valuable. Not only must they devote a big slice of each day to reviewing new proposals, but they have portfolios to monitor, board meetings to attend, tasks to do for portfolio companies—and in recessions most of their time is spent playing Red Cross nurse to their portfolios and not reviewing new proposals—and finally, making on-site inspections of new deals. Therefore, when a new business plan floats in the door, the first areas reviewed are the hockey stick, the amount required, and the management team. If the hockey stick suggests the kind of ROI they are interested in, they will read management's track record to see if the projections were prepared by qualified managers or merely good hockey stick artists. If the former, the package will get a thorough reading. If the managers have short track records in the turnaround business, the other aspects of the business plan must be extremely interesting, including the ROI, market size, growth rate, and product niche.

Credibility of the Projections.   What makes the projections believable? Normally it is the credibility of the projection maker in concert with the facts. Lee Iaccoca had a combination of experience and management skills, plus bubbling enthusiasm, to convince the federal government to guarantee $500 million of loans to Chrysler Corporation in 1980. John DeLorean, who had previously run the Chevrolet Division of General Motors, convinced sophisticated investors pulled together by Oppenheimer & Company, plus the government of Ireland, to invest and loan $165 million to launch, to their regret, DeLorean Motor Company. Fred Smith, at the age of 29, on the strength of a paper he had written at Yale and no previous business experience, raised $96 million in venture capital and joint-venture funds to launch Federal Express. Jeffrey Roloff, at the age of 23, raised $600,000 of venture capital from two funds and $600,000 in Industrial Revenue Bonds to expand Central Data Corporation, a computer manufacturer that he began at the age of 19. The task of each of these entrepreneurs was to convince lenders, guarantors, and investors that the projections would be realized.

Let us begin with the key line in an operating statement projection— revenues. If declining sales were the precursor of the troubled company's problems, why do sales increase in the projections? These questions may seem naive, but they must be answered at some point in the business plan.

The plan for achieving those sales must be carefully thought out and expressed in the business plan. If the company is manufacturing a product, the traditional channels for reaching customers may be added to. Perhaps the company plans to change from shotgun to direct response marketing. Perhaps it intends to begin census-based telemarketing, or other unique strategies such as air space marketing.*

The boneyard investor is concerned with cash flow, not profitability. The owner or manager must provide cash flow projections to supplement his or her operating statement projections. The cash flow statement projections will

---

*These and other strategies for generating cash flow from multiple channels are described and explained in A. David Silver, *The Inside Raider* (New York: Harper & Row, 1990).

describe the company's ability to service the creditors, who presumably will have been convinced to compromise the amounts owing them or to stretch them out. The investor wants to see if there will be cash available after all payments to new suppliers for operating expenses and to pay old debts; and he or she will go through every item in the projections. The numbers based on assumptions will be suspect. The prospects for raising money for a troubled company are based on the credibility of the projections, and that begs the question: who is the projection-maker? Who is responsible for making these numbers happen? This is the "Who says you're good at what you do?" question.

How Much Can I Lose?   The answer to this question lies partially in the structure of the financing and partially in an assessment of the riskiness of the deal. In regard to financing structure, the weakest instrument an investor can purchase is a limited partnership interest, and the second weakest is a minority common stock position. A senior common stock or preferred stock position is the third weakest, providing only preferences to the investor in liquidation and in receiving dividends prior to any dividend payments on the common stock. The fourth weakest instrument is an unsecured loan, usually referred to as a subordinated debenture. Finally, the strongest instrument is a secured loan.

In all of these securities the investor and the company can enter into agreements that spell out how they will treat one another over the course of the relationship. But the investors can enforce their position if they must if their investment vehicle is strong rather than weak. The purchase agreement entered into between the company and the investor at the closing contains a litany of the things that the company must do ("positive covenants") and the things that it must not do ("negative covenants") to and for the investor. Failure to comply places the company in default, and the remedies in the event of default are the determining factor in measuring the risk of loss of the investment. One remedy useful in protecting an investor's principal is the ability to take control of the company's board of directors. This permits the investor to bring in new management to try to turn the company around.

Other remedies, which may include demanding immediate repayment of the investment, are difficult to enforce on strapped companies but serve as a threat of the lengths to which the investor will go in order to protect his or her principal.

The second measure of the downside of a deal is a calculation of the inherent risks. There are three major risks in every troubled company:

1. Production—Can the product be produced?
2. Marketing—Can the product be sold?
3. Management—Can the product be produced and sold at a positive cash flow?

For the troubled company operating at break-even or at a loss *on a cash flow basis* (profits are irrelevant in a workout situation), all three risks are relatively large, hence the projections lack credibility. When the workout specialist's capabilities are placed in front of the old management team's, the projections take on the sound of hard currency.

One very strong plus is going for the troubled company when it is seeking financing. More wealth has been created by investing in bankrupt or seriously troubled companies than in rapidly expanding ones, for which the investment price is steep. Milton S. Petrie acquired roughly 10 million shares of Toys 'R' Us at prices below 50 cents a share when it was in bankruptcy in 1974–78. The stock is worth nearly a billion dollars today.

Charles Schwab bought his discount stock brokerage firm back from Bank of America at a "steal" when the bank was coughing blood, and he has turned it into a thrilling success story while overbuilt and over-leveraged multinational stock brokerage firms cut back and looked for dimes in the parking lot.

The overworked investment motto of the legendary Rothschilds says it best: "Buy when blood is running in the streets. Sell when the fatted lamb is lowing in the fields."

How Do I Get My Money Out?   The normal means of achieving liquidity in a venture or boneyard investment are by public offering or acquisition by a larger company for cash or stock.

The business plan should indicate that the owners are indeed interested in arranging for an exit route such as this for the investors. If they have another means in mind for achieving liquidity such as participation in earnings, this too should be mentioned, but it is rarely as attractive as selling out at a high p/e ratio. Large industrial corporations for whatever reason are not successful developers of new products. Their research and development efforts over the years have been poorer at generating valid new products (except in the pharmaceutical industry) than has the entrepreneurial process. Thus, the troubled high-tech company has more options than the insolvent manufacturer or distributor to take its investors out at a high p/e ratio.

If you plan to offer stock to creditors to compromise a portion of their accounts payable, it may be a practical idea to merge your company with a public shell. A little-known loophole in the Bankruptcy Act of 1978 *makes their stock free-trading*—that is, immediately exchangeable for cash. I will describe this unique tactic in chapter 9.

Who Says this Deal Is Any Good?   Investors like endorsements and testimonials. Professional venture capitalists will call dozens of references before investing—customers, suppliers, and personal references. "Why did you buy the product? What do you think about it? Will you buy more? How was the service?" are a few of the typical questions asked of customers.

Personal references include bankers, previous employers, and previous co-workers.

The reference checks on entrepreneurs are not always glowing. Burt McMurtry, a specialist in high-tech investments, says:

> Quite often when I check on a prospect, his former subordinates say they worshipped him. He was dynamic, the high-energy type. His peers, however, were often irritated with him because he was something of a prima donna, always trying to get his project funded first. And his former bosses? Some of them will say they like what he accomplished, but he nearly drove them crazy. Didn't take no for an answer easily, and had zero grasp of corporate politics.*

Some venture capitalists ask for seven personal references—five good ones and two bad ones. The business plan should offer to make these available, but they should be referred to only and handed out at meetings with interested investors.

The business plan should include many of the endorsements received by the product in trade journals, letters from customers, and customer responses at demonstrations and trade shows. Investors should be given a hands-on demonstration of the product or service by going to a trade show, visiting the company at its plant, or, at a minimum, through product photographs. In attempting to convey enthusiasm about a business to an investor, the manager should bear in mind the plight of the first person who ate a lobster and tried to convince others that it was good. "You mean you ate that strange thing that crawls on the bottom of the sea?" they were likely to ask. "Yes, and let me explain why it was good." Clearly, the lobster eater could have used the endorsement of others who ate it and did not die.

Who Else Is in It?   Investors like to have company in a deal. They want to know that other institutions or corporations are involved with the company in either a risk-taking capacity or as lenders, suppliers, or customers.

When Fred Smith raised $96 million to launch Federal Express, he first got General Dynamics excited about selling him hundreds of Falcon jets. Then he hired an investment banker to endorse the business plan and himself. Next he showed that he was investing all of his net worth. Afterward he convinced Prudential Insurance to supply a middle tier of long-term financing subject to the venture capital being raised. Then he went back to General Dynamics and enhanced the terms of their deal to signify to others an improving relationship.

The investment bankers needed $26 million of venture capital to support the debt structure, and they landed some important names first: First

---

*Forbes, 3 August 1981.

National Bank of Chicago, Allstate Insurance, and Citicorp. The rest of the financing came together quickly because of the endorsement factor. Endorsement makes the difference between the Masters Tournament and the local pro-am. Further, in the event that the company will need more capital in the future, there will be more than one person pulling the oars.

The business plan or the workout specialist's cover letter should indicate whether other institutions or corporations are financially involved with the company. Endorsements are very important in the rather small world of business, where with a few telephone calls an investor can check out the credibility and integrity of an owner or manager.

Jobs Are Leveragable.   One asset of a troubled company that is frequently overlooked is *jobs*. Over half of the states offer loans, guarantees, and grant programs to assist in the saving (or creation) of jobs in their region. If the troubled company is seeking financing of, for instance, $1 million and if the money arrives in time to save 100 jobs, the company can attract a loan guarantee for all or a large percentage of the loan from a state or local government. That is an endorsement backed by hard dollars.

The Likelihood that a Trustee Will Be Appointed to Run the Company

One great fear that envelopes owners or managers of troubled companies is that they will be replaced by a trustee during bankruptcy proceedings, which means that they will be removed from the day-to-day operations of the company and lose their salaries. But that fear can be alleviated by turning over day-to-day operations to a *workout manager*.

I have used the term workout consultant to describe the physician who diagnoses and treats troubled companies. However, a handful of these doctors only take clients who hire them to manage their business. One of these, Suren G. Dutia, 48, assumes the role of chief executive officer when he is hired to effect a workout and turnaround.

"I don't take on two or three clients at a time and live on airplanes flying from one to the other," says Dutia.

"When I take an assignment, it has to be as Chief Executive Officer with all the duties and responsibilities that go with the job." Dutia and workout managers who operate in this manner receive handsome equity incentives that produce significant financial rewards if they succeed.

"My specialty is the entrepreneurial, high-technology company that has been managed by an engineer and gotten itself into trouble when its growth slows and it hasn't developed Act 2 to follow Act 1."

The appointment of a trustee signifies the loss of credibility by the owner or manager in the eyes of his or her creditors. "He's lied to us one time too many," shout the enraged creditors. Or, "Your honor, we cannot negotiate with the president. She's completely inflexible and unyielding," the creditors protest to the judge.

It is only in the thoroughly dysfunctional companies that the creditors attempt to replace the CEO with a trustee. This occurs when the CEO is stuck in the "blame" stage of crisis: the "they-did-it-to-me-and-they're-going-to-pay-for-it" stage. Frank Lorenzo, the former CEO of Eastern Airlines, was replaced by a trustee when he was fixated on the negative attributes of working out a plan of reorganization.

In order to avoid the cacophonous call for a trustee, the owner or manager must either call in a workout manager or plan to address creditor demands with an open and flexible attitude.

The Prospects for Selling the Company

Experienced workout consultants say that the asset they seek to maximize above all others is *options*—the fewer the options to save the company, the smaller their probability of success. And like a physician whose death rate is higher than the norm, a workout consultant with a high rate of failure will receive fewer referrals. After all, if there are no survivors to give positive references to potential clients, a workout consultant who buries his clients will bury himself.

"There are two overriding goals that workout specialists strive for," says William Gano, a Memphis, Tennessee problem-solver: "To achieve a financing and to accomplish an informal plan of reorganization."

A financing and an acquisition are similar but in most situations a company loses its identity when it is acquired and the acquisition price is "down and dirty." If a company is sold out at the bottom of the roller coaster and then recovers and rebounds to a higher level of success, the acquirors receive the benefits. On the other hand, if it accomplishes a financing at a boneyard price and then rockets back to life, the stockholders, although seriously diluted, have the opportunity to recapture their investment and perhaps make a small gain.

With the excessive high-tech investments in the 1970s, many venture capital funds formed to invest in start-up and rapidly emerging companies in the 1980s changed their objectives to become vulture capital funds. These are investment companies that prey on wounded companies having proprietary markets, definable niches, and demonstrable economic validity but that have exhausted their capital and their credibility with their investors.

In many instances, the "technoids" who started these companies are ill-equipped to manage the company in a crisis and must be replaced. It is difficult to change existing management without a change in ownership; thus when the vulture capitalists offer to invest $2 million, for example, to rescue the company, they usually seek control. It is a foregone conclusion that they will bring in a workout manager to run the company. A change in control coupled with a change in management is a *de facto* acquisition.

There are many shrewd acquirors who realize that the acquisition price of a troubled company will be less if the acquisition is made through the bankruptcy courts than before the company files for protection. This is not the most desirable result for the stockholders, who will receive nothing in that circumstance, or for the workout specialist, who will not be able to put another notch on the gun handle if the client slides into bankruptcy. Beware the anxious suitor who proposes an acquisition pre-Chapter 11 and then continually pushes back the wedding date until the beleaguered company has no choice but suicide.

To enhance the prospects for selling a crisis-torn company, the workout consultant must be hired as early as possible in order to begin managing the crisis and the company's operations. If the crisis overwhelms a management team unprepared for battle, the prospects for selling the company will evaporate as will its price.

Selling the troubled company is a backdoor option: not a first choice and not a second choice, but an option for preserving the company nonetheless. Those managers who, like Dylan Thomas, "rage, rage against the burning of the light," rather than formulating a survival plan virtually shut the back door, eliminating their option of selling the company.

In my workout and turnaround assignments, I make it very clear up front that acquirors and sources of financing will be pursued simultaneously and with equal energy. I want the client to have as many options to choose from as possible. Thus I telephone my staff from the client's office and ask them to run searches through two data bases: public and private companies in industries that have acquired companies similar to the client and venture capital funds that list the client's industry, size, and region among their criteria.* By the time I return to the office, stacks of annual reports, 10-Ks, Standard & Poor's tear sheets, and photostated directory pages are on my desk waiting for me to qualify a dozen potential investors and a like number of acquirors.

The Courage of the Owner or Manager

It requires a wheelbarrow full of courage hoisted in front of the owner or manager in crisis to get through difficult times. If you have never been there, you cannot imagine the asynchronous din of threats, process servers in the outer office, collection calls, lawyers screaming, creditors telling you what part of your anatomy they're going to "sue off," key personnel resigning, managers begging for product, and deathly silence in the wee hours of the morning except for nightmares of liquidating auctions in the company's

---

*My principal data bases are A. David Silver, *The Middle-Market Leveraged Financing Directory and Source Book* and *The Middle-Market Business Acquisition Directory and Source Book* (New York: HarperCollins, 1990).

parking lot. Few have the amount of courage necessary to get them through this period. One way they get it is to hire the services of a workout specialist who fears nothing that a creditor, collector, or lawyer can do to the company because the specialist has stared them down before and they blinked first.

The Economy's New Hero.   If the decade of the 1990s is going to bear witness to tough economic times, the workout specialist is going to emerge as America's new business hero. My definition of "hero" is someone who is great, someone who has achieved an authentic instance of greatness. A hero is someone who has intentionally taken a large step, one far beyond the capabilities of most persons, in solving a problem that affects many people. A hero brings about something that is unlikely to have happened by the mere force of events, by the trends or tendencies of the time—that is, something that is unlikely to occur without his or her intervention. The economy's new heroes are distinguished, in the first instance, because their intervention makes the highly improbable happen.

Workout specialists do not seek publicity and as a result are not widely known. They are essentially shy and imprisoned within driven, fanatical personalities. In this involuntary confinement, the heroes have developed a certain independence of outlook. Questions of status, social position, and relative degrees of economic standing—so common in many people—have not affected them. Until recently, workout specialists and bankruptcy lawyers held the short, dirty end of the economic stick, when entrepreneurs and raiders held the long, sleek stick that stirred the drink.

"Shoot at me," our heroes say to their enemies. "I'm going to succeed anyway."

Workout specialists know they are stronger, more imaginative, and more effective fighters than the managers they replace or supplement and the creditors they fend off. They are fearless, understanding, and indifferent to praise or blame.

Our heroes build groups of followers within the companies they help by convincing them that the hero's view of the future will become reality. Joining the heroes will improve the follower's lives and shelter their companies from failure and obscurity. Workout specialists have become their powerful, self-confident champions who are unafraid of the future. Workout specialists have immense natural authority, dignity, and strength.

The peculiar quality of greatness and a sense of the sublimity of the occasion stems from a delight in being alive at "the right time" and in control of events at a critical moment in history. With companies self-destructing like so many Mrs. O'Leary's cows, *the* time for the workout consultant has arrived. Workout consultants thrive on change and the instability of things. The infinite possibilities of the unpredictable future offer endless opportunities for spontaneous moment-to-moment improvisation and for large, imaginative, bold strokes causing important events that change the course of a company, an industry, or a region. Although strength comes to our heroes from their clear, brightly colored vision of—and passionate faith in—their views of a reconstructed future and in their power to mold it, they know where they are going, by what means, and why. This strength enhances their energy and drive as it did Winston Churchill's during the Battle of Britain, when he said: "It is impossible to quell the inward excitement which comes from a prolonged balancing of terrible things."*

These new American heroes are usually in their late 40s or 50s and casual in their appearance. They wear no jewelry and disdain lace-up shoes, which require time. They are almost always married or divorced—the latter if the spouses were too frequently left out of things while our heroes made night calls on terminally ill patients. Their language, images, and turns of phrase are rooted in strength and individual imagination. They are excellent communicators; these new heroes can convince people to do things that they never intended to do before. They have an extraordinary variety of humor—some of it, but not all, of the gallows variety. After all, our heroes perform their duties on the bottom rung of the economic ladder and have felt the boot for years of those who took over companies with pyramidal funny money and slapped seven figure fees into their wallets. Our heroes have distinctive physical characteristics, sometimes carried over from childhood. The unique aspects of their appearances include herky-jerky physical movements—the rapid manner in which they walk and the way they stand, seemingly unable to sit down—their gestures, and the features of their exceedingly expressive faces. Above all is the tone of voice; it is controlled, calm, and self-assured. It does not know bitterness, even when failures seem imminent. Our heroes have an ironical awareness of the shortcomings of all people.

The workout specialist deals with the minds of his or her opponents—those who would deep-six the company—and the minds of those who might put cash into the troubled company. They focus their knowledge, determine how to use it, then drive toward the turnaround goal they choose. They do not childishly strive for wealth or power or to overcome the fear of failure. They have outgrown certain experiences in their homes, schools, and corporations, where these strivings were once important. No longer. Power, wealth, and the fear of failure are not valid reasons for work. They have a single-minded purpose: save the patient; chalk up a "W."

It is unusual to find these characteristics in an owner or manager, but not out of the question. As we shall see, to become heroic the owner or manager of a crisis-riven company must recognize from the outset that he or she is no longer in the widget business. No. Not for awhile. He or she is in the workout business. Once that transformation is made, which is difficult, it is possible that the owner or manager can effect a turnaround without the assistance of a workout specialist.

---

*From Isaiah Berlin, *Personal Impressions* (New York: Viking, 1981).

The Economic Validity of the Business

The business your company has been in may no longer be valid. It may not be worth saving. The saddle may have been shot out from under you, and the horse may have hightailed it into the hills.

You can still save the company, however, and enter a new business, as I will describe in chapter 8. But the first step is to determine if you should fetch the old horse, re-saddle it, and try to ride it again. This means determining your company's likelihood of success once Humpty Dumpty is put back together again.

Will It Be Successful if I Turn It Around?   Prior to saving the existing business, the workout specialist performs the DEJ (demonstrable economic justification) factor test (see Exhibit 2.8). The workout specialist asks: Does this business meet all the requirements of the DEJ factor test? If it possesses all eight of the following factors, it is my experience that *the workout specialist or owner/manager can be almost assured of success*. Plus, *the cost of saving the company will be less than $500,000.*

Managers who fail to ask these eight questions may refinance the troubled company only to have it fail again. The DEJ factor test is a predictor of success and a measure of the cost of seizing the opportunity. Here's the rule:

> *Super DEJ*. If the business possesses all eight DEJ factors, refinancing it will cost less than $500,000, and the probability of success will be about 90 percent.
>
> *Majority DEJ*. If the business possesses seven out of eight DEJ factors, saving it will cost up to $2 million, and the probability of success will be about 80 percent.
>
> *Marginal DEJ*. If the business possesses six out of eight DEJ factors, saving it will cost up to $20 million, and the probability of success will be about 60 percent.
>
> Below 6 DEJ factors, the business is a reject and the manager should think in terms of creating a new vehicle. (See chapter 8.)

As you review the eight DEJ factors, think of the marketing failures within your company. Which two or more DEJ factors nailed its coffin shut? If you can't come up with an example inside your company, remember DeLorean Motor Company, a $165 million fatal plunge.

Imagine trying to save a defense contractor (Lockheed) or an automobile manufacturer (Chrysler). The former has institutional barriers to entry and needs to wait years to be paid for contracts. The latter needs mountains of advertising and a large dealership organization to sell its products to consumers. Is there any reason why these companies required government

Exhibit 2.8   The DEJ Factor Test

DEJ Factor	Ask Yourself These Questions	The Cost
1. Existence of qualified buyers	Are the consumers to whom the product or service is marketed *aware* that they have a need for it?	Advertising
2. Large number of buyers	Are there lots of consumers who need this product or service?	Competitive pressure on *price*
3. Homogeneity of buyers	Will the market accept a standardized product or service or must it be customized?	Manufacturing, tooling, die costs
4. Existence of competent sellers	Is the product or service so complex to explain that customers will need 90 days or more to test it?	Salespersons' salaries and expenses
5. Lack of institutional barriers to entry	Is there a requirement for governmental or industry association approval before the product or service can be marketed?	Working capital that burns while approval is awaited
6. Easy promotability by word of mouth	Can the product's or service's merits be described by word of mouth?	Advertising
7. Invisibility of the inside of the company	Is there a need to reveal profit margins to the public?	Competitive pressure on price
8. Optimum price/cost relationship	Is the selling price at least five times the cost of goods sold?	Restriction of the number of marketing channels

bailouts? Both companies have six out of eight DEJ factors and their refinancings required nine-figure refinancings. Where would the capital have come from if not from the government? Existing stockholders would have been diluted to a fare-thee-well.

The workout specialist can assist the owner or manager in assessing his or her company's demonstrable economic justification. It is a valid question to ask, although not always asked by managers or owners in crisis. But workout consultants are objective and impartial observers. They are like the field surgeons in the Civil War movies who grit their teeth, hold back their fear, and tell the wounded soldier, "Son, I have to take off your leg to save your life. Take a swig of this and hold on."

While we're on the subject of economic validity, the workout specialist's *raison d'etre* is the sum of the 13 factors that we have just reviewed at length. If upon reviewing them once again you can see at least 10 reasons out of the 13 for how a workout specialist may help you, then use the directory in the back of this book and find the doctor whose track record and experience fits your company's illness.

13 Valid Reasons for Hiring a Workout Specialist

1. Time: You've run out of it.
2. The personal exposure of the owner or manager: You could go down with the ship.
3. Choosing the best bankruptcy lawyer: If your company is too far gone, you will need to consider this course of action.
4. The existence of free cash flow: Can you find cash in the assets and overhead?
5. The crisis readiness of the management team: Are your middle managers battle-scarred?
6. The characteristics of the bankruptcy judges in your jurisdiction: What are your chances in Chapter 11?
7. The reputations of the creditors with debtor companies: You may have bent the credibility branch too far.
8. The capitalization of the company: If you are such a good manager, why did you borrow so much money?
9. The prospects for raising capital: Can you develop a winning Redirect and Grow Plan?
10. The likelihood that a trustee will be appointed to run the company: Are you severely disliked and mistrusted by creditors?
11. The prospects for selling the company: This is a backdoor option but you need time to probe it.
12. The courage of the owner or manager: Do you have the guts to take the blows and keep on going?
13. The economic validity of the business: Does your company solve problems for people better than any competitor?

CHAPTER 3

The Primary Causes
of Business Failures

It's like setting your hair on fire and trying to put it out with a hammer.
— The Manager of a company in crisis

Every company is as different from every other company as a thumb print. How then can one cite the primary causes of business failures? One thread that can lead to failure runs through all troubled companies: *managers are unprepared for crisis*.

Business schools, experience in a large corporation, and being part of an entrepreneurial team do not teach battlefield survival tactics. Knowing how to turn around a company racing toward failure is a systematic process known to a very few people in the business community. Thus, managements cause businesses to fail, at least according to several score of the top workout specialists in the country, who play the role of emergency room doctor to the nation's troubled companies.

I asked the leading workout specialists in the country to validate their business existence. This means, in effect, what are the factors that go wrong in a given company, causing your telephone to ring with anxious client calls? Exhibit 3.1 illustrates how they ranked the causes of business failures.

In the view of workout consultants, 7 out of 10 causes of business failures can be linked to management, one to the capital structure, and two to marketing. Others may disagree with this assessment. After all, workout consultants are surrogate managers generally hired by the stockholders. Their loyalty is to the stockholders who hire them and not necessarily to the managers who they frequently replace. Notwithstanding, the opinions of these experts are worth exploring.

Exhibit 3.1   Workout Consultants' Ranking of Causes of Business Failures

1. Managers are unprepared for crisis.
2. Managers tiptoe around stressors until they become crises.
3. Managers do not know where and how to slash expenses and raise cash.
4. Many of today's managers have never lived through seriously difficult times.
5. Managers think sales growth can disguise problems within their organization.
6. Undercapitalization.
7. Failure to be responsive to the market by continually reviewing products or services.
8. Failure to stay in contact with customers and to continually ask them what they want.
9. Lack of depth of talented people in middle management.
10. Owners and managers become emotionally involved with their companies.

PREPARING FOR A CRISIS

As the top vote getter was management's unpreparedness for a crisis, how could that factor be mitigated or eliminated as a cause of business failures? The answer: *fire drills*.

Managers are trained to run companies in good times, not in hard times. In some instances, they do not know the warning signals of approaching hard times, or they do but choose to ignore them. Every manager learns that undercapitalization (or over-leveraging) is a knife that cuts both ways; but knowing the relationship of excessive leverage to the variables that can throw a company into crisis—product obsolescence, regional disaster, industry downturn, and national recession—does not make a manager battle ready.

I have recommended elsewhere* and I reiterate here that to teach crisis-preparedness to management you have to hold fire drills with about the same frequency that we had them in school. Only then can management role-play a crisis and learn how to handle the real thing when it occurs. Further, I advocate hiring a workout specialist for a day to lead the dress rehearsal. After all, who knows better than the workout consultant the effects of a crisis in a given company.

The fire drill idea may not seem appropriate to you, but it is if you do not know the answers to these questions:

---

*A David Silver, *The Business Bible for Survival* (Rocklin, CA: Prima Publishing, Inc., 1989).

- If our company's bank is acquired by a large out-of-state bank, could our line of credit be suddenly called?

- If our principal supplier goes into Chapter 11, can it continue selling to us? Would quality deteriorate? Would shipments slow down or become irregular?

- Could our company survive the accidental death of a senior manager? What steps would it take to effect a smooth transition?

- Could our company survive a massive product recall or a cease-and-desist order from a regulatory agency regarding product toxicity? What steps would it take?

- If our principal customers suddenly stop ordering products because they are the subject of junk bond failures, do we have alternate channels of distribution?

- Could we survive a simultaneous postal rate increase, a direct mail marketing campaign that is "lost" by the post office, or a telephone strike or power outage that cancels a telemarketing campaign?

- If our company's top five salespeople suddenly left to start their own company, could we survive a steep sales decline?

If you have done fire drills to practice the steps your management team would take in the event of these crisis scenarios, then you may be ready to handle all the trouble the market can throw at you. If not, it's time to take to the practice field.

"DRESS REHEARSAL FOR A CRISIS"

The setting for the fire drill is your company's conference room on a Saturday. The props are the conference room table, the chairs, some legal pads and pencils, and a blackboard and chalk. The managers whom you invite to the play, entitled "Dress Rehearsal for a Crisis," are not permitted to bring any records or documents with them.

Before you have called the managers into the conference room for their auditions, write on the board these questions:

1. What events could happen to throw our company into a crisis?
2. What would be the effects of a crisis?
3. What steps would we take to work out of a crisis?

Whether the possibility of a crisis may be remote or stressors may be building up within the company that are about to boil over into a crisis, you are looking for weak links among key managers: those who believe the company is immune to crises and those who cannot role-play the crisis dress rehearsal with you because they are afraid of speaking out about their stressors.

Do not alert your managers to the subject of the meeting; surprise is the key element of your overall plan.

Invite your key managers into the conference room. Tell them you want to do some downside forecasting. Then ask them to sound out all of the crises that could affect their divisions. When you write them on the blackboard the list will appear something like the following:

Marketing

1. Customers will send back shipments protesting that they never placed the orders.

2. Potential customers currently testing our newest products will fail to order them, claiming that they do not have sufficient information, that their budget has been cut, or that someone above them has scotched the project.

3. Our top salespeople will leave us and join a competitor.

4. Customers will fall on hard times and delay payments from 30 to 90 days.

5. Customers will demand a higher service component with each sale, more training of our personnel, a longer warranty, and other services, so they go to our competitors who offer them.

6. The demand for our product will shift and our sales and profit margins will decline, leaving us strapped for cash.

Production

1. Our principal suppliers may go out of business, and we do not have second sources for components lined up.

2. Certain suppliers may demand faster payments for critical components; if we do not maintain our payments on a current basis, they may put us on C.O.D. terms.

3. Our key suppliers will become insolvent, so we will experience a decline in quality of the parts we are receiving.

4. A decline in the value of the dollar could make the cost of our imported components prohibitively expensive.

5. We may have to lay off production workers, which could diminish our ability to produce or to maintain our quality standards.

6. A regulatory agency may shut us down for environmental violations.

Human resources

1. The threat of strikes and work stoppages is our biggest fear. If we go into a lay-off period, we could be struck.

2. A wrongful termination lawsuit could affect our ability to hire.

3. We cannot find skilled people to hire and train.

4. Our best workers may suddenly leave to join a competitor or start-up.

5. Health insurance costs could increase 20 percent per year and wipe out profitability.

Controller

1. Our bank could fail, the deposits we maintain could be tied up, and amounts above $20,000 are not insured.

2. Our bank officer could leave the bank or be relocated. He or she has been giving us instant credit on all deposits, rather than holding them for five days. We could lose this favorable treatment if he or she leaves the bank.

3. Our bank could be acquired by a megabillion dollar bank from another state, and we could become just a number. Employees' payroll checks may not be cashable, or we may lose other privileges.

4. Accounts receivable collections could suddenly dry up and we would have to litigate to collect; the litigation expense could eat us up.

Chief Financial Officer

1. Our loans could be suddenly called due to FDIC takeover of our lender. Our access to capital markets could dry up.

2. Our stock price could fall, and although we may want to buy back our own stock, if the loan window shuts, we could be prey to a corporate raid.

3. We could be struck by a class action suit arising from a flagrant accounting error, driving our stock price down.

4. Our expansion plans for the coming year require that we raise $20 million in fresh capital. Conventional sources of financing may disappear and leave us with a half-built plant and half-developed new products. We could miss the market.

5. We are over-leveraged in relation to the industry. A down tick in cash flow due to slow sales could weaken our competitiveness.

6. Our competitors are making vertical acquisitions. We do not have anything going in that area; if we did, our stock price is too low to use, and we have too much debt to use more for acquisitions.

DEALING WITH THE EFFECTS OF A CRISIS

Once you have elicited this plethora of potential crises, ask the managers how they might go about solving them. Look for the words "preparedness," "slash expenses and raise cash," or "set up a strategic planning team." It is likely that your managers are unprepared, that they do not have effective strategies. Do you fire the ones who are not ready? It depends. There are three kinds of managers you will want to terminate: the "woe is me," the "no problem," and the "cannot cooperate" types.

As you discuss the potential crises with your key managers, asking them questions about their readiness, you will find some who will say "no problem." I cannot emphasize this enough: be very careful of these unrealistic types and get rid of them. If their values are permitted to permeate the organization so that no one stands up to say, "Hey! This could be serious," then by the time your problem is recognized, your company will be paralyzed. When this happens, the day-to-day activities of the company will become suffused with accusations, retaliations, general contentiousness, demoralization, and, eventually, ruin.

Sanford C. Sigoloff, 58, is the most widely known corporate turnaround expert in the country—Republic, Daylin, Wickes, which filed the third largest bankruptcy ever in 1982, and most recently L.J. Hooker, the junk bond laden department store chain. His first step in engineering workouts is to look for his most loyal lieutenants. He does not want to hear "no problem" from middle managers. He wants details of their problems. Says Bruce Spector, a Los Angeles bankruptcy lawyer who worked on Wickes with Sigoloff: "It's the complexity. He's got to have it. His love is problem solving and synthesizing information. He lives on it."*

Toughness may not be your historical management style, and I am not encouraging you to adopt an uncomfortable persona. But you must get at the truth: you must be critical of your managers, you must be clear with them, and you must seek clarity from them in pre-crisis periods.

Unless you encourage candor and confidence you will not be able to convince your managers to put all of their problems on the table. The emperor must be told he is not wearing clothes if that is the case. "Am I part of the problem?" you might ask. "Speak freely. There will be no beheadings." Yet it is your responsibility to show that you will be merciless with any middle manager who does not bring you the unvarnished truth with complete details of his or her fears, problems, and uncertainties. You must then determine which of the managers will be your companions on the journey through the tough times, should they come.

The head of marketing is likely to cite as one of the effects of a crisis that news of the company's woes could leak out to the trade press and cause

---

Fortune, 5 January 1987, 105.

customers to withhold orders. "Well, that's true," you or the workout expert says. "How would you handle it?" you ask.

The answer is quite complex. Communications are a critical factor during crises. Communication is the means of carrying messages to the various members of the company (internal communication) and to the outside community (external communication). The unvarnished truth is communicated among your teammates within the company. We'll address forms of communication with your employees shortly.

External communication is quite a different matter. Sun Tzu advises as follows:

> All warfare is based on deception. A skilled general must be master of the complementary arts of simulation and dissimulation. While creating shapes to confuse and delude the enemy he conceals his true dispositions and ultimate intent. When capable he feigns incapacity; when near he makes it appear that he is far away; when far away, that he is near.*

To accomplish Sun Tzu's prescription you have to write a hymn and have every person in the company who communicates with outsiders sing out of the same choir book. There is a need-to-know rule that applies to the company's bank, key customers, key suppliers, and the trade press. These outsiders need to know that a blow has struck the company, that the company is prepared to handle it, and that the company has mobilized all of its appropriate resources to deal with it. If you're not clear with these people, whose company could suffer if your company goes down, they will demand more information. It is wise to cut them in with a second layer of information in exchange for their cooperation in helping you resolve the problem. At that point you can peel away another layer of the problem, along with one level of your strategic plan to resolve it. Outsiders will either join with you or plan to join the enemy camp. Ask them which side they're on. Gain their loyalty or plan to count them in the enemy camp.

RESPONSE TO CRISIS WITHIN THE COMPANY

Gerald Caplan defined crisis as an "upset in a steady state."† The company strives to maintain a state of equilibrium with a series of adaptive maneuvers and problem-solving activities. Over the course of days and weeks many situations occur that disturb the equilibrium. These discontinuities are dealt with by implementing a crisis response plan within the company. This plan has three parts: *perception, nomination,* and *delegation.*

---

*Sun Tzu, p.41.

†Cited in Lydia Rapoport, "The State of Crisis: Some Theoretical Consideration," *The Social Service Review*, 27(a) (1962).

Perception

Keep the problem in front of you and the appropriate personnel at all times. Do not ignore relevant data that defines, amplifies, or circumscribes the problem. Absorb it fully. There may be shadows in the data that distort the information. Like the artisans in Plato's cave, we are chained in place staring at shadows on the wall. We cannot see the shadow-casters, but we are asked to make judgments about them by analyzing the shadows—the description of the problem—and to act accordingly. Something in our memory triggers our perception of the shadows, gives it new meaning. To rush into forming judgments as to the correct perception of a situation could yield incorrect data. The key to perceiving data accurately is a technique known as *problem-formulating* which the following examples illustrates.

Jacob Getzels and Mihaly Csikszentmihalyi studied young art students over a seven-year period.* At the onset, each participant in the study completed a still life for the researchers based on an arrangement made from a collection of objects provided. Afterwards, the artists answered several questions.

One question was "Could any of the elements in the drawing be eliminated or altered without destroying its character?" The objective of the investigations was to determine whether students considered their works fixed or flexible.

The answers to this question enabled Getzels and Csikszentmihalyi to draw a correlation between ability and recognition of the possibility of change. A panel of judges rated each artist's drawing. Those who received the highest ratings overall were the ones who said their work might be changed. A follow-up study seven years later by the same investigators indicated that more success had come to the artists who earlier had seen the possibility for change.

When a crisis strikes a company it carries information that in its sum and substance makes up the problem. The loan window may shut, forcing the company to cut back on new product development, a new plant, an acquisition, or needed capital expenditures. But is that the crisis-provoker? Formulate it. Remove objects. Is it a signal to kill the new product development, to delay the acquisition, and to cut back or slash expenses and get liquid? Add objects. Is there more to the problem than one bank's willingness to loan money? Is there a regional banking crisis? Is the problem more than localized with just your company? Should you be thinking about a larger bonfire and preparing for it accordingly? It's all in perception. Keep the problem in front of you and formulate it daily.

---

*Jacob Getzels and Mihaly Csikszentmihalyi, *The Creative Vision: A Longitudinal Study of Problem Finding in Art* (New York: John Wiley & Sons, Inc., 1976).

Nomination

Your managers are unlikely to know the primary morale booster strategy during the depth of a crisis. But the "name game" is a favorite technique among family therapists to lighten the load and ease tension.

Give names or assign symbols to the crisis-provoking events. Make them memorable and important sounding. Greek gods are useful for this purpose, along with well-known professional wrestlers and historical butchers and assassins. The personnel who take the most heat from creditors will need the cleverest names for their enemies. In a workout that I was called in on recently, we labeled the guy who was going to nail our whatevers to the wall, "Curt Lemay," after the well-known general who wanted to bomb Vietnam off the map.

"Hey, it's Lemay on the telephone. Who wants to take old Bombs Away this time?" we would shout to one another in the accounts payable section.

Soon all of the creditors will receive nicknames and the personnel who hold them off will be awarded monikers for their warlike prowess. The tiniest wisp of a payables clerk may come to work one day and find an Incredible Hulk doll on the desk, clutching a fifty-dollar bill in his hands, courtesy of the department head, for holding off Godzilla the Gorilla, the meanest bill collector in the industry.

In time, the name game spreads internally. A salesperson who collects cash with an order becomes "Sly Fox." The human resources officer assigned the unpleasant task of laying off 200 workers becomes "Atilla the Hun." He finds a stuffed teddy bear in his office one day, courtesy of his boss with a note that says, "I know I stuck you with a terrible job, but you did it with kindness and I'm grateful to you."

The objective of the name game is to discharge tension; to make the company a pleasant place to be in the midst of turmoil and problems. It uplifts everyone's spirits and makes them feel part of a drama. In doing this, you demonstrate mastery of the problem.

Delegation

Every employee wants to be an insider, wants to have inside information about what is going on in the company, especially when there is a cash crunch or a roaring, three-alarm fire. Once they know what is going on, they will welcome taking on additional assignments.

You will need to delegate much more than you ever have in the past because your time will be taken by the bullets and developing the survival plan. You will doubtless have more critical meetings than you ever imagined, and they will require hours of preparation. Thus, many of the routine tasks that you once assigned to yourself or to senior people will have to be delegated.

The weekly cash flow statement projection, the company's road map through the crisis, will have to be delegated. The bullet control list—the bills that *must* be paid within 24 hours—must be delegated. Key account sales, one of the jobs you may have enjoyed the most because it got you out into the market, will probably have to be assigned to a senior marketing person.

After you have delegated responsibility, it is essential to remain in touch. Not only will you need to keep close tabs on the duties you have delegated, but it is important that you demonstrate your concern for the people to whom the tasks were given. This means face-to-face contact, coupled with encouragement and more than just a lean in and a "how ya' doin'?" In troubled times, you will need to spend more time than ever delegating responsibility and following up continually with the battle-scarred soldiers, who may be holding the company's future in their hands.

I will discuss in detail in chapter 4 crisis management strategies, including selecting the right teammates to go through the war with you and cash-generating strategies. But at this point, step back and reflect on the "Dress Rehearsal for a Crisis." Did you know before you read this section on role-playing a crisis before it happens that behavior modification on this scale is required? What management team that you know of is able to explain the process of battle readiness? It is a systematic process because crises, like other stages in a company's growth, development, and change have a beginning, a middle, and an end. They can be managed but only by a trained, crisis-ready team.

CAPITALIZATION

I asked approximately 200 of the nation's leading debtor-advocate bankruptcy lawyers to rank the causes of business failures. Bankruptcy lawyers are generally hired by company managers and consequently have a degree of loyalty to them. They cite *capitalization* as the principal cause of business failures. Their rankings appear in Exhibit 3.2.

Excessive Debt

In the opinion of bankruptcy lawyers it is excessive leverage or insufficient financing that kills companies. They are absolutely right in *their* perspective, which, using a medical analogy, is surgical rather than treatment oriented. The debtor-advocate bankruptcy lawyer understands his or her task very well: that debt must be surgically removed from the right-hand side of the company's balance sheet in order to save the patient.

The headlines of the financial pages encourage the reader to believe that excessive debt is the primary factor in the current high rate of corporate

---

Exhibit 3.2   Debtor-Advocate Bankruptcy Lawyers' Ranking of the Causes of Business Failures

1. Excessive debt.
2. Inadequate sources of financing.
3. Breakdown in communication between debtor and creditors.
4. Managers are not prepared for crisis.
5. Managers wait too long to seek help.
6. Managers don't know how to cut expenses.
7. Lack of sales.
8. Poor accounting records.
9. Neglect of marketing.
10. Sudden changes in the market makes the company's products obsolete.

---

failures. Certainly in the case of the January 15, 1990 bankruptcy filings of Allied Stores and Federated Department Stores, which were acquired via the junk bond-backed leveraged buyout of Robert Campeau a year earlier, an excessive debt to worth ratio was the alleged culprit. *The Wall Street Journal* headline on the day after Campeau put his two department stores into bankruptcy read: "Behind the Bankruptcies: Heavy Debt, Little Equity." And, indeed, the debt to worth and debt to asset ratio of Allied and Federated show a heavy financial load borne by very little net worth, as underscored in Exhibit 3.3.

It is clear that there is some relation between excessive leverage and business failures, but, as many battle-scarred entrepreneurs will tell you, they have lived through tough times when their companies' debt to worth ratio was 20 times and more. However, they were turning their assets rapidly and generating enough cash every day to bounce the bullets away from the companies' hearts. Empirical studies of bankruptcy and workout specialists make the case that leverage ratios in and of themselves are not predictive of business failures. You have to look at liquidity ratios as well. These include sales/working capital, current assets/current liabilities, and cash plus short-term investments/current liabilities, the so-called "Acid Test" ratio. This means that companies with a higher percentage of their assets in cash, near cash, accounts receivable, and inventory, rather than in machinery, equipment, plant, and land, can sustain higher leverage ratios without teetering on the brink of failure because their assets are more quickly converted into cash; and cash stops bullets.

But you argue, Campeau's takeover candidates were department store chains, which have a higher percentage of current assets than fixed assets on their balance sheets. Why were they unable to carry the junk bond debt? The answer seems to lie with Campeau's management team's unpreparedness for crisis. Reports of the hubris of the Campeau team, their plans for new store openings as accounts payable stretched beyond 90 days in the chains, and

Exhibit 3.3   Leverage Ratios: Allied Stores and Federated Department Stores

($ millions)	1989	1990	Projected 1991
Allied Stores			
Total assets	$3,687	$3,727	$3,814
Long-term debt	2,606	2,953	3,240
Total liabilities	3,290	3,633	3,952
Stockholders' equity	396	94	(138)
Total debt/total assets	.9x	1.0x	1.0x
Debt/worth	8.3x	38.6x	infinite
Federated Department Stores			
Total assets	$7,672	$7,618	$7,759
Long-term debt	4,773	5,175	5,516
Total liabilities	6,657	7,028	7,402
Stockholders' equity	1,015	590	357
Total debt/total assets	.9x	.9x	1.0x
Debt/worth	4.7x	11.9x	20.7x

Source: *The Wall Street Journal*, February 12, 1990.

their ineffectiveness in generating cash by spin-offs and other strategies be-speak a management team proud of their purchases and unwilling to address the issue of an awesome debt load.

The same stories have surfaced in the L.J. Hooker bankruptcy (Bonwit Teller, B. Altman, Sakowitz, and other retail chains) and in the Revco Drug-store bankruptcy. As Thucydides reported of the Peloponnesian War 2,000 years ago, the Spartans were carried from battle on their shields, killed or wounded, not by the weapons of the Atheneans, but by their *koros, até,* and *hubris*: conceit, insouciance, and pride.

Junk Bonds

A bond is classified as a "junk bond" if it is rated less than investment grade by either Standard & Poor's or Moody's. They typically carry a higher interest rate, or yield, than do bonds of higher quality to compensate for the higher level of risk.

Until the late 1970s, the high-yield market consisted primarily of issues of high-quality companies, known in Wall Street parlance as "investment grade," that had become "fallen angels," or companies that had sustained losses for several years in a row. Standard & Poor's and Moody's downgraded their debt below BBB−. In 1977, the entire high-yield public bond market was a mere $24 billion.

Exhibit 3.4   Buyers of Junk Bonds 1908–1988

	Percentage
Mutual funds/money managers	30%
Insurance companies	30
Pension funds	15
Savings & loans	8
Foreign institutions	5
Individuals	5
Corporations	3
Securities dealers	3
Other	1

Source: Compiled by ADS Financial Services, Inc. from various published sources.

Today, there is approximately $160 billion in public junk bonds outstanding, or 25 percent of the entire public corporate bond market, and approximately three fourths of it was used to finance takeovers. That means they came to the market below investment grade.

The eager buyers of Campeau, L.J. Hooker, and other junk bonds were principally experienced money managers in prestigious financial institutions, some of which institutions themselves have become fallen angels. The appetites of this elite club are as depicted in Exhibit 3.4.

Notwithstanding the puffed up rhetoric in the press that links the high rate of business failures with junk bond financed takeovers, in reality there is not much substance to the correlation. The total failure rate of junk bonds is less than 5 percent, and there are no signs of its rising to precipitous levels. Many corporate raiders are experienced in raising cash quickly, and they have been able to carry their debt loads without visible strain. For example, to underpin its $26.5 billion leveraged buyout of RJR/Nabisco, the venerable raiders at Kohlberg, Kravis, Roberts & Co. (KKR) raised $1.7 billion from their institutional investors. Naturally, that diluted the ownership of KKR in RJR/Nabisco, but it maintained the firm's integrity in the financial community. Further, KKR, prior to the equity injection into RJR/Nabisco, returned a stunning capital gain to its investors when it took another of its companies, supermarket giant Safeway, public at approximately 13 times its takeover price just three years ago.

YOU CAN DROWN IN AN INCH OF WATER

The business school libraries have many elaborately researched books and theses on the subject, which are intellectually illuminating but do not represent life rafts to a drowning sailor. If you were admitted to a hospital because of a heart attack, the last information you would want to know is that the taste you developed in your grandmother's kitchen for bacon, eggs, cakes, cookies, and milk—all high cholesterol foods—was the probable cause of your heart disease. Theories have their place *a priori*. But when you are the head of a troubled company you want to know the 911 numbers of the workout consultants nearest the company. That's what this book is all about: emergency services to drowning companies.

However, until the doctor arrives, it will be of inestimable value to know how to crisis manage and how to raise cash quickly.

CHAPTER 4

Crisis Management Strategies

His rage and despair and the shock of the blow had so quieted and sobered him that now he was beyond even self-hatred. He felt gentle and dear. The sadness grew and became all but insupportable, and for the first time that evening, one of the few times in his life, he began to see things more or less as they were.

—James Agee, *A Death in the Family*

After the blow, when the knowledge of your illiquidity crisis sets in, there comes a time, usually in the quiet and lonely part of the early morning, when you begin to see things clearly. It occurs to you that you are involved in events that you may have some control over. Sure there may have been external forces at work beyond your control—a change in legislation, the failure of a large customer, product obsolescence—that landed you in the soup. But the time for blame and rage has gone. You are a manager. Your company is out of cash. What steps can you take without the help of outsiders to turn your company around?

There are several:

- Select a crisis management team
- Sell assets to raise cash
- Slash expenses
- Turn morale around

SELECT A CRISIS MANAGEMENT TEAM

If you are the kind of manager for whom year-to-year sales and earnings growth through traditional marketing channels is a fairly established pattern, the sudden jolt of an illiquidity crisis will probably unsettle you considerably and require an outsider or another member of management to take over the leadership and form the crisis management team. At the other end of the spectrum, if your management style is innovative—entrepreneurial—and you are the kind of person who requires the unceasing renewal of the daily "chase," who scorns the beaten track, and who thrives on management-by-improvisation, then doubtless you will probably not be able to build and lead a crisis management team either.

Neither the *traditional manager* nor the *improvisational manager* is well suited to pull his or her company through the dangerous mine field of an informal reorganization. The former is likely to be too unsettled by events; and the latter too scattered and unfocused for the detailed work and patience necessary to accomplish a workout.

The optimum management style to lead a workout team is the *inside raider*, a person who is atavistic in his or her search for cash wherever it may be. The raider management approach, which I describe and explain in *The Inside Raider,** is to locate the leverage points within to get the cash out, pay down debt, and generate multiple cash flow channels. Inside raiders are highly focused on slashing expenses, raising cash, and leveraging others, while avoiding others inversely leveraging them. Their approach requires clarity up front, a relentless curiosity as to how much a vendor, lender, or customer can be leveraged, and a devotion to the core business.

Whereas the traditional manager and the entrepreneurial manager are always planning for the upside, the inside raider is always concerned with avoiding the downside. The inside raider thinks defensively. In opposition to the entrepreneurial manager, the inside raider is more sanguine about what tomorrow will bring but has a good idea that it will bring more problems in need of solutions. Exhibit 4.1 compares management approaches in more detail.

The differences in form and rhythm of the three archetypical managers run through every activity within the company, and like Goldilocks sampling the porridge of the Three Bears, in a troubled company environment, the traditional manager is *too rigid*, the entrepreneurial manager is *too improvisational*, but the inside raider is *just right*. Goldilocks ate baby bear's porridge "all up," until there was no more. There are no more inside raiders to bring in to manage your workout and turnaround—they are busy taking over companies from within or without for fun and profit.

The closest facsimile of the inside raider's management approach is that of the workout specialist. And one of the reasons that the best of the bunch are expensive, indeed ask for fees plus success bonuses, is that they can get the job done where traditional or entrepreneurial managers cannot. Because of the short supply of workout specialists and the long supply of companies in trouble, fees for workout specialists' services are at an all-time high. Fees will drift down as more people and firms hang out workout specialist shingles.

---

*A. David Silver, *The Inside Raider* (New York: Harper & Row, 1990), p. 92.

Exhibit 4.1   Types of Management Styles

Traditional	Entrepreneurial	Raider
The objective of business is to maximize return on stockholders' equity.	The objective of business is to develop and convey innovative solutions to consumers who will pay more than cost.	The objective of business is to generate maximum cash flow from the core products or service for a minimum expenditure.
The means to achieve this objective is capital investment to build a base, hire qualified people, and create demand through mass marketing.	The means to achieve this objective is to fire in all directions and if something falls run toward it.	The means to achieve this objective is to find the leverage points within and outside the company and squeeze them.
The teammates selected to deliver the objectives are experienced and qualified managers who think and act linearly.	The most important people are those who can clean up after the entrepreneur and keep the scorecard accurately.	The teammates are strategic thinkers and careful implementers who can think and act both linearly and associationally.
The ultimate plan for our company's product is to capture significant market share in every developed country in the world.	The ultimate plan for our company's product is to develop a better one in 2–3 years that outsells the initial one.	The ultimate plan for our company's product is to take niche products and sell them through 5 or 6 channels to avoid reliance on any single means of distribution.
Ownership of assets and production capability is a measure of our success.	The minds of our creative people are the true measure of our success.	Maximizing cash flow is how we measure success.
To lick the competition, outsell them by pouring resources into marketing.	To lick the competition, bring more innovative products to market more frequently.	To lick the competition, gather and use information better, but cooperate with and even sell to competitors if it generates cash flow.

The Workout Team

The leader of the firefighting brigade within your company is most likely going to be the workout specialist whom you engage or the manager whose approach is most like that of the inside raider. The chief executive officer may have to step back, as did Jerry Geist, the CEO of Public Service Company of New Mexico, who spent the utility's every spare nickel on expansion of the electricity delivering capacity as well as forays into real estate development and venture capital investing. In a workout situation, the company is in the workout business, which requires an entirely different mind-set than typically found among company builders.

The leader, whether hired from within or without, will need a small band of warriors to find cash, defend the company from enemies, manage operations, and ultimately develop and implement the redirect-and-grow plan. If the teammates' qualifications were sought in the animal world, the workout leader might choose the following creatures:

Ferret	To find cash among the assets, in overhead expenses, and in other unique places.
Lion	To defend the company against predator and creditor attacks.
German Shepherd	To guide the operations through the rocky shoals of a workout period and not lose anything of value.
Beaver	To build a new and better operating plan once the debt is pared down and stretched out.

When I go in as a workout consultant, I establish with the CEO in advance that my role is consultative rather than decision-making, except in those instances where the CEO authorizes me to commit the company. I ask to interview the heads of finance, marketing, and production to determine whether or not they have the stamina to contribute to and survive a workout situation. I can also learn during the interview process if the problem may be a Pirandello complex—that is, middle managers are afraid to tell the boss the truth—and if the CEO or owner is his own worst enemy. I may advise him or her to yield some responsibility to the senior officers and to me if he or she is too rigid or too improvisational to contribute to the turnaround process.

Notice that I do not consider heads of engineering or new product development (or new locations, or new anything) to be important members of the workout team because their departments will be wound down. In addition, at least one-half of the administrative staff will probably be terminated with the remaining personnel in those departments carrying double loads. The core team that will steer the company through the mine field will include perhaps five people, as shown in Exhibit 4.2.

This is not your typical organizational chart, but a military operation is not, after all, the typical business condition. The German Shepherd is essentially monitoring the core operations while he or she and the Ferret sell, liquidate, and spin off every division, hard asset, and off-balance sheet asset that will produce cash in a hurry. The Lion is speaking with, visiting, cajoling, and passing a few coins to the creditors and maintaining the bullet list. The German Shepherd is maintaining the weekly cash flow statement

Exhibit 4.2 Core Members of the Workout Team

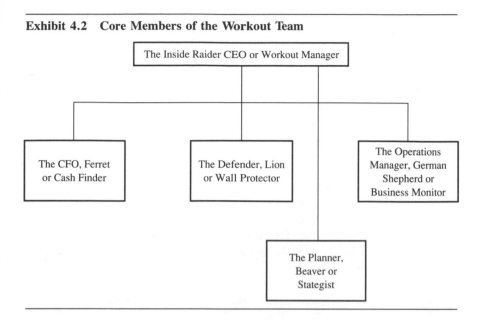

projections, informing the Ferret, the Lion, and the Beaver when they are ahead or behind schedule and gathering data from these lieutenants to keep the road map as accurate as possible. At the bottom of the well, when the worst of the crisis is passed, when the debts are compromised, settled, and/or stretched out, the Beaver will provide ideas and strategies for financing the redirect-and-grow plan.

The leader selects the best people within the company to handle these four assignments and, if they do not exist, brings them in from outside the organization, from other companies and other turnarounds. This situation resembles a classic Western movie like *Gunfight at the O.K. Corral*, where Burt Lancaster pulls in an expert rifleman, a highly regarded six-shooter, the retired sheriff who joins the team for one last great shoot-out, and a skilled horseman to head up the retreat, if needed. There are many parallels between the modern-day workout team and the movie versions of successful bands of outlaws or Mafia families.

In addition to the skill areas that must be capably covered, the small band of teammates must possess the characteristics of heart and courage, the ability to cooperate, and an understanding of leverage that are pretty rare in the homogenized culture of the corporate world. Once again, if the senior officers and middle managers do not have these characteristics, the team leader must hire from the outside.

Heart refers to the inner drive that impels a person to make sacrifices to save the company.

Courage derives from the internal strength to stand up to the most severe attacks without blinking or backing off.

The ability to cooperate flows from the awareness of when to push and when to pull back in negotiations in order to evolve rather than break down communications.

An understanding of leverage entails an internal sense that the company needs time, cash, and supporters, coupled with a divining rod for locating all three in the most unsuspected places.

I have written elsewhere about these qualities and how to test for them and how to identify them during the interview process and when selecting your teammates. You may not think the inception of a crisis period is a jolly good time to curl up in your favorite easy chair with a book or two, but, if you have never been someplace before, you need road maps and the crisis equivalent of a Michelin Guide to help you steer the course, at least until the workout consultant arrives.

There are two conditions to manage in a troubled company: the emotional distress and the battle to survive. In *The Business Bible for Survival*, I provide an in-depth explanation and description of the former, including tests for the qualities you will need in your war buddies. I underscore the importance of carefully selecting your teammates at the outset because the battle to save a company is the closest approximation to war that you are likely to see, and your enemies are larger and better financed than you and are able to hire the best creditor-advocate lawyers in the country to make your life miserable.

Litigation Is a Weapon

As if the cash crunch, personnel defections, and the injuries to your image in the marketplace aren't enough to damage your company, the creditor lawsuits will sail over the parapets of your company's walls and explode in the center of your office like a thousand sticks of dynamite going off in tandem. The objective of litigation, particularly in the early stages of crisis, is to severely weaken the opponent. Workout consultants call the early round litigation "cannons," which are meant to tear down the defenses of the already shell-shocked company and force a settlement with the creditor company on extremely unfavorable terms to the debtor.

Some of the litigation will likely charge the company with fraud and racketeering and the most egregious acts of malevolent behavior one can conceive. Although these are civil offenses, dischargeable in court or by settlement by the payment of money, some creditors will reconstruct the events that induced them to ship goods, provide services, or lend money to the company as acts of criminal fraud and urge the attorney general to bring a criminal action against the company. This is the weaponry of the battlefield of companies in crises, and I have been there and I can report from first-hand experience that it takes certain kinds of people to stand up to the battering ram of litigation, to take the blows, and to pursue a game plan to survive and thrive amidst the chaos.

Fraud Is Not Dischargeable in Bankruptcy. The second objective of litigation is to prevail with a cause of action that, should the debtor company seek protection under the bankruptcy code, will not be discharged by the court for cents on the dollar but must be paid in full in an amount to be determined by a court of law. If a company borrows $20 million from financial institutions several months prior to hitting the wall, the financial institutions in many instances will examine the books of the borrower, uncover some transactions in the checking account that seem questionable at first glance, and allege 20 to 50 counts of fraud and racketeering. If the company cannot develop a survive and thrive plan outside of Chapter 11, then the $20 million claim for fraud sticks to the company through the bankruptcy proceedings, and the plaintiffs are *not* treated like other unsecured creditors. Indeed, if racketeering is added to the causes of action, Congress has determined that the plaintiffs, should they prevail, are entitled to treble damages plus legal fees; and if the debtor company loses the racketeering case at trial, the plaintiffs may be awarded over three dollars for their one dollar loan, while the unsecured creditors receive, say, 20 cents on the dollar.

Accordingly, the arrows in the quiver of creditors can be menacing and intimidating, and although skilled workout consultants understand them as howitzers designed to break the will of the managers of the company in crisis, many managers cannot withstand the attack so they crack. Thus, it is significant to pull together a loyal band of warriors within the troubled company who possess hefty reserves of heart, courage, the ability to cooperate, and an understanding of leverage.

Racketeering. "Civil filings under the Racketeer Influenced and Corrupt Organizations law have increased more than eight-fold over the past five years to nearly a thousand cases in 1988," wrote William H. Rehnquist, Chief Justice of the Supreme Court.*

Chief Justice Rehnquist continued:

> Virtually everyone who has addressed the question agrees that civil
> RICO is now being used in ways that Congress never intended when it
> enacted the statute in 1970. Most of the civil suits filed under the statute
> have nothing to do with organized crime. They are garden-variety civil
> fraud cases of the type traditionally litigated in state courts. Why does

---

*"Get RICO Cases Out of My Courtroom," *The Wall Street Journal*, 19 May, 1989.

the statute work this way? In part, because it creates a civil counterpart for criminal wire fraud and mail fraud prosecutions. It does this by stating that acts indictable under those provisions, as well as many other types of criminal acts, are capable of establishing the "pattern of racketeering" that is the predicate for a civil RICO action.

Justice Rehnquist went on to cite misuses and abuses of the civil RICO statute:

> In its present form, civil RICO has a tremendous reach. Civil RICO claims have been raised in actions relating to divorce, trespass, legal and accounting malpractice, inheritance among family members, employment benefits and sexual harassment by a union.
>   In one case, elderly "life care" residents of a religious retirement community claimed that the owner had used fraud to induce them to sign contracts and had mismanaged community finances. Because the owner was judgment-proof, the residents relied on a clause in the RICO statute that permits actions not only against the owners or operators of a criminal enterprise, but against persons "associated" with it. Among others, they sued Prudential Insurance Co., the community's mortgagee, and ultimately, secured a large settlement from Prudential.

Notwithstanding the Chief Justice's plea to reform civil RICO legislation, Congress seems unable to come to grips with this or other burning societal issues. Consequently RICO will probably remain a burden that debtor companies must carry, despite the taunts and jeers of the company's community of customers, vendors, employees, and fellow citizens who are likely to "convict" the company of mobsterism before a trial. Creditors have learned the military aspects of collecting the full amount owing them: drive gaping holes through the walls of the debtor company, smear its management with charges of fraud and racketeering, and force them into financial despair with the most expensive litigation the law will permit.

Who within your company has the heart and courage to stand shoulder to shoulder with you when the walls come tumbling down? If these people do not exist, find the workout consultants who can join you in battle.

The Damage Trail.   Among the assignments to be given to your Lion—the defender of the walls—is the maintenance of a damage trail: a chronological listing of the damaging events that result from aggressive litigation. Lawsuits are filed with public courts and anyone, including reporters, has access to them. In fact, many newspapers station people full-time in the courts to collect stories of disputes and disagreements that become news a day or two later. Other self-appointed watchdogs of the community's ethical fabric photostat the stories of litigation and send them to the defendant's customers or vendors in other cities and to national publications, so, before the debtor company knows it, the inability to pay a vendor or lender becomes a RICO lawsuit described in minute detail in trade journals and national newspapers distributed all over the country.

A national or trade publication typically will investigate the local dispute more thoroughly and telephone a spokesperson for your company, as well as the plaintiff. The Lion should be the person who fields those telephone calls and should be trained in his or her response. Many libel lawyers will advise not to contribute to the article. "It only makes it worse," they say. The plaintiff or its counsel is likely to make a statement to the trade journal or national publication. It would be hard-pressed not to answer the question, "What is the substance to your claim of racketeering?" Its response might be something like, "We found several instances of misappropriation of money and accounting irregularities."

That is a damaging statement, and the Lion should enter it in his or her Damage Trail Notebook. A large customer may read the article and comment on the statement made by the plaintiff and tell the debtor company that it cannot do business any further until the charges made by the plaintiff are cleared up. The Lion should ask the customer for a letter to that effect, in order to provide a direct causal relationship between the plaintiff's statement and the loss of business from a valued customer. The customer's letter is filed in the Damage Trail Notebook.

Other companies may recoil from servicing the company upon reading the article. Credit card companies may send cancellation notices; banks may shut down the company's accounts; other vendors may stop shipping except on a C.O.D. basis. The Lion should dutifully record all of these events in the Damage Trail Notebook.

The entries in the Damage Trail Notebook will form the bases of bringing counterclaims for damages related to the plaintiff's statements to the press. These counterclaims may take the form of libel, tortuous interference, business interference, and more. It may be costly to counterclaim and pursue the counterclaimant. It may require expensive, litigation-experienced lawyers and months of depositions and document requests, but it puts litigants on notice that their cannons did not knock out your cannons. Try to find a lawyer who believes so strongly in your case that he or she will work on a contingency, rather than an hourly, basis.

You may not pursue your causes of action to trial, for that depends upon the probability of winning your case, its merits, the predilections of the judge, and the amount of cash you can rustle up to stay the battle. In many instances that I have been involved in, if the debtor company can find cash and build a litigation war chest, it can destroy the cannons of the opponent and negotiate a settlement and withdrawal of the damaging litigation with a powerful counterclaim. Without cash to fund a litigation war chest and the operations of the business, even in a shrunken size, the enemies may prevail simply because they have more cash. In the business battlefield, soldiers march on cash.

SELL ASSETS TO RAISE CASH

It is the principal assignment of the Ferret to raise cash. Most companies are corpulent with assets and overhead expenses, which is one reason why they get into trouble (or become takeover targets) in the first place. The inside raider management approach is to sell assets, slash expenses, and generate multiple cash flow channels toward the objective of maximizing liquidity and cash flow return on stockholders' equity. But it is traditionally managed and entrepreneurially improvised companies that get into trouble. If a person with Ferret skills exists in one of these companies, I would be surprised. Thus, the skill typically is brought in when the workout consultant is hired. Parenthetically, if each of the four skill areas must be hired along with the workout consultant—the Ferret, the Lion, the German Shepherd, and the Beaver—is there any wonder why the average workout assignment, as reported in the Directory in the back of the book, is 12 months in length and costs anywhere from $100,000 to several million dollars plus success bonuses?

I will summarize several cash-raising tactics, but for details on this subject, see *The Inside Raider*.

Have Customers Supply Raw Materials

If your company manufactures equipment, machinery, or a product sold under contract to a vendor that resells it to industrial or individual consumers, you may be tying up cash in raw materials, which is a service that does not earn your company a dime. Change your manufacturing process to a value-added manufacturer that provides the labor content only. Have your customers purchase the raw materials and deliver it to you just in time for producing their goods. You can charge for the cost of labor, plus a profit markup, and for delivery. For a $25 million (revenues) company with a cost of goods sold of 65 percent, half of which is raw material, you will free up $8,125,000 in cash. The Ferret should be rewarded a bonus for achieving this, but the German Shepherd should be charged with the responsibility of putting the cash in a safe place. This could mean a savings account outside of the county in which the company is headquartered to prevent the Sheriff's garnishments and attachments.

Sale-Leaseback Fixed Assets

One of the most common ways to squeeze cash out of fixed assets is to sell them to a leasing company and lease them back. This tactic is called the sale-leaseback, and it is routinely done by traditional corporations whenever the wolf is seen off in the distance approaching the door. There are many equipment leasing companies that seek sale-leasebacks, including Chase Manhattan Leasing, Ford Credit Corp., General Electric Capital Corp., Greyhound Financial Corp., and more. See *The Middle-Market Leveraged Financing Directory and Source Book* for a detailed Directory of sources of financing.

Sale-Leaseback of Office Space

To find sale-leaseback investors for your office building or warehouse, begin with investors who seek high-quality buildings and run through the field down to low quality; along the way you should find the right match. Insurance companies are the premier real estate investors.

In addition, corporate pension funds, college endowment funds, and association or small pension funds make good sale-leaseback candidates. At the lower end of the quality spectrum are wealthy individuals herded into syndicates by investment bankers. But individuals die, get divorced, and want special reports sent hither and thither. Thus, there is a risk in selling your asset to individuals and leasing it back from them; however, it frees up cash and without cash you may end up on your back like a Pee Wee League quarterback in the Super Bowl.

Sell Your Vans or Trucks and Hire the Service

Let's assume you own a fleet of 20 delivery vans, each of which costs you $15,000 and which you can sell for $7,500 each, or $150,000. The operating costs of the 20 vans are shown in Exhibit 4.3.

If your company delivers goods to customers, doing it the most cost-effective way is a major concern. The choices are owning, leasing but providing the drivers, leasing the vans and leasing the drivers, using common carriers, and reducing the number of personnel in your fleet management department.

Selling your vans or trucks and subcontracting the delivery function to a common carrier represents a significant cash savings. The common carrier costs are estimated in Exhibit 4.4.

Exhibit 4.3 The Costs of Owning and Operating 20 Vans

	20 Vans
Approximate monthly payment for a 60-month loan at 10.75% with 15% down payment	$ 5,520.00
Liability insurance	2,500.00
Maintenance	2,000.00
Gas (1,500 miles per month, 15 miles/gallon @ $.85/gallon)	1,700.00
Driver (20 hours/week @ $8/hour)	12,800.00
Worker's compensation	2,040.00
Driver's health insurance	2,400.00
Total	$28,960.00

Exhibit 4.4   Common Carrier

	20 Vans
Charges for a delivery service range from per mile charges to flat fees that are determined by weight and value of shipment. The average cost is $.95 per mile. 50 miles @ $.95, 20 loads/month	$19,000.00
Insurance averages $.40 per $100 of value (cost for a $5,000 load)	400.00
Total	$19,400.00

A comparison of owning (or leasing) versus hiring common carriers in this example demonstrates that the latter provides a cash savings of about $10,000 per annum. If your company leases or owns and operates 200 vans or trucks, the savings will be about 10 times higher.

Spin-offs

The cash-generating artillery in the Ferret's bag of tricks must include knowing how to spin off assets that are not essential to the company's *core*. To achieve success, the Ferret must know the mechanics of the spin-off and the different kinds of spin-offs and have the ability to profit in several ways from the spin-off while giving up risk and costs.

Selling the manufacturing subsidiary that was never part of the company's core is a simple judgment call and should be done quickly. The Ferret needs to get more creative than that. He or she will have to make tougher calls such as spinning off divisions that service the company such as data processing, human resources, advertising, and others for strategic purposes, not because they do not fit but because spinning them off raises cash. These three spin-offs are done all too infrequently by traditional managers or, if done at all, not too well.

The optimum facilities management spin-off is of a precocious service department that manages an internal generic activity extremely well. Other corporations that have a need for these services would hire the department to provide them, if the department were freestanding. The majority of facilities management spin-offs have involved the data processing departments of large and medium-sized corporations. Some commercial banks are spinning off their data processing departments into stand-alone companies in order to raise cash.

In the facilities management spin-off, the budget of the department leaves the parent, thus freeing up cash, and the spun-off division contracts with the parent to provide its usual services. The spun-off division incorporates and the former employees of the parent become employees of the new entity. It is free to provide services to other companies, and the endorsement of the parent assists the new company in obtaining contracts. Working capital for the spun-off division is provided by service contracts from the parent company and others. Smart Ferrets will hold onto some equity in the spun-off company because occasionally these companies have a way of becoming valuable. For example, Oryx Energy Corporation, which was spun off by Sun Oil Company to manage its depleted oil reserves in the Austin Chalk area of West Texas, found oil using a new technology known as horizontal drilling. Oryx's market value in two years vaulted to more than $2 billion. This is a case of the foal becoming a better runner than the sire. Would that Sun had held onto some of Oryx's stock.

The Ferret should review the various divisions carefully to determine which have the most spin-off possibilities. Successful facilities management spin-offs need to provide a service that other companies can use, be made up of an enthusiastic, high-energy entrepreneurial group of employees, and be willing to take the risk when the umbilical cord is cut. The trust department of Chemical Bank became a successful management spin-off under the name Favia-Hill & Co., Inc., the names of its senior managers. The data processing department of Uniroyal, Inc., was spun off as a stand-alone, Computeristics, Inc., in a transition that I worked on several years ago. And McKesson-Robbins, the largest drug and health and beauty aids company in the country, spun off its pharmaceutical services company and held onto a chunk of its equity, which became valuable when the stand-alone company achieved an initial public offering.

Sell Slow-Paying Accounts Receivable

Your company's slow accounts receivable may be "stone" to you, but they are "diamonds" to someone who knows how to leverage them. If you have a large enough cache of paper, say over $10 million, it may pay to form a captive finance subsidiary, put some key personnel into it with equity incentives, and help them finance the subsidiary with bank loans or private placements. This is known as "securitizing" your assets and selling an interest in them to public investors. But securitizing your company's accounts receivable takes time, of which you have precious little.

If your accounts receivable staff has been unable to collect efficiently, sell the paper for whatever you can raise. Interview several agencies to collect the receivables and select one of them. American Guaranty Factors in Arlington, Texas generally collects about 10 percent of charged off accounts receivable and splits that with its clients. You may raise 5 cents on the dollar on bad debts, 15 cents on the dollar for over 180-day-old paper but as much as 50 cents on the dollar for 90- to 180-day old receivables.

Sell Obsolete Inventory

Every industry has its liquidators and barter companies listed in its trade journals as well as in the Yellow Pages. They provide the flotsam and jetsam of products that we see in flea markets on Sunday morning strolls. The liquidator in the B. Altman bankruptcy paid 50 cents on the dollar for the retailer's inventory. Of course, the purchase included salable as well as slow-moving items. If your intent is to sell only slow-moving items, don't look for 50 cents on the dollar but a price nearer 30 cents.

Several well-known consumer electronics catalogs and direct mail merchandiser firms, including JS&A (for Joe Sugerman & Associates) and DAK (for Dean A. Kaplan), buy discontinued and overstocked items from cash-poor manufacturers at distressed prices. They buy cheap—but pay cash—then advertise the products heavily in their direct response ads or in their catalogs and sell them at 25 to 30 percent off retail list. The strapped manufacturer can generate $10 quickly and with certainty for an item that it might otherwise sell for $50 in time.

Have a "Yard Sale"

The Ferret should go through the company's warehouses, offices, and closets, gather all of the accumulated, but no longer used, desks, chairs, lamps, computers, calculators, file cabinets, carpets, coatracks, typewriters, and other relics and sell them to a junk collector.

If your company's machinery and equipment is not being used full-time, offer contract manufacturing services to other manufacturers in your community. You might be able to squeeze two of your manufacturing shifts into one and rent machinery services to others, using your second-shift personnel, or rent the equipment to others using their personnel.

If your company carries inventory over from one season to the next, sell it to a going-out-of-business company to generate cash at the end of the season. These companies move from town to town, locate empty retail stores, plaster their windows with "Going Out of Business" signs and unload nonsalable inventory purchased from many overstocked companies. People walk by these stores and say, "I can't remember the store that was there." The companions usually reply, "That's why they're going out of business."

Rent Freed-Up Space

The process of generating cash from languid and peripheral assets can be accomplished completely in 45 to 60 days, and the Ferret can be reassigned to gathering cash from operating expenses, which I will get to in the next section. Prior to moving on, the Ferret should be assigned to rearranging the office and warehouse space. I have not gone into detail about the sale of peripheral divisions and subsidiaries because it goes without saying that as the company metamorphoses into the workout business from whatever business it was in, the peripheral operations are the first to be sold.

If the data processing department has been spun off via a facilities management contract, the fleet management department shrunk to a few people when the vans and trucks are sold, the maintenance staff let go when the buildings are sold, the purchasing division shut down when the company becomes a value-added labor provider, and half the administrative staff terminated as various peripheral divisions and subsidiaries are sold, there is a considerable amount of freed-up space that can be rented to other companies to generate additional cash flow.

SLASH EXPENSES

The second and equally important assignment of the Ferret is to slash expenses. This is an all-encompassing task because no expense item should be safe from the Ferret's scrutiny. The line items to be cut include the following:

Management salaries

Management perqs

Space

Administrative personnel

Vehicles

Lawyers

Auditors

Health insurance

Commercial insurance

Telephone

Postage

Courier

Travel and entertainment

Advertising

The fundamental question that the Ferret must ask is, "Can I pay less?" Surprisingly few managers ask for discounts, lower prices, datings, installment payments, and barter. But people who live in humble circumstances do; and a company teetering on the edge of bankruptcy is in humble circumstances. You can always get something for less money, and there is always a less expensive vendor. You just have to ask.

Salary Reductions

Across the board salary reductions for all personnel are a mandatory first step. The biggest cuts should be made in the largest salaries. The salary cuts for key people should be discussed one-on-one and not be announced with an impersonal form letter. Some people may be at the most expensive years in their working lives with children in college, while others may be in less expensive years. Some may be able to endure 33 percent cuts, while for others a 20 percent cut may be the maximum endurable limit. Cuts at the production worker level cannot be impersonal because these people tend to feel, and rightly so in most instances, that they are like mushrooms kept in the dark, but from time to time manure is thrown on them.

A tactic that I found useful in a workout of a manufacturing company was to go into the factory for a shirt-sleeve meeting with the head of production, explain the situation, and request everyone's extra effort. The head of production and I fielded questions for an hour and then asked for a voluntary 20 percent pay cut. A few hands were raised from the first volunteers, and then when all hands were up we pulled out a wad of crisp fifty dollar bills and passed them around to everyone. "You see," the head of production said, "we're going to pull through these dark days if we all pull together."

We routinely passed out $50 bills whenever the production workers came in on Saturdays or did an exceptional job at getting out an order without flaws or providing warranty and repair work in record time. Some workout consultants recommend spreading shares of the company's stock around to all employees to compensate for longer hours and lower pay.

Health Insurance Expenses

One could argue that in a crisis the managers and employees should be willing to forego their health insurance costs. After all, the proponents of this line of reasoning contend, it is a luxury the company can ill afford. The counterargument is that employees will be putting in longer hours during the difficult months of a crisis and their families will object to a simultaneous reduction in pay and reduction in benefits.

A middle-ground solution is to self-insure the risk of employee (and the employee's family) medical needs. This sometimes works, depending on the hazards of the job itself and the climate, when coupled with a wellness program including smoke-ending and exercise. But crises cause physical stress and fatigue, which some people convert into drivers and motivators but from which others fall prone to illness.

Nonetheless, if your company is paying $120 per employee per month (or $360 for the employee and his or her family) for health insurance, and if it employs 250 people, after cutbacks, the monthly bill is $73,800. The

Ferret's job is to slash expenses and raise cash, and no expense item is safe from his machete.

If health care actuarial tables can be retrieved rapidly from the carrier, the Ferret may be able to determine that the actual cost of employee medical care for the preceding 12 months was only $45,000 per month, or 61 percent of out-of-pocket costs. He or she could recommend to the crisis management team that the company cancel its health insurance plan and self-insure by setting aside $45,000 in a savings account each month. The cost would drop from $360 per employee-family per month to $180 (or $60 per person), and interest would accrue on the savings. If the company's back were ever thrust against the wall with no options, it could use the health care savings to keep the doors open, as long as the employees understand and approve the emergency measures.

But a self-insured program requires at least one full-time employee to monitor it. Some employees have "extended families" that try to use the company's insurance plan. Others have medical treatment on organs or tissues that were removed years ago. Others visit health care providers who add multiple unnecessary diagnoses and treatments so that they will be reimbursed handsomely. Can the company afford the time of an in-house health maintenance person? Once again, it depends on the overall fairness of the workers and the community to pull together for a win-win; if they act selfishly, they will try to get what they can out of a sinking ship.

Shop the Health Insurance Plan

The health insurance industry has many carriers and it is intensely competitive. Many of the carriers lose money each year, while the U.S. health care bill rises inexorably at a 10 to 20 percent annual rate. Thus, someone is making out like a bandit, and it is probably the providers.

An entrepreneurial industry has emerged to act as a gatekeeper to prevent providers from overdiagnosing and overtesting patients. Companies in this industry, known as utilization review (UR), are hired by corporations and carriers or by carriers pulled together into associations by Preferred Provider Organizations (PPOs) or Health Maintenance Organizations (HMOs) to maintain a vigil over the costs of treatment presented by providers prior to the treatment (except in cases of emergency surgery, where it is done after the fact).

Utilization review companies are sleuths that use computers to track the procedures of physicians who are members of PPOs or HMOs. When they spot a blip on their screens, such as when more than half of the babies delivered by an ob-gyn within a certain period are by cesarean section, they pay the doctor a visit to "remind" him or her to bring costs back into line. The UR is the "enforcer" of lower health care costs. Elliot A. Segal, president of National Capitol Preferred Provider Organization of Washington, DC, told *The Wall Street Journal* that the woodshed talk that URs have with physicians is "a way of putting somebody on notice in a subtle but telling way."*

Healthcare Compare Corporation (HCCC), Lombard, Illinois, a publicly held utilization review company with 1989 revenues of $36 million and earnings of $2.2 million, has been monitoring physicians for six years on behalf of PPOs and insurance companies to eliminate unnecessary procedures. It is backed by the Pritzker family, owners of The Marmon Group and Hyatt Hotels Corporation. It was recently hired by American Airlines to monitor their health care expenditures. HCCC helped Murray Industries, the Florida manufacturer of pleasure boats, reduce its health care costs by 22 percent. Another client, Park 'n Fly Service, a parking lot operator in St. Louis, reported a reduction of 27 percent, without sacrificing quality of care.

Under UR, physicians use their traditional system of charging a fee for services rendered, but the procedures have to be approved by either HCCC or one of the other 300 UR companies (or divisions of PPOs) currently in operation. A typical UR fee is $1.25 to $2.00 per employee per month. URs have staffs of nurses and doctors, and in 60 percent of the cases the UR's nurses approve the procedures. The other diagnoses are reviewed by the UR's staff physicians. Emergency operations are done immediately, without consultation.

Employee Leasing

These innovative companies are capable of lowering health insurance costs to $60 per employee per month. They take all of your employees on their payroll and rent them back to you. The employees will receive improved health benefits and when you want to terminate them, the employee-leasing company will find them another job. You can save the payroll costs of your human resources department by at least $20,000 per person. The employee-leasing company will fill out all of the government and insurance forms for the employees and handle all terminations, and you will gain back extra time for other management tasks.

Tempting? That's the offer an employee-leasing company makes, and thus far 20,000 U.S. companies have taken up that offer. How do employee-leasing companies make money?

They charge their clients the sum of payroll plus benefits plus a fee. They make an additional profit by negotiating substantially less expensive benefit packages for their employees. However, the fee charged to clients is small in comparison with the savings in management time and employee hassles.

---

*The *Wall Street Journal*, September 28, 1989.

Following are the services that employee-leasing companies provide for your people:

- Process payroll checks.
- Provide you with weekly payroll and billing reports.
- File and pay all state and federal employer taxes.
- Prepare W-2 forms at year-end for all employees.
- Provide a comprehensive employee health insurance program.
- Process Section 125 benefits deductions.
- Process all insurance claims.
- Offer and administer COBRA (Comprehensive Omnibus Benefits Retirement Act) benefits.
- Provide coverage for workmen's compensation; issue certificates and administer claims.
- Administer state employment claims.
- Provide a credit union.
- Provide an in-house human resources consultant.
- Provide in-house legal counsel.

GTE, Holiday Corp., Greyhound, Hospital Corp. of America, and thousands of other companies are leasing some or all of their employees from the 400 employee-leasing companies trolling for clients in the United States. The average size of a company leasing its employees is 30 people, and many of them are rapidly expanding companies whose managers are too busy steering their companies' growth to pay necessary attention to government and insurance compliance forms.

One of the largest employee-leasing companies, Action Staffing (Tampa, Florida) has revenues of $69 million. It leases the 11,000 employees on its payroll to 450 companies. Larry Jones, the ex-military man who runs Action Staffing, likens his company to a "collection agency for the IRS." Some companies with chronic withholding tax problems must be assigned a tax auditor to monitor them on a weekly basis. Clearly, it takes fewer IRS auditors to observe the payroll records of one company with 11,000 employees than it does 450 companies of 25 employees each.

Insurance companies are also fans of employee leasing, for two reasons. First, they can bill one company for their services rather than several hundred, and they can monitor the insurance records with far fewer auditors. Second, they need fewer sales persons to call on 400 employee-leasing companies than on the nearly 20,000 companies in the United States that now lease their employees.

There are two primary savings to the lessee: the elimination of the salaries and related costs of its human resources department and a huge savings in management time.

Marvin R. Selter, chairman of National Staff Network, Inc., the nation's largest employee-leasing company, with approximately 35,000 employees, says that its typical client had been spending about 28 percent of its revenues on payroll, benefits, and employee administration costs and that it now spends 22 percent on employee leasing.

Other Insurance Expenses

The Ferret has several options in reducing employee health insurance costs, which apply to the company's commercial insurance policies as well: fire, casualty, and product liability insurance. These policies should all be reviewed by local agents, with the questions, "Do we need all of this coverage? And can you get the coverage that we need less expensively?"

The agents will doubtless bring in lower rates, particularly if they know they are in a competitive bidding situation. Then when the best deal is struck, the Ferret should tell the agent, "I would like to pay for this policy on a monthly basis."

Finally, it is an excellent time to cancel management life insurance policies paid for by the company. If the managers want to continue paying for them by themselves, they should be given that option.

Professional Fees

The second highest overhead burden after insurance expenses is usually professional fees. These include accounting, legal, and consulting costs. The workout specialist and bankruptcy lawyer, if you retain one, will be very expensive but necessary costs, and a fine line item to reduce are the professional costs of the accountants and lawyers who failed to warn you that trouble was just around the corner.

Has your company competitively bid for these services in the past? Did you ever examine what you were getting for what you were paying in the way of accounting and legal fees? If not, listen to the timely poem of Edna St. Vincent Millay, who wrote of living too high on the hog:

> My candle burns at both ends,
> It will not last the night;
> But, ah, my foes, and oh, my friends —
> It gives a lovely light.*

---

* "Trip from Thistles," in *Modern American and British Poetry,* edited by Louis Untermeyer (New York: Harcourt Brace and Company, 1955).

Where's My Discount?   A story is told about the workout consultant and his young son. The child approached his father one day and asked, "Dad, may I please borrow $10?"

The father replied, "Sure, $10, or maybe $9, of course I'll loan you $8."

The workout consultant never accepts the first price. He asks for a discount price for everything. If you never ask, you never receive.

When we have very little cash, we tend to ask the price of things. But if we are affluent or when we are on vacation, we accept most prices as stated, frequently without asking if there is room for negotiation. Without cash we ask who pays for delivery, are payment terms available, if price is negotiable, if the product comes with a warranty, if training is free, and if service is free; we also ask for rain checks of all sorts.

The same applies in business. When business is good, some of us stop asking questions. But when things get tight, we become Sam Spade, master detective. No question goes unasked. If you want your Ferret to find cash, he must begin by demanding lower rates from lawyers, accountants, advertising firms, marketing consultants, and other providers of professional services.

Slashing Accounting Charges.   Here are some questions to ask your company's accounting firm to lower their audit fees:

1. What is the price of this year's audit?
2. Does it include the tax filings?
3. Who is assigned to it?
4. What are their billing rates?
5. Are they experienced in this kind of business?
6. Does the audit price include the management letter?
7. What work can we do on the books internally to lower the audit cost?
8. Does the cost include the defense of your work in the event of an IRS audit or litigation?

Let's look at what is behind these questions. Accounting firms sell their time. They hire intelligent young people, train them, and mark up their cost by a multiple of two to five times. Let's assume that one junior accountant, one senior accountant, and one partner are assigned to perform your company's audit, that they earn $40,000, $60,000, and $125,000 per annum, and that they each work 2,500 hours each year. Accordingly, their "raw material" costs are $16 per hour, $25 per hour, and $50 per hour respectively.

In order for the accounting firm to bid your job intelligently, it must estimate the number of hours that the job will take. At the pre-audit meeting, if you *ask* for an estimate of the number of hours the job will take, the accounting firm will tell you. Then you will have a pretty fair idea of the markup factor which will help you negotiate the fee. For example, if the accounting firm bids $40,000, estimates 100 hours, or $400 per hour, and if you assume 33 hours per auditor, then you are probably being high bid:

					Acounting Firm's Cost
33	×	Jr. accountant	×	$16	$ 528.00
33	×	Sr. accountant	×	$25	725.00
34	×	Partner	×	$50	1,700.00
100					$2,953.00

Rather than a 500 percent markup, the accounting firm is trying to achieve a 3,300 percent markup. You have much room to negotiate—in fact, all the way down to $16,000.

Another way to cut audit expenses is to ask how your accounting department may assist in order to reduce the time involved in data collection. Some companies, particularly those in which the chief financial officer was formerly with an accounting firm, do such an extensive audit prep that the accounting firm actually only performs a review. Leaving a detailed paper trail for all money transfers in and out is one of the best ways to cut audit expenses.

The same type of analysis is required when negotiating the cost of legal services. Lawyers and accountants sell their time at markups above the actual cost of the skilled labor employed. If your law firm routinely brings three lawyers to its meetings with you, your company is being triple-billed, and the Ferret should put a stop to it.

The scope of the legal services needed can be determined by one member of the firm, in less than 30 minutes. But lawyers frequently fill the conference room when it is obviously unnecessary. Most companies do not put their legal requirements out for bid and interview many lawyers at different firms, but your company should.

Control the Billing.   Discuss rates at the beginning of the engagement. Discuss the manner in which you wish to be billed—contingency, hourly rate paid monthly, or when an event occurs. Many lawyers prefer that you pay a retainer up front—bankruptcy lawyers quite properly want 90 percent of their expected fee up front—and then work the retainer off in hours. This is an appropriate arrangement for a complicated lawsuit or for a matter that has an uncertain ending, such as bankruptcy, but inappropriate for the drafting of a contract.

Be sure to specify that you want fully itemized bills, ones that break down how each hour or fraction thereof was spent. Question items in the bill that you do not understand. Your lawyer does not have to travel first class, for example. If he or she does not work for you while traveling, he or she should not bill you for travel time. Prepare a budget with your lawyer before the task begins, and monitor the budget frequently.

When to Go In-House.   If your company is consistently spending more than $75,000 a year on legal fees, it is time to consider hiring in-house counsel. However, most in-house lawyers cannot handle the "big case" or specialized issues such as environmental laws, tax, securities, antitrust, or litigation away from home.

If in-house counsel can be grafted onto other assignments such as helping the Beaver and the German Shepherd negotiate stretch-outs with creditors, you may get two tasks filled by the same person. Litigators in particular are actors at heart, and they are skilled at and have a flair for negotiating seemingly impressive assignments.

Panning for Gold in the Incoming Mail

In one recently troubled company that I was called in to help, I asked the secretaries to begin storing incoming third-class mail and catalogs. I visited the lunchroom and asked that aluminum cans be rounded up and saved. I also instituted an employee stock ownership plan to capture everyone's attention about *small costs that add up*. Here's what I told the stock-owning secretaries: "You're a cost center, you know. But you can become a profit center by combining the incoming paper trash, such as magazines, catalogs, and third-class mail, with the not-quite-outgoing mail—first drafts, bad photostats, mistakes—and by shopping for the best recycling price we can find on this category of paper, known as 'mixed paper.'"

There are certain rules of the road to maximize your trash. Most paper recyclers will put several Gaylord boxes on pallets outside your back door at no charge. A Gaylord is a 4 foot by 4 foot by 4 foot box and holds 600 to 800 pounds of paper. Four full Gaylords make a ton. The paper recyclers like to see you sort the computer printer paper from the other trash because it is the most valuable.

The range of value for your paper trash is approximately as follows (these prices vary between metropolitan areas and with economic conditions):

Computer printer paper $150/ton
Photostat paper   90/ton

Colored paper (catalogs)	20/ton
Newspapers	10/ton
Corrugated boxes	5/ton

After you presort the paper trash into categories, make certain you keep it dry. Put covers on the Gaylords or bring them inside if it looks like rain. Once paper becomes wet it loses its value.

Uses of Recycled Paper.   Computer printer paper is recycled into the highest quality stationery. Photostat paper is recycled as medium-grade bond. Mixed paper, your incoming mail, is recycled as inexpensive paper. And, in some markets, corrugated paper boxes and newspapers have a second life as cardboard and napkins. The recyclers in Miami, Florida, are no longer picking up newspapers because there is an excess of it.

How Much Can You Make?   Depending on the size of your company and its paper consumption, as well as its incoming mail, you might be able to fill your four to eight Gaylords 20 times a year and generate $3,400 to $6,800 annually. That's about the volume that several heavily computerized firms of 250 to 400 employees told me they're generating each year.

There's More to the Story.   Aluminum cans are worth 56 cents per pound in most cities across the country, and 28 cans to make a pound. If your company has 280 employees who swig one soft drink per day, their sugar addiction is worth $5.60 per day, or nearly $1,600 per year, to the company. For some companies, that is a meaningful savings.

DuPont Co. and Waste Management, Inc. recently announced a joint venture to recycle plastic waste at a plant that will open in 1990. There are 11 million tons of plastic trash thrown out by Americans each year. The joint venture expects to pay 15 cents a pound for plastic. A new savings area is around the corner.

Double-Sided Photostating.   One of the largest savings in paper costs can be generated by photostating reports on the front and back of each piece of paper. At $15.00 per pound of photostat paper, by using both sides your company might save $1,000 per year or more.

Cut Fax Cover Sheets in Half.   Most fax messages are sent with a cover sheet that has your company's logo on it, the name of the receiver, its fax number, the date of the message, the time of the message, the sender's name and number, and the total number of pages being faxed. This entire gaggle of information can be put on one half of an $8\frac{1}{2}$-inch by 11-inch piece of paper.

There is a triple savings here. You will save 50 percent on cover sheets, 50 percent on storage space for used cover sheets (to be reconciled against the monthly telephone bills), and 50 percent on fax charges. Assuming that one full page costs 17 cents to send in the United States and that your company sends 5,000 fax messages per annum, each with its own cover sheet, by going to half sheets the savings is $425 per year. Double that number for the value of the other two savings—paper and storage.

Roll Back Rental Expenses

The Ferret should pull a copy of the company's real estate leases out of the files, bring in a tape measure from home, and read this section in detail in order to cut your company's office, plant, and warehouse rental expenses. You are probably paying for "rentable" space when you should be paying for "usable" space. The difference between the two is common areas in the building. Common areas include tenant's pro-rata share of the lobbies, corridors, restrooms, janitorial and electrical closets, vending, and other areas that are shared by all tenants. If you are on an upper floor, your pro-rata usage of the lobby is less than that of a first-floor tenant. Thus, your firm should pay less for the common area. Is it paying less for the lobby? Read the lease.

Most landlords and leasing agents are reluctant to discuss the "common area factor" with tenants, but you should be armed to the teeth with all of the facts. To the landlord, the common area is the "loss factor," and you want to absorb as little of it as possible.

Common Area Factor. This is the square footage differential between rentable area and usable area. Rentable area includes the entire finished interior of a building's floor, including common areas. Usable area is the entire interior square footage of office space available for the private use of the tenant. The Building Owners and Managers Association (BOMA) has established standards for measuring usable space. These standards state that usable space should be calculated by measuring from the inside surface of the dominant portion of the permanent outer building walls to the office side of the corridor or other permanent walls to the center of partitions that separate the office from other usable areas.

Landlords typically calculate a pro-rata share of the common area for each tenant and add that amount of space to usable area in order to create a number for rentable area. Then they base the rent on the larger number. The landlord's "loss factor," which properly should be called "excess profit factor," arises from charging for common area factors that the tenants simply never use. These include the janitor's closet and the air conditioning equipment room, among others.

Internal Space Measurement.   The second problem is that the measurement of the space your company is occupying for its office, plant, or warehouse is probably inaccurate. The landlord more than likely took measurements from a blueprint or from the outer walls. Remeasure the space from the inner walls; carefully go around the buttresses with your tape measure; exclude the electrical and telephone boxes. Then compare your total square footage number with the number in the lease. I will bet dollars to doughnuts that your number is the smaller one.

Postage

If your business uses direct mail as a common advertising medium, wasted postage costs can add up to several hundred-thousand dollars per year. Here are some tips to save postage costs:

1. *Use an electronic scale* to avoid the need for adding extra postage "just to be safe."

2. *Use a postage meter* rather than stamps to limit your expense to the exact amount required.

3. *Use "Forwarding and Return Postage Guaranteed and Address Correction Requested"* on all mail. This is a relatively inexpensive way to keep your mailing lists current.

4. *Save unused postage stamps that were printed in error.* They can be redeemed at 90 percent of their face value.

5. *Use first-class presort when possible.* For those mailings that qualify, savings can be as much as 25 percent. More on presort later in this chapter.

6. *Third-class bulk rates can save more than 60 percent* for mailings of 200 pieces or more. In addition, sorting by carrier routes eliminates three United States Postal Service handlings, allowing faster delivery. More on carrier route sorting later in this chapter.

7. *Include promotional pieces in your regular mailings of invoices and statements.* Most letters mailed at the one-ounce rate weigh much less, so take advantage of this.

8. *Keep a variety of envelopes on hand and always use the smallest possible size.* This will lower weight and avoid postage surcharges.

9. *Use registered mail only when insurance is necessary.* Certified mail is less expensive.

10. *For promotional mailings, use a first-class postcard rather than a first-class letter.* A $4\frac{1}{2}$-inch by 6-inch single-fold piece will double your message area and can even accommodate a business reply card.

Presorting Services.   Major mailers, such as credit card companies and mail order houses, sort their mail by zip code before taking it down to the post office. The U.S. Postal Service offers them a 25 percent discount, or 4 cents off of a 25 cent mailing. The American Postal Workers Union, a 350,000 member union, argues that they could do the job just as well and they would like to see $2\frac{1}{2}$ cents of the discount in their paychecks. However, an independent government commission that reviews postal rates says that the presorting discount is a bargain.

But what about companies that generate 500 pieces of mail per day or less? If that is your situation, you can call on one of 250 privately owned presorters located throughout the country. These innovative companies save your company most of the 4 cents, which can add up to several thousand dollars per year, depending on volume.

Overnight Couriers.   The average cost to an ordinary user to send a one-pound package overnight is $14.50. Federal Express Corporation charges $20.25 for the same package, but it guarantees delivery by 10:30 A.M. the following morning. AT&T and other large corporations are offered discounts by the air freight companies of up to 40 percent.

The Ferret can achieve the AT&T-size discount by using a repackager, such as UniShippers Association, Salt Lake City, Utah, that can achieve the same discount for your company. Exhibit 4.5 compares UniShipper's rates with three of its competitors.

Exhibit 4.5   Rate Comparison for Overnight Air Freight Service

Weight (pounds)	UniShippers	Federal Express	DHL Express	Emery Express
Letter	$ 8.50	14.00	14.00	14.00
Package	14.00	20.25	25.00	23.00
1	14.00	20.25	25.00	23.00
2	15.00	23.00	25.00	23.00
3	18.00	25.75	28.00	25.75
4	21.00	28.50	31.00	28.56
5	23.00	31.25	34.00	31.25
50	68.00	95.00	89.00	95.00
90	103.00	145.00	129.00	145.00

What does this mean to your company? Let's say that your company ships 200 packages per year, or about one every other day, and that the average weight is 2 pounds. If you use one of the carriers in the above exhibit, you will pay $4,600 per annum. But if you ship via a repackager, you will pay $3,000—a savings of $1,600 per annum. The real savings occur with big packages. Another way to reduce courier expenses is to ask the recipient for his or her courier credit card number. There are circumstances in which the receiver needs the contents of the package more than you need to send them.

Be especially aware of lawyers, advertising agents, and other company agents who add a surcharge above conventional courier rates. A public relations firm that one of my client companies used briefly added a 17.5 percent surcharge to communications costs. You should insist that these "handling charges" be rolled back. Then introduce your agent to UniShippers.

Telephone Costs

There are several means to reduce telephone costs. As you know, there are alternatives to using AT&T as your company's primary carrier. Your company can purchase lease interconnect telephone systems with a feature known as *least cost* routing. (AT&T offers equipment that is competitive in most areas with those of interconnect or competitive telephone equipment manufacturers.) This feature relies on a microchip that automatically selects the least costly carrier for a particular long distance call—WATS, AT&T, ALC, MCI, Sprint, or Telenet. If you are in the service business and your telephone calls are billed to a client or customer—law firm, hotel, hospital— you can select an interconnect system with *call accounting/cost accounting* that assigns each call to a specific telephone.

Repackagers of Telephone Services. There are 125 repackagers in the country. Each month they buy from the major long distance carriers hundreds of trunks of telephone lines at a reduced price, which the carriers sell for 11 cents per minute. The repackagers pay a price of 5 cents per minute, and resell them for 8 cents per minute. You can use a repackager and buy (or lease) interconnect systems that offer cost-saving features. Let your Ferret's fingers walk through the Yellow Pages to find repackagers in your area, and slash the cost of long-distance calls.

Codes Toll Restriction. Interconnect systems also offer the ability to block certain telephones from calling certain area codes. For instance, this service restricts the accounts receivable department from calling the West Coast or from making calls to the other regions of the country to check in with Aunt Tillie and Uncle Mel. Codes toll restriction will slash another 5 percent off the monthly telephone bill.

Reducing Advertising Costs

Your company does not have to advertise at its current level. Leads can be generated inexpensively, customer response can be measured and weighed using the customer's money, and sales can be achieved through word-of-mouth or testimonial selling. The important distinction to bear in mind is that between finding potential customers—lead generation—and selling the prospects—marketing. The function of advertising is generally assigned to the former task. In certain instances, such as when a product's utility cannot be easily distinguished from the utility of its competitors, advertising has its role. If that situation obtains with some of the products or services of your company, you can supplement advertising with public relations or video news releases.

Let There Be No Substitute. The function of marketing a product is to persuade the customer that your product is a substitute for all competitive products, but that none of the competitive products is a substitute for yours. It is foolhardy to think that an advertisement can put this message across. It cannot. Whatever gains you think may be derived from placing advertisements in trade journals, you are probably being misled (unless you have a one-in-a-million ad, like the brilliant Avis ad, "We Try Harder").

Public Relations. As you know, generating interesting articles about your product or service in national media is more effective and far less expensive than advertising. A magazine or newspaper article may sit around awhile or be passed around, but it is read by many people and the information is retained more than in an advertisement.

What will this kind of consumer research cost you? Perhaps a $1,000 retainer paid to the public relations agent and postage handling to mail your story to reporters.

Other Ferret Targets

Once the Ferret gets the hang of finding cash in the company's selling, general, and administrative expenses, nothing will be sacred. Travel, business entertainment, sales commissions, utilities—all will be examined, lowered, and, when possible, paid for over time. It is a challenging assignment, and one that the Ferret should work out of in 120 days, so as to be of use to one of the other lieutenants while monitoring the cash function through a well-organized management information system.

IMPROVING EMPLOYEE MORALE

Crises are turn-ons! As you have seen, the Ferret assignment is an exciting task, producing daily victories—some in the tens of thousands of dollars and others for a fraction of that amount. Yet turn-ons all.

But other employees may not be having that much fun. The key to the turnaround is spreading the wealth of the excitement of the chase—the chase to save the company. When all the employees become as involved as the Ferret, the workout and turnaround may cause one of the more humorous employees to say, "Hey, boss! That was fun. Let's get into trouble again."

Crisis as a Turning Point

In charting development through crisis, the social psychologist Erik H. Erikson said that a heightened vulnerability signals the emergence of a potential strength, creating a dangerous opportunity for growth, which Erikson calls "a turning point for better or worse."*

Another student of crises, Hans Selye, provides the following three basic rules for adapting to stress:

1. Find your own purpose in life that fits your own personal stress level.
   - separate leisure from work; "if work is what you have to do then leisure is what you want to do."

2. Control your emotional level by recognizing situations as being either life-threatening or non–life-threatening.
   - anger results from threatened values due to low self-esteem.

3. Collect the goodwill and appreciation of others.
   - persuade others to share our natural desires for our own well-being.

It is the third Selye dictum that must be shared with the less directly involved, "mushroom-growing" employees. Share with them some of the company's wins, involve them in the turnaround mission, and interject some humor into the turnaround process.

The Pregnancy

Following is a humorous event from a turnaround that I worked on a few years ago. I was advising a company in a workout situation, and I got into the picture a little late. The creditors were enraged, and many of the obligations

---

*Erikson, Erik H., *Insight and Responsibility* (New York: W.W. Norton, 1964), p.139.

had been turned over to lawyers. We needed all the creditors to back off for two months to permit management to develop and implement an informal plan of reorganization. How do you buy two months?

We installed a new controller and she was in her seventh month of pregnancy. She introduced herself on the telephone and very appropriately said that the invoices would have to be pulled together so that within a week or so she would know the accounts pretty well. There were 400 individual obligations, and she was familiar with them so it would not take her too long.

"By the way," she added, "I'm going to have a baby fairly soon."

There is no credit manager, collection agent, or commercial lawyer that I know of who does not love babies or revere the miracle of giving birth. The thought that they might adversely affect the successful delivery of a baby changed their entire approach to the matter of collecting the money owed.

"A baby? And you're doing this job?" they asked.

"Yes, my first."

"When is it due?"

"In two months."

The die was cast. The creditors realized they were not going to hassle this sweet young woman who would have her first child in 60 days. Many stopped calling. A handful hung in there and scratched away for nickels and dimes; but, for the most part, the company bought the two months it needed.

When the controller left two weeks before the baby was due, another voice handled the calls. More questions were asked about Donna's condition than about possible payment and payment dates. By the time the baby was born, the company was well on its way with a stretch-out plan.

Ethics

Do you invent a pregnant controller if you do not have one? Do you invent a recovery plan if you do not have one? What are the ethics of dealing with creditors?

The Golden Rule and the Ten Commandments provide the ethical baseline. If you are trying to convert suppliers and lenders to long-term partners or convince them to own your stock or to take 10-year notes, there is no way to succeed unless your ethics are of the very highest order. A lie, a misrepresentation, a flim-flam, or any other form of trickery will be transparent to your creditors. The only solution is to be perfectly honest. Never promise anything you cannot deliver. Stick to the truth; it is easier to remember.

On the other hand, just as you would not tell the referee in a hard-fought basketball game that you walked or that you fouled a player on the other team, so you would not reveal every nuance of your crisis to your creditors. They do not need to know, and, if they did know, you could foul out of the game. As in any sport, you are playing to win, and you can play as hard as you like as long as you play fair.

The company needs to change the voices that talk to creditors in order to buy time. You have put several cash-generating plans into play, but they need time to light up the scoreboard. You have designed a stretch-out plan, but you need time to sell it to creditors and their lawyers. New voices gain time. New controller stories shared with employees improve morale.

CHAPTER 5

Workout Consultants' Views of Troubled Companies

Upset receptionist to CEO: "Sir, there are 20 outraged creditors in the reception area and they're breaking up the furniture."

CEO: "Tell them . . . tell them . . . oh, that the person who handles the checkbook is out sick today; you know, make something up that we haven't used before."
                                   —A frequently repeated pre-attack conversation

WOLVES IN SHEEPS' CLOTHING

The very first thing the owner or manager should know about workout consultants is that they have different views of troubled companies. Some owners and managers have hired workout specialists without proper investigation of their *modus operandi* and have been bought out and thrown out of their companies without a legal leg to stand on to reverse the ill treatment of the intrepid interlopers. Others have hired workout specialists on the recommendation of their senior secured lenders only to find their companies set up for an asset strip by the lenders, while the business is laid waste and the stockholders are left holding the bag. A particular workout consultant may be recommended to you as your salvation from bankruptcy. He or she may be heralded as an angel sent from heaven to wipe out the blot on the family escutcheon and to save you from disgracing the family record by being the third generation of ownership whose blood was too thin to keep the company from filing for protection under the bankruptcy code. "Bankruptcy," a judge once said to me during a difficult workout, "is the last refuge of scoundrels."

Beware the workout consultants who say they have come to aid you, but in reality represent cathartidas, turkey vultures who thirst for carrion, the carcasses of dead companies that they can salvage only by possession of their entrails.

THE VULTURES WHO WORK IN THE BONEYARD

It does not require a financial genius to come to the aid of a struggling company, make a deal with its distressed owner to trade a cash infusion for equity, and then take control, kick out the owner, and change the locks on the door. This type of transaction happens all the time and is based on financial slight of hand that deceives the owner and his or her business advisors. To avoid this occurring in your company, I will explain how it works.

Assume that the financial statements in Exhibit 5.1 describe a seriously troubled company, called Carrion, Inc., owned by George Gullible and managed by him and his children.

The balance sheet of Carrion does not suggest a deeply troubled company, although it is heavily leveraged. The debt to worth ratio is approximately 19 times. But, on the other hand, Carrion's current ratio is a positive 1.2 times. To create a little tension in the atmosphere, assume that $350,000 of the company's $700,000 of accrued expenses represents unpaid employees' withholding taxes. The Gullible family elected to use the government's money a few months ago to pay some bullets and hasn't been able to repay the loan thus far.

The precursor of Carrion's difficulty is a prolonged decline in sales. You can detect some indication of this because inventories exceed accounts receivable in the balance sheet in Exhibit 5.1. Carrion is a manufacturer of

---

Exhibit 5.1   Balance Sheet of Carrion, Inc.

Assets		Liabilities & Stockholders' Equity	
Cash	$ 100,000	Notes payable—bank	$1,000,000
Accounts receivable	2,500,000	Accounts payable	3,000,000
Inventory	3,400,000	Accrued expenses	700,000
		Current portion LTD	400,000
Total current assets	6,000,000	Total current liabilities	5,100,000
Plant & equipment—net	1,500,000	Long-term debt	2,500,000
Other assets	500,000	Total liabilities	7,600,000
		Stockholders' equity	400,000
		Total liabilities &	
Total assets	$8,000,000	stockholders' equity	$8,000,000

---

apparel or dry goods or industrial parts—that is, a product that normally turns over six times a year and with average accounts receivable outstanding of 45 days, or nine times. You can see in Exhibit 5.2 that the accounts receivable are turning a little more slowly, about 6.6 times, or 55 days, the inventory has slowed to 4.3 times, or 85 days, which indicates that customers aren't ordering, or even worse, Carrion's product line is becoming obsolete.

The 12-month operating statement, as is so often the case, does not tell the whole story. The monthly cash flow statement is more revealing because it shows how much cash comes in each month and how much cash goes out. For example, Carrion's monthly "nut," or fixed cost, is the sum of operating and interest expenses divided by 12, or in this case $7,460,000/12 or $622,000 per month. Add to this the cost of producing the goods shipped in a particular month—that is, labor and materials—which in the case of Carrion is a little over $1.2 million per month. Thus, $1.8 million in cash is going out of Carrion each month, or *less* than the anticipated accounts receivable collections. Compounding the problem is that about $1 million of accounts payable are long in the tooth, several hundred thousand dollars of withholding taxes are in arrears, and the wheels could come off the bus if *only one* of the following events happened:

1. A key supplier stops shipping until its account is paid in full, an immediate need for $500,000.
2. The bank calls the $1 million note payable.
3. A customer with a $350,000 account receivable owing the company goes out of business, leaving the debt uncollectible.
4. The IRS demands immediate payment of the withholding tax arrearage, say $300,000.
5. A production jam creates a week's delay in shipments, and $400,000 worth of orders are cancelled after they are produced.

Exhibit 5.2   Operating Statement of Carrion, Inc.

	%	12 months
Sales	100.0	$22,500,000
Cost of goods sold	65.0	14,620,000
Gross profit	35.0	7,880,000
Operating expenses	30.7	6,900,00
Net operating income	4.3	980,000
Interest expenses	2.4	560,000
Net profit before taxes	1.9	420,000
Provision for taxes	.8	190,000
Net profit after taxes	1.1	$ 230,000

LEGAL VULTURES

Carrion may appear profitable, but in reality it is a heartbeat away from serious trouble, particularly if one of the triggering events occurs and pulls Carrion's monthly cash receipts below its $1.8 million monthly "burn rate" or "nut." If Carrion's owners have personally guaranteed the loans, what typically follows is that one of the family members telephones the company's accountant or lawyer and asks for advice.

Typically neither professional has heard of the existence of the workout consultant industry, and it would be unusual for the professional to recommend a workout consultant even if he or she has heard of the breed, although this is changing as a result of greater information such as this book. That may sound crass and unfair to lawyers and accountants, but law firms and accounting firms are run like businesses, and each lawyer and accountant has 2,500 hours to sell per year. If George Gullible calls to say that he has run into a serious cash crunch and that he is beginning to lose credibility with certain suppliers, there is a very strong probability that George's lawyer or accountant will recommend a consultation with a bankruptcy specialist in the firm or in another firm which has a reciprocity understanding with George's lawyer or accountant. It is also likely that George's lawyer and an associate in the firm will sit in with George and the bankruptcy lawyer in order to sell some hours. If George is persuaded to put Carrion, Inc., into Chapter 11 based on the circumstances that I have just related to you, a great disservice will have been done because Carrion is *not* a Chapter 11 candidate.

We will examine very shortly the relative ease by which Carrion can be turned around. However, it bears pointing out that, although workout consultants resent losing business opportunities to lawyers, and occasionally to accountants, the fault lies with workout consultants who have not done a particularly notable job of getting the word out that they exist. A public relations effort to spread the word in leading business magazines, financial newspapers, and trade journals, done frequently to remind managers that an industry of specialists exists to service them in troubled times, would make the playing field more even.

VULTURE CAPITALISTS

Let's take another vantage point from which Carrion, Inc., is viewed. This time we will perch on the shoulder of Cathartida Capital Corp., a $35 million venture capital fund: "one that invests in distressed companies with the objective of turning them around via the implementation of skillful management, fresh capital and leverage." Assume that Cathartida hears of George Gullible's distress through George's accountants and asks to be sent current financial statements and a brief description of the operations. The information is dutifully sent to Cathartida, where it is read by the partners whose arms fill with goose bumps, signifying a fly on its way into the web.

A Cathartida partner telephones George and arranges an appointment to visit the company. The partner persuades George that Carrion's problem is that it is desperately short of capital and that, with capital, Chapter 11 can be avoided (or Cathartida will fund the company's plan of reorganization if its lawyer has filed for protection). George is delighted that the company's problems and his distress can be wiped away so quickly. He agrees to a due diligence analysis by Cathartida, which is done quickly, and the Cathartida partners ask to meet with George and his family privately.

The next scene is so rapacious that it belongs on the plains of Kenya, where the lion stalks and kills the wildebeest, the hyenas then feast on the leftovers, and finally the vultures pick the bones clean.

"George," the Cathartida partner says in his most solemn voice, the one used when paying condolence calls, "the problems at Carrion are bigger than I thought."

"How big?" George asks.

"George, you could lose everything," the lizard-lidded Cathartida partner inaudibly croaks.

"What?" George asks.

"Everything. The whole company could be liquidated for the benefit of creditors, and you and your family may not get a dime out of it. Not a dime," the vulture capitalist adds for effect.

The melodrama goes on and on with spreadsheets and due diligence reports and financial mumbo-jumbo that confuses George and his family until finally one of them asks what Cathartida can do to help.

The trap is sprung. Cathartida will invest the necessary capital to save Carrion from certain death, but it must have voting control of the company's stock.

"Why do you need voting control to make an investment?" George astutely asks.

"Because you have damaged Carrion's relationship with certain vendors and possibly your bank and others. Cathartida must be prudent with its money; after all, we are fiduciaries of the money provided by our investors. We need to roll up our sleeves and follow our investment with some hard work to turn your company around," the partner argues.

George protests, but his family is less concerned with 49 percent ownership if the company, their meal ticket, can be saved. Tennis at the club next Sunday morning may not be as pleasant if the Saturday newspaper announces "Carrion's Financial Woes Continue" or worse. The meeting drags on until the wildebeest becomes exhausted and the lion goes for his throat.

George caves in and sells treasury stock to Cathartida equal to 51 percent of its total issued and outstanding shares of voting common stock, for $1 million. A couple of days later, Cathartida refinances Carrion's $1 million note payable with a $3 million revolving line of credit, uses the $2 million net cash to pay withholding taxes and accounts payable, and swings its $1 million capital investment back out to itself via 12 monthly consulting fees of $100,000 each. George protests that the capital should have remained in the company, and arguments erupt at a series of board meetings. Eventually, George agrees to sell his family's remaining 49 percent interest for a distressed price. Or, as George will tell the story months later, to eliminate his distress.

The moral of the story is that greed lurks around the corner of every troubled company. Vulture capitalists posing as workout consultants prey on the distress of companies whose owners or managers perceive their difficulties as beyond their ability to control. The principal factor that the worried manager overlooks is inertia: the tendency of an object in motion to remain in motion. Troubled companies have a community of allies that will go down if the company goes down. Vendors will lose a customer. Lenders will lose a borrower. Customers will lose a source of supply. The troubled company has more people who will stretch themselves to keep the company afloat than it has adversaries who will seek its liquidation.

But to many owners such as George Gullible, the hassle factor is too much for them to handle; they toss the keys over to a bankruptcy lawyer or a vulture capitalist and walk away with a few dollars and injured pride.

THE UTILITY OF VULTURE CAPITAL FUNDS

Many vulture capital funds do not practice deception. Rather they invest in and purchase distressed companies with the agreement up front that new management will be installed. These vulture capital funds raise their capital from the same sources that have invested in venture capital and LBO funds since the early 1970s. These institutional investors, such as Yale University Endowment Fund, Rockefeller Foundation, General Motors Pension Fund, and Warner-Lambert Pension Fund, have invested in one or more of the vulture capital funds that have put together capital pools in the last two years. They are seeking annual returns of 30 percent, which is a typical venture capital return, according to Ann Johnson, president of Tremon Partners, Inc., New Canaan, Connecticut, which organized a pool of capital to be managed by several vulture capital funds. However, unlike venture capital and LBO funds, vulture funds must occasionally maneuver their portfolio companies through the rocky shoals of bankruptcy court, which can stretch the actual return of capital to the funds' investors and reduce the annualized rate of return somewhat.

At least 20 vulture capital funds have raised $1.1 billion in the last 24 months, with another $1 billion in capital sought after by a like number of vulture fund managers. *Buyouts*, a Needham, Massachusetts, newsletter, keeps score on the nascent industry's fund-raising efforts.

The funds come in two breeds: control buyers and small chunks buyers. The former take over control of troubled companies and install their own handpicked management. The latter take small bites of many troubled companies, usually publicly held, and sometimes assume board or creditor committee seats; but they do not operate the companies, preferring instead to bet on the skills of the workout specialist hired by the board.

Institutional investors such as the University of Michigan Endowment Fund spread the risk and invest in several vulture capital funds having different operating styles.

THE WORKOUT MANAGER'S VIEW

There are two breeds of animal that do not view the anguish and distress of the troubled company with atavistic glee: the workout manager and the workout consultant. The former goes about the task as a live-in physician. The latter puts the company in bed and makes frequent house calls. Both receive fair compensation for their time and generally leave the patient far better off than when they first arrived.

"I make a long-term commitment to my client," says Suren G. Dutia, currently chief executive officer of Xscribe Corp., San Diego, California.

"In most cases I will stay with them 18 months to three years. When I leave, the company is consistently profitable; it has a solid business and strong middle management with a clear line of succession to replace me," Dutia continued.

When Dutia was called into Xscribe by its stockholders, it had been losing about $800,000 a month for several quarters, in the computer-aided transcription/litigation business.

"I only take an assignment if I can be chief executive officer with all the rights and duties that go with the title," Dutia said.

"It's a question of style. I'm not comfortable making recommendations and then seeing them carried out partially or not in a timely manner. I think of a strategy and act on it immediately. I can commit the company to an action and the creditors know that the commitment is binding.

"If I were a consultant," Dutia added, "and if I made an offer to the creditors which they accepted, I would then have to get the CEO to go along with it. He may agree with me, or he may disagree with me and ask me to counter with some other offer. There is too much room for communications error and slip-up and the turnaround plan can slip away. I much prefer control."

The workout manager is compensated in the same manner as a CEO is, receiving salary, bonuses, and equity. If he or she turns the company around and the equity becomes valuable, the rewards can range into eight figures.

Perhaps the best-known workout manager is Sigoloff & Associates, whose President, Sanford C. Sigoloff, 58, is credited with such well-known turnarounds as Republic, Daylin, and Wickes, which filed the second largest bankruptcy ever in 1982. Sigoloff is currently involved in the workout and turnaround of L.J. Hooker (Bonwit Teller, B. Altman, Sakowitz, and other retail brand names). His staff has given Sigoloff the nickname "Ming the Merciless" because of his prodigious attention to detail.

In the early days of crisis intervention at Wickes, he called his managers together on Saturday mornings and floored them with the incredible amount of detail he had absorbed in his first 30 days as CEO. He knew the number of feet from the conveyor belt to the loading dock, whether there was a ladies room on the first floor and how far it was from the elevators, and how many items were on the shelves. On a home computer, working far into the night, Sigoloff had produced cash flow models. No detail failed to catch his eye or to find a cell in his memory bank.

To ease tensions among middle managers during the Daylin turnaround, Sigoloff gave names to the company's crises. Each one was called a "ticking time bomb," and he gave his managers mock bombs complete with alarm clocks. He also addressed their most urgent needs; for example, he rebalanced inventory to make certain the company could fill orders so as to make life bearable for the marketing managers while they carried out his instructions to lay off thousands of employees and sell every unnecessary asset for cash.

THE WORKOUT CONSULTANT'S VIEW

Whereas the workout manager drives the troubled car and controls the accelerator, brakes, clutch, gears, and on/off switch, the workout consultant rides shotgun and makes recommendations, sometimes strong ones, to the driver. But the shotgun riding workout consultant is free to open the passenger-side door and bail out if the driver begins heading for the cliff with a stuck accelerator.

"A consultant," the brilliant advertising executive Carl Ally once said, "borrows your watch to tell you the time, then charges you for it." Although the remark seems humorous when one considers the large number of consultants who tell us things we already knew but perhaps needed clarification, for the first-time crisis manager the workout consultant is as essential as Diogenes in separating truth from fiction and in sorting bullets from BBs and plotting a map out of the jungle of wretched despair and danger. Few owners or managers have the courage or knowledge to perform a workout and turnaround on their own. Plus there are far more companies in trouble than there are workout specialists to go around. Thus, the preferred mode of operation of 90 percent of the nation's workout specialists is the consulting assignment.

Gary Brooks of Allomet Partners, New York, became a workout consultant after he and three other employees at Eastman Kodak turned around a Long Island subsidiary. Brooks claims it is often easier to effect a workout when the owner has personal guarantees outstanding to creditors because he can be more easily persuaded to yield the CEO position to someone with greater credibility in order to protect the core business and its employees.

Many workout consultants learned their craft while employed at a large corporation with troubled divisions or at a smaller company with serious operational problems.

"MY HOME? OR WHERE I SLEEP?"

To follow workout consultant Robert L. Sind around for a day means rising at 6:00 A.M. for a 6:45 breakfast near the midtown Manhattan office of Recovery Management Corp., the workout and turnaround firm that Sind formed in 1983, after 20 years in the investment banking industry—interrupted from time to time with workout assignments at Oxford Industries, Inc., Columbia Pictures Corp., and Commodore International Corp., the large recreational vehicle manufacturer, and six years as chief financial officer with Beker Industries, Inc.

"Beker had sales of $200 million in phosphate fertilizers when I joined them, and it had invested an inordinate amount of money, something like $100 million, much of it borrowed, in the ammonia sector of the fertilizer industry," Sind said.

"Phosphate sales headed south quickly followed by the ammonia business, and the company entered a serious crisis. I negotiated standstill agreements with the creditors and sold off the ammonia business to pay down debts."

Sind stayed on at Beker until it was completely turned around. Calls came from banks, stockholders of troubled companies, venture capitalists, and crisis-riven managers for Sind to come fix their troubled situations. In 1983, he formed Recovery Management Corp. to provide workout and turnaround services to large and complex situations on a full-time basis. Since then, Recovery Management's staff has expanded to 20, including part-time associates whom Sind hires under his contracts with clients according to their industry-specific skills.

Recovery Management's client list reads like a who's who of fallen angels: Knoll International, Pettibone, Tosco, Thomas Homes, Mack Truck, Globe Distributors, LCP, Gulfstream Land, and Hudson General. The company manages several workouts at a time, "so long as they are not all in the beginning stage," says Sind.

"If you handle several clients at once and they're located in different sections of the country, where is your home?" I asked Sind.

"My home? Or where I sleep?" Sind responded with a wry smile.

A Week in the Life of a Workout Consultant

As you will be able to see from the following travelogue, a week in the life
of a company physician is not for the homebody who knits baby blankets.
This is a rigorous, difficult to schedule, travel intensive, body-wearying way
to make a living. But ask a workout consultant if they would have it any
other way, and they will say, "Absolutely not."

Monday.   Rise at 6:00 A.M., catch cab to the airport for flight to Chicago,
where client A is making substantial changes in production schedules and
shipping terms. Need to observe customer reactions and production workers'
reactions to the changes at the plant. Make interventions where appropriate.
Lunch with client A's senior secured bank and client A's CEO to present new
cash flow statements and assure lender that the payment schedule provided
several weeks ago can be met. Back to the client's office; read my faxes
from the office and fax back responses and comments. Meet with client
A management involved in selling assets and provide input and direction.
Review product order rates and discuss marketing strategies to try to improve
cash flows. Meet with client A managers involved in negotiating stretch-outs
with creditors. Get involved with some of the tougher cases. Take litigation
to my hotel to read that night. Pick up pressed and cleaned clothes in Chicago
hotel maintained there for these extended visits.

Tuesday.   Up at 6:00 A.M., and at client A's office by 7:00. Make calls to
my associates at headquarters. Get details on situations at clients B, C, and
D. Call clients B, C, and D to make interventions and suggestions. Fax
my office to set appointments. Meet with CEO of client A and client A's
litigation counsel to review litigation strategy. Decide to settle some, defend
others. Back to creditor negotiations of previous afternoon. Then review
the marketing strategies and spin-off plans. Review offer to sell a division.
Telephone broker for the buyer and negotiate terms. Follow up with lawyer
to see how the morning's plans fared. Catch cab to airport. Fly to New York
and check into hotel where a fresh set of clothes awaits me, plus faxes from
the office and clients.

Wednesday.   Up at 5:00 A.M. to call the office to respond to the prior
evening's faxes and take morning messages. Breakfast with venture capitalist whose portfolio has several troubled companies. Second breakfast with
senior credit officer of large New York bank to discuss possible creditor
committee assignment on $500 million nonperforming loan. Catch cab to
client B, which is in early stages of trouble and do a full-day's diagnostic
work-up. Take files to hotel and read until midnight.

Thursday.   Up at 5:00 A.M. and call headquarters to discuss incoming faxes slipped under the door that morning. Call clients A, C, and D and make interventions, set appointments, and call C and D creditors that need some attention. Catch cab to client B's office and have meeting with client B managers to follow up on the previous day's diagnostic session. Meet with CEO to outline my preliminary plans and the time line for getting things done. Discuss my feelings and his about middle management and their strengths and weaknesses. Review faxes from the office and respond. Fed Ex client B's files to headquarters. Then catch cab to LaGuardia and fly to Boston.

Friday.   Rise at 6:00 A.M. and review faxes. Fax responses to office and clients. Have breakfast with creditor of client A to discuss workout plans. Second breakfast with creditor of client B—same topic. Catch cab to client C to meet with management to discuss the progress of the workout plan previously set up. Spin-offs and asset sales going well. Lunch downtown with stockholders of client D to discuss possible changes in senior management to enable turnaround plan to go more smoothly. We also discuss the option of selling the entire company or raising capital from institutional lenders. Meeting lasts until 2 P.M. Catch cab to large Boston bank to negotiate standstill agreement with client C's principal lender. Catch cab to Logan, and fly to a weekend on the beach away from telephones, fax machines and hordes of creditors.

The Conveyor Belt

To the outside observer, handling crises of multiple clients may appear to be a less precise craft than working on one at a time. But, according to Harvey Nachmann, Vice President of PBR Associates, Baltimore, it depends on where the clients are situated along the conveyor. "The work is very difficult and time consuming at the beginning," says Nachmann, "but when we begin to take control of events, it isn't that rigorous and we can take on other assignments." PBR Associates at this writing had workouts underway in Maryland (3), New Jersey (2), Pennsylvania (2), New York and Ohio. Note the regional concentration which shortens the time to get from one client to the other.

CHAPTER 6

How to Select a
Workout Consultant

All happy families resemble one another; every unhappy family is unhappy in its
own way.

—Count Leo Tolstoy

A DIFFICULT SELECTION PROCESS

There is no heading for "workout specialists" in the Yellow Pages. There is a
paucity of directories of workout specialists because they have only recently
become popular. If you ask for advice from your lawyer, he or she is likely to
recommend a bankruptcy lawyer. If you ask your accountant to recommend
a workout specialist, he or she is likely to recommend a bankruptcy lawyer
or the consulting division of the accounting firm, if it has one.

Finally, if someone introduces you to a workout specialist, it may be a
vulture capitalist who visits you, carrying a physician's black bag but whose
true purpose is to transfer ownership from your family to his.

And even if you get by these hurdles and actually get to interview an
honest-to-gosh workout specialist who has the experience, the interest, and
the industry criteria to assist you, he or she may be too expensive, have a
conflict of interest—that is, in a relationship with your largest lender, which
precludes representing your company—or not have the time to help you
immediately.

However, if we assume that these possible deterrents can be worked out,
the specialist's preferred form of representation and your desires may differ.
For instance, you may not wish to relinquish CEO powers and issue 10
percent of the company's common stock to attract the services of a certain
workout manager; but those are his or her terms. Or, if the board of directors
is doing the hiring, it may want a workout manager to come aboard as CEO
with an equity interest, but the only people it has interviewed to date are

workout consultants who are paid with a retainer up front then sell their time by the hour.

The directory in the back of the book will certainly make your life easier and save you the *cost of search*, but you will have to conduct interviews of the workout specialists whose names you select from the directory.

RESTRUCTURING CONSULTANTS

The deck is stacked against you in the sense that the creditors have been through many workouts and this is probably your first one. The creditors know the most experienced workout specialists and bankruptcy lawyers, whereas you may know very few. Moreover, the creditors will move very quickly to hire the services of the best *restructuring consultant* whom they can get and the best creditor-advocate bankruptcy lawyer available.

A restructuring consultant is a workout consultant who takes the bulk of his or her assignments from lenders and creditor committees. You may be very well served by hiring a restructuring consultant as your workout consultant because they usually have enormous credibility with creditors, and that will transfer to you. Workout specialist Frank Zolfo, one of the pioneers of the workout industry and who heads up a 30-person firm of workout specialists, says, "It is the integrity of the workout consultant that is paramount to obtaining creditor approval for a plan of reorganization." It is not uncommon, therefore, for a workout consultant to take assignments from creditors because in so doing, he or she is gaining their respect. Of more importance to you, the consultant is learning how they think, how much of a haircut they will take on the amount owing them, and whether or not the line they draw in the sand can be moved back or if it is Custer's last stand.

POSSIBILITY OF CONFLICT OF INTEREST

Assume that you hire a workout team known best for creditor assignments. Further assume that the team is helping five major banks collect their loans, and, although none of the banks have loans to your company, they do have loans to your suppliers. Carrying this hypothetical situation further, let's say you cannot offer more than 20 cents on the dollar to your creditors, and this slim sum causes sufficient pain to your suppliers because their loans from subject banks are jeopardized and cannot be paid in a timely manner.

Now put yourself in the seat of the restructuring consultant whom you have hired. Is he likely to receive a telephone call or two from the banks, questioning the inadequacy of your 20-cent offer? You can be sure he will. What will be his response to you?

He could ask you to dig a little deeper. He could ignore the banks' requests. Or he could resign from your assignment. The latter leaves you in a dangerous position. The creditors will become disconcerted that a workout consultant whom they respect has left you.

It is critical in hiring a workout consultant to establish up front that conflicts of interest, if they arise, will be decided in your favor. You simply cannot afford to be naked in front of your creditors for any period of time and for any reason.

WORKOUT CONSULTANT VERSUS WORKOUT MANAGER

As you know, the workout consultant is a professional who sells you his or her time and brains. A workout manager is a principal who replaces you as CEO and becomes a stockholder in your company responsible to the company's board of directors and stockholders. Which one should you hire?

You have little choice in the matter if you have given incorrect information of a material nature, no matter how innocently, to the company's creditors. If your credibility is damaged, even the most highly respected workout consultant may not be able to gain back the respect of creditors. Whenever you read that Sigoloff & Associates has been called into a company, you can be fairly certain that the creditors have insisted that management be replaced.

Additionally, if you have read Grimm's Fairy Tales to your board of directors at too many meetings, they may hire a workout manager to replace you. Even the creditors committee may give you a Samuel Goldwynism: "Would I let you remain in the CEO spot? I'll give you my answer in two words: Im Possible."

THE INVESTMENT BANKER WORKOUT CONSULTANT

"The people who loaded you up with debt," Frank Zolfo told me, "may be the people you hire to get rid of the debt." Investment banks are jumping into the workout and turnaround business. Some of them know what they are doing, and others are hanging out shingles to attract clients who will teach them.

A survey of workout consultants produced a list of the five best investment bank workout-consulting divisions (see Exhibit 6.1).

Exhibit 6.1 The Best Investment Bank Workout-Consulting Divisions

Name of Firm	Head Office	Department Head
1. Smith Barney Harris Upham, Inc.	New York	Nicholas J. Sakellariadis
2. Bear Stearns & Company	New York	Daniel Celantano
3. Rothschild, Inc.	New York	Wilbur Ross
4. Chilmark	Chicago	David M. Schulte
5. Gruntal Finance Corp.	New York	Michael Koblitz

"The unique feature that we bring to the field of crisis management is the ability to raise money rapidly," says Michael Koblitz, who runs the workout department for Gruntal Finance Corp., an old-line investment banking and brokerage firm that was recently involved in the Cuisinarts workout and sale and that sits on the Drexel Lambert & Company creditors committee. The absence of cash is symptomatic of most crisis-riven companies but not the cause of the problem, as we have seen. Therefore, there are risks attendant in raising good money after bad; if old management is boxed out and new management understands the proper balance between leverage and growth, access to capital is not a major obstacle.

THE SPECIAL REQUIREMENTS OF
FAMILY-OWNED BUSINESSES

In family-owned businesses, on the other hand, there is much moving of bishops, pawns, kings, and queens before the workout consultant can focus on cash, production, marketing, or whatever affliction has brought the company to its knees. The need to remove family members from daily decision making and control of the checkbook before restructuring the company's capitalization and bringing in new money is a sixth sense of certain workout consultants and frequently not the purview of investment bankers turned crisis managers.

"Sometimes the owner of a company is absolutely certain that his son should succeed him," says Diane M. Freaney of Triage, Inc., "even though the son wants to be an artist or music composer."

"When we relieve the son from the responsibility of plant supervision or overseeing the sales reps, he wants to kiss and hug us. His face fills with joy," adds Freaney.

Can you imagine trying to solve the problems of the dysfunctional Loman family of Arthur Miller's *The Death of a Salesman* with a dollop of cash? Here's a snapshot from a scene near the end of the play with which many players in the drama of family-owned business can identify:

> *Biff:* Pop, I'm nothing! I'm nothing, Pop. Can't you understand that? There's no spite in it any more. I'm just what I am that's all.
>
> *Willy:* What're you doing? What're you doing?
> *To Linda*: Why is he crying?
>
> *Biff:* Will you let me go, for Christ sake? Will you take that phony dream and burn it before something happens?*

It seems obvious that family-owned businesses have special needs, far removed from those of a $20 billion bank whose real estate loans are pulling

---

*Arthur Miller, *The Death of a Salesman* (New York: Viking Press, 1949), p. 133.

it into a morass of red ink to the sound of bleating federal bank examiners clamoring for answers to their shrill cries of "What're you doing? What's happening to your loans?"

In both situations, family-owned or publicly held monoliths, the process of hiring the workout specialist is the same: act quickly, interview methodically, and make sure you get what you bargain for.

THE TELEPHONE INTERVIEW

Five or six appropriate workout specialists can be located by referring to the directory in the back of the book. Appropriateness can be determined by the directory information: the length of time the company has been in the workout field; industries in which the company specializes; size of companies with which the workout specialist has familiarity; and affordability. Clearly, the Recovery Managements and the Sigoloff & Associates need head-turner retainers in the middle to high six figures or more, and they are not appropriate for the troubled company with no more than $5,000 to $25,000 to pay a doctor. Further, a workout consultant who specializes in real estate disasters is inappropriate to offer aid and comfort to a direct mail vitamin and health care delivery firm.

The key to using the directory is to telephone the workout consultants who appear, on the surface, to fit your needs and ask them the following initial screening questions:

1. Do you have experience with companies in the (fill in the blank) industry?
2. Do you have experience with companies of our size that are in illiquidity crises?
3. What is your typical fee structure?
4. May I interview some of your references?

You can provide preliminary financial information to the consultant via fax or overnight courier to enable her to perform a preliminary diagnosis. If your bank loan has been called or if suppliers have shut you down, be certain to add that to the preliminary data that you send to the workout consultant. She may not be able to fit your needs into her time constraints or fee schedule without knowing the extent and scope of the crisis.

In the initial telephone interview it is important to screen out vulture capitalists and workout specialists who are overly committed and unable to concentrate their full attention on your company's immediate needs. A workout consultant who takes five days to return your call is probably too busy to assist you right away. Bear in mind that to a workout consultant troubled companies are her *inventory* and she and her staff see them in stages along a conveyor belt. If the workout consultant with a three-person staff has three other clients coming off the assembly line into *finished goods* inventory and well past the pit of their crises, then there should be ample time and resources to deal efficiently with your company's crisis. Your company represents *raw material*, and its consulting needs are very much hands-on, personnel-oriented meetings with creditors and Johnny-on-the-spot. If the workout consultant needs to make one or two telephone calls from your office to look in on how a redirect and grow plan is progressing at another of her clients, that is not inappropriate behavior. After all, there are more troubled companies than there are workout consultants to go around.

THE HONESTY FACTOR

Once you have narrowed down the list to two or three candidates, 90 percent of the selection process can be done before the in-depth interviews. This assumes that you have provided the candidates sufficient information to enable them to respond. It is up to you to be very clear. If your company represents the sole employer in a small community and if filing for protection under Chapter 11 could destroy the local economy, it is extremely important that you provide that information to the candidates up front. If one of your company's requirements is to avoid a filing, then the workout consultant will have to be on-site within 48 hours and remain on site for one to two weeks to arrest the crisis and settle down the howling tempest of employees, customers, suppliers, and lenders.

For your part, references should be checked before the in-depth interview. Take full and complete notes of your conversations with reference contacts. If the references seem too good to be true, always ask, "Do you know anyone who has something less flattering to say about Charlie?" There are no saints in the workout business; but there are many very good people who love their work and carry it out with speed, efficiency, and rock-solid honesty.

The honesty factor will be an area that lenders and creditors will be able to comment on. In your reference checking, you might interview several creditors of companies that the candidates have rescued. The key question to ask them is, "Did the candidate make any promises to you that he couldn't or didn't keep?" The answer to this question could hold the key to the candidate's ability to rescue your company. Above all else, the workout consultant substitutes his or her credibility for yours—or for the people in your company who have been speaking with creditors and vendors—in order to convince them to *stand still* while a rehabilitation plan is sculpted. Imagine the consequences to your company if the workout consultant has made optimistic promises in previous assignments to some of the same creditors that your company owes money to. The "How do you spell relief?" commercial will end with "D-I-S-A-S-T-E-R" in the annals of your company's history.

THE IN-DEPTH INTERVIEW

When you have narrowed down the candidates to two or three by reference checking and have supplied the candidates with financial and descriptive information, the next step is to bring them in for in-depth interviews. It is not appropriate to inform the candidates in a detailed memorandum before the fact exactly what your expectations are; although you could set these out in the in-depth interview as well.

Although the candidates should not expect a consulting fee for the interview day, they are entitled to receive reimbursement of their expenses for visiting you. If your company is in Chapter 11, your company will need court approval to pay the consultant's retainer, although you can pay the consultant personally.

The candidates should be prepared to cover the following ground with you during the in-depth interview:

- The initial findings.
- The expectations of senior management or owners as to the criticality of avoiding a filing, removing the owners' personal guarantees, or retaining family ownership.
- The consultant's fee structure, particularly as to success bonuses and equity features, but also whether it is per diem, per hour, or some other arrangement.
- A PERT chart or time schedule in which the consultant's actions are plotted against time.
- The associates whom the consultant will assign to the task and some background on their experience and skills.
- The length of time that the workout consultant anticipates spending on the assignment. (This will enable you to assess the overall costs and determine the candidates' relative affordability.)
- The extent to which the work will be done on-site and the extent to which it will be done from the workout consultant's office. There is a great deal of benefit in having the consultant on-site a large portion of the time, not least of which has to do with crisis management and managing the distress.
- The percentage of the work to be done by the workout consultant and the percentage to be done by his staff. If you pay for a hand-tailored Turnbull & Asher shirt, you don't want to be given a standard brand J.C. Penney, even if the candidate persuades you that the shirt is really "Jacques Penné."
- A clear definition of the consultant's role. Will he or she make all decisions or advise you? Will he or she do the firing when that is called for? Or will he or she make personnel reduction recommendations to you? Will he or she tell customers that the

company can only ship to them on a C.O.D. basis, or will he or she advise you that C.O.D. status is called for and help you negotiate these terms with customers?

- Finally, a formal consulting agreement in which the scope and function of the assignment are outlined in writing.

Let's examine some of these criteria in more detail.

THE LENGTH OF TIME OF THE ASSIGNMENT

The candidate's projection of the length of time required to effect a workout and turnaround of your company will ultimately depend on the stage at which your company is in the crisis roller coaster. For instance, if it has bottomed out and has no credit, no shippable inventory and no suppliers, the consultant may recommend that he or she come in and effect standstill agreements with creditors while he or she finds a buyer for the company. Most consultants will estimate a three- to six-month assignment to hold back the dike and sell the company, for there are few options at this stage. It would be appropriate to build a success fee into this difficult assignment as well.

On the other hand, if the firefighter is called to the scene before the blaze gets out of hand, the workout consultant's assignment will require more time and more steps, including implementing an informal plan of reorganization and possibly monitoring the plan on an infrequent basis to make certain that the steps set in motion are being carried out. After all, the consultant's credibility was put on the line and he or she doesn't want to see it compromised. You can expect at least a 15-month assignment to rehabilitate and reorganize your company if it is in an early stage of crisis and if the management team is not lazy about the problems.

By referring to the information in the Workout Consultant's Directory, you can see that 82 percent of the consultants report that their typical assignments last 18 months or less. Exhibit 6.2 provides more detail.

**Exhibit 6.2   Workout Consultants'
Estimates of the Length of a
Typical Assignment**

Time	Percentage
2 years or more	18.0
18 months	18.0
1 year to 18 months	15.0
6 months to 1 year	12.0
Under 6 months	37.0
Total	100.0

The exhibit is illuminating in that there is a gap between up to 18 months and 24 months or more. Certainly, some workout assignments last more than 18 months and less than 24 months. However, it is worth noting that 8 out of 10 workout consultants put the end date at 18 months for a full assignment. The bulge in the 6-month time period represents primarily the *transfer* function—that is, negotiating standstill agreements and finding a buyer for the company. This is an excellent role for an investment bank workout consultant with a long history of successful merger and acquisition experience.

THE EXPERIENCE FACTOR

Credibility is one of the most important ingredients that you are buying when shopping the market for a workout consultant. This is particularly true if the people in your company who have been promising payment or promising delivery or promising to live up to a warranty agreement have sacrificed their credibility to try to buy time because you told them, perhaps too optimistically, that help is on the way.

One way to determine how credible a workout consultant is regarded—in addition to the interview and reference checking—is to examine the length of time he or she has been in the workout and turnaround field.

"I sometimes think I've been in the business since I was two years old," says Robert L. Sind, one of the most experienced workout and turnaround experts.

"When I got into the field over 20 years ago," remembers Frank Zolfo, "there was Ernst & Young and me and very few others."

Experience and price are correlative factors. If you want a Sind or a Zolfo to rescue your company, you're going to pay up for it. But then, you will doubtless hire a workout consultant whose credibility with the major lenders and creditors in the country is bluer than blue chip.

The industry is relatively new, with 25 years cited by the workout consultants in the directory as the maximum length of time they have trod the boneyards of American industry. Surprisingly, there is relatively little burnout in the industry. Very few workout consultants report having left the industry for a little R and R. This underscores the axiom that stress is a downer, but crisis is a turn-on.

The workout consultants in the directory cluster in the 1- to 10-year experience range, with nearly 30 percent in the 1- to 5-year range. Exhibit 6.3 amplifies on the experience factor.

The more experience that you hire, the more credibility with creditors you will purchase. This translates into more time to effect a turnaround or, in trade jargon, the longer the standstill period you can arrange. These precious commodities translate into dollars. Time is a precious commodity when the firing squad of creditors is in the "Ready-Aim . . ." position.

**Exhibit 6.3   Amount of Experience
in the Workout Industry**

Years of Experience	Percentage
Over 20 years	15.0
15 to 20 years	9.0
10 to 15 years	9.0
5 to 10 years	59.0
1 to 5 years	28.0
Total	100.0

FEE STRUCTURE

Workout consultants' fee structures are fairly evenly disbursed, as you can see by referring to the directory. Approximately 54 percent work on an hourly basis, and approximately 46 percent work on a retainer basis. The latter is also expressed as a retainer against an hourly fee basis.

The key to estimating the cost of a workout and turnaround assignment is to determine how much money your company owes. If it owes $200 million, the retainer to attract an experienced workout consultant might be $500,000 or more. If it owes $20 million, the retainer might be $40,000 or more. But if your company owes $2 million or less, a $5,000 retainer or a flat hourly fee may be the amount you are looking at. All workout consultants will insist on expense reimbursements.

The hourly fee will depend on how much debt your company owes, the depth of the crisis, the estimated length of the assignment, and the region of the country. If your company is located in a major metropolitan area, it may have to pay a higher hourly fee—say, $250 per hour—because salary structures are higher in those markets. In a small, less populated region, hourly fees may be as low as $125 per hour.

Hiring a workout consultant should not be a price-sensitive business. It would be foolhardy to lose your company in order to save $15,000 in fees.

Approximately 27 percent of the workout consultants charge success fees. Again, this is a function of the stage of crisis that your company is in. Some consultants may be willing to charge a smaller hourly fee and retainer in order to obtain a success fee. The latter may be stated as a function of increasing the company's cash position or returning it to positive cash flow of a certain monthly or quarterly level. Beware of a success fee that is based on increasing net worth to a certain level. Even the lamest of consultants should be able to do that by simply negotiating settlements with creditors and issuing them company stock. Then you would owe the consultant a cash bonus but not have the cash to pay it with.

THE CONTRACT

The language of the contract, or *consulting agreement* as it may be referred to, and the scope of the assignment should track each other on each point. Some consultants may sell with the virtues of Jacob but deliver with the cunning and guile of Esau. Be certain that the contract provides for a written summary of what the consultant did, at least every three weeks, and then match his or her performance against the PERT chart or time line.

Also allow for an inexpensive divorce fee if you become dissatisfied with the consultant's performance. You might provide for a 15-day notification period. Be sure to pay the consultant all amounts owing when and if you divorce. You do not want him or her among your large creditors.

Finally, *cover the details*. For instance, does the consultant charge for the time en route to your company? If so, make certain that he or she is doing work for you en route. Ask for details in the billing statement such as how each hour was spent. Review the billing statement before you sign the contract, and set forth the frequency and detail that you expect to see.

A crisis period is intense and many details can slip through the cracks. You do not want *any* misunderstandings to arise between you and your workout consultant, who will hold your company in his or her hands.

Therefore, before signing the consulting agreement always ask the following question: "What question have I overlooked that you would have asked?"

An experienced workout consultant will probably smile and say: "There is one that you left out."

And you will ask, "Which one is that?"

"Can we win?"

"Well, can we?" you ask.

"Yes, we can."

CHAPTER 7

How the Workout
Consultant Operates

Beware
Of entrance to a quarrel, but being in,
Bear't that the opposed may beware of thee.
Give every man thy ear, but few thy voice;
Take each man's censure, but reserve thy judgment.

—Shakespeare, *Hamlet*

There are six stages in the workout and turnaround process. The six steps follow sequentially and although the workout consultant may double-back when on step number five to reexamine the information and conclusion filed away in step number one, the sequence must be followed in a systematic manner in order for the company to be rehabilitated outside of a Chapter 11 or 7 filing.

First, I will summarize the steps then provide you with an example from the case histories of one of the more experienced workout consulting firms; next we will examine the steps in greater detail.

STEP ONE: DIAGNOSIS

The workout consultant, who is normally a quick learner, will find out as much as possible about the nature and extent of the company's crisis in order to assess the present circumstances and plan the course of remedial action.

STEP TWO: CRISIS MITIGATION

The consultant will meet with the people who are the gatekeepers at the flash points, calm their fears, and win their support. These people will probably include employee groups (or union leaders), the company's principal lender, key suppliers, and possibly important customers. The operative phrase is "negotiate standstill agreements" or buy time, and, if the workout consultant has credibility, this stage of the workout process, which is central to its success or failure, will go very well and buy time.

STEP THREE: CASH GENERATION

The workout consultant will next turn his or her attention and experience to generating a pool of cash. This will be done by slashing expenses, selling off unused assets, sale leasebacks, spin-offs of divisions, production changes, adding new channels of distribution, changing the terms by which customers pay, and possibly raising bridge capital.

STEP FOUR: PREPARATION OF A TURNAROUND PLAN

Before the ink is dry on Step Three, the workout consultant begins to develop a rehabilitation plan that will return the company to normalized operations. The plan will include restructuring debt, negotiating new terms with suppliers, redeploying assets and personnel, and raising capital (if the cash on hand is inadequate).

STEP FIVE: NEGOTIATION OF THE PLAN

The workout consultant will present the plan to the largest and most important creditors first, who may request modifications and changes. They may even refuse to accept it, which means back to Step Four or call in the bankruptcy lawyer to prepare a filing. The plan must be negotiated quickly with a great deal of clarity and in a manner that leaves the company enough backdoors and circuit breakers to make alterations or to find cash if the plan cannot be lived up to.

STEP SIX: IMPLEMENTATION OF THE PLAN

Once the plan has the acceptance of all creditors, it is implemented and carefully monitored for two to three months to make sure that it is working smoothly. This is a critical period that tests the company's and the workout consultant's abilities to do in fact what they said they could do on paper. A downtick in revenues or cash receipts could seriously upset the company's plan and cause the creditors to grow restless. The workout consultant may have to back pedal to Step Four to see if he or she made some incorrect assumptions, then renegotiate a new plan in Step Five and implement the revised plan, all of which will test the patience of creditors.

THE TARHEEL FURNITURE CASE

Harry was your typical "hail fellow-well met," a natural-born salesperson. But he had never done much of anything with his life, even after he was married, because daddy and daddy's businesses were always there to take care of him. One day he talked daddy into putting him into his own business. A local furniture manufacturing company was for sale, and Harry figured he would be good at drumming up orders.

So his father, a well-known, wealthy local businessman, went to his bank and borrowed $400,000 to buy the business for Harry and his wife. Then he decided that while he was about it, he'd also make Harry's sister Sheila and her husband owners of the business too. Sheila and her husband didn't really want to be part of the business; they didn't know anything about furniture making and they didn't want to learn. They had their own things going and would rather have had the cash instead, but to no avail. They become involuntary owners of Tarheel Furniture.

In no time at all, Harry had drummed up orders from many of the country's leading chains, including K-Mart, Wal-Mart, and others. Two years later, despite the huge orders, Tarheel Furniture was losing money. Worse still, it wasn't even shipping orders on time. Debts mounted and on the very day a business workout specialist from Triage, Inc., arrived in the North Carolina town, the bank called its $400,000 loan. This was the state of the crisis that greeted consultant Carol Mann, one of the Triage partners.

The first thing Mann did was go directly from the airport to the bank to seek a loan extension. Without it, there was no point in her staying to try to turn the company around. In fact, she had not even been to the Tarheel plant to get a first-hand look at what the problems might be. She asked the bank for two weeks to give her time to analyze the situation and see whether the company could be saved. Reluctantly, the bank agreed.

Making matters worse, the family had told Mann that the option of seeking Chapter 11 protection during reorganization was out of the question. The family was very prominent locally and word of its present situation would be most embarrassing.

When Mann got to Tarheel, she found things even worse than she had imagined. The company had no idea how much inventory it had. It didn't know what its manufacturing costs per unit were. It had no formal production process; most people did not even know all of the parts or steps required to produce the ladder-back and shaker-back chairs and rockers that were the firm's specialty. Orders were being shipped late, if they were being shipped at all. There was no uniform pricing policy. There were no floor leaders, no supervisors, no managers. Employees came and went at will.

Not only that, physically the plant was a disaster-in-waiting. The local fire marshall and the EPA had just cited Tarheel the day Mann arrived for safety and environmental violations. More than five inches of sawdust covered the floors. Aisles were clogged with materials. Hundreds of 55-gallon drums filled with no-one-knew-what littered the back yard. Unused painting tanks were filled with sludge.

The first thing Mann did was to shut down the plant and call an employee meeting. "Before we do anything else," she told the assembled workers, "we're going to shut down for two days and clean and straighten up this plant." She also spelled out new work rules that were to go into effect immediately, such as being on the job on time and until quitting time, wearing safety goggles and safety shoes, no more eating and drinking while operating machinery—in effect, the basics that any normal employer would expect of employees. She explained that she was now in charge.

Next, she took inventory. "They had stock coming out of their ears," she recalled, "but nothing that could be shipped to fill existing orders."

Mann then cut the company's product line in half, offering special pricing on the closed-out products. She taught one of the office workers how to cost out each of the company's remaining product lines per unit. Then she set new prices.

She met with production employees and codified manufacturing procedures. Where the firm had used four different types of woods to make chairs, she used two. She took inventory of pieces for chairs. During a personal inspection tour she discovered that many perfectly good pieces, items which cost the company $2 and $3 each, were routinely being thrown into a trash dumpster. Mann put an immediate stop to that.

She appointed several individuals as floor leaders and supervisors, then held training meetings each morning to teach them basics of supervision.

Mann next took the unprecedented step of calling the firm's customers and telling them she was canceling their orders, unless they were willing to wait 12 weeks for shipment.

By this time, Mann's two weeks were up. She called the bank to warn them that they weren't going to get their financial statement.

"My priority was to make products for shipment to generate money so we could pay our bills," said Mann.

But she also invited the banker to visit—and he was amazed at the progress. He felt that Mann had made great strides and that many of Tarheel's problems were on their way to being solved.

Once the production problems were resolved, she then tackled the firm's financial problems. She found the firm had been using a factor to raise immediate cash. But the factor was charging the equivalent of approximately 23 percent interest a year. Mann dropped the factor and instituted her own credit and receivables plan. It called for a down payment at the time of the order; in addition, no orders would be shipped to customers who had unpaid balances over 30 days.

Vendors were another problem. The company owed them almost $500,000. One nearby supplier of specialty wood had already refused to ship the company

any more supplies. Mann met with the vendors and told them they were not going to be paid half in 30 days and the remaining half 30 days later as a trade association had indicated to them. In fact, she told them, they were not likely to be paid anything they were owed.

Having said that, she then told the vendors she wanted to continue doing business with them, but on a C.O.D. basis from now on. "I reminded them that they needed us as a customer as much as we needed them as suppliers; we were mutually dependent." When one vendor became recalcitrant, she set up a meeting with him at a time that "just happened to coincide" with an appointment she had to meet the sales representative of the manufacturer of machinery used by that particular vendor. The vendor decided to continue doing business with Tarheel rather than risk having Tarheel manufacture its own parts.

During all of this, Mann also sought to have Harry removed from the company. He would antagonize financially distressed vendors and workers by driving up to the plant in his new, expensive sports car. Finally, she agreed to keep him in sales and give him an added 2 percent commission to help him repay his outstanding loans. During the period, Harry had taken out a second loan—a personal loan of $180,000 to be repaid over five years and to be used toward paying off the $400,000 note. (This latter loan, which Harry's father personally guaranteed, eventually became $250,000.)

Two and one-half months later, with production and financial problems being straightened out and with the firm on a solid footing with new orders and cash flowing in, the bank agreed to restructure the two outstanding loans, which now totaled $650,000.

Tarheel was a dramatically different company than the one that greeted Carol Mann the day the bank decided to call in the loan. The relationship with the bank was much improved and the company was making money. There were two managers and supervisors in place, and Mann had taught them how to run the operation and manage money. Sometime later, Harry sold the business to a syndicate. When, afterward, his father died, Daddy's money went to pay off the loans he had personally guaranteed for Harry.

CAROL MANN AND TRIPLE BYPASS SURGERY

As you can see from the Tarheel Furniture case, in a real-life situation the six-step process for rescuing and rehabilitating a company does not always go according to Hoyle. Carol Mann got off the airplane in a small North Carolina town and was told that the bank had pulled the plug on Tarheel Furniture. Mann may have planned a day of detailed diagnosis and fact collecting, but, instead of having a morning cup of coffee in the company's conference room while taking a legal pad full of notes, she had to go into the enemy's camp and negotiate a standstill agreement to permit her time to carry out her assignment. Fortunately, Mann had done a considerable amount of diagnosis before she arrived on the scene. In the car on the way to the bank, Mann was briefed on the details of the default notice, and she knew whether or not the bank could collect on the loan or if the company could tie its hands with a lender liability complaint, or if a threatened Chapter 11 filing would delay the collection process for six months to a year.

Mann demonstrated in 30 minutes at the bank some of the extraordinary ways in which experienced workout consultants earn their money. If turning around a default notice into a standstill agreement and then engineering a workout and turnaround plan isn't a Picasso for this difficult profession or isn't the equivalent of a heart transplant or a triple bypass surgery that restores the life of the patient, then I don't know what is.

STEP ONE: DIAGNOSIS

The key to a successful rehabilitation lies in the homework. Company management and its owners in most instances will have confused symptoms with the locus of pathology that is killing the company. Management and owners will be blaming half a dozen dragons that are responsible for the company's crisis as well. As they say in engineering, the workout consultant will receive more noise than signals and will have to differentiate the two so as to quickly cut to the chase.

The workout consultant's first step in most situations is a diagnostic interview with the CEO and subsequently with other key members of management. The purpose of the interview is to assess the stage of crisis and the symptomatic issues. These could be in all or a few of the following areas:

- Sales
- Production
- Credit
- Overhead expenses
- Personnel

The manner in which the CEO presents his or her view of the crisis can be very telling. In many cases, the CEO is part of the problem or at least a conflictual player in the crisis. This occurs when the CEO believes the crisis can be resolved with more sales or raising more debt, when the locus of the disease is obsolete products or inefficient production. An experienced workout consultant will bring two or three members of senior management, who have identified the problems in precise detail, into a joint interview with the CEO and attempt to exacerbate the conflict beyond the management team's usual threshold of tolerance; and then, when the conflict is at its height, the consultant will hypothesize strategies that the group can explore. The workout consultant looks for levels of conflict, crisis avoidance, detouring around the crisis, protection offered the CEO out of loyalty, cognitive dissonance, and courage to put the conflicts aside and explore a workout and turnaround plan.

As we saw in chapter 3, problem formulation is the most creative aspect of the workout process. The teammates who carefully diagnose the elements of the situation, turn them this way and that and examine them from all angles, will be the most effective actors in the drama that lies before them. The teammates who rush into action with a set plan might easily overlook some conflictual issues that were not resolved in the diagnostic step. The teammates who profess unwavering fealty to the chief, with the idea that the workout consultant will never be able to resolve the conflicts, will probably be given their walking papers. The interaction of the senior managers during the diagnostic interview will provide the workout consultant with the heart of the problem, the symptoms, the areas in which the cannon balls will strike the company's walls, and which of the teammates will play the key roles of Ferret, Lion, and Beaver.

After a day or two of diagnosis, the workout consultant has a plan for remedial action in mind.

STEP TWO: CRISIS MITIGATION

By the third day, the workout consultant and the Ferret and Lion are ready to swing into action. The Ferret's role, as we discussed in chapter 4, is to find cash. He or she finds it in the company's overhead, in its assets, and in its unused channels of distribution. He or she and the workout consultant devise a timetable during which the Ferret will raise a targeted amount of cash. If no Ferret is available, the workout consultant may bring in an associate or a free-lance consultant to work with him.

The Lion and the workout consultant will turn their attention to damage control. They will meet with the major creditors, the angriest ones first, and negotiate standstill agreements. These are verbal pledges, committed to writing if necessary, in which the creditors agree to stand back and not pull the plug on the company while the workout consultant and the company devise a rehabilitation plan. The workout consultant will *interview* the major creditors while negotiating with them to determine if their pistols are cocked, if their rifles are in the ready-aim position, and what circumstances might cause them to squeeze the trigger.

Workout consultants have a keen ear for conflictual issues. They can hear when the creditors have been seriously lied to. They can hear when lenders feel abused by the company's having ignored them. And they can sense when the creditors are at the end of their tethers. The interviews will enable the consultant, and the Lion, whom he or she will train to listen acutely as well, to discern the bullets from the serious problems. An experienced workout consultant will stay in touch with all of the key creditors on at least a once a week basis to assure them that the standstill agreement they entered into is enabling the company to produce results.

Once trained in negotiating and interviewing, the Lion can be turned loose to negotiate and interview all of the other creditors who can damage the company. If the company cannot produce a Lion, the workout consultant can nominate an associate or free-lancer to join the team for this critical assignment.

With the standstill agreements in place, the workout consultant can turn attention to crisis mitigation within the company. Things may not be going smoothly with cash ferreting and creditor negotiations, so the workout consultant may be in an unmitigated dither in the early stages of the crisis. This is known as "buzzard's luck": when you can't kill nothin', and ain't nothin' won't die. The crisis could be in full boil and the workout consultant may have to back pedal to the diagnostic step and see where the plan may have gone awry.

The consultant may have to help the Ferret generate cash more rapidly and use some of it to bring the bank loan current in order to negotiate a standstill agreement with the lender. Or he or she may have to shut down production for two weeks and give all plant workers a brief vacation so as to collect accounts receivable and apply the proceeds to overextended creditors in order to obtain their willingness to stand still.

It is not unusual for the lenders and creditors to test the workout consultant's mettle in the early going. Students do the same thing to substitute teachers all the time. The creditors want to let workout consultants know early on that they can't sneak the sun by the rooster. The creditors are on the alert and they want to see tremendous speed and a high degree of activity on the part of workout consultants. Stated another way, workout consultants had better produce some early, stunning results if they want to gain the respect and attention of the creditors.

Once relations are normalized, the workout consultant can meet with the employees and provide them with inside information, hear their concerns, answer their questions, and persuade them to rally behind the plan.

STEP THREE: GENERATE CASH

As you have seen, the need to generate cash is in many cases as necessary immediately after the diagnostic step as crisis mitigation. "The absence of cash is not what causes the crisis," says Frank Zolfo; "It is symptomatic of the crisis."

If the company's overhead level is twice that of any competitor, if its profits per employee are one third of any competitor, and if its debt to worth ratio is three times that of any competitor, *but* if the company's cash position is strong, the owner and manager might never call the workout consultant. But once the company's cash position sinks to a discouragingly low level, you can bet that the telephones will ring in the offices of several workout specialists. Cash is not only King, its absence is the signal that the company has been struck with a disease.

The rooting out of cash, the search for dimes in the parking lot, the collection and sale of the company's paper trash—all of these tactics for raising cash quickly—were enumerated in chapter 4. The workout consultant and the Ferret will search for cash in a peripatetic yet systematic method.

The Lion may need to make a call on some of the cash horde in order to negotiate standstill agreements or to persuade suppliers to continue shipping product. The workout consultant and teammates will examine all of the Lion's requests and respond immediately. But the bulk of the cash will be stored in a safe place.

STEP FOUR: PREPARATION OF A TURNAROUND PLAN

With the major surgery completed, the workout consultant and teammates (or associates) can begin planning what the company is going to do for a living when it comes out of its informal reorganization. The metamorphosis is in its beginning stage.

The fundamental aspect of the turnaround stage is to negotiate an informal plan of reorganization with creditors. This means compromising and stretching out the money owing them in a manner similar to what they would have received in a formal reorganization, but more rapidly and at less cost to them than in a Chapter 11 proceeding. The creditors may have formed a committee and hired a restructuring consultant or a creditor-advocate bankruptcy lawyer to negotiate for them, but a turnaround plan that is sculpted without the auspices of bankruptcy court and armies of lawyers moves along faster, the pace having been determined by the standstill agreement and the responsiveness of the workout team in meeting its proscribed time commitments.

Negotiating the plan of reorganization is a game of leverage, with the rules circumscribed by the Federal Bankruptcy Act of 1978. In round one of the game, the debtor normally submits a plan that is somewhat less than its best offer. For example, it might offer its senior secured lender 60 cents on the dollar repayable immediately if the company has lined up a replacement lender; and it may offer its large unsecured creditors 40 cents on the dollar payable over three years, its medium-sized unsecured creditors 30 cents on the dollar repayable over five years, and its small creditors 10 cents on the dollar, payable immediately.

The workout consultant may huddle with the Beaver, or an associate brought in to devise a redirect and grow plan, to assist in constructing the plan of reorganization. The Beaver may have come up with some acquisition candidates, an opportunity for a public offering, a merger with a public company, or a novel source of financing—all of which are interesting options for the debtor company, which is now very lean, has a small pile of cash, and is operating in a cash flow positive manner.

These options, one or more of which may become part of the company's redirect and grow plan, can be factored into the turnaround plan so that the debtor company's offer holds out an upside potential factor. Following are two reconstructions of the initial plan offered creditors:

Plan A: Possible Acquisition of a Company with Twice the Cash Flow of the Debtor Company

Secured creditor: Will receive 60 cents on the dollar payable immediately, plus 5 percent of the amount owing every six months for four years if the company's proposed acquisition is consummated.

Large unsecured creditors: Will receive 40 cents on the dollar repayable over three years, plus an additional 20 cents on the dollar payable in years five through eight if the company's proposed acquisition is consummated.

Medium-sized unsecured creditors: Will receive 30 cents on the dollar repayable over five years, plus an additional 20 cents on the dollar payable in years six through eight if the company's proposed acquisition is consummated.

Small unsecured creditors: Will receive 10 cents on the dollar payable immediately, plus an additional 10 cents on the dollar payable in years three through five if the company's proposed acquisition is consummated.

Another variation of a turnaround plan that offers a definite payment plus an upside potential might be offered if the company plans to achieve a public market for its common stock by a new issue or by merger with a publicly held company.

Plan B: Possible Creation of a Public Market for the Company's Common Stock

Secured creditors: Will receive 60 cents on the dollar payable immediately or 40 cents on the dollar of the company's common stock such that, if the stock trades at $10 per share, the overall payment will be 80 cents on the dollar.

Large unsecured creditor: Will receive 40 cents on the dollar repayable over three years or 25 cents on the dollar plus a number of shares of the company's common stock, which at $10 per share would result in an overall payment of 55 cents on the dollar.

Medium-sized unsecured creditors: Will receive 30 cents on the dollar repayable over five years or 15 cents on the dollar plus a number of shares of the company's common stock, which at $10 per share would result in an overall payment of 42.5 cents on the dollar.

Small unsecured creditors: Will receive 10 cents on the dollar payable immediately or 5 cents on the dollar payable immediately plus a number of shares of the company's common stock, which at $10 per share would result in an overall payment of 17.5 cents on the dollar.

There are numerous variations on the plan of reorganization, but they are all academic unless they can be sold to the creditors. The ability of the company to sell its plan will depend on the credibility with which it has treated its creditors, the cash that it has managed to generate, sources of financing it has been able to identify, other options that the Beaver has located, and whether or not all of the debtor's assets are pledged to one or more secured lenders.

STEP FIVE: NEGOTIATING THE PLAN

Typically, the creditors will reject the first plan that is submitted to them. They may know that the debtor is sandbagging them 20 to 30 percent. Thus, they might hold out for a plan that is 50 percent higher. The workout consultant may then counter with the argument that the company will do better in Chapter 11 and the creditors will receive less than they would in the initial plan.

The creditors may then counter with their opinion that they would realize more in a Chapter 7 liquidation.

Both sides present their liquidation value appraisals. The debtor company's appraisals show that the Chapter 7 alternative will result in payments to creditors of far less than the workout consultant offered them in the initial plan. The creditors' appraisal points to higher values in liquidation. The creditors may have also identified a possible buyer for the company at a price greater than the $10 per share that the company estimated its stock would be worth in an acquisition by a public company or via a new issue.

Who has the leverage? If all of the company's assets are pledged to one or two secured creditors and there are hundreds of unsecured creditors, the company has a great deal of leverage. In this circumstance the secured creditor is likely to wind up with 50 cents on the dollar in liquidation and the unsecured creditors zero. In Chapter 7, it is frequently difficult to collect all of the debtor company's accounts receivable, and inventories become stale and some of them unsalable. Thus, the spectre of a Chapter 7 filing becomes the shibboleth that the workout consultant plays off of.

But if there are many secured creditors, each with different collateral, and only a handful of unsecured creditors, the creditors have more leverage. In Chapter 7 they will be able to attach and sell their collateral quickly or whenever they feel they can obtain the best price. The workout team has less wiggle room and it will have to make its plan of reorganization more attractive than liquidation. The workout team will have to operate with a very sharp pencil and do so quickly. It must also identify new sources of financing that are willing to take out the hard-nosed secured creditors for more money than they would receive in liquidation. The Ferret and the Beaver will have their work cut out for them because lenders to companies in an informal reorganization or in a chapter proceeding are difficult to find.

The workout consultants in the directory were asked to name the best lenders to troubled companies in the United States. Their votes were counted and appear in Exhibit 7.1.

The consultants listed a total of 41 lenders to troubled companies. The ten lenders that received the second largest number of votes were Bankers

---

Exhibit 7.1   The Best Lenders to Troubled Companies in the United States*

Name	Locations
1. Fidelcor Business Credit Corp.	New York, Philadelphia, Chicago, Los Angeles, San Francisco, Miami, Atlanta, Dallas
2. Heller Financial, Inc.	Chicago, New York, Glendale, CA, Atlanta
3. Congress Financial Corp.	New York, Chicago, Dallas, Los Angeles, San Ramon, CA, Miami, Portland, OR, Hato Rey, PR, Atlanta, Columbia, MD
4. Citicorp	Englewood Cliffs, NJ, Dallas, Schaumburg, IL, Atlanta, Irvine, CA
5. Chemical Bank	Morristown, NJ
6. Foothill Capital Corp.	Los Angeles
7. General Electric Capital Corp.	Stamford, CT, New York, Atlanta, Chicago, Dallas, Los Angeles, San Francisco, Charlotte
8. CIT Group, Inc.	New York, Livingston, NJ
9. First National Bank of Chicago	Chicago
10. Manufacturers Hanover Trust	New York

*For details on these and several hundred other lenders including names of key decision makers, addresses, telephone numbers, fax numbers, minimum and maximum loan sizes, preferred collateral, and industries of interest, see *The Middle-Market Leveraged Financing Directory and Source Book*, A. David Silver (New York: Harper & Row, 1990).

Trust Co., Continental National Bank, Fremont Financial Corp., National
Westminster Bank, LaSalle Group, Chase Manhattan Bank, Westinghouse
Credit, Security Pacific Business Credit, Inc., Fleet Financial Corp., and
Prudential Capital Corp.

Locating the most appropriate lender, presenting a financing plan, and
negotiating a refinancing in an informal or formal reorganization is the subject of another book. And *The Middle Market Leveraged Financing Directory and Source Book* is the most complete text and directory on the subject.
It also contains a directory of equity investors, some of whom do turnaround
financings.

It is essential in negotiating a turnaround plan with creditors to have
identified sources of financing. If the creditors play hardball with the plans
that you offer, you want to be able to replace them with new sources of
financing.

STEP SIX: IMPLEMENTATION OF THE PLAN

The workout consultant has steered the company into its synthesis or re-
building stage. The company has avoided the graveyard and the costs and
time delays of a Chapter 11 filing. The consultant has helped the company
raise cash, slash expenses, spin off peripheral divisions, negotiate a standstill plan, buy time to develop a plan, structure the plan, and negotiate the
plan with creditors.

The company is much smaller than before the crisis, but it is cash flow
positive and has managed to store a small cash stockpile. The workout
consultant and teammates have identified alternative sources of financing.

The final step before full-steam ahead is to codify the agreements with
creditors with promissory notes and releases. For the contract step, the
workout consultant will usually call on the services of a debtor-advocate
bankruptcy counsel who has been on standby and who perhaps has prepared
a Chapter 11 filing as a backstop.

The implementation of the plan depends on the company's redirect and
grow plan. This is essentially the company's business plan for its second
life.

CHAPTER 8

The Redirect and Grow Plan

A rare old bird is the pelican,
His beak holds more than his belican.
He can take in his beak
Enough food for a week
I'm darned if I know how the helican!

—Anonymous

If the Ferret finds cash in the company's overhead, assets, and unused marketing channels and if the Lion protects the company from damage by a neglected and annoyed creditor, then the workout consultant must be the Pelican. The company that is successfully turned around, we frequently read, becomes an agile predator, buying up cash flow positive and asset rich companies, using leveraged buyout financing techniques, stock swaps, and other financial artistry that dazzles the eye. "Hey! Wasn't that company talking Chapter 11 just a year ago?" we ask, as the once left for dead Itel Corp., Penn Central, or Wickes rebuilds itself as a new kind of company. What is it about turnarounds with Pelicans at the helm that makes them so fascinating during the redirect and grow phase? How can they take over companies 5 to 10 times their size or dominate an industry at the speed of light so soon after their stay in the intensive care ward?

They are born-again entrepreneurial companies under the guidance of battle-scarred managers who are masters of leverage and cash flow management.

THE ATTRACTIVENESS OF THE REFORMED DRUNK

Companies that stumble into crisis or file for protection under Chapter 11 do not fall victim to external circumstances or bad luck. They fall because they get drunk on cash-consuming peripheral assets and overhead expenses, and their drunken spree is usually financed with debt. However, after they are salvaged and rehabilitated by a professional workout consultant, they emerge with the most positive characteristics in the annals of industry. Their features include most of the following:

- A stockpile of cash.
- A small management structure with short lines of communication.
- A battle-scarred and experienced management team that has stood over its grave and survived the most severe fusillade of verbal threats and the most inflamed battles for control.
- Month-to-month positive cash flow produced by a core business that is demonstratably economically justifiable.
- Pre-crisis debt stretched out over four to eight years, and sometimes longer, with low interest payments, easily serviced by the company's cash flow.
- A tax loss carry forward that can be used to shelter the company's earnings for up to five years.

A successfully rehabilitated company under the management of an experienced workout team is like a record album about to go platinum or a movie that is about to smash all box office records. Smart money gravitates to it like sunlight to a solar dish.

Sigoloff & Associates, the most well-known workout consulting firm, was known prior to the 1980s for its turnarounds of Republic Corp. and Daylin Corp. It then moved into Wickes Lumber Corp., which filed for protection under Chapter 11 in 1982, the second largest filing at the time. All the steps that we have been discussing were taken in a timely and efficient manner, and Sigoloff's plan of reorganization for the company was approved in 1985. Wickes had a $500 million tax loss carry forward, a clean balance sheet, and positive cash flow. Its redirect and grow plan was to acquire consumer products companies that sold their wares through channels similar to Wickes lumber yards and do-it-yourself centers.

The shrewdest investment bankers and high-rolling investors acquired Wickes stock upon its emergence from Chapter 11. Saul Steinberg acquired 10.4 percent of the company through his Reliance Group Holdings, Inc. Michael Milken bought 5 percent through Drexel Burnham Lambert, Inc. When Sigoloff announced that he wanted to float a $500 million junk bond issue to make acquisitions, Milken offered to do the financing and to raise an additional $1.2 billion in a blind pool for Sigoloff to make whatever acquisitions he desired. Salomon Brothers, arguably a more prestigious underwriter, asked Sigoloff for the privilege of raising the money as well; thus, the financing became co-managed.

Wickes acquired the consumer and industrial products division of Paramount Communications, Inc. and Collins & Aikman, the carpet manufacturing company. Never willing to rest on their laurels, once Wickes had digested its acquisitions, the Sigoloff workout team sifted through the myriad offers to rehabilitate other troubled companies, and in 1989 it moved to New York to perform surgery on L.J. Hooker, the fallen retail conglomerate.

LEVERAGE? OR THE LAW OF RECIPROCITY?

Operating in the rarefied atmosphere of a Sigoloff may not be your style, and the company that you have just rehabilitated may not be a national chain or multimillion dollar operation like Wickes. But you can springboard your once left for dead company, no matter how small it is, into a much more valuable enterprise through the means of a redirect and grow plan and the careful use of *leverage*.

You may have noticed as we took the path of the workout consultant in the previous chapters that this person is rarely *inversely leveraged*. That is, he or she categorically and absolutely refuses to part with cash (or goods or services) first, but rather persuades others to pay first and then he or she will deliver. What was one of the first things that Carol Mann did when she became the workout consultant to Tarheel Furniture? She had the staff notify the customers that shipments would be made only to those customers who paid in advance.

And the message workout consultants deliver to suppliers is "We want you first to stand still, then to agree to take a stretch out on the money we owe you, then to take a percentage of what we owe you, but to keep shipping to us on conventional terms." Does it work? Yes, most of the time, because business operates under the Law of Reciprocity.* This law, which relies on clarity and the credibility of the players is as follows: I'll cooperate with you on the first move if you cooperate in turn. And I will keep cooperating so long as you do. But if you defect, then I will defect as well until you begin cooperating again.

It seems that managers who run their companies into crises become so caught up with their *koros*, *até*, and *hubris* that they overlook the Law of Reciprocity and bully their lenders, boss their creditors around, and defect on promises they make to customers, suppliers, lenders, and employees. Is there any wonder that the workout consultant can turn around the opinions of the community of companies and people who supply goods, services, time, and money to the crisis-riven company? They want clarity, which the workout consultant gives them. They want credibility, which the workout consultant is cloaked in. And they want to return to the Law of Reciprocity because those are the rules that they understand: indeed, clarity up front, cooperate until the other side defects, and forgive when it begins to cooperate

---

*See *The Inside Raider*.

once again. The Law of Reciprocity is a sixth sense, perhaps biologically inbred in our species.

Thus, the implementation of a standstill agreement followed by a negotiated settlement of debt a few months later at a fraction of the amount owed is not a mysteriously engineered or ingeniously crafted piece of mysticism known only to Sigoloff, Sind, Zolfo, Mann, and a handful of other workout geniuses. It follows that the customers, suppliers, vendors, and employees were routinely and regularly alienated, again and again, with voodoo explanations concocted by a hubritic CEO who was busy leaping into his Beamer-7 and pressing his new Gucci loafers on the pedal of fame and fortune.

The workout consultant, a humbler soul with a gaggle of credit managers as her list of references, apologizes to the abused community of company supporters and promises to see that they (1) get some of their money back and (2) continue to have the company as their customer or supplier; but first, the abused community must cooperate with the company, under new management, *one last time*. Call it leverage, if you like; but isn't it really the spirit of reciprocity under which all of us run our businesses?

LAWYERS HAVE TO EAT TOO

When a company defects from a cooperative arrangement with a lender, supplier, customer, or employee, a low-density signal is heard across the land, but its tone can be captured, amidst the cacophony of a million other signals, only by lawyers. The signal says, "Someone has defected. Who can we represent in a lawsuit?" The LLD degree is a license that canonizes the lawyer with the exclusive ability to "Listen for Low Density" signals. No other member of our species has this capability, which is so profitable that U.S. law schools are graduating approximately 35,000 new LLD's a year. They have to eat; so they bring lawsuits.

The litigation keeps the two sides apart, continues the defection, and rewards the lawyers with fees, while the two economic units cease the commerce between them, which benefited society in one way or another.

Sometimes the lawyers persuade alienated creditors that debtors have caused much more harm to the creditors than simply stiffing them on a bill. The lawyer finds two or more instances of failure to pay, conjures up a "pattern of racketeering" coupled with mail fraud, and then files a petition with other creditors to drive the debtor into bankruptcy, where fraud claims are not dischargeable. This becomes very serious and very costly litigation, and the woebegone manager who waits too long to call in the workout consultant eventually turns over the company to the doctor with hardly a breath of life left in it.

Again, in a seemingly miraculous fashion, the workout consultant performs open heart surgery on the victim of fraud and racketeering litigation, slashes expenses, finds cash in the trash, spins off divisions, and using the automatic standstill provisions of Chapter 11 gains the time needed to meet with the well-fed lawyers and their clients and begins to persuade them that cooperation is superior to defection. To prove it, he or she asks the court for permission to sell an asset and to disburse the proceeds to the angriest creditors.

Once having gotten those expensive problems out of the way, the work-out consulting team can return to their map room and devise a redirect and grow plan.

FOXMEYER'S COUP

Not knowing anything about the workout business, Bill Tauscher, Richard Bard, and I mounted the pharmaceutical industry's credit managers' stage on Lexington Avenue in New York City in 1978 and told the alienated credit managers that the only way that Lag Drug Company could repay them $12 million was for Lag Drug to acquire Fox Vliet Drug Company, which also owed them $12 million but was current with its obligations.

The credit managers came unglued. They could see themselves losing $24 million to these three young "thieves." But as unsecured creditors they had little to say in the matter because we had lined up financing to acquire the $85 million (revenues) Fox Vliet, and its cash flow, even after debt service, would be able to repay $24 million over time. The $12 million that Lag Drug Company owed the agitated group of credit officers could not be repaid in any other way. Citicorp had a lien on all of its assets and, in Chapter 7, Citicorp alone would be paid.

Tauscher, Bard, and I may have done the first LBO using the carcass of an insolvent buyer, but nobody kept score back then. I knew precious little about the workout and turnaround business, and I billed accordingly— $1,500 per month plus a success fee based on raising fresh capital. But Lag Drug Company had nothing to lose since it had fallen so far, and the creditors had quite a bit to lose since they were extended to the tune of $12 million with a lien on their inventory in the name of Citicorp.

We were precocious in submitting our redirect and grow plan—Step Six, you will recall—ahead of Steps Two through Five. In other words, our plan to repay the creditors was set forth amidst a mild retort of guffaws and shouts of horror *before* we asked for a standstill agreement, generated cash, and persuaded the creditors that we were more credible than the original Lag Drug management team that got them into this mess in the first place. The cart was way out in front of the horse.

But we had one very persuasive tool at our disposal. We had pre-pared cash flow statements that were sufficiently convincing to the trade that they would receive $24 million over time. We left the stage winners and FoxMeyer (its new name) merged with National Intergroup Corporation, a New York Stock Exchange company, a few years later at a value of $350 million to FoxMeyer stockholders.

CASH FLOW STATEMENTS AS GOSPEL

In every battle plan there is a map of the area. The map points out the enemy position and topographic elements. Similarly, the cash flow statement points out the most serious bills, the next most serious, and all the others. It also indicates your sources of cash to meet these obligations. It is your battle plan, and the workout consulting team updates it weekly throughout the crisis period.

The objective is to carry out a strategy so as to preserve the company in some form and to propel it forward as an exciting new business. It is the survive and thrive game. I call the chase the *redirect and grow* plan. Simultaneously, the workout consulting team negotiates a stretch-out plan for the liabilities that the company will pay with the cash flow generated by the accomplishments of the redirect and grow plan. The stretch-out process is the *informal reorganization*.

The two plans operate in tandem. The weekly cash flow statement is the playing field; the ball, bat, and gloves will be the tools that you have learned in this book; and the character of the players will include the heart, courage, judgment, and business acumen that the workout consultant and his or her teammates have developed in their business careers. Those careers were spring training compared with the contest of rehabilitating a company and relaunching it on a new path.

THE LBO STRATEGY

Let's assume that the workout team decides that the redirect and grow plan will be a leveraged buyout of a company in a similar line to the core business preserved from the debtor company's workout. This decision seems appropriate because the core business has excess manufacturing capability, skilled people, responsive marketing channels, and very low overhead. Acquiring a company in a similar line of business will have the effect of increasing cash flow per dollar of goods sold because you will not need the acquired company's plant, administrative overhead, or two-thirds of its personnel. Further, you have persuaded lenders to provide 90 percent of the purchase price and you will invest 10 percent.

The LBO redirect and grow plan looks good on paper and in the cash flow statements, but can you sell it to the creditors and convince them that this is how they will get paid more than if the company sticks to its knitting?

THE STRETCH-OUT PLAN

The day has come to sell the plan to the creditors: how you plan to pay them and when. As a first step, the 400 creditors should be organized according to the following categories of criticality:

A—Priority claims, taxes

B—Secured creditors

C—Unsecured creditors, over $25,000

D—Unsecured creditors, $10,000 to $24,999

E—Unsecured creditors, $1,000 to $9,999

F—Unsecured creditors, under $999

G—Special exceptions

You may have another arrangement in mind, particularly if there is a bulge in the $1,000 to $9,999 group, and it must be broken up into two categories. The object of grouping the creditors into categories is to offer them differing repayment plans.

Assume that the LBO target will be able to provide a post-acquisition cash flow of $200,000 per month to the company. To leave some wiggle room, plan on having only half, or $100,000 per month. Then use half of that number, $50,000, to pay the salaries and benefits of the survival team and another $25,000 for utilities, legal fees, and general and administrative expenses.

The cash available to service the LBO debt is one half of the LBO's cash flow, or $100,000 per month. If all creditors are paid equally, it will take 38 months to repay $3.8 million (say, 48 months to leave yourself a cushion and to pay interest). However, the smaller creditors may not go along with a 48-month plan because the individual payments to them will be very small and their need for cash is usually very great. You may have to offer them cents on the dollar up front or a 12-month stretch. Creditors owed $5,000 to $10,000 are usually difficult to deal with. They will need some careful negotiating. The larger creditors can take a longer stretch plus an interest rate and perhaps an upside opportunity, such as warrants, in consideration for their forbearance. Therefore, an effective stretch-out plan recognizes the needs of all the creditors as well as the degree to which they can be leveraged.

Common Stock

Do not rule out the possibility of offering common stock to your creditors for all or part of the amount owing. If the workout team has been clear, intelligent, open, and forthright, and if the LBO target has an interesting story—hopefully a solid, dependable cash flow without a requirement for capital expenditures—there is absolutely no reason not to try selling your stock to your creditors. They know that fortunes are made in adversity. The creditors who will be supplying twice the amount of product they used to sell because of the LBO are the most likely to accept common stock rather than a promissory note paid out over 48 months.

Promissory Note

Another plan might include five series of promissory notes—with or without options to convert them into common stock—with interest at a very low rate: 5 to 7 percent, payable in the 48 months. The larger the creditor, the longer the term. However, there may be special exceptions such as the creditor with a fraud claim whose lawyer won't take his or her teeth out of your ankle without special consideration. This creditor is in category G. The upside, or sweetener, might be to accelerate the note if the company's earnings increase dramatically. An alternative upside might be to have the balance of the note convertible into common stock; then, if earnings drop dramatically, the loyal creditors who convert a large portion of their note into stock could make a pile of money on your adversity.

Communicating the Stretch-Out Plan

We have discussed the frequent visits by the workout consultant to the bank and to the large, important creditors. We have also discussed the most effective means of presenting the stretch-out plan in person to the bullets, to the serious, and to the not as serious. What follows then is the promissory note and release that you would like them to sign and return to you, plus the cover letter that accompanies it. A sample promissory note has been tailored to the size company that we have been discussing, and it is provided in Exhibit 8.1.

Exhibit 8.1   Nonnegotiable Promissory Note and Release

Holder: _____

Address: _____

                _____

Principal
Amount: $_____ Due: _____

FOR VALUE RECEIVED, Survive and Thrive Corporation, a Delaware corporation (hereinafter "the Company" or "STC"), its successors, and assigns, whose address is *Your Address, City, State, Zip Code,* hereby promises to pay, subject to the conditions set forth below, to Holder* above at the address set forth above, or such other place(s) as the Holder shall direct, the principal sum set forth above plus interest of seven and one-half percent (7.5%) per annum for four (4) years payable as follows: forty-eight (48) equal monthly installments of $_____ each, the first installment to be paid December 31, 19____, subsequent installments to be paid monthly thereafter;

plus

if the Company's pretax annual earnings for any of the next 10 years exceed $5 million, a payment of $_____, representing the balance of the principal and interest due and unpaid for the period of four (4) years beginning December 31, 19____, to be paid ninety (90) days after the thirty-sixth (36th) monthly payment is made hereunder.

In the event of default by the Company in performance of this Note and Release or in payment of any amount or installment of principal and interest to the Holder of this Note, the Holder of this Note shall be entitled to acceleration of the balance of principal and interest of this Note. Upon declaration of acceleration by the Holder hereof, the entire balance of principal and interest shall become due and payable in full, subject to the conditions set forth below. Other rights, powers, privileges, and remedies of the Holder of this Note are cumulative and not exclusive of any rights, powers, remedies, and privileges that the Holder might have.

Notwithstanding anything herein to the contrary, the Company covenants and agrees with the Holder, and the Holder covenants by acceptance hereof, expressly for the benefit of the present and future holds of "Senior Indebtedness," defined as any debt due and owing in connection with the acquisition of entities to be acquired by STC, that the payment of the principal and interest of this Note is expressly subordinated in right of payment to the payment in full of up to $3 million in principal and interest of Senior Indebtedness of the Company. Upon any terminating liquidation of assets of the Company, upon the occurrence of any dissolution; winding up; liquidation, whether or not in bankruptcy; insolvency; or receivership proceedings, the Company shall not pay thereafter, and the Holder of this Note shall not be entitled to receive thereafter, any amount in respect of the principal and interest of this Note unless and until the above specified amount of Senior Indebtedness shall have been paid or otherwise discharged.

The Holder hereof, by its acceptance of this Note, covenants and agrees for itself, its successors, and assigns that in the event of the Company's default hereunder and if the Holder obtains judgment thereon in a court of competent jurisdiction, the Holder shall not execute such judgment upon the assets of the Company, its successor, and assigns unless and until, and only to the extent that, the then book value of such assets exceeds the total amount of Senior Indebtedness, not to exceed $3 million.

This Note may be prepaid at any time without penalty.

The Company hereby waives presentment for payment, protest, notice of protest, notice of nonpayment, and diligence in bringing suit. The Company agrees to pay all costs of collection, including reasonable attorney's fees, if a default shall occur under this Note.

The Holder, upon acceptance hereof, shall have no further claims against the Company or any surviving or successor entity, should the Company be sold or acquired, or against the Company's subsidiaries or against their employees for payment and specifically no claims against the subsidiaries (or their assets) of the Company presently owned, or hereafter acquired, except as set forth herein. The Holder specifically releases the Company and its subsidiaries from any further claim except the amount specified by this Note.

IN WITNESS WHEREOF, the undersigned has executed and delivered this Note the day and year written below.

ACCEPTED AND AGREED TO:

By: _____   Date: _____
Your Name, Chairman
Survive and Thrive Corporation

By: _____   Date: _____
Holder's Name

Title: _____
Holder's Title

Company Name: _____

*The word *Payee* may be used in place of *Holder*.

CHAPTER 9

A Bankruptcy Primer

Meekness, n. Uncommon patience in planning a revenge that is worthwhile.
—Ambrose Bierce

That which your company can accomplish in an informal reorganization it can accomplish in a formal reorganization, but at considerably more expense and time and under guidelines set forth by the Federal Bankruptcy Act of 1978 and enforced by 286 bankruptcy judges throughout the land. As you know, a Chapter 11 filing is generally required or chosen if (1) you do not know of the availability of workout consultants to rehabilitate the company outside of Chapter 11; (2) if you attempt to deny or skirt around the problems affecting your company; (3) if your credibility is completely shot with creditors and they join hands to force you into Chapter 7; or (4) if the workout consultant is unable to persuade the creditors to accept the plan of reorganization and he or she sees no option other than letting a bankruptcy judge force the creditors to accept it or a version of it.

Because you may end up in Chapter 11, even with the best of intentions and the most highly skilled workout consultant in your camp, you need to understand some of the fundamentals of the Act.

THE LAWS OF SUPPLY AND DEMAND

One of the reasons that there are over 600,000 annual Chapter 11 filings in America is that there are fewer than 200 workout consultants to catch the falling objects, fix them up, wind them up, and send them back into the stratosphere. Yet there are over 350,000 lawyers; although not all of them are trained in bankruptcy law, they each know of someone who is, while few of them know or choose to recommend, if they know, a workout consultant. Thus, it is high cotton time for bankruptcy lawyers.

Legal Fees

Until the early 1980s, the major U.S. law firms were content to leave bankruptcy law to smaller firms that specialized in the area. But lately, they have changed their minds. The fees are too large to pass up, and the volume of clients is mind-numbing. You can expect to pay a major city debtor-advocate bankruptcy lawyer $300 to $450 per hour and his or her associates $150 to $200 per hour.

When Manville Corp. filed for protection to block claims against it while under asbestos litigation, the legal fees aggregated telephone book numbers, as can be seen in Exhibit 9.1.

These fees are enough to turn the heads of lawyers who used to think bankruptcy work was the dirty end of the stick. Today, companies that file for protection are not always broke; their managers or their workout consultants just haven't found the cash yet. But they will.

Trolling

It isn't just the fat fees that are attracting lawyers to bankruptcy work. Bankruptcy court is a remarkable arena in which to troll for new clients. At a typical hearing in bankruptcy court there may be 50 creditors present, including banks and vendors. A bankruptcy lawyer can display his or her

---

Exhibit 9.1   Manville Asbestos Litigation

Lawyers	Client	Fees
Levin & Weintraub & Crames	Manville	$ 5,850,000
Davis, Polk & Wardwell	Manville	12,757,012
Heller, Durman, White & McAuliffe	Manville	28,269,727
Milbank, Tweed, Hadley & McCloy	Creditors	4,672,449
Caplin & Drysdale	Plaintiffs	1,750,000
Gilbert, Segall & Young	Plaintiffs	589,062
Moses & Singer	Plaintiffs	4,197,902
Latham & Watkins	Plaintiffs	156,475
Fried, Frank, Harris, Shriver & Jacobson	Future plaintiffs	4,500,000
Hahn & Hessen	Shareholders	2,808,630

Source: White & Case court documents.

---

skills in front of a very receptive audience—people who are always on the look out for skilled professionals.

Rare is the debtor-advocate bankruptcy lawyer who doesn't do creditor-advocate work as well. And that isn't at all bad for debtors because their lawyers bring fresh news from the "enemy camp."

The key is to hire the best debtor-advocate bankruptcy lawyer before the creditors hire him or her. You will need to pay them an up-front retainer of at least 3 to 5 percent of the amount of your company's debt, before they will represent you. Their names, addresses, telephone numbers, and fax numbers appear in the second directory at the back of the book.

THE RULES OF THE ROAD IN CHAPTER 11

Following is a summary of the guidelines that your company will have to follow if it files for protection under Chapter 11. I do not cover the rules of Chapter 7 in this book because, as you know, that is a liquidation scenario in which a trustee is appointed to sell the company's assets. The trustee acts unemotionally and with dispatch because he or she earns a fee of 3 percent of the amount of money that is collected from the sale of the assets. There is not much in the way of "process" to say about Chapter 7.

Restriction on Payments

In Chapter 11, the debtor company is not permitted to pay for services, if its assets are collateralized, unless it obtains court approval. Even payments to its legal firm must be approved by the court. This is the reason why the debtor's counsel asks for a retainer up-front because counsel may not see another payment until the end of the case, when the bill is tossed into the priority payment basket called "administrative costs of the estate." These costs include, in addition to legal fees, income tax obligations incurred after the filing.

Probability of Reorganizing under Chapter 11

A plan of reorganization requires the approval of two thirds of each class of creditor and 51 percent in number. The probability of getting a plan approved depends on the options. If Chapter 7 produces a smaller return than Chapter 11, a plan will usually be confirmed. But to ensure that a plan will be confirmed the debtor company will need to have found unencumbered cash during its workout period, or it will need to raise fresh financing.

A company faced with the prospect of a Chapter 11 filing should stop paying creditors and start stockpiling cash. The bank that has a lien on the company's accounts receivable will argue that the cash belongs to the bank.

It may win the argument. Thus, cash must be found elsewhere in addition to cash from accounts receivable and stowed away because the company will need cash (plus a redirect and grow plan) to come out of Chapter 11.

Payments Prior to Filing and After

Payments made to creditors within three months prior to filing can be reversed by the court. Payments made to managers or significant stockholders, such as a large management fee, within 12 months prior to filing, can be reversed by the court. The latter is a good law because it prevents self-dealing in a manner that injures creditors. But the reversal of payments to suppliers of goods and services within three months of filing can harm the company in Chapter 11. The creditor will demand that the reversed payment be made good before it will pick up the company's garbage or service its computers.

But if the company pays a pre-petition debt to one or two creditors but not all, it commits a criminal act. Therefore, all of the small and important bills should be paid in full before filing; and, certainly, all credit cards should be paid down to zero because, after filing, the prefiling bills cannot be paid and services will be shut down.

Due Process

The United States Constitution provides that no person shall "be deprived of life, liberty, or property without due process of law." This means that courts should act promptly prior to the deprivation.

Unfortunately, the judicial process in this country is extremely backed up, and these delays can work to the detriment of the debtor company. Assume that the debtor company has been injured by another company. It sues the other company, but the damage is so great and the case is so long in coming to trial that the company must file for protection in order to avoid further damage. Then, once in Chapter 11, confirmation of the plan of reorganization depends on the previous case and it drags further, until the company's creditors give up and file for Chapter 7.

Personal Attacks on the CEO

The CEO is the lightning rod who takes most of the shots from creditors and the press for the company's problems. Many CEOs have to change their home telephone numbers to unlisted numbers. Their spouses and other family members take nasty calls from angry creditors and insidious people unrelated to the case.

The smaller the company, the greater are the personal attacks because the filing is an embarrassment in the community and causes disruption and unemployment throughout the community. Even hairdressers and service station owners are affected and sometimes these people are not afraid to tell the beleaguered CEO what they think.

Raising New Capital in Chapter 11

A bankruptcy prospect does *not* dim the debtor company's prospects for raising new capital. Asset-based lenders, in fact, frequently prefer lending to a Chapter 11 company than to a company in an informal reorganization because the former cannot be surprised by a blitzkrieg from an angry creditor. In a Chapter 11 filing, the creditors are backed off and are in a court mandated standstill. Thus, new lenders make loans secured by post-petition receivables and inventory, which then finance the plan of reorganization.

Equity investors are not dissuaded from investing fresh capital in a Chapter 11 company. They typically rely on the strength of management and, in most instances, they will not back the management team that caused the company to become insolvent.

Debtor-in-Possession

Yes you can manage your company in Chapter 11, which is known as debtor-in-possession, unless the creditors become so angered that they file a motion with the court to have a trustee appointed. This happened to Frank Lorenzo in the Eastern Airlines, Inc., Chapter 11 proceeding.

Creditors may become angered if the management of the debtor is dilatory in filing a plan of reorganization, or if the plan gives them significantly less than they expected to receive.

Unpaid Payroll Taxes

If your company files for protection with federal withholding taxes owing—and, as you know, cash-deprived companies frequently fail to pay these taxes—there is no compromising with the Internal Revenue Service. The full amount is owed when you emerge from Chapter 11; however, the IRS gives you up to six years to repay the debt.

Are you liable for these taxes if the company cannot pay them? The answer is yes if your name is on the signature card for the payroll account and if you were in direct control of that account. Thus, a CEO who does not sign the payroll checks and who does not directly control those people who do is probably not liable for unpaid federal and state withholding taxes.

The worst scenario involves a company that goes into Chapter 7 (liquidation of assets rather than reorganization) unable to pay its obligation to the IRS, and the IRS comes after the CEO, the chief financial officer, and the members of the board of directors. In this instance, there is bad news and good news. First, the bad news: the IRS will garnishee 10 percent of your salary for the rest of your life, or until it is paid in full. Now, the good news: you can have only one garnishee at a time. So if you see this event coming, remember that the IRS will have to wait in line if another garnishment is filed ahead of it.

Say that you are in Chapter 11, that your business turns down, and that you are unable to pay post-petition payroll taxes, in addition to pre-petition taxes. How do these get paid? The rule is that the plan of reorganization, in order to be acceptable to this class of creditor, must include payment in full of post-petition taxes upon emerging from Chapter 11 along with other "administrative costs" while the pre-petition payroll taxes may be paid over time.

Cram Down Provision

The creditors of a company in bankruptcy are arranged into classes according to the priority of their claims. The priority class of creditor includes the IRS and administrative claims—that is, legal bills from your bankruptcy lawyer and others who have been approved by the bankruptcy court to do work for your Chapter 11 company, plus post-petition taxes. These must be paid in full in order to emerge from Chapter 11. Fully secured creditors are next in line, and lenders usually fill this category. Partially secured creditors, or those with "impaired" collateral, represent the third class; it is important to have an ally among the creditors in this class, as will be explained momentarily. Finally, there is the unsecured class of creditors, those without any collateral.

Fifty percent of all creditors and two thirds of each class of creditor must approve the debtor's plan of reorganization before the company is permitted to emerge from Chapter 11. Some creditors continually reject the plans of reorganization submitted by the debtor. Recalcitrant creditors feel that if they keep leaning on the company to improve its plan, the company will indeed do so. They are right in some cases; they are nit-picking nuisances in others.

The authors of the 1978 Bankruptcy Code must have felt that nit-picking nuisances should be punished because they introduced the "cram down" provision. If at least one impaired creditor—that is, partially secured or unsecured creditor—accepts the plan of reorganization, the bankruptcy court can cram it down the throats of all creditors. Thus, virtually any reasonable plan of reorganization will be approved by the court if the debtor persuades one impaired creditor to accept. How might you do this? You must pay the creditor promptly and efficiently while in Chapter 11, showing that creditor your good faith and your attention to its needs.

Go Public

Yes, you can go public via a Chapter 11 filing. The expression once applied to companies that save their lives by an initial public offering—"go broke *or* go public"—has become obsolete. It is now possible to "go broke *and* go public." The 1978 Bankruptcy Code provides that creditors may be offered stock in settlement of their claims. Moreover, the stock is exempt from registration under the Securities and Exchange Act of 1933, which means that the stock is *free trading* (the holder can sell it through a broker the minute he or she receives it). This creates an extraordinary opportunity for troubled companies to raise cash.

Why might you want to issue stock to creditors? First, it saves cash and enhances the company's liquidity. Second, if debt is replaced with equity, the company's net worth increases. Third, much of the stock will be dumped at distress prices and you or your key employees might be able to buy up stock (issued as one share for each one dollar of debt) at 16 cents or less per share. Fourth, if the company's story is a good one, upon its emergence from Chapter 11, the stock will rise in price, and in two years the insiders—you, your key employees, and your investors under 10 percent—can sell some stock to create personal wealth.

Compumed Corp. was founded in 1983 by Robert O. Stuckelman, a former Litton Industries executive, and by Howard S. Mark, M.D., to rent electrocardiograph (EKG) devices to physicians. Over 2,600 EKG devices were installed throughout the country and tied to Compumed's central computer in Los Angeles. Compumed charged its physician clients a rental fee and a processing fee. By 1985, the company was very profitable but highly leveraged due to $8 million in borrowings to buy the EKG devices. To alleviate its debt, Compumed filed a registration statement with the SEC in 1985 for an initial public offering, but the SEC told Compumed that it had violated the law. The SEC claimed its EKG rentals were franchises, and Compumed was selling them to the public without filing a prospectus with the SEC. The initial public offering was derailed, and under the weight of its debt, Compumed filed for protection under Chapter 11. It was a classic Bobby McGee Chapter 11—three large secured creditors and hundreds of unsecured creditors. Rental fees were sufficient to pay interest and operating expenses, but the company was prohibited by the SEC from placing more units in the field; thus Compumed had to change the nature of its business.

Because their clients' rental payments would run out in three years, Stuckelman and Mark felt that they could grow only if the company acquired other medical devices to sell or to rent to its 2,600 physician clients. To make acquisitions, Compumed would have to be public because it had no cash. To do this, Compumed paid all unsecured creditors with stock, creating in the process a large net worth sufficient to obtain a NASDAQ listing, which means a daily listing of its stock price in the newspapers. Moreover, because its expansion story was pretty well accepted by its new stockholders, there was not much selling of the stock. Compumed has roughly 8 million shares of stock outstanding and was trading over-the-counter at about 25 to 50 cents per share in mid-1990.

Compumed is a perfect example of two axioms: (1) when you're broke, buy something, and (2) go broke to go public.

The Tax Loss Carry Forward

The use of the tax loss carry forward to shelter the earnings of the company your loss company acquires has lost some of its effectiveness, but it is still a potent tool. Prior to the Tax Reform Act of 1986, if the buyer had accumulated losses over the last few years and was acquiring a company that had earnings, the seller's earnings could be sheltered for five years by carrying the buyer's losses forward. For example, if the buyer had a $1 million loss in 1989 and acquired a company that produced a combined income of $1 million in 1989, there would be no tax payment on 1989 combined earnings.

But this privilege has been removed and in its place is the following: the buyer multiplies the interest rate on seven-year government notes—say, 8 percent—by the acquisition price, and, if the buyer indeed has losses, it can still carry them forward but to a smaller degree. For example, using the above case and assuming an acquisition price of $4 million, the annual savings would be $320,000 per annum, or 8 percent of the acquisition price. If the seller owes $400,000 in taxes on $1 million of profits, it will only pay $80,000 if acquired by a loss carry forward buyer.

WRAP-UP

If you have hired an experienced workout consultant, chances are your company will not have to file for protection under Chapter 11. Even if your company is in Chapter 11, the workout specialist can help you avoid a liquidation and help you rehabilitate your company by designing, raising money for and implementing an acceptable plan of reorganization. But if you have not hired a company doctor, then there is a high probability that you will be just another statistic: an economically viable company that died for lack of cash. There are plenty of heroes in the cemetery, and fewer, although growing, happy owners and managers who hired the services of a workout specialist in the nick of time.

To find the best consultant and bankruptcy lawyer for your company, use the directories in the back of the book and narrow the lists to the ones that understand your business, that have done rehabilitations in your industry, and whose references glow with high marks from managers in whose footsteps you are following.

Directory of Workout Consultants

INDEX OF WORKOUT CONSULTANTS

Codes for Industries Specialization:

A:	Agriculture	L:	Lodging
B:	Banking, finance	M:	Manufacturing
C:	Construction	Mktg.:	Marketing
Cl.:	Clothing	NR:	Not reported
CR:	Computer-related	P:	Publishing
D:	Distribution	Pr.:	Printing companies
DC:	Defense contractors	Prj.:	Capital projects
Diver.:	Middle market	R:	Retail
E:	Electronics	RE:	Real estate
En.:	Energy	S:	Service
Eng.:	Engineering	T:	Transportation
Ent.:	Entertainment	Tel.:	Telecommunications
F:	Food processing	U:	Utilities
HC:	Health care	UD:	Urban development
HF:	Home furnishings	VC:	Venture capital-backed
HT:	High-tech	U:	Utilities

Minimum Client Size:

Under $5 million:	Sm.
$5 million to $50 million:	Med.
$50 million and above:	Lg.

Name	Headquarters	Industries Specialization	Min. Size
ADS Financial Services, Inc.	Sante Fe, NM	CR,D,E,R,M	Sm.
AJM Consulting Group	Orange, CA	M,D,S	Sm.
Accounts Unlimited	Ardsley, NY	M,B	Med.

Name	Headquarters	Industries Specialization	Min. Size
Advanced Planning Associates	Dunwoody, GA	M,D,S	Sm.
Advent Management Associates, Ltd.	West Chester, PA	M,C	Sm.
Advisors to Banks and Businesses	Vallejo, CA	NR	Sm.
Alderman Associates, Inc.	Londonderry, NH	HT,M,D	Sm.
Alix (Jay) & Associates	Southfield, MI	All	Med.
Allomet Partners, Ltd.	New York, NY	M,D	Sm.
Alvarez & Marsal, Inc.	New York, NY	M,D	Med.
American National Bank and Trust Company of Chicago	Chicago, IL	Diversified	NR
Andersen (Arthur) & Company	Los Angeles, CA	Several	Med.
Anderson, Bauman, Tourtellot, Vos & Co.	Greensboro, NC	M	Med.
Argus Management Corp.	Natick, MA	All	Sm.
Aspetuck Capital Partners, Inc.	Westport, CT	M,D	Med.
Austin & Associates	Delray Beach, FL	M	Med.
Bahr International, Inc.	Dallas, TX	M,D,L,R,T	Med.
Bantam Group	Westwood, MA	CR,HT	Sm.
Beacon Management Group, Inc.	Pompano Beach, FL	NR	Sm.
Bear Stearns & Co., Inc.	New York, NY	Diversified	NR
Bird & Co., Inc.	Stamford, CT	CR,HT,RE, Mktg.	Sm.
Bodington, J.	San Francisco, CA	T,U,En.	Sm.
Branch Office, The	Midland, MI	NR	Sm.
Breakiron (R.) & Associates	Glendale, AZ	M,S	Sm.
Brennen Consultants, Inc.	South Bend, IN	M,T	Sm.
Brincko Associates, Inc.	Los Angeles, CA	M,S,R,HT	Med.
Brown (Stan) Associates	Ft. Lauderdale, FL	RE,M,HC	Med.
Buccino & Associates, Inc.	Chicago, IL	All	Med.
Bunker Hill Associates, Inc.	Houston, TX	En.,B,M,S,RE	Sm.
Burns (P. J.) & Associates	Kentfield, CA	D,C,Eng.,HT	Med.
Caslin Group Business Consultants, The	Washington, DC	M,R,S,D	Sm.
Chicago Consulting	Lake Bluff, IL	M,D	Sm.

Name	*Headquarters*	*Industries Specialization*	*Min. Size*
Chilmark Partners	Chicago, IL	None	Lg.
Cohen & Rogozinski, CPAs	Allentown, PA	None	Sm.
Coloney Company, The	Tallahassee, FL	DC	Sm.
Continuum Associates	Baltimore, MD	CR,DC	Sm.
Conway & Youngman	Wilmington, MA	HT,S,D,R,RE	Med.
Conway MacKenzie & Dunleavy Consultants, Inc.	Birmingham, MI	M,S,R,C,T,Tel.	Med.
Coopers & Lybrand	New York, NY	Various	All
Corporate Restructuring Group, Inc.	San Jose, CA	HT,C,M,RE,A	Med.
Cowherd Consulting Group (The), Inc.	Darien, CT	M	Lg.
Crisis Management Associates	St. Charles, MO	M,R,T,HT,HC	Sm.
DKM Management, Inc.	Atlanta, GA	M,D	Med.
Deloitte & Touche	Baltimore, MD	All	All
Delta Management Group (The), Inc.	Memphis, TN	M,S,D	Med.
Diogenes Group (The), Inc.	Los Angeles, CA	M,D,R,S	Sm.
Distribution Investment Associates	Oakland, CA	D	Med.
Diversicorp, Inc.	Dallas, TX	M,D	Med.
Dorgan (William E.) Associates, Inc.	Tucson, AZ	M,S,B	Sm.
Dutia, Suren G.	Del Mar, CA	E,CR,HC	Med.
EIG Management, Inc.	Santa Monica, CA	R	Med.
Effective Management Systems, Inc.	Snellville, GA	T	Med.
Eisner (Richard A.) & Co.	New York, NY	NR	Sm.
Ernst & Young	New York, NY	M,B,D,R,C, HC,L	Sm.
Executive Sounding Board Associates, Inc.	Philadelphia, PA	M,D,HC,RE	Sm.
Executrex International, Inc.	Milltown, NJ	HT,M,HC	Sm.
Federer (Frank) Associates	San Antonio, TX	M,HT,S	Med.
Finley Group (The), Inc.	Charlotte, NC	R,D,M	Med.
First National Bank of Chicago (The)	Chicago, IL	NR	Lg.
Frieze (Stanley B.) Company	Great Neck, NY	All except R,RE	Med.

Name	Headquarters	Industries Specialization	Min. Size
Gayl & Gutnick, Inc.	Chadds Ford, PA	M,D,HC,RE	Sm.
Getzler (A.E.) & Co., Inc.	New York, NY	All except T,A	Med.
Gilbert Thomas, Ltd.	Boca Raton, FL	M,R,D,E,B	Sm.
Gillings & Company	Bay City, MI	A,M,D,R	Sm.
Glass & Associates, Inc.	Canton, OH	M,S,D,T	Med.
Grandwest & Associates	Atlanta, GA	All except RE,HT,Tel.	Med.
Grisanti Galef & Goldress	Torrance, CA	R,M,S	Med.
Gruntal & Company, Inc.	New York, NY	NR	Lg.
Hamstreet, Stumbaugh & Co.	Portland, OR	M,F,S,HT	Med.
Hankin & Company	Los Angeles, CA	M,D,S,R	Sm.
Heller Equity Capital Corp.	Chicago, IL	M,D,S	Med.
High-Point Schaer	New York, NY	C,En.,T,M,Prj., Eng.,L,U,D	Med.
Holtz Rubenstein & Co.	Melville, NY	M,D,C,RE	Lg.
Honig & Associates, Inc.	Waban, MA	NR	Sm.
Horwath Consulting	Houston, TX	HC,L,RE	Sm.
Hospitality Source (The), Inc.	Lake Geneva, WI	L	Sm.
I.M. Systems Group, Inc.	Rockville, MD	S,F,L,RE	Med.
Inglewood Associates, Inc.	Pittsburgh, PA	M,D,R,S	Med.
Iowa Consulting, Inc.	Des Moines, IA	Tel.,M,S	Med.
JCi Consultants	Lake Wylie, SC	M,D,S,B	Sm.
James, D.A.	Albuquerque, NM	U	NR
Johnston & Co.	Manchester, NH	CR,HC,Tel.	Sm.
KL Industries, Inc.	Bloomfield, NJ	M,E	Med.
Kakde Group	Dayton, OH	M	Sm.
Kearney, A.T.	New York, NY	M,D,S,HT	Med.
Kellogg Corporation	Littleton, CO	C,M	Med.
Kibel, Green, Inc.	Santa Monica, CA	M,D,RE	Med.
Kurt Salmon Associates, Inc.	Atlanta, GA	HF,Cl.,R	Med.
LEK Partnership (The)	Boston, MA	M	Lg.
Lambda Group, Inc.	Glendale, CA	Tel.,P,D,S,RE	Sm.
Locke Venture Management, Inc.	Lake Forest, IL	VC	NR
Lustig Warner Associates	Lawrence, NY	M,D,S,En.	Sm.
MESA Corporation	San Diego, CA	M,D,R,S	Sm.
MacKenzie, Hovey & Associates, Inc.	Denver, CO	M,RE	Med.

Name	Headquarters	Industries Specialization	Min. Size
Makarowski (Bob) & Associates, Inc.	New York, NY	B,Advertising	Sm.
Management & Investment Group	Waco, TX	M,D	Sm.
Management Assistants	Marina del Ray, CA	M,S	Med.
Management Control Services	Pleasant Hill, CA	NR	NR
Management Resource Partners	Atherton, CA	M,D,R,HT	Med.
Maner, Jr. (Doland C.)	San Francisco, CA	D,S	Sm.
Maxey International	Roanoke, VA	HF,R	Sm.
McLaughlin Associates, Inc.	New York, NY	HC,HT,T,Tel.	Sm.
McShane & Company	Reisterstown, MD	D,M,S	Sm.
McTevia (James V.) & Associates, Inc.	East Detroit, MI	All	Med.
Nathaniel Bigelow Holdings, Inc.	Boston, MA	M,B,HC	Med.
Naulty Associates	Huntington Beach, CA	M,D,S	Sm.
Nelson & Company	Atlanta, GA	M,HT,RE,R,S	Med.
New England Ventures	Scottsdale, AZ	M,D,HT	Med.
Nightingale & Associates, Inc.	New Canaan, CT	All	Med.
Osnos (Gilbert C.) & Company, Inc.	New York, NY	M,R,D,S	Med.
PBR Group	Elkins Park, PA	R,M,D,E,HT, CR	Sm.
Pacifica Management Advisors, Inc.	Los Angeles, CA	D,S	Sm.
Peat Marwick, Main & Company	Chicago, IL	T,M	Lg.
Pegasus Industries, Inc.	Cary, IL	D,RE,M	Sm.
Phoenix Management Group (The)	Chapel Hill, NC	M,T,D,HC,C	Sm.
Planitech	Medford, OR	M,S	Med.
Powers & Associates	Fort Worth, TX	All	Med.
Profit Development	Paris, France	HT,T,Tel.	Lg.
Purcell Associates, Inc.	Palatine, IL	M,S,B,Pr.	Med.
Quinn, Whitwer & Company, Inc.	Bethesda, MD	M,D,S,HT,C	Sm.
Quintero (R.G.) & Company	New York, NY	M,R,RE	Sm.

Name	Headquarters	Industries Specialization	Min. Size
RDR Group (The), Inc.	New York, NY	B,Eng.,M,T, Tel.	Med.
Raymond Group (The), Inc.	Chappaqua, NY	HT	Med.
Recovery Management Corporation	New York, NY	M,D,B,RE,En., Ent.	Med.
Regent Pacific Management Corp.	Cupertino, CA	All	Sm.
Sciotto (Bruce A.) Company	Charlotte, NC	M	Sm.
Seidman, Friant, Levine Ltd.	New York, NY	M	Med.
Shepherd's Group (The), Inc.	Oldwick, NJ	M,HT,S,B	Med.
Sigoloff & Associates	Santa Monica, CA	R,RE	Lg.
Singer (Alan M.) Company	Buffalo, NY	M	Med.
Smith Barney, Harris Upham Company, Inc.	New York, NY	NR	Lg.
Sponaugle, S. Woodrow	Rye Beach, NH	S,M	Sm.
Stafford Group (The)	Hebron, IN	Ent.,L	Sm.
Stengel (R.F.) & Company, Inc.	Wayne, PA	M,D,HT,T	Lg.
Stone (Jack R.) & Associates, Inc.	Dallas, TX	M,S,D	Sm.
Strategic Planning and Research Corporation	Plano, TX	HT,M,Tel.,CR	Sm.
Stratford Partners, Inc.	Chicago, IL	B,T,R	Med.
Sugarman & Company	San Francisco, CA	M,D,Tel.,R, HC	Sm.
Sullivan Associates, Inc.	Minneapolis, MN	M,D,R,RE	Med.
Texas Corporate Recovery	Weslaco, TX	B,R	Med.
Triage, Inc.	Lafayette Hill, PA	Family-owned	Sm.
Tripp Associates	Windham, NH	HT	Sm.
Turnaround Effect Associates	Dallas, TX	En.,M,RE,HC	Med.
Turnaround Resources, Inc.	Sandy, UT	CR,HC,M	Sm.
Turnmark Corporation	Colleyville, TX	M,D,C,S, Mktg.	Sm.
Tyson, Weisser, Fortune & Associates	Tampa, FL	M,D,RE	Med.
Viking Capital Partners	Cleveland, OH	M,R,Mktg.	NR
Walquist & Associates	Portland, OR	M,A	Med.
Westwick Consultants	Vancouver, B.C.	R,D	Sm.

Name	Headquarters	Industries Specialization	Min. Size
Wheeler & Rubin, Inc.	Philadelphia, PA	M,HT,D	Med.
Wilson Phelps Group	Beverly Hills, CA	M,T,E	Med.
Yocum Consulting Associates, Inc.	Toledo, OH	M,CR,Eng.	Sm.
Zimmerman Company (The)	Minnetonka, MN	M	Sm.
Zolfo, Cooper & Company	New York, NY	All	Med.

NAME:	ADS Financial Services, Incorporated
ADDRESS:	524 Camino del Monte Sol Santa Fe, NM 87501
TELEPHONE:	505-983-1769
FAX:	505-983-2887
PRINCIPAL(S):	A. David Silver
NUMBER OF YEARS IN BUSINESS:	17
INDUSTRIES SPECIALIZED IN:	Computer-related Distribution Electronics Retail Manufacturing
MINIMUM CLIENT SIZE:	$3 million
MAXIMUM CLIENT SIZE:	$100 million
FEE STRUCTURE:	Retainer or hourly
SUCCESS BONUS:	Yes
EQUITY PARTICIPATION:	No
CLIENT REFERENCES:	William Y. Tauscher, CEO Computerland Corporation 415-734-4000
	Roger Main, CEO IEC Electronics Corp. 315-331-7742
LENGTH OF TYPICAL ASSIGNMENT:	6–9 months
BRANCH OFFICE(S):	None

NAME:	AJM Consulting Group
ADDRESS:	1763 North Warbler Place, #201
	Orange, CA 92667
TELEPHONE:	714-974-4218
FAX:	714-637-6957
PRINCIPAL(S):	Arnold J. Mensch, CPA
NUMBER OF YEARS	
IN BUSINESS:	4
INDUSTRIES	
SPECIALIZED IN:	Manufacturing
	Distribution
	Service
MINIMUM CLIENT SIZE:	None
MAXIMUM CLIENT SIZE:	$100 million
FEE STRUCTURE:	Hourly
SUCCESS BONUS:	No
EQUITY PARTICIPATION:	No
CLIENT REFERENCES:	Confidential
LENGTH OF TYPICAL	
ASSIGNMENT:	4–12 weeks
BRANCH OFFICE(S):	None

NAME:	Accounts Unlimited
ADDRESS:	29 Concord Road
	Ardsley, NY 10502
TELEPHONE:	914-693-2009
FAX:	Call first
PRINCIPAL(S):	Barry L. Kasoff
NUMBER OF YEARS IN BUSINESS:	7
INDUSTRIES SPECIALIZED IN:	Manufacturing
	Finance
MINIMUM CLIENT SIZE:	$40 million
MAXIMUM CLIENT SIZE:	$150 million
FEE STRUCTURE:	Project fee (firm quotation)
SUCCESS BONUS:	If acceptable with client
EQUITY PARTICIPATION:	If acceptable with client
CLIENT REFERENCES:	Bedford Financial Corporation
	HPM Acquisition Corporation
	Psychology Today Magazine
LENGTH OF TYPICAL ASSIGNMENT:	6–30 months
BRANCH OFFICE(S):	None

NAME:	Advanced Planning Associates
ADDRESS:	5025 Redcliff Court,
	Suite 100
	Dunwoody, GA 30338
TELEPHONE:	404-451-7775
FAX:	Same
PRINCIPAL(S):	Daniel A. Wilkens
NUMBER OF YEARS IN BUSINESS:	6
INDUSTRIES SPECIALIZED IN:	Manufacturing
	Distribution
	Service
	Other
MINIMUM CLIENT SIZE:	None
MAXIMUM CLIENT SIZE:	$50 million and up
FEE STRUCTURE:	Hourly plus retainer
SUCCESS BONUS:	Yes
EQUITY PARTICIPATION:	Yes
CLIENT REFERENCES:	The Brill Corporation
	6525 The Corners Parkway,
	Suite 214
	Norcross, GA 30092
	404-662-5588
	Wesley International
	3680 Chestnut Street
	Scottdale, GA 30079
	404-292-7441
	Sports Flipp Tipps, L.P.
	2240 Norcross Parkway,
	Suite 240
	Norcross, GA 30091
	404-441-5772
LENGTH OF TYPICAL ASSIGNMENT:	9 months
BRANCH OFFICE(S):	None

NAME:	Advent Management Associates, Ltd.
ADDRESS:	P.O. Box 3203
	West Chester, PA 19381-3203
TELEPHONE:	215-431-2196
FAX:	215-431-2641
PRINCIPAL(S):	John J. Reddish, CMC
NUMBER OF YEARS IN BUSINESS:	12
INDUSTRIES SPECIALIZED IN:	Manufacturing
	Construction
	Certain others
MINIMUM CLIENT SIZE:	$500,000
MAXIMUM CLIENT SIZE:	None
FEE STRUCTURE:	Retainer
SUCCESS BONUS:	Sometimes
EQUITY PARTICIPATION:	Rarely
CLIENT REFERENCES:	Available to prospective clients
LENGTH OF TYPICAL ASSIGNMENT:	Up to 3 years
BRANCH OFFICE(S):	None

NAME:	Advisors to Banks and Businesses
ADDRESS:	585 Fairhaven Way
	Vallejo, CA 94591
TELEPHONE:	707-645-8160
FAX:	707-746-0153 (Fax to be used with prior permission)
PRINCIPAL(S):	Prem M. Dhawan
NUMBER OF YEARS IN BUSINESS:	2
INDUSTRIES SPECIALIZED IN:	Diversified
MINIMUM CLIENT SIZE:	$2 million
MAXIMUM CLIENT SIZE:	Unlimited
FEE STRUCTURE:	Flexible (depends on projects, usually time plus)
SUCCESS BONUS:	Yes
EQUITY PARTICIPATION:	Not yet
CLIENT REFERENCES:	Confidential
LENGTH OF TYPICAL ASSIGNMENT:	No limit (depends upon the project)
BRANCH OFFICE(S):	None

NAME:	Alderman Associates, Inc.
ADDRESS:	23 Industrial Drive
	Londonderry, NH 03053
TELEPHONE:	603-668-3400
FAX:	603-668-9383
PRINCIPAL(S):	Walter A. Alderman, Jr.
NUMBER OF YEARS	
IN BUSINESS:	22
INDUSTRIES	
SPECIALIZED IN:	High-tech
	Manufacturing
	Distribution
MINIMUM CLIENT SIZE:	$5 million
MAXIMUM CLIENT SIZE:	$120 million
FEE STRUCTURE:	Varies
SUCCESS BONUS:	Yes
EQUITY PARTICIPATION:	Yes
CLIENT REFERENCES:	Bedford Computer Corp.
	Londonderry, NH
	Saxon Industries
	Business Products Division
	Miami Lakes, FL
	Petricca Industries
	Pittsfield, MA
LENGTH OF TYPICAL	
ASSIGNMENT:	Turnaround: 3–6 months
	Rebuild: 3–12 months
	Transfer: 3–6 months
BRANCH OFFICE(S):	None

NAME:	Jay Alix & Associates
ADDRESS:	400 Town Center, Suite 500
	Southfield, MI 48075
TELEPHONE:	313-358-4420
FAX:	313-358-1969
PRINCIPAL(S):	Jay Alix
	Lawrence Ramaekers
	Thomas Cross
	Elmer Heupel
	Michael Cantwell
	Robert Dangremond
NUMBER OF YEARS IN BUSINESS:	9
INDUSTRIES SPECIALIZED IN:	All
MINIMUM CLIENT SIZE:	$5 million
MAXIMUM CLIENT SIZE:	$5 billion
FEE STRUCTURE:	Hourly
SUCCESS BONUS:	Yes
EQUITY PARTICIPATION:	No
CLIENT REFERENCES:	Wang Labs
	Lowell, MA
	TIE Communications
	Shelton, CT
	Cardinal Industries
	Columbus, OH
LENGTH OF TYPICAL ASSIGNMENT:	6 months to 1 year
BRANCH OFFICE(S):	None

NAME:	Allomet Partners, Ltd.
ADDRESS:	325 East 77th Street 2H
	New York, NY 10021
TELEPHONE:	212-249-3935
FAX:	212-861-9772
PRINCIPAL(S):	Gary Brooks, CMC
	Raleigh C. Minor, CMC
NUMBER OF YEARS IN BUSINESS:	21
INDUSTRIES SPECIALIZED IN:	Manufacturing
	Wholesale distribution
MINIMUM CLIENT SIZE:	$5 million
MAXIMUM CLIENT SIZE:	$100 million
FEE STRUCTURE:	Project fee (firm quotation)
SUCCESS BONUS:	No
EQUITY PARTICIPATION:	No
CLIENT REFERENCES:	Cuisinarts, Inc.
	Stamford, CT
	Renaissanace Greeting Cards
	Sanford, ME
	Tibbetts Industries, Inc.
	Camden, ME
LENGTH OF TYPICAL ASSIGNMENT:	Diagnostic/plan: 10–12 weeks
	Interim Management: 4–6 months
BRANCH OFFICE(S):	12 Main Street
	Ashburnham, MA 01430

NAME:	Alvarez & Marsal, Inc.
ADDRESS:	885 Third Avenue, Suite 1700
	New York, NY 10022
TELEPHONE:	212-230-3304
FAX:	212-230-3307
PRINCIPAL(S):	Antonso C. Alvarez
	Bryan P. Marsal
NUMBER OF YEARS	
IN BUSINESS:	8
INDUSTRIES	
SPECIALIZED IN:	Crisis management
MINIMUM CLIENT SIZE:	$35 million
MAXIMUM CLIENT SIZE:	$4 billion
FEE STRUCTURE:	
SUCCESS BONUS:	
EQUITY PARTICIPATION:	
CLIENT REFERENCES:	Resorts International
	Republic Health
	Integrated Resources
LENGTH OF TYPICAL	
ASSIGNMENT:	9 months to 1 year
BRANCH OFFICE(S):	None

NAME:	American National Bank and Trust Company of Chicago
ADDRESS:	33 North LaSalle Street Chicago, IL 60603
TELEPHONE:	312-661-5078
FAX:	312-661-5341
PRINCIPAL(S):	W. S. Kirkland
NUMBER OF YEARS IN BUSINESS:	N.A.
INDUSTRIES SPECIALIZED IN:	Diversified
MINIMUM CLIENT SIZE:	NR
MAXIMUM CLIENT SIZE:	NR
FEE STRUCTURE:	NR
SUCCESS BONUS:	NR
EQUITY PARTICIPATION:	NR
CLIENT REFERENCES:	Confidential
LENGTH OF TYPICAL ASSIGNMENT:	NR
BRANCH OFFICE(S):	None

NAME:	Arthur Andersen & Company
ADDRESS:	633 West Fifth
	Los Angeles, CA 90071
TELEPHONE:	213-614-6592
FAX:	213-614-6670
PRINCIPAL(S):	David Nolte
NUMBER OF YEARS	
IN BUSINESS:	14
INDUSTRIES	
SPECIALIZED IN:	Several
MINIMUM CLIENT SIZE:	$10 million
MAXIMUM CLIENT SIZE:	None
FEE STRUCTURE:	Hourly
SUCCESS BONUS:	No
EQUITY PARTICIPATION:	No
CLIENT REFERENCES:	Confidential
LENGTH OF TYPICAL	
ASSIGNMENT:	Over 1 month
BRANCH OFFICE(S):	All major U.S. cities
	33 W. Monroe St.
	Chicago, IL 60603
	312-507-6660
	312-507- 6748
	Attn: Tom Allison

NAME:	Anderson, Bauman, Tourtellot Vos & Co.
ADDRESS:	230 N. Elm Street Suite 1550 Renaissance Plaza Greensboro, NC 27401
TELEPHONE:	919-275-9110
FAX:	919-275-1551
PRINCIPAL(S):	Neal A. Anderson Edward J. Bauman Peter L. Tourtellot Gerardus "Gary" Vos
NUMBER OF YEARS IN BUSINESS:	1
INDUSTRIES SPECIALIZED IN:	All manufacturing
MINIMUM CLIENT SIZE:	$5 million
MAXIMUM CLIENT SIZE:	$100 million
FEE STRUCTURE:	Hourly
SUCCESS BONUS:	Yes
EQUITY PARTICIPATION:	Sometimes
CLIENT REFERENCES:	Confidential
LENGTH OF TYPICAL ASSIGNMENT:	2 years
BRANCH OFFICE(S):	None

NAME:	Argus Management Corporation
ADDRESS:	19 West Central Street
	Natick, MA 01760
TELEPHONE:	508-651-3777
FAX:	508-651-7072
PRINCIPAL(S):	David J. Ferrari
	Thomas E. Brew, Jr.
	Marshall Brem
NUMBER OF YEARS IN BUSINESS:	20
INDUSTRIES SPECIALIZED IN:	All
MINIMUM CLIENT SIZE:	$3 million
MAXIMUM CLIENT SIZE:	Unlimited
FEE STRUCTURE:	Hourly basis
SUCCESS BONUS:	No
EQUITY PARTICIPATION:	No
CLIENT REFERENCES:	CB Sports
	Glen Falls, NY
	Malden Mills
	Lawrence, MA
	GCA Corp.
	Andover, MA
LENGTH OF TYPICAL ASSIGNMENT:	1–12 months
BRANCH OFFICE(S):	None

NAME:	Aspetuck Capital Partners, Inc.
ADDRESS:	6 Sipperley's Hill Road
	Westport, CT 06880
TELEPHONE:	203-454-4625
FAX:	203-454-7901
PRINCIPAL(S):	Terrance J. Bruggeman, President
NUMBER OF YEARS	
IN BUSINESS:	8
INDUSTRIES	
SPECIALIZED IN:	Manufacturing
	Distribution
MINIMUM CLIENT SIZE:	$35 million
MAXIMUM CLIENT SIZE:	$1 billion
FEE STRUCTURE:	Flat monthly fee
SUCCESS BONUS:	Yes
EQUITY PARTICIPATION:	Yes
CLIENT REFERENCES:	Harley Davidson
	Milwaukee, WI
	Steiger Tractor
	Fargo, ND
	Worlds of Wonder
	Fremont, CA
LENGTH OF TYPICAL	
ASSIGNMENT:	Restructuring plan: 2–3 months
	Implementation: 4–18 months
BRANCH OFFICE(S):	None

NAME:	Austin & Associates
ADDRESS:	#1 Harbourside Drive
	Delray Beach, FL 33483
TELEPHONE:	407-276-3452
FAX:	Call first
PRINCIPAL(S):	W. F. Austin
NUMBER OF YEARS	
IN BUSINESS:	6
INDUSTRIES	
SPECIALIZED IN:	Manufacturing—Building
	products
	Manufacturing—Machinery
	Manufacturing—Paper products
MINIMUM CLIENT SIZE:	$5 million
MAXIMUM CLIENT SIZE:	$30 million
FEE STRUCTURE:	Hourly and flat
SUCCESS BONUS:	Yes
EQUITY PARTICIPATION:	Sometimes
CLIENT REFERENCES:	Simpson Estates
	33 North Dearborn
	Chicago, IL
	Photo-Marker
	212 National
	Spartanburg, SC
	A & T Industries
	209 17th Street
	Ft. Lauderdale, FL
LENGTH OF TYPICAL	
ASSIGNMENT:	6 months
BRANCH OFFICE(S):	None

NAME:	Bahr International, Inc.
ADDRESS:	12221 Merit Drive, Suite 1305
	Dallas, TX 75243
TELEPHONE:	214-980-7070
FAX:	214-980-7072
PRINCIPAL(S):	C. Charles Bahr, III
NUMBER OF YEARS	
IN BUSINESS:	12
INDUSTRIES	
SPECIALIZED IN:	Manufacturing
	Retail
	Wholesale
	Hospitality
	Transportation
MINIMUM CLIENT SIZE:	$20 million
MAXIMUM CLIENT SIZE:	$800 million
FEE STRUCTURE:	Hourly
SUCCESS BONUS:	In certain cases
EQUITY PARTICIPATION:	No
CLIENT REFERENCES:	Confidential
LENGTH OF TYPICAL	
ASSIGNMENT:	3–7 months
BRANCH OFFICE(S):	None

NAME:	Bantam Group
ADDRESS:	50 Bay Colony Drive
	Westwood, MA 02090
TELEPHONE:	617-329-2028
FAX:	617-329-2238
PRINCIPAL(S):	Joseph J. Caruso
NUMBER OF YEARS	
IN BUSINESS:	4
INDUSTRIES	
SPECIALIZED IN:	Software
	Industrial automation
	High-tech
MINIMUM CLIENT SIZE:	No minimum
MAXIMUM CLIENT SIZE:	$100 million
FEE STRUCTURE:	Weekly retainer
SUCCESS BONUS:	Yes
EQUITY PARTICIPATION:	Yes
CLIENT REFERENCES:	Available to prospective clients
LENGTH OF TYPICAL	
ASSIGNMENT:	6 months to 1 year
BRANCH OFFICE(S):	None

NAME:	Beacon Management Group, Inc.
ADDRESS:	1000 West McNab Road
	Pompano Beach, FL 33069
TELEPHONE:	305-782-1119
FAX:	305-782-1199
PRINCIPAL(S):	Michael J. Donnelly
NUMBER OF YEARS	
IN BUSINESS:	5
INDUSTRIES	
SPECIALIZED IN:	First-generation companies where the founder still owns a majority of the company
MINIMUM CLIENT SIZE:	$1 million
MAXIMUM CLIENT SIZE:	$50 million
FEE STRUCTURE:	Hourly
SUCCESS BONUS:	Not normally/may consider
EQUITY PARTICIPATION:	Not normally/may consider
CLIENT REFERENCES:	Confidential
LENGTH OF TYPICAL	
ASSIGNMENT:	No typical length (depends on type of involvement)
BRANCH OFFICE(S):	None

NAME:	Bear Stearns & Co., Inc.
ADDRESS:	245 Park Avenue
	New York, NY 10167
TELEPHONE:	212-272-3644
FAX:	212-272-3088
PRINCIPAL(S):	Daniel A. Calentano
NUMBER OF YEARS	
IN BUSINESS:	Over 10
INDUSTRIES	
SPECIALIZED IN:	Diversified
MINIMUM CLIENT SIZE:	Varies
MAXIMUM CLIENT SIZE:	Varies
FEE STRUCTURE:	Retainer, no hourly fees
SUCCESS BONUS:	Varies
EQUITY PARTICIPATION:	Varies
CLIENT REFERENCES:	Confidential
LENGTH OF TYPICAL	
ASSIGNMENT:	NR
BRANCH OFFICE(S):	None

NAME:	Bird & Co., Inc.
ADDRESS:	88 Mountainwood Road
	Stamford, CT 06903
TELEPHONE:	203-322-0235
FAX:	203-322-0754
PRINCIPAL(S):	Bill Bird
NUMBER OF YEARS	
IN BUSINESS:	12 years
INDUSTRIES	
SPECIALIZED IN:	Computer related
	Software
	High-tech
	Real estate
	Marketing
MINIMUM CLIENT SIZE:	No minimum
MAXIMUM CLIENT SIZE:	No maximum
FEE STRUCTURE:	Retainer
SUCCESS BONUS:	Yes
EQUITY PARTICIPATION:	Yes
CLIENT REFERENCES:	Citicorp
	Shared Medical Systems, Inc.
	Lincolnshire Management Corp.
	55 East 52nd Street
	New York, NY 10022
LENGTH OF TYPICAL	
ASSIGNMENT:	6 to 12 months
BRANCH OFFICE(S):	None

NAME:	J. Bodington
ADDRESS:	120 Montgomery Street, #1776
	San Francisco, CA 94104
TELEPHONE:	415-391-3280
FAX:	415-391-3056
PRINCIPAL(S):	Jeffrey C. Bodington
NUMBER OF YEARS	
IN BUSINESS:	11
INDUSTRIES	
SPECIALIZED IN:	Energy
	Transportation
	Utilities
MINIMUM CLIENT SIZE:	$500,000
MAXIMUM CLIENT SIZE:	$3 billion
FEE STRUCTURE:	Hourly
SUCCESS BONUS:	Sometimes
EQUITY PARTICIPATION:	Sometimes
CLIENT REFERENCES:	ETSI
	San Francisco
	"Confidential"
	San Diego
	"Confidential"
	Menlo Park, CA
LENGTH OF TYPICAL	
ASSIGNMENT:	None are typical (One took
	2 weeks & another 5 years)
BRANCH OFFICE(S):	None

NAME:	The Branch Office
ADDRESS:	415 Jerome
	Midland, MI 48640
TELEPHONE:	517-832-8831
FAX:	517-631–8632
PRINCIPAL(S):	Sharon Miller
	Michael P. Thomas
NUMBER OF YEARS IN BUSINESS:	5
INDUSTRIES SPECIALIZED IN:	
MINIMUM CLIENT SIZE:	$100,000
MAXIMUM CLIENT SIZE:	$100 million
FEE STRUCTURE:	Hourly
SUCCESS BONUS:	No
EQUITY PARTICIPATION:	No
CLIENT REFERENCES:	Available to clients upon request
LENGTH OF TYPICAL ASSIGNMENT:	15 months to 2 years
BRANCH OFFICE(S):	903 North Jackson
	Bay City, MI 48708
	517-893-4547

NAME:	R. Breakiron and Associates
ADDRESS:	5113 West Sanna Street
	Glendale, AZ 85302
TELEPHONE:	602-435-1448
FAX:	602-937-2285
PRINCIPAL(S):	Robert Breakiron
NUMBER OF YEARS	
IN BUSINESS:	1
INDUSTRIES	
SPECIALIZED IN:	Manufacturing (low- and high-tech)
	Service (plumbing and electrical contractors, construction equipment dealers)
MINIMUM CLIENT SIZE:	Under $5 million
MAXIMUM CLIENT SIZE:	$75 million plus
FEE STRUCTURE:	Hourly or flat (depending on job)
SUCCESS BONUS:	No
EQUITY PARTICIPATION:	No
CLIENT REFERENCES:	Arizona Pioneer Museum
	Box 1677, Black Canyon Stage
	Phoenix, AZ 85027
LENGTH OF TYPICAL	
ASSIGNMENT:	6–24 months
BRANCH OFFICE(S):	None

NAME:	Brennen Consultants, Inc.
ADDRESS:	300 North Michigan Street
	South Bend, IN 46601-1239
TELEPHONE:	219-234-8780
FAX:	219-282-4344
PRINCIPAL(S):	William E. Brennen
	James G. Perkins
NUMBER OF YEARS IN BUSINESS:	16
INDUSTRIES SPECIALIZED IN:	Manufacturing
	Transportation
MINIMUM CLIENT SIZE:	$2–5 million
MAXIMUM CLIENT SIZE:	$75–80 million
FEE STRUCTURE:	Flat & Overrides
SUCCESS BONUS:	Yes
EQUITY PARTICIPATION:	Infrequently
CLIENT REFERENCES:	Food processing
	Dairy operation
	Funeral service
LENGTH OF TYPICAL ASSIGNMENT:	1–3 years
BRANCH OFFICE(S):	None

NAME:	Brincko Associates, Inc.
ADDRESS:	1801 Avenue of the Stars, Suite 1054
	Los Angeles, CA 90067
TELEPHONE:	213-553-4523
FAX:	213-553-6782
PRINCIPAL(S):	John P. Brincko
	John Knopf
	Frank Brancale
NUMBER OF YEARS IN BUSINESS:	11
INDUSTRIES SPECIALIZED IN:	Service
	Manufacturing
	Retail
	High-tech
MINIMUM CLIENT SIZE:	$5 million
MAXIMUM CLIENT SIZE:	$4+ billion
FEE STRUCTURE:	Hourly and monthly retainer
SUCCESS BONUS:	Yes
EQUITY PARTICIPATION:	Yes
CLIENT REFERENCES:	Confidential
LENGTH OF TYPICAL ASSIGNMENT:	Varies
BRANCH OFFICE(S):	None

NAME:	Stan Brown Associates
ADDRESS:	1620 S.W. 4th Court
	Fort Lauderdale, FL 33312
TELEPHONE:	305-760-9141
FAX:	305-760-9136
PRINCIPAL(S):	Stanley C. Brown
NUMBER OF YEARS IN BUSINESS:	3
INDUSTRIES SPECIALIZED IN:	Real estate
	Manufacturing
	Health care
MINIMUM CLIENT SIZE:	$10 million
MAXIMUM CLIENT SIZE:	$50 million
FEE STRUCTURE:	Hourly
SUCCESS BONUS:	Sometimes
EQUITY PARTICIPATION:	Sometimes
CLIENT REFERENCES:	None
LENGTH OF TYPICAL ASSIGNMENT:	3 to 6 months
BRANCH OFFICE(S):	None

NAME:	Buccino & Associates, Inc.
ADDRESS:	208 South La Salle Street, Suite 510 Chicago, IL 60604
TELEPHONE:	312-782-1239
FAX:	312-782-0766
PRINCIPAL(S):	Gerald P. Buccino, President
	Edward C. Hall, Executive Vice President/Managing Director–Southwestern Region
	Arnold H. Dratt, Executive Vice President/Managing Director–Midwestern Region
	Robert R. Starzyk, Executive Vice President/Managing Director–Southeastern Region
	William L. McMahon, Executive Vice President/Managing Director–Western Region
NUMBER OF YEARS IN BUSINESS:	10
INDUSTRIES SPECIALIZED IN:	Work in all
MINIMUM CLIENT SIZE:	$5 million
MAXIMUM CLIENT SIZE:	$500 million
FEE STRUCTURE:	Hourly
SUCCESS BONUS:	Sometimes
EQUITY PARTICIPATION:	No
CLIENT REFERENCES:	Tallgrass Technologies Corp. Overland Park, KS
	Johnson Products Co., Inc. Chicago, IL
	Chicago Housing Authority Chicago, IL
LENGTH OF TYPICAL ASSIGNMENT:	2–6 months

BRANCH OFFICE(S):

13355 Noel Road, #500
Dallas, TX 75240

4 Houston Center, #1459
Houston, TX 77010- 3028

300 Galleria Parkway, #400
Atlanta, GA 30339

445 South Figueroa, #2600
Los Angeles, CA 90071

475 Park Avenue South
New York, NY 10016

NAME:	Bunker Hill Associates, Inc.
ADDRESS:	707 Travis, # 1700
	Houston, TX 77002
TELEPHONE:	713-223-5730
FAX:	713-223-5379
PRINCIPAL(S):	Michael M. Fowler
	C. Kingswell-Smits
	J. A. Chaffee
NUMBER OF YEARS IN BUSINESS:	7
INDUSTRIES SPECIALIZED IN:	Oil & gas
	Manufacturing
	Services
	Real estate
	Financial institutions
MINIMUM CLIENT SIZE:	$1 million
MAXIMUM CLIENT SIZE:	$200 million
FEE STRUCTURE:	Hourly
SUCCESS BONUS:	Yes
EQUITY PARTICIPATION:	Sometimes
CLIENT REFERENCES:	Kaneb Services, Inc.
	Paramount Refinery Partners
	Consolidated Petroleum
	Industries
LENGTH OF TYPICAL ASSIGNMENT:	3 months to 2 years
BRANCH OFFICE(S):	None

NAME:	P. J. Burns & Associates
ADDRESS:	101 Blacklog Road
	Kentfield, CA 94904
TELEPHONE:	415-461-6963
FAX:	415-925-0574
PRINCIPAL(S):	Patrick J. Burns
NUMBER OF YEARS	
IN BUSINESS:	8
INDUSTRIES	
SPECIALIZED IN:	Distribution
	Construction
	Engineering
	High-tech
MINIMUM CLIENT SIZE:	$5 million
MAXIMUM CLIENT SIZE:	$600 million to $1 billion
FEE STRUCTURE:	Hourly and retainer
SUCCESS BONUS:	Yes
EQUITY PARTICIPATION:	Yes
CLIENT REFERENCES:	DHL Cargo Operations
	Honolulu, HI
	International Systems
	& Control, Inc.
	Houston, TX
	Atlantic Pacific Marine Corp.
	Houston, TX
LENGTH OF TYPICAL	
ASSIGNMENT:	3 months to 3 years
BRANCH OFFICE(S):	None

NAME:	The Caslin Group Business Consultants
ADDRESS:	1200 19th Street NW, Suite 602 Washington, DC 20036
TELEPHONE:	202-659-0541
FAX:	202-331-1894
PRINCIPAL(S):	Michael J. Caslin III
NUMBER OF YEARS IN BUSINESS:	5
INDUSTRIES SPECIALIZED IN:	Manufacturing Retail Wholesale Service Public administration
MINIMUM CLIENT SIZE:	Nothing under $200,000
MAXIMUM CLIENT SIZE:	$10 million
FEE STRUCTURE:	Hourly and flat, depending upon negotiations and client needs
SUCCESS BONUS:	Yes
EQUITY PARTICIPATION:	Yes
CLIENT REFERENCES:	Mr. Steve Mariotti, President National Foundation for Teaching Entrepreneurship to Handicapped & Disadvantaged Youth, Incorporated 171 West 23rd Street, Suite 4C New York City, NY 10011
	Mr. Michael Aubert, Director Dartmouth Early Learning Center, Incorporated 487 Smith Neck Road South Dartmouth, MA 02748
	Mr. Michael Hill, President Excel Environmental Systems, Incorporated 1445 Main Road Tiverton, RI 02878

LENGTH OF TYPICAL
ASSIGNMENT: 3 months to 2 years
BRANCH OFFICE(S):   New England Division
                             1445 Main Road
                             Tiverton, RI 02878
                             401-625-1030

NAME:	Chicago Consulting
ADDRESS:	404 West Hawthorne Court
	Lake Bluff, IL 60044
TELEPHONE:	708-234-5347
FAX:	708-346-7206
PRINCIPAL(S):	William Avellone
	Jere Brown
NUMBER OF YEARS	
IN BUSINESS:	15
INDUSTRIES	
SPECIALIZED IN:	Manufacturing
	Distribution
MINIMUM CLIENT SIZE:	No limit
MAXIMUM CLIENT SIZE:	No limit
FEE STRUCTURE:	Hourly or flat
SUCCESS BONUS:	Sometimes
EQUITY PARTICIPATION:	Sometimes
CLIENT REFERENCES:	$200 million industrial parts
	producer
	$30 million manufacturer
	$30 million software company
LENGTH OF TYPICAL	
ASSIGNMENT:	120 days to 18 months
BRANCH OFFICE(S):	8 South Michigan Avenue,
	Suite 3600
	Chicago, IL 60603
	312-346-5080

NAME:	Chilmark Partners
ADDRESS:	333 West Wacker Drive
	Chicago, IL 60606
TELEPHONE:	312-984-9711
FAX:	312-984-0317
PRINCIPAL(S):	David M. Shulte
NUMBER OF YEARS IN BUSINESS:	6
INDUSTRIES SPECIALIZED IN:	None
MINIMUM CLIENT SIZE:	$100 million
MAXIMUM CLIENT SIZE:	None
FEE STRUCTURE:	Monthly retainer
SUCCESS BONUS:	Only in M & A assignments
EQUITY PARTICIPATION:	Depends on nature of assignment
CLIENT REFERENCES:	ITEL Corporation
	Horsham Corporation
	Global Marine Incorporated
LENGTH OF TYPICAL ASSIGNMENT:	12–18 months
BRANCH OFFICE(S):	None

NAME:	Cohen & Rogozinski, CPAs
ADDRESS:	1427 Chew Street
	P.O. Box 4376
	Allentown, PA 18105-4376
TELEPHONE:	215-433-3220
FAX:	215-435-3111
PRINCIPAL(S):	Howard S. Cohen, CPA
	Ronald W. Rogozinski, CPA
NUMBER OF YEARS IN BUSINESS:	23
INDUSTRIES SPECIALIZED IN:	None
MINIMUM CLIENT SIZE:	$1 million
MAXIMUM CLIENT SIZE:	$25 million
FEE STRUCTURE:	Hourly
SUCCESS BONUS:	No
EQUITY PARTICIPATION:	No
CLIENT REFERENCES:	Mr. Bart Kline
	Jacob Kline Cooperage
	701 East Highland Street
	Allentown, PA 18103
	Mr. Neil Hartman
	Buck Electric
	P.O. Box 13217
	Reading, PA 19612-3217
	Mr. Frank R. Fasching
	Allen Supply Co., Inc.
	P.O. Box 1288
	Allentown, PA 18105-1288
LENGTH OF TYPICAL ASSIGNMENT:	6 months to 1 year
BRANCH OFFICE(S):	3800 William Penn Highway
	Easton, PA 18042

NAME:	The Coloney Company
ADDRESS:	1014 North Adams Street
	P.O. Box 668
	Tallahassee, FL 32302
TELEPHONE:	904-222-8193
FAX:	904-222-9824
PRINCIPAL(S):	Wayne H. Coloney, President
	Lt. General Maurice F. Casey
	(USAF Ret.), Vice President
NUMBER OF YEARS IN BUSINESS:	8
INDUSTRIES SPECIALIZED IN:	Small defense contractors
MINIMUM CLIENT SIZE:	$2 million
MAXIMUM CLIENT SIZE:	$40 million
FEE STRUCTURE:	Hourly
SUCCESS BONUS:	Not generally
EQUITY PARTICIPATION:	Not generally
CLIENT REFERENCES:	Confidential
LENGTH OF TYPICAL ASSIGNMENT:	In excess of 9 months
BRANCH OFFICE(S):	None

NAME:	Continuum Associates
ADDRESS:	7222 Ambassador Road
	Baltimore, MD 21207
TELEPHONE:	301-281-0900
FAX:	301-281-0909
PRINCIPAL(S):	Stanley Bielak
NUMBER OF YEARS IN BUSINESS:	6
INDUSTRIES SPECIALIZED IN:	Computer software/services
	Federal contractors
MINIMUM CLIENT SIZE:	$1 million
MAXIMUM CLIENT SIZE:	$125 million
FEE STRUCTURE:	Flat
SUCCESS BONUS:	Yes
EQUITY PARTICIPATION:	Yes
CLIENT REFERENCES:	Wasaydon Resource Corp.
	Washington, DC
	Waldent Smallen & Bloomg
	Baltimore, MD
	Maldem International
	Alexandria, VA
LENGTH OF TYPICAL ASSIGNMENT:	6–24 months
BRANCH OFFICE(S):	None

NAME:	Conway & Youngman
ADDRESS:	355 Middlesex Avenue
	Wilmington, MA 01887
TELEPHONE:	617-646-2200
FAX:	508-658-6712
PRINCIPAL(S):	Carl M. Youngman
	Thomas H. Conway
	Leslie Charm (Mr.)
NUMBER OF YEARS IN BUSINESS:	20
INDUSTRIES SPECIALIZED IN:	High-tech
	Service/distribution
	Retail
	Franchising
	Real estate
MINIMUM CLIENT SIZE:	$5 million
MAXIMUM CLIENT SIZE:	$1 billion
FEE STRUCTURE:	Flat
SUCCESS BONUS:	Yes
EQUITY PARTICIPATION:	No
CLIENT REFERENCES:	Ben & Jerry's Ice Cream
	Waterbury, VT
	Samuel Adams Beer Company
	Boston, MA
	Metallon Engineered Materials
	Corporation
	Pawtucket, RI
LENGTH OF TYPICAL ASSIGNMENT:	3–9 months
BRANCH OFFICE(S):	None

NAME:	Conway MacKenzie & Dunleavy Consultants, Incorporated
ADDRESS:	999 Haynes Street, Suite 340 Birmingham, MI 48009
TELEPHONE:	313-433-3100
FAX:	313-433-3143
PRINCIPAL(S):	Van E. Conway Donald S. MacKenzie Patrick G. Dunleavy
NUMBER OF YEARS IN BUSINESS:	16
INDUSTRIES SPECIALIZED IN:	Manufacturing Service Paper Retail Construction Communications Transporation
MINIMUM CLIENT SIZE:	$5 million
MAXIMUM CLIENT SIZE:	$1 billion
FEE STRUCTURE:	Hourly
SUCCESS BONUS:	Occasionally
EQUITY PARTICIPATION:	Possibly
CLIENT REFERENCES:	ALC Communications 30300 Telegraph Road, Suite 350 Birmingham, MI 48010
	Commercial Contracting Corporation 1743 Maplelawn Troy, MI 48099
	Kapaco Group, Incorporated 279 Paw Paw Avenue Watervliet, MI 49098
LENGTH OF TYPICAL ASSIGNMENT:	2 weeks to 3 months
BRANCH OFFICE(S):	None

NAME:	Coopers & Lybrand
ADDRESS:	1251 Avenue of the Americas New York, NY 10020
TELEPHONE:	212-536-2357
FAX:	212-642-7110
PRINCIPAL(S):	1,200 partners
NUMBER OF YEARS **IN BUSINESS:**	Numerous
INDUSTRIES **SPECIALIZED IN:**	Various
MINIMUM CLIENT SIZE:	No minimum
MAXIMUM CLIENT SIZE:	No maximum
FEE STRUCTURE:	Hourly
SUCCESS BONUS:	No
EQUITY PARTICIPATION:	No
CLIENT REFERENCES:	Confidential
LENGTH OF TYPICAL **ASSIGNMENT:**	Depends upon assignment
BRANCH OFFICE(S):	Principal offices in 95 U.S. cities and 100 countries

NAME:	Corporate Restructuring Group, Incorporated
ADDRESS:	10 Almaden Boulevard, Suite 1600 San Jose, CA 95113
TELEPHONE:	408-295-1020
FAX:	408-292-1382
PRINCIPAL(S):	J. Sydney Whalen William D. Parker, Jr.
NUMBER OF YEARS IN BUSINESS:	7
INDUSTRIES SPECIALIZED IN:	High-tech Construction Leasing Agriculture Manufacturing Real estate
MINIMUM CLIENT SIZE:	$5 million
MAXIMUM CLIENT SIZE:	$200 million
FEE STRUCTURE:	Hourly
SUCCESS BONUS:	Yes
EQUITY PARTICIPATION:	Yes
CLIENT REFERENCES:	Cap Concrete Company Fremont, CA
	Minton Company Mountain View, CA
	Mariani Financing Los Altos, CA
LENGTH OF TYPICAL ASSIGNMENT:	1–2 years
BRANCH OFFICE(S):	3000 Sand Hill Road Menlo Park, CA 94025
	3158 Danville Boulevard Alamo, CA 94507

NAME:	The Cowherd Consulting Group, Inc.
ADDRESS:	106 Stephen Mather Road Darien, CT 06820
TELEPHONE:	203-655-2150
FAX:	609-584-3305
PRINCIPAL(S):	Edwin R. Cowherd, CMC
NUMBER OF YEARS IN BUSINESS:	18
INDUSTRIES SPECIALIZED IN:	Manufacturing Process
MINIMUM CLIENT SIZE:	$100 million
MAXIMUM CLIENT SIZE:	Unlimited
FEE STRUCTURE:	Monthly/annually/flat
SUCCESS BONUS:	Usually yes
EQUITY PARTICIPATION:	No, but would consider
CLIENT REFERENCES:	Buffalo Color Corp. Teepak, Inc. Congoleum Corp.
LENGTH OF TYPICAL ASSIGNMENT:	1–3 years
BRANCH OFFICE(S):	None

NAME:	Crisis Management Associates
ADDRESS:	2069 Zumbehl Road, Suite 13
	St. Charles, MO 65503
TELEPHONE:	314-947-9487
FAX:	314-723-2932
PRINCIPAL(S):	Larry G. Coons, President
NUMBER OF YEARS IN BUSINESS:	9
INDUSTRIES SPECIALIZED IN:	Manufacturing
	Retail
	Transportation services
	High-tech
	Health/medical
MINIMUM CLIENT SIZE:	Open
MAXIMUM CLIENT SIZE:	$10 million
FEE STRUCTURE:	Firm quotation basis
SUCCESS BONUS:	Negotiable
EQUITY PARTICIPATION:	Negotiable
CLIENT REFERENCES:	Confidential
LENGTH OF TYPICAL ASSIGNMENT:	6 months
BRANCH OFFICE(S):	None

NAME:	DKM Management, Incorporated
ADDRESS:	7155 Roswell Road, #4
	Atlanta, GA 30328
TELEPHONE:	404-671-1239
FAX:	404-434-8083
PRINCIPAL(S):	Charles A. Soule, Jr.
NUMBER OF YEARS IN BUSINESS:	5
INDUSTRIES SPECIALIZED IN:	Manufacturing
	Distribution
MINIMUM CLIENT SIZE:	$5 million
MAXIMUM CLIENT SIZE:	$150 million
FEE STRUCTURE:	Flat—monthly or weekly
SUCCESS BONUS:	Yes, if possible
EQUITY PARTICIPATION:	If possible & feasible
CLIENT REFERENCES:	AID Corporation
	Clayton, GA
	Executive Transportation
	Atlanta, GA
	Continental Plastics
	Avenel, NJ
LENGTH OF TYPICAL ASSIGNMENT:	Minimum 6 months
BRANCH OFFICE(S):	None

NAME:	Deloitte & Touche
ADDRESS:	2 Hopkins Plaza, Suite 1111
	Baltimore, MD 21202
TELEPHONE:	301-576-6700
FAX:	301-837-0510
PRINCIPAL(S):	W. E. Kuntz
NUMBER OF YEARS	
IN BUSINESS:	125
INDUSTRIES	
SPECIALIZED IN:	All
MINIMUM CLIENT SIZE:	$2 million
MAXIMUM CLIENT SIZE:	None
FEE STRUCTURE:	Hourly
SUCCESS BONUS:	N.A.
EQUITY PARTICIPATION:	N.A.
CLIENT REFERENCES:	Confidential
LENGTH OF TYPICAL	
ASSIGNMENT:	Varies (usually months)
BRANCH OFFICE(S):	Throughout the United States

NAME:	The Delta Management Group, Incorporated
ADDRESS:	4990 Poplar Avenue, Suite 215 Memphis, TN 38117
TELEPHONE:	901-685-8671
FAX:	901-763-2506
PRINCIPAL(S):	C. William Gano III, M.B.A. J. Slavick
NUMBER OF YEARS IN BUSINESS:	10
INDUSTRIES SPECIALIZED IN:	Manufacturing Service Wholesale distribution
MINIMUM CLIENT SIZE:	$5 million
MAXIMUM CLIENT SIZE:	$50+ million
FEE STRUCTURE:	Flat (monthly retainer or fixed fee)
SUCCESS BONUS:	Yes
EQUITY PARTICIPATION:	No
CLIENT REFERENCES:	Confidential
LENGTH OF TYPICAL ASSIGNMENT:	6–12 months
BRANCH OFFICE(S):	None

NAME:	The Diogenes Group, Incorporated
ADDRESS:	12121 Wilshire, #1103 Los Angeles, CA 90025
TELEPHONE:	213-207-6444
FAX:	213-826-2306
PRINCIPAL(S):	Lawrence McNamee Peter Bundy Walter Wentz
NUMBER OF YEARS IN BUSINESS:	14
INDUSTRIES SPECIALIZED IN:	Manufacturing Wholesale Retail Service
MINIMUM CLIENT SIZE:	$3 million
MAXIMUM CLIENT SIZE:	$250 million
FEE STRUCTURE:	Hourly or flat
SUCCESS BONUS:	No
EQUITY PARTICIPATION:	Yes
CLIENT REFERENCES:	Confidential
LENGTH OF TYPICAL ASSIGNMENT:	9–12 months
BRANCH OFFICE(S):	None

NAME:	Distribution Investment Associates
ADDRESS:	1939 Harrison Street, #401 Oakland, CA 94612
TELEPHONE:	415-763-9535
FAX:	415-465-8689
PRINCIPAL(S):	Edmond F. Trainer Robert J. Wikse
NUMBER OF YEARS IN BUSINESS:	5
INDUSTRIES SPECIALIZED IN:	Wholesale distribution
MINIMUM CLIENT SIZE:	$20 million
MAXIMUM CLIENT SIZE:	$600 million
FEE STRUCTURE:	Hourly and flat
SUCCESS BONUS:	At times
EQUITY PARTICIPATION:	At times
CLIENT REFERENCES:	Confidential
LENGTH OF TYPICAL ASSIGNMENT:	Varies with assignment
BRANCH OFFICE(S):	None

NAME:	Diversicorp, Inc. Diversified Consulting Associations Division
ADDRESS:	7540 LBJ Freeway, Suite 634 Dallas, TX 75251
TELEPHONE:	214-991-9813
FAX:	214-490-9047
PRINCIPAL(S):	Jim Mayer, CEO George Thorson, C.O.O.
NUMBER OF YEARS IN BUSINESS:	6

**INDUSTRIES
SPECIALIZED IN:**
	Manufacturing
	Wholesale distribution
	Specific interest in: steel,
	   furniture, concrete, and
	   masonry

MINIMUM CLIENT SIZE:	$5 million
MAXIMUM CLIENT SIZE:	$200 million

FEE STRUCTURE:	Negotiated; dependent upon
	   length of anticipated
	   engagement

SUCCESS BONUS:	Not normally
EQUITY PARTICIPATION:	Never
CLIENT REFERENCES:	Savage Industries Builders Concrete Manufacturing Company, Inc.
LENGTH OF TYPICAL ASSIGNMENT:	Highly variable 1 week–2 years
BRANCH OFFICE(S):	Tampa, FL King of Prussia, PA Omaha, NE

NAME:	William E. Dorgan Associates, Inc.
ADDRESS:	4400 East Broadway, Suite 600 Tucson, AZ 85711
TELEPHONE:	602-791-3000
FAX:	602-795-4753
PRINCIPAL(S):	William Dorgan
NUMBER OF YEARS IN BUSINESS:	6
INDUSTRIES SPECIALIZED IN:	Manufacturing Services Financing
MINIMUM CLIENT SIZE:	$1 million
MAXIMUM CLIENT SIZE:	$50 million
FEE STRUCTURE:	Hourly
SUCCESS BONUS:	Yes, when appropriate
EQUITY PARTICIPATION:	No
CLIENT REFERENCES:	Confidential
LENGTH OF TYPICAL ASSIGNMENT:	2 weeks to 4 months
BRANCH OFFICE(S):	None

NAME:	Suren G. Dutia
ADDRESS:	12917 Caminito del Canto
	Del Mar, CA 92014
TELEPHONE:	619-792-5190 (Home)
	619-457-5091 (Office)
FAX:	619-457-3928
PRINCIPAL(S):	Suren G. Dutia (only accepts assignment as President/CEO)
NUMBER OF YEARS IN BUSINESS:	10
INDUSTRIES SPECIALIZED IN:	Medical instruments
	Electronic equipment
	PC-based software
MINIMUM CLIENT SIZE:	$10 million
MAXIMUM CLIENT SIZE:	$50 million
FEE STRUCTURE:	Flat fee/As an employee, require annualized compensation and expenses/benefits
SUCCESS BONUS:	Yes
EQUITY PARTICIPATION:	Yes
CLIENT REFERENCES:	PM America, Incorporated
	Dynatech Corporation
	(5 subsidiaries)
	Xscribe Corporation
LENGTH OF TYPICAL ASSIGNMENT:	18 months to 3 years
BRANCH OFFICE(S):	None

NAME:	EIG Management, Incorporated
ADDRESS:	501 21st Place
	Santa Monica, CA 90402
TELEPHONE:	213-394-4779
FAX:	213-394-8356
PRINCIPAL(S):	Eliot I. Green
	Elayne L. Green, Esq.
NUMBER OF YEARS IN BUSINESS:	4
INDUSTRIES SPECIALIZED IN:	Retail
MINIMUM CLIENT SIZE:	$20 million
MAXIMUM CLIENT SIZE:	$200 million
FEE STRUCTURE:	Daily or monthly
SUCCESS BONUS:	Where practicable
EQUITY PARTICIPATION:	Where practicable
CLIENT REFERENCES:	Merksamer Jewelers, Incorporated
	Sacramento, CA
	Plymouth Lamston Stores Corporation
	Saddle Brook, NJ
LENGTH OF TYPICAL ASSIGNMENT:	6 months
BRANCH OFFICE(S):	None

NAME:	Effective Management Systems, Inc.
ADDRESS:	P.O. Box 1540
	Snellville, GA 30278
TELEPHONE:	404-985-6844
FAX:	404-972-0582
PRINCIPAL(S):	Robert L. Sullivan
NUMBER OF YEARS IN BUSINESS:	$3\frac{1}{2}$
INDUSTRIES SPECIALIZED IN:	Motor carrier (trucking)
MINIMUM CLIENT SIZE:	$5 million
MAXIMUM CLIENT SIZE:	$180 million
FEE STRUCTURE:	Hourly plus retainer
SUCCESS BONUS:	No
EQUITY PARTICIPATION:	No
CLIENT REFERENCES:	Service Transport, Inc.
	Nashville, TN
	Fredrickson Motor Express
	Charlotte, NC
	Greenwood Motor Lines
	Greenwood, SC
LENGTH OF TYPICAL ASSIGNMENT:	12 months
BRANCH OFFICE(S):	None

NAME:	Richard A. Eisner & Co.
ADDRESS:	575 Madison Avenue
	New York, NY 10022
TELEPHONE:	212-355-1700
FAX:	212-355-2414
PRINCIPAL(S):	Richard A. Eisner
NUMBER OF YEARS	
IN BUSINESS:	27
INDUSTRIES	
SPECIALIZED IN:	Diversified
MINIMUM CLIENT SIZE:	No limit
MAXIMUM CLIENT SIZE:	No limit
FEE STRUCTURE:	Hourly
SUCCESS BONUS:	Open
EQUITY PARTICIPATION:	Open
CLIENT REFERENCES:	Confidential
LENGTH OF TYPICAL	
ASSIGNMENT:	Varies
BRANCH OFFICE(S):	Long Island
	New Jersey

NAME:	Ernst & Young
ADDRESS:	277 Park Avenue
	New York City, NY 10172
TELEPHONE:	212-773-3000
FAX:	212-773-1959
PRINCIPAL(S):	Over 2,000 partners
NUMBER OF YEARS	
IN BUSINESS:	Over 60
INDUSTRIES	
SPECIALIZED IN:	Manufacturing
	Financial services
	Wholesale/distribution
	Retailing
	Insurance
	Construction
	Hospitality
	Health care
MINIMUM CLIENT SIZE:	$2 million
MAXIMUM CLIENT SIZE:	No maximum
FEE STRUCTURE:	Hourly
SUCCESS BONUS:	No
EQUITY PARTICIPATION:	No
CLIENT REFERENCES:	
LENGTH OF TYPICAL	
ASSIGNMENT:	3–18 months
BRANCH OFFICE(S):	150 South Wacker Drive
	Chicago, IL 60606
	One North Charles Street
	Baltimore, MD 21201

NAME:	Executive Sounding Board Associates, Inc.
ADDRESS:	Public Ledger Building, Suite 1025 Philadelphia, PA 19106
TELEPHONE:	215-592-9880
FAX:	215-592-0639
PRINCIPAL(S):	Martin I. Katz, President Neil E. Leary, Senior Vice President Marc D. Feldman, Vice President
NUMBER OF YEARS IN BUSINESS:	13
INDUSTRIES SPECIALIZED IN:	Various
MINIMUM CLIENT SIZE:	No minimum
MAXIMUM CLIENT SIZE:	No limit
FEE STRUCTURE:	Hourly
SUCCESS BONUS:	No
EQUITY PARTICIPATION:	No
CLIENT REFERENCES:	Confidential
LENGTH OF TYPICAL ASSIGNMENT:	2–6 months
BRANCH OFFICE(S):	ESBA Capital Group, Inc. Court Square Building, Suite 800 200 E. Lexington Street Baltimore, MD 21202

NAME:	Executrex International, Inc.
ADDRESS:	440 South Main Street
	Briar Ridge Plaza
	Milltown, NJ 08850
TELEPHONE:	201-390-4202
FAX:	201-390-4202
PRINCIPAL(S):	Gary A. Griffin
	Dr. Jerry T. Justus, Ph.D
NUMBER OF YEARS IN BUSINESS:	5
INDUSTRIES SPECIALIZED IN:	Health care/medical
	High-tech
	Manufacturing
MINIMUM CLIENT SIZE:	$3 million
MAXIMUM CLIENT SIZE:	$140 million
FEE STRUCTURE:	Hourly (flat in some cases)
SUCCESS BONUS:	Yes
EQUITY PARTICIPATION:	Yes
CLIENT REFERENCES:	N.A.
LENGTH OF TYPICAL ASSIGNMENT:	3–24 months
BRANCH OFFICE(S):	2101 East Broadway, Suite 28
	Tempe, AZ 85282

NAME:	Frank Federer Associates
ADDRESS:	370 East Sunset
	San Antonio, TX 78209
TELEPHONE:	512-822-9501
FAX:	
PRINCIPAL(S):	Frank Federer
NUMBER OF YEARS	
IN BUSINESS:	5
INDUSTRIES	
SPECIALIZED IN:	Manufacturing
	High-tech
	Service
MINIMUM CLIENT SIZE:	$5 million
MAXIMUM CLIENT SIZE:	$50 million
FEE STRUCTURE:	Hourly or flat
SUCCESS BONUS:	Yes
EQUITY PARTICIPATION:	No
CLIENT REFERENCES:	Available upon request
LENGTH OF TYPICAL	
ASSIGNMENT:	4–12 months
BRANCH OFFICE(S):	None

NAME:	The Finley Group, Incorporated
ADDRESS:	1650 Charlotte Plaza Charlotte, NC 28244
TELEPHONE:	704-375-7542
FAX:	704-342-0879
PRINCIPAL(S):	Timothy F. Finley Robert R. Dunn R. Carter Pate Wayne T. Stephens
NUMBER OF YEARS IN BUSINESS:	5
INDUSTRIES SPECIALIZED IN:	Retail Distribution Certain manufacturing
MINIMUM CLIENT SIZE:	$6 million
MAXIMUM CLIENT SIZE:	$500 million
FEE STRUCTURE:	Hourly
SUCCESS BONUS:	Yes
EQUITY PARTICIPATION:	No
CLIENT REFERENCES:	Baddour, Incorporated Memphis, TN Forshaw Industries Charlotte, NC
LENGTH OF TYPICAL ASSIGNMENT:	8 months
BRANCH OFFICE(S):	1201 Main Street Dallas, TX

NAME:	The First National Bank of Chicago
ADDRESS:	Three First National Plaza, Suite 0610 Chicago, IL 60670
TELEPHONE:	312-732-1227
FAX:	312-732-7483
PRINCIPAL(S):	Lawrence E. Fox Peter B. Sweet Geoffrey R. McConnell
NUMBER OF YEARS IN BUSINESS:	15
INDUSTRIES SPECIALIZED IN:	All
MINIMUM CLIENT SIZE:	$50 million
MAXIMUM CLIENT SIZE:	No limit
FEE STRUCTURE:	Flat
SUCCESS BONUS:	Yes
EQUITY PARTICIPATION:	Yes
CLIENT REFERENCES:	Abercrombie & Fitch Allied Technology/Technology Service Zapata
LENGTH OF TYPICAL ASSIGNMENT:	6 months
BRANCH OFFICE(S):	1150 S.E. King Avenue Portland, OR 97200
	555 S. Flower Street, 33rd Floor Los Angeles, CA 90071-2487
	153 W. 51 Street, 8th Floor New York, NY 10019

NAME:	Stanley B. Frieze Company
ADDRESS:	45 Shore Park Road
	Great Neck, NY 11023
TELEPHONE:	516-487-1959
FAX:	516-829-5993
PRINCIPAL(S):	Stanley B. Frieze, President
NUMBER OF YEARS IN BUSINESS:	12
INDUSTRIES SPECIALIZED IN:	All industries except retailing and real estate
MINIMUM CLIENT SIZE:	$10 million
MAXIMUM CLIENT SIZE:	$250–$300 million
FEE STRUCTURE:	Project fee
SUCCESS BONUS:	No
EQUITY PARTICIPATION:	No
CLIENT REFERENCES:	Footwear Manufacturer Toronto, Canada
	Furniture Manufacturer New York
	Housewares Distributor New Jersey
LENGTH OF TYPICAL ASSIGNMENT:	Diagnostic Assessment: 3–8 weeks
	Interim Management: 3 months to 3 years
BRANCH OFFICE(S):	None

NAME:	Gayl & Gutnick, Inc.
	J. C. Gayl, Inc.
ADDRESS:	P.O. Box 1128
	Chadds Ford, PA 19317
TELEPHONE:	215-388-2000
FAX:	215-388-1208
PRINCIPAL(S):	Jonathan F. Gayl
NUMBER OF YEARS IN BUSINESS:	15
INDUSTRIES SPECIALIZED IN:	Recycling
	Paper
	Health/medical services
	Commercial real property
	Manufacturing
	Wholesale distribution
MINIMUM CLIENT SIZE:	$1 million
MAXIMUM CLIENT SIZE:	$100 million
FEE STRUCTURE:	Varies
SUCCESS BONUS:	Sometimes
EQUITY PARTICIPATION:	Sometimes
CLIENT REFERENCES:	Confidential
LENGTH OF TYPICAL ASSIGNMENT:	6 months to long term
BRANCH OFFICE(S):	None

NAME:	A. E. Getzler & Co., Inc.
ADDRESS:	295 Madison Avenue
	New York, NY 10017
TELEPHONE:	212-697-3616
FAX:	212-370-5822
PRINCIPAL(S):	A. E. Getzler
NUMBER OF YEARS	
IN BUSINESS:	20
INDUSTRIES	
SPECIALIZED IN:	All except trucking and
	agriculture
MINIMUM CLIENT SIZE:	$8 million
MAXIMUM CLIENT SIZE:	$200 million
FEE STRUCTURE:	Hourly
SUCCESS BONUS:	On occasion
EQUITY PARTICIPATION:	No
CLIENT REFERENCES:	None
LENGTH OF TYPICAL	
ASSIGNMENT:	3 weeks to 2 years
BRANCH OFFICE(S):	None

NAME:	Gilbert Thomas, Ltd.
ADDRESS:	621 N.W. 33rd Street, #330
	Boca Raton, FL 33487
TELEPHONE:	407-994-9797
FAX:	407-997-9557
PRINCIPAL(S):	Melvin Gilbert
	Thomas Mitlelsteadt
NUMBER OF YEARS IN BUSINESS:	2
INDUSTRIES SPECIALIZED IN:	Manufacturing
	Retail/wholesale
	Electronics
	Financial
MINIMUM CLIENT SIZE:	$1 million
MAXIMUM CLIENT SIZE:	$15 million
FEE STRUCTURE:	Hourly
SUCCESS BONUS:	No
EQUITY PARTICIPATION:	No
CLIENT REFERENCES:	Grove Optical
	Boca Raton, FL
	Logical Devices
	Ft. Lauderdale, FL
	Graphics Plus of Florida
	Delray Beach, FL
LENGTH OF TYPICAL ASSIGNMENT:	6 months to 1 year
BRANCH OFFICE(S):	None

NAME:	Gillings & Company
ADDRESS:	721 Washington Avenue, Suite 504
	Bay City, MI 48707-0650
TELEPHONE:	517-895-5818
FAX:	517-895-5112
PRINCIPAL(S):	Donald W. Gillings
NUMBER OF YEARS IN BUSINESS:	10
INDUSTRIES SPECIALIZED IN:	Agriculture
	Manufacturing
	Distribution
	Retail
MINIMUM CLIENT SIZE:	No minimum
MAXIMUM CLIENT SIZE:	No limit
FEE STRUCTURE:	Varies
SUCCESS BONUS:	No
EQUITY PARTICIPATION:	Occasionally
CLIENT REFERENCES:	Confidential
LENGTH OF TYPICAL ASSIGNMENT:	6 months
BRANCH OFFICE(S):	None

NAME:	Glass & Associates, Inc.
ADDRESS:	4571 Stephen Circle N.W., Suite 130
	Canton, OH 44709
TELEPHONE:	216-494-3252
FAX:	216-494-2420
PRINCIPAL(S):	Kenneth E. Glass, President
NUMBER OF YEARS IN BUSINESS:	6
INDUSTRIES SPECIALIZED IN:	Manufacturing
	Service
	Distribution
	Transportation
MINIMUM CLIENT SIZE:	$10 million
MAXIMUM CLIENT SIZE:	$2 billion
FEE STRUCTURE:	Hourly
SUCCESS BONUS:	Yes
EQUITY PARTICIPATION:	Yes
CLIENT REFERENCES:	McNally, Inc.
	Pittsburgh, PA
	Knudsen Foods
	Los Angeles, CA
	Monon Corporation (Evans Transportation)
	Monon, IN
LENGTH OF TYPICAL ASSIGNMENT:	9–12 months
BRANCH OFFICE(S):	None

NAME:	Grandwest & Associates
ADDRESS:	945 East Paces Ferry Road, Suite 2525
	Atlanta, GA 30326
TELEPHONE:	404-841-9500
FAX:	404-841-0374
PRINCIPAL(S):	Arch D. Granda
NUMBER OF YEARS IN BUSINESS:	2
INDUSTRIES SPECIALIZED IN:	All except high-tech, environmental, real estate, and communications
MINIMUM CLIENT SIZE:	$5 million
MAXIMUM CLIENT SIZE:	$300 million
FEE STRUCTURE:	Hourly plus retainer
SUCCESS BONUS:	Yes
EQUITY PARTICIPATION:	Yes (also provides equity investment)
CLIENT REFERENCES:	American Directory Co.
LENGTH OF TYPICAL ASSIGNMENT:	4 to 8 months
BRANCH OFFICE(S):	None

NAME:	Grisanti Galef & Goldress
ADDRESS:	19701 Hamilton Ave.
	Torrance, CA 90502
TELEPHONE:	213-532-9990
	404-396-7557
FAX:	213-329-8420
PRINCIPAL(S):	Marvin Davis
	Jerry Goldress
NUMBER OF YEARS IN BUSINESS:	40
INDUSTRIES SPECIALIZED IN:	Retail
	Manufacturing
	Service
	All types
MINIMUM CLIENT SIZE:	$5 million
MAXIMUM CLIENT SIZE:	Over $2 billion
FEE STRUCTURE:	Weekly or monthly
SUCCESS BONUS:	Yes
EQUITY PARTICIPATION:	Depends on company size and our role
CLIENT REFERENCES:	L. B. Foster Corporation
	Pittsburgh, PA
	Wherehouse Entertainment, Inc.
	Los Angeles, CA
	Stoody Corporation
	Los Angeles, CA
	Folger Adams Corporation
	Lemont, IL
LENGTH OF TYPICAL ASSIGNMENT:	6 months
BRANCH OFFICE(S):	80 Seville Chase
	Atlanta, GA 30328
	San Francisco
	Detroit
	Miami
	Chicago

NAME:	Gruntal & Company, Incorporated
ADDRESS:	14 Wall Street
	New York City, NY 10005
TELEPHONE:	212-225-4256
FAX:	212-608-3290
PRINCIPAL(S):	Michael J. Koblitz, Managing
	Director
NUMBER OF YEARS	
IN BUSINESS:	Firm—110; MJK—20
INDUSTRIES	
SPECIALIZED IN:	All
MINIMUM CLIENT SIZE:	$50 million
MAXIMUM CLIENT SIZE:	None
FEE STRUCTURE:	Flat
SUCCESS BONUS:	Sometimes
EQUITY PARTICIPATION:	Sometimes
CLIENT REFERENCES:	Confidential
LENGTH OF TYPICAL	
ASSIGNMENT:	$2\frac{1}{2}$ years
BRANCH OFFICE(S):	35 nationwide

NAME:	Hamstreet, Stumbaugh & Co.
ADDRESS:	One S.W. Columbia, Suite 1000 Portland, OR 97258
TELEPHONE:	503-299-6633
FAX:	503-323-7330
PRINCIPAL(S):	Clyde Hamstreet Brent Stumbaugh
NUMBER OF YEARS IN BUSINESS:	5
INDUSTRIES SPECIALIZED IN:	Manufacturing Broadcasting High-tech service distributor Food processing
MINIMUM CLIENT SIZE:	$5 million
MAXIMUM CLIENT SIZE:	No limit
FEE STRUCTURE:	Hourly or incentive
SUCCESS BONUS:	Sometimes
EQUITY PARTICIPATION:	Occasionally
CLIENT REFERENCES:	Metheus (Al Kennedy, Attorney) Ft. Vancouver Broadcasting (Heritage Media Corp.) McCormick & Baxter
LENGTH OF TYPICAL ASSIGNMENT:	6–9 months
BRANCH OFFICE(S):	Hamstreet, Stumbaugh & Co. Newport, OR

NAME:	Hankin & Company
ADDRESS:	12400 Wilshire Boulevard, Suite 320
	Los Angeles, CA 90025
TELEPHONE:	213-207-4466
FAX:	213-207-8565
PRINCIPAL(S):	Rock Hankin, Senior Partner
	Elden Westhusing, Partner
NUMBER OF YEARS IN BUSINESS:	6
INDUSTRIES SPECIALIZED IN:	Manufacturing
	Retail
	Wholesale
	Distribution
	Service
MINIMUM CLIENT SIZE:	$4 million
MAXIMUM CLIENT SIZE:	$300 million
FEE STRUCTURE:	Depends upon situation
SUCCESS BONUS:	Yes
EQUITY PARTICIPATION:	No
CLIENT REFERENCES:	Data Design Laboratories California
	Manna Pro California
	Bridgeport Brass Indiana
LENGTH OF TYPICAL ASSIGNMENT:	3 months
BRANCH OFFICE(S):	None

NAME:	Heller Equity Capital Corp.
ADDRESS:	Turnaround Investment Division
	200 North LaSalle Street
	Chicago, IL 60601
TELEPHONE:	312-621-7340
FAX:	312-621-7208
PRINCIPAL(S):	Erwin A. Marks, Managing Director
	Colin P. Cross, Principal
	James A. Skelton, Principal
NUMBER OF YEARS IN BUSINESS:	1
INDUSTRIES SPECIALIZED IN:	Value-added or niche manufacturers, distributors, and service companies; avoids high-tech or heavily regulated industries
MINIMUM CLIENT SIZE:	$25 million
MAXIMUM CLIENT SIZE:	$250 million plus
FEE STRUCTURE:	N.A.
SUCCESS BONUS:	N.A.
EQUITY PARTICIPATION:	Makes equity investments in troubled companies
CLIENT REFERENCES:	N.A.
LENGTH OF TYPICAL ASSIGNMENT:	Average holding period: 3 years
BRANCH OFFICE(S):	42 offices worldwide

NAME:	High-Point Schaer
ADDRESS:	888 Seventh Avenue, Suite 202A
	New York City, NY 10106
TELEPHONE:	212-315-5860
FAX:	212-315-5663
PRINCIPAL(S):	Joel K. Pondelik
NUMBER OF YEARS IN BUSINESS:	150
INDUSTRIES SPECIALIZED IN:	Capital projects
	Construction
	Engineering
	Energy
	Transportation
	Infrastructure
	Leisure & tourism
	Urban & regional development
	Manufacturing in general
MINIMUM CLIENT SIZE:	$5 million
MAXIMUM CLIENT SIZE:	$2 billion
FEE STRUCTURE:	Hourly
SUCCESS BONUS:	Often
EQUITY PARTICIPATION:	No
CLIENT REFERENCES:	NR
LENGTH OF TYPICAL ASSIGNMENT:	1 year

BRANCH OFFICE(S):

International:
London
Abu Dhabi
Hong Kong
Singapore
Taipei
Wellington, New Zealand

United States:
Alexandria, VA
Boston, MA
Laconia, NH
San Diego, CA
Clearwater, FL
Williamsburg, VA
Los Angeles, CA
San Francisco, CA
Irvine, CA
Phoenix, AZ
Seattle, WA
Dallas, TX
Roseland, TX
New York, NY
Philadelphia, PA

NAME:	Holtz Rubenstein & Co
ADDRESS:	445 Broad Hollow Road
	Melville, New York 11747
TELEPHONE:	516-752-7400
FAX:	516-752-1742
PRINCIPAL(S):	William J. Holtz
	Frank Candia
	Alan E. Weiner
	Howard Weiner
	Daniel A. Segal
	Paul Rubenstein
NUMBER OF YEARS IN BUSINESS:	15
INDUSTRIES SPECIALIZED IN:	Manufacturing
	Distribution
	Construction
	Real estate
	Non-profit organizations
MINIMUM CLIENT SIZE:	$3 million
MAXIMUM CLIENT SIZE:	$100 million
FEE STRUCTURE:	Hourly
SUCCESS BONUS:	If appropriate
EQUITY PARTICIPATION:	No
CLIENT REFERENCES:	NR
LENGTH OF TYPICAL ASSIGNMENT:	4 to 8 weeks
BRANCH OFFICE(S):	None

NAME:	Honig & Associates, Inc.
ADDRESS:	63 Neshube Road
	Waban, MA 02168
TELEPHONE:	617-244-7650
FAX:	617-244-8062
PRINCIPAL(S):	Ross G. Honig
NUMBER OF YEARS IN BUSINESS:	10
INDUSTRIES SPECIALIZED IN:	Diversified
MINIMUM CLIENT SIZE:	$2 million
MAXIMUM CLIENT SIZE:	$300 million
FEE STRUCTURE:	Hourly
SUCCESS BONUS:	Yes
EQUITY PARTICIPATION:	No
CLIENT REFERENCES:	Superior Teltec, Inc.
	Atlanta, GA
	Louis McGerson Company, Inc.
	Middleboro, MA
	Arthur Blaun & Company
	Boston, MA
LENGTH OF TYPICAL ASSIGNMENT:	18 months to 1 year
BRANCH OFFICE(S):	None

NAME:	Horwath Consulting
ADDRESS:	1100 Louisiana,
	Suite 800
	Houston, TX 77002
TELEPHONE:	713-658-7071
FAX:	713-654-8835
PRINCIPAL(S):	Thomas Lattin plus 400 partners
	in 50 offices in major cities
NUMBER OF YEARS	
IN BUSINESS:	73
INDUSTRIES	
SPECIALIZED IN:	Hotels
	Health care
	Real estate
MINIMUM CLIENT SIZE:	No minimum
MAXIMUM CLIENT SIZE:	No maximum
FEE STRUCTURE:	Retainer plus hourly fee
SUCCESS BONUS:	When appropriate
EQUITY PARTICIPATION:	No
CLIENT REFERENCES:	Mayfair House
	Miami, FL
	Key Biscayne Hotel
	Miami, FL
	Tucson National
	Tucson, AZ
LENGTH OF TYPICAL	
ASSIGNMENT:	6 months to 1 year
BRANCH OFFICE(S):	50 major cities; listed in
	the telephone directory as
	Laventhol & Horwath.

NAME:	The Hospitality Source, Incorporated
ADDRESS:	P.O. Box 97 Lake Geneva, WI 53147
TELEPHONE:	414-248-8811
FAX:	414-248-3192
PRINCIPAL(S):	Don G. Willey Michael S. Wien Michael Harman
NUMBER OF YEARS IN BUSINESS:	18
INDUSTRIES SPECIALIZED IN:	Hotels, motels, and resorts
MINIMUM CLIENT SIZE:	$2 million
MAXIMUM CLIENT SIZE:	$20 million
FEE STRUCTURE:	Flat fee
SUCCESS BONUS:	No
EQUITY PARTICIPATION:	No
CLIENT REFERENCES:	Wells Fargo Realty 1222 Merit Drive Dallas, TX 75251
	Tara Hotels Fifty Braintree Hill Office Park Braintree, MA 02184
	JMB Realty Corporation 900 North Michigan Chicago, IL 60611
LENGTH OF TYPICAL ASSIGNMENT:	Diagnostic: 1 week Turnaround: 6 months to 1 year
BRANCH OFFICE(S):	1032 Crofton Court Highland Park, IL 60035 FAX: 708-674-1022

NAME:	I. M. Systems Group, Inc.
ADDRESS:	1401 Rockville Pike, Suite 110
	Rockville,MD 20852
TELEPHONE:	301-217-0300
FAX:	301-279-7926
PRINCIPAL(S):	Vance Y. Hum
	Jon Luther
NUMBER OF YEARS IN BUSINESS:	4
INDUSTRIES SPECIALIZED IN:	Professional services
	Technical services
	Food
	Property (resort, retail, commercial)
MINIMUM CLIENT SIZE:	$10 million
MAXIMUM CLIENT SIZE:	$100 million
FEE STRUCTURE:	Flexible
SUCCESS BONUS:	Yes
EQUITY PARTICIPATION:	Yes
CLIENT REFERENCES:	Centech
	Silver Spring, MD
	Benchmark Services
	Mentor, OH
LENGTH OF TYPICAL ASSIGNMENT:	3 months to 4 years
BRANCH OFFICE(S):	None

NAME:	Inglewood Associates, Inc.
ADDRESS:	1910 Cochran Road
	Manor Oak One, Suite 105
	Pittsburgh, PA 15220
TELEPHONE:	412-343-0126
FAX:	412-343-6957
PRINCIPAL(S):	Herb Ailes
	Mark DuMars
	John O'Brien
NUMBER OF YEARS IN BUSINESS:	7
INDUSTRIES SPECIALIZED IN:	Manufacturing
	Distribution
	Retail
	Service
MINIMUM CLIENT SIZE:	$8 million
MAXIMUM CLIENT SIZE:	$100 million
FEE STRUCTURE:	Hourly
SUCCESS BONUS:	Sometimes
EQUITY PARTICIPATION:	Yes
CLIENT REFERENCES:	Tactec Systems
	Meadowlands, PA
	Mathews Marble Manufacturing
	Pittsburgh, PA
	National Waterbeds, Inc.
	Harrisburg, PA
LENGTH OF TYPICAL ASSIGNMENT:	Analysis: 1–3 months
	Management: 2–3 years
BRANCH OFFICE(S):	14 Water Street
	Chagrin Falls, OH 44022

NAME:	Iowa Consulting, Inc.
ADDRESS:	100 Court Avenue, Suite 225
	Des Moines, IA 50309
TELEPHONE:	515-282-8019
FAX:	515-282-0325
PRINCIPAL(S):	Mark Esbeck
	Joe Bustin
NUMBER OF YEARS	
IN BUSINESS:	2
INDUSTRIES	
SPECIALIZED IN:	Manufacturing
	Communications
	Service
MINIMUM CLIENT SIZE:	$5 million
MAXIMUM CLIENT SIZE:	$25 million
FEE STRUCTURE:	Hourly or negotiable
SUCCESS BONUS:	Will consider
EQUITY PARTICIPATION:	Will consider
CLIENT REFERENCES:	Oak Cable
	Hurley, IA
	Shrivers, Inc.
	Corydon, IA
	Fairfield Aluminum
	Fairfield, IA
LENGTH OF TYPICAL	
ASSIGNMENT:	4–6 months
BRANCH OFFICE(S):	None

NAME:	JCi Consultants
ADDRESS:	P.O. Box 7051
	Lake Wylie, SC 29710
TELEPHONE:	803-831-7815
FAX:	803-831-2979
PRINCIPAL(S):	Charles Jaco
	J. E. Jaco
NUMBER OF YEARS IN BUSINESS:	14
INDUSTRIES SPECIALIZED IN:	Manufacturing
	Distribution
	Services
	Financial
MINIMUM CLIENT SIZE:	None (but $2.5 million/year)
MAXIMUM CLIENT SIZE:	None (but range upwards to $150 million)
FEE STRUCTURE:	Hourly
	By phase
	By job
SUCCESS BONUS:	Occasionally
EQUITY PARTICIPATION:	No
CLIENT REFERENCES:	Confidential; available only to serious prospects
LENGTH OF TYPICAL ASSIGNMENT:	12 weeks to 18 months
BRANCH OFFICE(S):	None

NAME:	D. A. James
	c/o Gas Company of New Mexico
ADDRESS:	2444 Louisiana Blvd., N.E.
	Albuquerque, NM 87110
TELEPHONE:	505-888-8704
FAX:	505-883-6211
PRINCIPAL(S):	D. A. James
NUMBER OF YEARS IN BUSINESS:	$2\frac{1}{2}$
INDUSTRIES SPECIALIZED IN:	Utilities
MINIMUM CLIENT SIZE:	N.A.
MAXIMUM CLIENT SIZE:	N.A.
FEE STRUCTURE:	N.A.
SUCCESS BONUS:	N.A.
EQUITY PARTICIPATION:	N.A.
CLIENT REFERENCES:	Gas Company of New Mexico
LENGTH OF TYPICAL ASSIGNMENT:	N.A.
BRANCH OFFICE(S):	None

NAME:	Johnston & Co.
ADDRESS:	355 W. Mitchell Street
	Manchester, NH 03103
TELEPHONE:	603-627-2434
FAX:	Call first
PRINCIPAL(S):	James W. Johnston
NUMBER OF YEARS IN BUSINESS:	4
INDUSTRIES SPECIALIZED IN:	Computer hardware
	Software
	Health care
	Biotechnology
	Communications
MINIMUM CLIENT SIZE:	No minimum
MAXIMUM CLIENT SIZE:	$50 million
FEE STRUCTURE:	Flat per month
SUCCESS BONUS:	Yes
EQUITY PARTICIPATION:	Sometimes
CLIENT REFERENCES:	Handi Van
	Lowell, MA
	Cadec System
	Londonderry, NH
	Aurora Technology
	Cambridge, MA
LENGTH OF TYPICAL ASSIGNMENT:	1 year
BRANCH OFFICE(S):	None

NAME:	KL Industries, Inc.
ADDRESS:	300 Broadacres Drive
	Bloomfield, NJ 07003
TELEPHONE:	201-893-1144
FAX:	201-893-1295
PRINCIPAL(S):	Fred Kann
	Owen Leonard
	Myron Bregman
NUMBER OF YEARS IN BUSINESS:	5
INDUSTRIES SPECIALIZED IN:	Manufacturing of electronics
	Electromechanical
MINIMUM CLIENT SIZE:	$15 million
MAXIMUM CLIENT SIZE:	$40 million
FEE STRUCTURE:	N.A.
SUCCESS BONUS:	N.A.
EQUITY PARTICIPATION:	N.A.
CLIENT REFERENCES:	EOG, Inc.
	Concair Rotron
LENGTH OF TYPICAL ASSIGNMENT:	Varies with assignment
BRANCH OFFICE(S):	None

NAME:	Kakde Group
ADDRESS:	1976 Tait Circle Road
	Dayton, OH 45429
TELEPHONE:	513-226-1900
FAX:	513-226-1623
PRINCIPAL(S):	Suhas Kakde
NUMBER OF YEARS IN BUSINESS:	10–12
INDUSTRIES SPECIALIZED IN:	Manufacturing
MINIMUM CLIENT SIZE:	$0.5 million
MAXIMUM CLIENT SIZE:	$25 million
FEE STRUCTURE:	Hourly or daily, unless project fee
SUCCESS BONUS:	No
EQUITY PARTICIPATION:	No
CLIENT REFERENCES:	Available upon request
LENGTH OF TYPICAL ASSIGNMENT:	6 months
	Diagnostic plan: 8–10 weeks
BRANCH OFFICE(S):	None

NAME:	A. T. Kearney
ADDRESS:	875 Third Avenue, 27th Floor New York, NY 10022
TELEPHONE:	212-751-7040
FAX:	212-751-1262
PRINCIPAL(S):	Numerous
NUMBER OF YEARS **IN BUSINESS:**	12
INDUSTRIES **SPECIALIZED IN:**	Manufacturing Wholesale Service businesses High-tech
MINIMUM CLIENT SIZE:	$20–50 million
MAXIMUM CLIENT SIZE:	$200 million
FEE STRUCTURE:	Flat or monthly
SUCCESS BONUS:	No
EQUITY PARTICIPATION:	No
CLIENT REFERENCES:	Confidential
LENGTH OF TYPICAL **ASSIGNMENT:**	2 months to 1 year or more

BRANCH OFFICE(S):   Chicago (World HQ)
                                      Amsterdam
                                      Atlanta
                                      Bebit
                                      Boston
                                      Brussels
                                      Cleveland
                                      Dallas
                                      Denver
                                      Dusseldorf
                                      London
                                      Los Angeles
                                      Madrid
                                      Milan
                                      Munich
                                      Paris
                                      San Francisco
                                      Stuttgart
                                      Tokyo
                                      Toronto
                                      Washington, DC

NAME:	Kellogg Corporation
ADDRESS:	26 West Dry Creek Circle
	Littleton, CO 80120
TELEPHONE:	303-794-1818
FAX:	303-797-6503
PRINCIPAL(S):	J. C. Kellogg
	Carl V. Carlson, Jr.
	William Dixon Shay, Jr.
NUMBER OF YEARS IN BUSINESS:	20
INDUSTRIES SPECIALIZED IN:	Construction
	Process plants
MINIMUM CLIENT SIZE:	$5 million
MAXIMUM CLIENT SIZE:	N.A.
FEE STRUCTURE:	Hourly
SUCCESS BONUS:	Yes
EQUITY PARTICIPATION:	No
CLIENT REFERENCES:	Confidential
LENGTH OF TYPICAL ASSIGNMENT:	3–24 months
BRANCH OFFICE(S):	Minneapolis
	San Diego
	Orlando
	Seattle

NAME:	Kibel, Green, Inc.
ADDRESS:	2001 Wilshire Blvd., Suite 426
	Santa Monica, CA 90403
TELEPHONE:	213-829-0255
FAX:	213-453-6324
PRINCIPAL(S):	Harvey R. Kibel
	Steven Green
NUMBER OF YEARS	
IN BUSINESS:	7
INDUSTRIES	
SPECIALIZED IN:	Real estate
	Distribution
	Manufacturing
MINIMUM CLIENT SIZE:	$6 million
MAXIMUM CLIENT SIZE:	$500 million
FEE STRUCTURE:	Hourly or flat
SUCCESS BONUS:	Sometimes
EQUITY PARTICIPATION:	Sometimes
CLIENT REFERENCES:	Marcy, Inc.
	Beehive International
	Snyder/Diamond
LENGTH OF TYPICAL	
ASSIGNMENT:	6 months
BRANCH OFFICE(S):	None

NAME:	Kurt Salmon Associates, Inc.
ADDRESS:	1355 Peachtree Street, Suite 900
	Atlanta, GA 30309
TELEPHONE:	404-892-0321
FAX:	404-898-9590
PRINCIPAL(S):	David Linch, et al.
NUMBER OF YEARS IN BUSINESS:	NR
INDUSTRIES SPECIALIZED IN:	Furniture, carpet, other home furnishings
	Apparel
	Textile
	Retail
MINIMUM CLIENT SIZE:	$25 million
MAXIMUM CLIENT SIZE:	None
FEE STRUCTURE:	Hourly or flat
SUCCESS BONUS:	Yes, occasionally
EQUITY PARTICIPATION:	No
CLIENT REFERENCES:	Confidential
LENGTH OF TYPICAL ASSIGNMENT:	3+ months
BRANCH OFFICE(S):	New York
	Los Angeles
	Nashville
	Princeton
	United Kingdom
	Hong Kong
	Singapore

NAME:	The LEK Partnership
ADDRESS:	101 Federal Street
	Boston, MA 02110
TELEPHONE:	617-951-9500
FAX:	617-951-9392
PRINCIPAL(S):	*Boston*:
	James A. Lawrence, Chairman
	Timothy J. Scholes, Partner
	London:
	Iain Evans, Partner
	Peter Johnson, Partner
	Chris Recny, Partner
	Steve Williams, Partner
	Peter Hansen, Partner
	Jayne Almond, Partner
	Jonathan Hale, Partner
	James Watt, Partner
	Michael Kennedy, Partner
	Los Angeles:
	Scott Shlecter, Partner
	Francis Hawkings, Partner
	Australia:
	Tim Sims, Partner
NUMBER OF YEARS IN BUSINESS:	15
INDUSTRIES SPECIALIZED IN:	Manufacturing
MINIMUM CLIENT SIZE:	$50 million
MAXIMUM CLIENT SIZE:	No limit
FEE STRUCTURE:	Hourly
SUCCESS BONUS:	No
EQUITY PARTICIPATION:	No
CLIENT REFERENCES:	Confidential
LENGTH OF TYPICAL ASSIGNMENT:	3 months

BRANCH OFFICE(S):

The Adelphi Building
1-11 John Adam Street
London WC2n 6BW

12100 Wilshire Blvd.,
    Suite 1000
Los Angeles, CA 90025

Level 10
155 George Street
Sydney
NSW 2000 Australia

Possart Strasse 22
8000 Munich 80

18 Boulevard Malesherbes
75008 Paris, France

NAME:	Lambda Group, Incorporated
ADDRESS:	217 South Orange Street, #2
	Glendale, CA 91204
TELEPHONE:	818-500-9877
FAX:	818-500-9301
PRINCIPAL(S):	T. Liam Leahy
	Jonathan Rich
	Eric Malm
NUMBER OF YEARS	
IN BUSINESS:	9
INDUSTRIES	
SPECIALIZED IN:	Mass media
	Publishing
	Wholesale distribution
	Service
	Real estate
MINIMUM CLIENT SIZE:	$0.5 million
MAXIMUM CLIENT SIZE:	$200 million
FEE STRUCTURE:	Hourly
SUCCESS BONUS:	Usually not
EQUITY PARTICIPATION:	If client requests this
CLIENT REFERENCES:	Confidential
LENGTH OF TYPICAL	
ASSIGNMENT:	Evaluation/plan/upturn:
	2–3 weeks
	Turnaround management:
	4–6 months
BRANCH OFFICE(S):	1250 Rogers Street, Suite C
	Clearwater, FL 34616
	2651 West 111th Street
	Chicago, IL 60655
	301-531 Yates Street
	Victoria, British Columbia
	V8W 1K7 Canada

NAME:	Locke Venture Management, Incorporated
ADDRESS:	595 East Illinois Road
	Lake Forest, IL 60045
TELEPHONE:	708-295-2400
FAX:	708-295-0983
PRINCIPAL(S):	E. L. (Buzz) Walsh
	William F. Geiger
	6 associates
NUMBER OF YEARS IN BUSINESS:	13
INDUSTRIES SPECIALIZED IN:	Growth companies
	Venture capital portfolio companies
MINIMUM CLIENT SIZE:	No minimum
MAXIMUM CLIENT SIZE:	No maximum
FEE STRUCTURE:	Typically flat
SUCCESS BONUS:	Where possible
EQUITY PARTICIPATION:	Where possible
CLIENT REFERENCES:	Confidential
LENGTH OF TYPICAL ASSIGNMENT:	18 months
BRANCH OFFICE(S):	None

NAME:	Lustig Wagner Associates
ADDRESS:	232 Juniper Circle East
	Lawrence, NY 11559-1914
TELEPHONE:	516-239-0611
FAX:	516-239-0813
PRINCIPAL(S):	Joel W. Lustig
NUMBER OF YEARS IN BUSINESS:	7
INDUSTRIES SPECIALIZED IN:	Manufacturing
	Distribution
	Services
	Energy
MINIMUM CLIENT SIZE:	$3.5 million
MAXIMUM CLIENT SIZE:	No limit
FEE STRUCTURE:	Case by case, typically flat
SUCCESS BONUS:	Case by case
EQUITY PARTICIPATION:	Case by case
CLIENT REFERENCES:	Confidential
LENGTH OF TYPICAL ASSIGNMENT:	3 months to 1 year
BRANCH OFFICE(S):	None

NAME:	MESA Corporation
ADDRESS:	9750 Miramar Road, #160
	San Diego, CA 92196
TELEPHONE:	619-549-2212
FAX:	619-549-2999
PRINCIPAL(S):	Thomas C. Lieberman
NUMBER OF YEARS IN BUSINESS:	5
INDUSTRIES SPECIALIZED IN:	Manufacturing
	Retail
	Wholesale
	Service
MINIMUM CLIENT SIZE:	$1 million
MAXIMUM CLIENT SIZE:	$25 million
FEE STRUCTURE:	Flat
SUCCESS BONUS:	Yes
EQUITY PARTICIPATION:	Sometimes
CLIENT REFERENCES:	Confidential
LENGTH OF TYPICAL ASSIGNMENT:	3 months to 1 year
BRANCH OFFICE(S):	Irvine, CA

NAME:	MacKenzie, Hovey & Associates, Inc.
ADDRESS:	695 S. Colorado Blvd. #480 Denver, CO 80222
TELEPHONE:	303-871-9100
FAX:	303-722-7281
PRINCIPAL(S):	William S. MacKenzie Christopher W. Hovey
NUMBER OF YEARS IN BUSINESS:	9
INDUSTRIES SPECIALIZED IN:	Manufacturing Real estate
MINIMUM CLIENT SIZE:	$10 million
MAXIMUM CLIENT SIZE:	$500 million
FEE STRUCTURE:	Hourly or daily
SUCCESS BONUS:	On occasion
EQUITY PARTICIPATION:	On occasion
CLIENT REFERENCES:	Confidential (but available with prior permission)
LENGTH OF TYPICAL ASSIGNMENT:	18 months
BRANCH OFFICE(S):	None

NAME:	Bob Makarowski & Associates, Inc.
ADDRESS:	301 East 85th Street New York, NY 10028
TELEPHONE:	212-628-1648
FAX:	212-628-1648
PRINCIPAL(S):	Bob Makarowski Philip Silverstein Alex J. Castro
NUMBER OF YEARS IN BUSINESS:	9
INDUSTRIES SPECIALIZED IN:	Banking Brokerage Investment banking Public relations Advertising
MINIMUM CLIENT SIZE:	$0.5 million
MAXIMUM CLIENT SIZE:	$10,000,000
FEE STRUCTURE:	Hourly
SUCCESS BONUS:	At times
EQUITY PARTICIPATION:	At times
CLIENT REFERENCES:	Citibank Management Services Westpac Banking Sydney Manufacturers Hanover Trust
LENGTH OF TYPICAL ASSIGNMENT:	8 months
BRANCH OFFICE(S):	None

NAME:	Management & Investment Group
ADDRESS:	6500 Depot Drive
	Waco, TX 76712
TELEPHONE:	817-776-6550
FAX:	817-753-7133
PRINCIPAL(S):	Terry W. Stevens
	Eugene C. Bredthauer
NUMBER OF YEARS IN BUSINESS:	2
INDUSTRIES SPECIALIZED IN:	Manufacturing
	Wholesale
MINIMUM CLIENT SIZE:	$1 million
MAXIMUM CLIENT SIZE:	$10 million
FEE STRUCTURE:	Flat
SUCCESS BONUS:	Yes
EQUITY PARTICIPATION:	Yes
CLIENT REFERENCES:	Amaco Products
	First Title Co.
	Triple S Sales
LENGTH OF TYPICAL ASSIGNMENT:	6 months to 1 year
BRANCH OFFICE(S):	None

NAME:	Management Assistants
ADDRESS:	702 Washington Street, #124
	Marina del Ray, CA 90292
TELEPHONE:	213-306-5774
FAX:	
PRINCIPAL(S):	Joe Curtin
NUMBER OF YEARS	
IN BUSINESS:	5
INDUSTRIES	
SPECIALIZED IN:	Manufacturing
	Service
MINIMUM CLIENT SIZE:	$5 million
MAXIMUM CLIENT SIZE:	$1 billion
FEE STRUCTURE:	The projected number of hours
	are listed in the project fee
SUCCESS BONUS:	Yes
EQUITY PARTICIPATION:	No
CLIENT REFERENCES:	Ashley Drew & Northern
	Crossett, AK
	Schwab's
	Oklahoma City, OK
	Wavelength
	El Segundo, CA
LENGTH OF TYPICAL	
ASSIGNMENT:	1 month
BRANCH OFFICE(S):	None

NAME:	Management Control Services
ADDRESS:	1645 Stanmore Drive
	Pleasant Hill, CA 94523-2156
TELEPHONE:	415-676-2010
FAX:	None
PRINCIPAL(S):	William R. Brink
NUMBER OF YEARS IN BUSINESS:	NR
INDUSTRIES SPECIALIZED IN:	NR
MINIMUM CLIENT SIZE:	NR
MAXIMUM CLIENT SIZE:	NR
FEE STRUCTURE:	NR
SUCCESS BONUS:	NR
EQUITY PARTICIPATION:	NR
CLIENT REFERENCES:	NR
LENGTH OF TYPICAL ASSIGNMENT:	NR
BRANCH OFFICE(S):	None

NAME:	Management Resource Partners
ADDRESS:	36 Irving Avenue
	Atherton, CA 94027
TELEPHONE:	415-321-2008
FAX:	415-328-4715
PRINCIPAL(S):	William Blaney
	Richard Baker
	Herbert Elliott
	Bernard Gutow
	Robert Jenkins
	Michael Ramelot
	John Roberts
	Jay Slaybaugh
	James Tucker
	Geoffrey Winkler
NUMBER OF YEARS IN BUSINESS:	10
INDUSTRIES SPECIALIZED IN:	Manufacturing (high-tech, low-tech)
	Distribution
	Specialty retail
MINIMUM CLIENT SIZE:	$25 million
MAXIMUM CLIENT SIZE:	$250 million
FEE STRUCTURE:	Estimated project cost
SUCCESS BONUS:	Yes
EQUITY PARTICIPATION:	Yes
CLIENT REFERENCES:	Inflated Products
	Williamstown, MA
	Laguna Manufacturing
	Irvine, CA
	Grandma Foods
	Portland, OR
LENGTH OF TYPICAL ASSIGNMENT:	6 months to several years
BRANCH OFFICE(S):	1824 Port Sheffield Place
	Newport Beach, CA 92660

NAME:	Doland C. Maner, Jr.
ADDRESS:	3145 Geary Blvd., Suite 031
	San Francisco, CA 94118
TELEPHONE:	415-773-3905
FAX:	415-752-3556 or 415-751-0947
PRINCIPAL(S):	Doland C. Maner, Jr.
NUMBER OF YEARS IN BUSINESS:	4
INDUSTRIES SPECIALIZED IN:	Wholesale
	Distribution
	Service operations
MINIMUM CLIENT SIZE:	$1 million
MAXIMUM CLIENT SIZE:	$10 million
FEE STRUCTURE:	Hourly
SUCCESS BONUS:	No
EQUITY PARTICIPATION:	No
CLIENT REFERENCES:	Confidential
LENGTH OF TYPICAL ASSIGNMENT:	1 week to 4 years
BRANCH OFFICE(S):	None

NAME:	Maxey International
ADDRESS:	P.O. Box 8804
	Roanoke, VA 24014
TELEPHONE:	703-345-8796
FAX:	703-982-8796
PRINCIPAL(S):	L. Keith Maxey
	Charles L. Haywood
NUMBER OF YEARS IN BUSINESS:	7
INDUSTRIES SPECIALIZED IN:	Furniture
	General merchandise
	Consumer products
MINIMUM CLIENT SIZE:	Case by case
MAXIMUM CLIENT SIZE:	Case by case
FEE STRUCTURE:	Case by case
SUCCESS BONUS:	Case by case
EQUITY PARTICIPATION:	Case by case
CLIENT REFERENCES:	High Point Furniture Industries
	Diversified Resources, Incorporated
	Virco Manufacturing
LENGTH OF TYPICAL ASSIGNMENT:	30–90 days
BRANCH OFFICE(S):	Maxey International
	P.O. Box 2076
	Southern Pines, NC 28387

NAME:	McLaughlin Associates, Inc.
ADDRESS:	2 Wall Street, Suite 503
	New York, NY 10005
TELEPHONE:	212-608-5560
FAX:	None
PRINCIPAL(S):	Charles W. McLaughlin
	Patricia A. Meding
NUMBER OF YEARS	
IN BUSINESS:	5
INDUSTRIES	
SPECIALIZED IN:	Health care,
	High-tech,
	Transportation
	Telecommunications
MINIMUM CLIENT SIZE:	$500,000
MAXIMUM CLIENT SIZE:	$5 million
FEE STRUCTURE:	Retainer
SUCCESS BONUS:	Yes
EQUITY PARTICIPATION:	Yes
CLIENT REFERENCES:	Confidential
LENGTH OF TYPICAL	
ASSIGNMENT:	6 months to 3 years
BRANCH OFFICE(S):	None

NAME:	McShane & Company
ADDRESS:	12912 Gent Road
	Reisterstown, MD 21136
TELEPHONE:	301-560-0077
FAX:	301-560-2718
PRINCIPAL(S):	Thomas P. McShane
NUMBER OF YEARS IN BUSINESS:	4
INDUSTRIES SPECIALIZED IN:	Distribution
	Manufacturing
	Service
MINIMUM CLIENT SIZE:	$1 million
MAXIMUM CLIENT SIZE:	$200 million
FEE STRUCTURE:	Hourly
SUCCESS BONUS:	Sometimes
EQUITY PARTICIPATION:	Rarely
CLIENT REFERENCES:	Confidential
LENGTH OF TYPICAL ASSIGNMENT:	4 months
BRANCH OFFICE(S):	None

NAME:	James V. McTevia & Associates, Inc.
ADDRESS:	18161 East Eight Mile Road East Detroit, MI 48021
TELEPHONE:	313-774-5580
FAX:	313-774-7098
PRINCIPAL(S):	James V. McTevia, President John D. Dupes, Vice President Joanne J. Vancour, Assistant Vice President
NUMBER OF YEARS IN BUSINESS:	31
INDUSTRIES SPECIALIZED IN:	All industries
MINIMUM CLIENT SIZE:	$10 million
MAXIMUM CLIENT SIZE:	$250 million
FEE STRUCTURE:	Hourly
SUCCESS BONUS:	No
EQUITY PARTICIPATION:	No
CLIENT REFERENCES:	Michigan Baptist Homes Bloomfield Savings & Loan Autodynamics Corporation of America
LENGTH OF TYPICAL ASSIGNMENT:	6 months to 1 year
BRANCH OFFICE(S):	1555 Palm Beach Lakes Blvd., Suite 1650 West Palm Beach, FL 33401

NAME:	Minter, Joseph and Thornhill
ADDRESS:	811 Barton Springs Road, Suite 800 Austin, TX 78704
TELEPHONE:	512-478-1075
FAX:	512-478-5838
PRINCIPAL(S):	William C. Davidson
NUMBER OF YEARS IN BUSINESS:	14
INDUSTRIES SPECIALIZED IN:	Real estate Retail sales
MINIMUM CLIENT SIZE:	$100,000
MAXIMUM CLIENT SIZE:	$20 million
CLIENT REFERENCES:	Texas Tool and Fastener Wesley Schreiber Dickchut Construction
LENGTH OF TYPICAL ASSIGNMENT:	1–2 years
BRANCH OFFICE(S):	None

NAME:	Nathaniel Bigelow Holdings, Incorporated (formerly Laughlin & Flynn, Inc.)
ADDRESS:	200 State Street Boston, MA 02109-1680
TELEPHONE:	617-439-0018
FAX:	617-439-4160
PRINCIPAL(S):	Richard Kimball, Managing Partner David Stuebe (key contact) Peter Worrell Phil Ryan
NUMBER OF YEARS IN BUSINESS:	50
INDUSTRIES SPECIALIZED IN:	Middle market, closely held businesses Manufacturing Financial services Regulated industries Health care
MINIMUM CLIENT SIZE:	$10 million
MAXIMUM CLIENT SIZE:	$200 million
FEE STRUCTURE:	Hourly or flat
SUCCESS BONUS:	Yes, when appropriate
EQUITY PARTICIPATION:	Yes, when appropriate
CLIENT REFERENCES:	Confidential
LENGTH OF TYPICAL ASSIGNMENT:	3 months to 2 years
BRANCH OFFICE(S):	1804 North M63 Benton Harbor, MI 49022 P.O. Box 239 Manchester, NH 03105

NAME:	Naulty Associates
ADDRESS:	16126 Tortola Circle
	Huntington Beach, CA 92649
TELEPHONE:	714-840-0266
FAX:	714-946-8730
PRINCIPAL(S):	Ricard D. Naulty
NUMBER OF YEARS	
IN BUSINESS:	10
INDUSTRIES	
SPECIALIZED IN:	Manufacturing
	Distribution
	Selected service
MINIMUM CLIENT SIZE:	$3 million
MAXIMUM CLIENT SIZE:	$50 million
FEE STRUCTURE:	Weekly
SUCCESS BONUS:	Yes
EQUITY PARTICIPATION:	Yes
CLIENT REFERENCES:	Hydril Corporation
	Los Angeles
	Hiac-Royco
	Menlo Park, CA
	Barden's Pest Control
	Long Beach, CA
LENGTH OF TYPICAL	
ASSIGNMENT:	3–18 months
BRANCH OFFICE(S):	None

NAME:	Nelson & Company
ADDRESS:	100 Galleria Parkway, Suite 400
	Atlanta, GA 30339
TELEPHONE:	404-951-4859
FAX:	404-256-4014
PRINCIPAL(S):	Robert E. Nelson, Jr.
	Joseph M. Cozzolino
NUMBER OF YEARS	
IN BUSINESS:	Established 1987; 20 years
	in practice
INDUSTRIES	
SPECIALIZED IN:	Manufacturing
	High-tech
	Real estate
	Retail
	Service
MINIMUM CLIENT SIZE:	$15 million
MAXIMUM CLIENT SIZE:	No limit
FEE STRUCTURE:	Hourly
SUCCESS BONUS:	No
EQUITY PARTICIPATION:	Yes
CLIENT REFERENCES:	Confidential
LENGTH OF TYPICAL	
ASSIGNMENT:	6 months
BRANCH OFFICE(S):	4500 Main Street, Suite 900
	Kansas City, MO 64111

NAME:	New England Ventures
ADDRESS:	9259 E. Raintree Drive, Suite 2031
	Scottsdale, AZ 85260
TELEPHONE:	602-951-7093
FAX:	602-951-7039
PRINCIPAL(S):	Howard Klemmer
NUMBER OF YEARS IN BUSINESS:	3
INDUSTRIES SPECIALIZED IN:	Manufacturing/distribution
	High-tech electronics
	Office products
MINIMUM CLIENT SIZE:	$25 million
MAXIMUM CLIENT SIZE:	$300 million
FEE STRUCTURE:	Hourly or flat
SUCCESS BONUS:	Yes
EQUITY PARTICIPATION:	Yes
CLIENT REFERENCES:	Dynatech Computer Systems
	Krof, Inc.
LENGTH OF TYPICAL ASSIGNMENT:	1–2 years
BRANCH OFFICE(S):	None

NAME:	Nightingale & Associates, Inc.
ADDRESS:	3 Forest Street
	New Canaan, CT 06840
TELEPHONE:	203-972-1417
FAX:	203-972-1322
PRINCIPAL(S):	William J. Nightingale
	Stephen J. Hopkins
	B. Arneberg
	Michael C. D'Appolonia
NUMBER OF YEARS	
IN BUSINESS:	15
INDUSTRIES	
SPECIALIZED IN:	No specific specialty
MINIMUM CLIENT SIZE:	$10–20 million
MAXIMUM CLIENT SIZE:	No limit
FEE STRUCTURE:	Per session
SUCCESS BONUS:	Yes
EQUITY PARTICIPAITON:	No
CLIENT REFERENCES:	Evans Product Company
	Worlds of Wonder, Inc.
LENGTH OF TYPICAL	
ASSIGNMENT:	6 months to 2 years
BRANCH OFFICE(S):	None

NAME:	Gilbert C. Osnos & Company, Inc. (dba Grisanti, Galef & Osnos, Associates)
ADDRESS:	230 Park Avenue, Suite C-301 New York, NY 10169
TELEPHONE:	212-370-4260
FAX:	212-370-4263
PRINCIPAL(S):	Gilbert C. Osnos
NUMBER OF YEARS IN BUSINESS:	12
INDUSTRIES SPECIALIZED IN:	Manufacturing Retail Distribution Service
MINIMUM CLIENT SIZE:	$40 million
MAXIMUM CLIENT SIZE:	$1 billion
FEE STRUCTURE:	Day rate
SUCCESS BONUS:	Sometimes
EQUITY PARTICIPATION:	No
CLIENT REFERENCES:	Barber Greene Plymouth Rubber IRT Corporation
LENGTH OF TYPICAL ASSIGNMENT:	9–12 months
BRANCH OFFICE(S):	None

NAME:	PBR Group
ADDRESS:	106 Susan Drive
	Elkins Park, PA 19117
TELEPHONE:	215-896-7456
FAX:	215-896-7587
PRINCIPAL(S):	Robert Riesner, President
	Harvey L. Nachman, Executive
	Vice President
NUMBER OF YEARS	
IN BUSINESS:	8
INDUSTRIES	
SPECIALIZED IN:	Retail
	Manufacturing
	Distribution (Electronic,
	High-tech)
	Computers
MINIMUM CLIENT SIZE:	$4 million
MAXIMUM CLIENT SIZE:	$125 million
FEE STRUCTURE:	Hourly
SUCCESS BONUS:	Yes
EQUITY PARTICIPATION:	Sometimes
CLIENT REFERENCES:	Scan Furniture, Incorporated
	Robert Bruce, Incorporated
	Frederick Computers Plus
LENGTH OF TYPICAL	
ASSIGNMENT:	3 months to 2 years
BRANCH OFFICE(S):	None

NAME:	Pacifica Management Advisors, Incorporated
ADDRESS:	10323 Santa Monica Boulevard, #108
	Los Angeles, CA 90025
TELEPHONE:	213-557-2708
FAX:	213-557-2710
PRINCIPAL(S):	Walter Kornbluh
NUMBER OF YEARS IN BUSINESS:	5
INDUSTRIES SPECIALIZED IN:	Wholesale
	Service
MINIMUM CLIENT SIZE:	$4 million
MAXIMUM CLIENT SIZE:	$100 million
FEE STRUCTURE:	Hourly
SUCCESS BONUS:	Yes
EQUITY PARTICIPATION:	Yes
CLIENT REFERENCES:	Traditional Industries
	5155 North Clareton Drive
	Agoura Hills, CA 91301
	RPM Rent-A-Car
	1336 East Holt Boulevard
	Ontario, CA
	Harrison-Ross Mortuaries
	1839 East Firestone Boulevard
	Los Angeles, CA 90001
LENGTH OF TYPICAL ASSIGNMENT:	4–6 months
BRANCH OFFICE(S):	None

NAME:	Peat Marwick, Main & Company
ADDRESS:	303 East Wacker Drive
	Chicago, IL 60430
TELEPHONE:	312-938-3270
FAX:	312-938-0449
PRINCIPAL(S):	John Atkinson
	Bill Ainsworth
NUMBER OF YEARS IN BUSINESS:	20
INDUSTRIES SPECIALIZED IN:	Transportation
	Manufacturing
MINIMUM CLIENT SIZE:	$50 million
MAXIMUM CLIENT SIZE:	$1.5 billion
FEE STRUCTURE:	Hourly
SUCCESS BONUS:	Case and client specific
EQUITY PARTICIPATION:	No
CLIENT REFERENCES:	Chicago, Milwaukee, St. Paul & Pacific Railroad Co.
	Other clients: confidential
LENGTH OF TYPICAL ASSIGNMENT:	Problem analysis/recovery plan: 1–3 months
	Workout/Turnaround: 1–3 years
BRANCH OFFICE(S):	Major cities worldwide

NAME:	Pegasus Industries, Inc.
ADDRESS:	8807 Cary–Algonquin Road
	Cary, IL 60013
TELEPHONE:	708-516-2000
	800-327-0897
FAX:	708-516-2112
PRINCIPAL(S):	Walter N. Tashjian
NUMBER OF YEARS IN BUSINESS:	6
INDUSTRIES SPECIALIZED IN:	Distribution
	Real estate
	Manufacturing
MINIMUM CLIENT SIZE:	$2 million
MAXIMUM CLIENT SIZE:	$25 million
FEE STRUCTURE:	Varies
SUCCESS BONUS:	Not usually
EQUITY PARTICIPATION:	Sometimes
CLIENT REFERENCES:	Tyke Corporation
	Chicago, IL
	General Steel & Wire Co.
	Lubbock, TX
	Country Estate Developers
	Gurnee, IL
LENGTH OF TYPICAL ASSIGNMENT:	3–6 months
BRANCH OFFICE(S):	None

NAME:	The Phoenix Management Group
ADDRESS:	207 Providence Road
	Chapel Hill, NC 27514
TELEPHONE:	919-493-0610
FAX:	919-490-6081
PRINCIPAL(S):	Richard B. Coxe
	John D. Grantham
NUMBER OF YEARS IN BUSINESS:	2
INDUSTRIES SPECIALIZED IN:	Manufacturing
	Transportation
	Distribution
	Medical
	Construction
MINIMUM CLIENT SIZE:	None
MAXIMUM CLIENT SIZE:	$50 million
FEE STRUCTURE:	Hourly plus % of results
SUCCESS BONUS:	Set objective, place value, and take percentage
EQUITY PARTICIPATION:	Only if we invest
CLIENT REFERENCES:	Carolina Table Company
	Lamar, SC
	Burton Equipment
	Columbia, SC
LENGTH OF TYPICAL ASSIGNMENT:	3–12 months
BRANCH OFFICE(S):	None

NAME:	Planitech
ADDRESS:	1825 Bristol Drive
	Medford, OR 92504
TELEPHONE:	503-773-6384
FAX:	503-773-3554
PRINCIPAL(S):	Bill Chaffee
NUMBER OF YEARS	
IN BUSINESS:	Consulting: 22 years
	Turnaround: 8 years
INDUSTRIES	
SPECIALIZED IN:	Manufacturing
	Service
MINIMUM CLIENT SIZE:	$10 million
MAXIMUM CLIENT SIZE:	$100 million
FEE STRUCTURE:	Hourly
SUCCESS BONUS:	No
EQUITY PARTICIPATION:	No
CLIENT REFERENCES:	Mark Industries
	Del Amo, CA
	Michael Barry & Company
	Los Angeles, CA
	Division of Magnavox
	Torrance, CA
LENGTH OF TYPICAL	
ASSIGNMENT:	4 months
BRANCH OFFICE(S):	None

NAME:	Powers & Associates
ADDRESS:	3500 City Center Tower II
	301 Commerce Street
	P.O. Box 100758
	Fort Worth, TX 76185-0758
TELEPHONE:	817-878-0724
FAX:	817-335-6935
PRINCIPAL(S):	Patrick E. Powers, Jr.
NUMBER OF YEARS	
IN BUSINESS:	6
INDUSTRIES	
SPECIALIZED IN:	All
MINIMUM CLIENT SIZE:	$5 million
MAXIMUM CLIENT SIZE:	$70 million
FEE STRUCTURE:	Hourly and bonuses
SUCCESS BONUS:	Yes
EQUITY PARTICIPATION:	Yes
CLIENT REFERENCES:	Confidential
LENGTH OF TYPICAL	
ASSIGNMENT:	6 months to 1 year
BRANCH OFFICE(S):	None

NAME:	Profit Development
ADDRESS:	19 rue d'Anjou
	Paris, France 75008
TELEPHONE:	33-1-4266-2017
FAX:	33-1-4266-0798
PRINCIPAL(S):	Robert Givens
NUMBER OF YEARS IN BUSINESS:	8
INDUSTRIES SPECIALIZED IN:	Telecommunications
	High-tech
	Transport
MINIMUM CLIENT SIZE:	$50 million
MAXIMUM CLIENT SIZE:	$1 billion
FEE STRUCTURE:	Flat
SUCCESS BONUS:	Yes
EQUITY PARTICIPATION:	Yes
CLIENT REFERENCES:	EGT
	Paris
	MORY
	Paris
	France Cables
	Paris
LENGTH OF TYPICAL ASSIGNMENT:	6–18 months
BRANCH OFFICE(S):	Corporate Development
	244 California Street
	San Francisco, CA

NAME:	Purcell Associates, Incorporated
ADDRESS:	800 East Northwest Highway, #700
	Palatine, IL 60067
TELEPHONE:	708-358-9404
FAX:	708-705-3850
PRINCIPAL(S):	Robert Purcell
NUMBER OF YEARS IN BUSINESS:	2 (10 years experience for principal)
INDUSTRIES SPECIALIZED IN:	Manufacturing
	Service
	Finance
	Concentration in printing
MINIMUM CLIENT SIZE:	$10 million
MAXIMUM CLIENT SIZE:	$150 million
FEE STRUCTURE:	Hourly
SUCCESS BONUS:	No
EQUITY PARTICIPATION:	No
CLIENT REFERENCES:	Confidential
LENGTH OF TYPICAL ASSIGNMENT:	4 months
BRANCH OFFICE(S):	None

NAME:	Quinn, Whitwer & Company, Incorporated
ADDRESS:	4550 Montgomery Avenue, #1125N Bethesda, MD 20814
TELEPHONE:	301-986-5855
FAX:	301-913-0253
PRINCIPAL(S):	Edward J. Quinn, Jr. Glen S. Whitwer
NUMBER OF YEARS IN BUSINESS:	13
INDUSTRIES SPECIALIZED IN:	Manufacturing Wholesale Service High-tech Contractors (construction)
MINIMUM CLIENT SIZE:	$1 million
MAXIMUM CLIENT SIZE:	$50 million
FEE STRUCTURE:	Hourly
SUCCESS BONUS:	Receive success fee for introducing investors and obtaining financing
EQUITY PARTICIPATION:	No
CLIENT REFERENCES:	Manor Montessori School Potomac, MD Maryland Pools Baltimore, MD SunLite Glass Capital Heights, MD
LENGTH OF TYPICAL ASSIGNMENT:	6 months
BRANCH OFFICE(S):	None

NAME:	The RDR Group, Inc.
ADDRESS:	630 Fifth Avenue, Suite 2518 New York, NY 10111
TELEPHONE:	212-969-9040
FAX:	212-586-4882
PRINCIPAL(S):	Ronald D. Rothberg Benjamin Rawls William Heller
NUMBER OF YEARS IN BUSINESS:	3
INDUSTRIES SPECIALIZED IN:	Accounting Alarm systems Architectural engineering Arena operators Asbestos removal Builders hardware distributors Business forms manufacturing Cable TV Contract bus transportation Corrugated shipping containers Electrical wire distributors Others
MINIMUM CLIENT SIZE:	$25 million
MAXIMUM CLIENT SIZE:	$400 million
FEE STRUCTURE:	Hourly plus retainer
SUCCESS BONUS:	Yes
EQUITY PARTICIPATION:	Yes
CLIENT REFERENCES:	Confidential
LENGTH OF TYPICAL ASSIGNMENT:	15 months
BRANCH OFFICE(S):	60 Fairway Ridge River Hills Plantation Lake Wiley, SC 29710
	5 Pine Court Pomona, NY 10970

NAME:	R. G. Quintero & Company
ADDRESS:	145 Fourth Avenue
	New York City, NY 10003
TELEPHONE:	212-505-9743
FAX:	212-533-9680
PRINCIPAL(S):	Ronald G. Quintero CPA, CMA, CFA
	John C. Reynolds
	Roger D. Timpson
NUMBER OF YEARS IN BUSINESS:	4
INDUSTRIES SPECIALIZED IN:	Manufacturing
	Retail
	Real estate
MINIMUM CLIENT SIZE:	$1 million
MAXIMUM CLIENT SIZE:	$1 billion
FEE STRUCTURE:	Hourly and flat
SUCCESS BONUS:	Sometimes
EQUITY PARTICIPATION:	Sometimes
CLIENT REFERENCES:	Available only to potential clients
LENGTH OF TYPICAL ASSIGNMENT:	1–4 months
BRANCH OFFICE(S):	None

NAME:	The Raymond Group, Inc.
ADDRESS:	P.O. Box 567
	Chappaqua, NY 10514
TELEPHONE:	914-241-1228
FAX:	Call first
PRINCIPAL(S):	Raymond V. Sozzi
NUMBER OF YEARS IN BUSINESS:	3
INDUSTRIES SPECIALIZED IN:	High-tech
MINIMUM CLIENT SIZE:	$5 million
MAXIMUM CLIENT SIZE:	$100 million
FEE STRUCTURE:	Flat
SUCCESS BONUS:	Yes
EQUITY PARTICIPATION:	No
CLIENT REFERENCES:	Decision Data
	Horsham, PA
	AVL
	Old Bridge, NJ
	Pansophic
	Syracuse, NY
LENGTH OF TYPICAL ASSIGNMENT:	18 months
BRANCH OFFICE(S):	None

NAME:	Recovery Management Corporation
ADDRESS:	1290 Avenue of the Americas, Suite 3405
	New York, NY 10104
TELEPHONE:	212-246-9292
FAX:	212-956-2134
PRINCIPAL(S):	Robert L. Sind
NUMBER OF YEARS IN BUSINESS:	20
INDUSTRIES SPECIALIZED IN:	Manufacturing
	Distribution
	Entertainment
	Real estate
	Energy
	Banking
MINIMUM CLIENT SIZE:	$35 million
MAXIMUM CLIENT SIZE:	Unlimited
FEE STRUCTURE:	Hourly plus retainer
SUCCESS BONUS:	N.A.
EQUITY PARTICIPATION:	N.A.
CLIENT REFERENCES:	Pettibone
	Tosco
	Commodore
	Associated Food Stores
	Beker
LENGTH OF TYPICAL ASSIGNMENT:	6 months–1 year
BRANCH OFFICE(S):	None

NAME:	Regent Pacific Management Corp.
ADDRESS:	10600 N. DeAnza Boulevard Cupertino, CA 95014
TELEPHONE:	408-973-0616
FAX:	408-973-8251
PRINCIPAL(S):	Gary J. Sbona William R. Krehbiel Jack S. Kenney
NUMBER OF YEARS IN BUSINESS:	17
INDUSTRIES SPECIALIZED IN:	Diversified
MINIMUM CLIENT SIZE:	No minimum
MAXIMUM CLIENT SIZE:	Several billion dollars
FEE STRUCTURE:	Fixed upon estimated intensity of management
SUCCESS BONUS:	Negotiable
EQUITY PARTICIPATION:	Negotiable
CLIENT REFERENCES:	Confidential
LENGTH OF TYPICAL ASSIGNMENT:	3 months to 3 years
BRANCH OFFICE(S):	None

NAME:	Bruce A. Sciotto Company
ADDRESS:	P.O. Box 2004
	Charlotte, NC 28247
TELEPHONE:	704-543-8311
FAX:	704-542-5380
PRINCIPAL(S):	Bruce A. Sciotto
NUMBER OF YEARS IN BUSINESS:	13
INDUSTRIES SPECIALIZED IN:	Manufacturing
MINIMUM CLIENT SIZE:	$1 million
MAXIMUM CLIENT SIZE:	$50 million
FEE STRUCTURE:	Weekly or monthly
SUCCESS BONUS:	Yes
EQUITY PARTICIPATION:	Yes
CLIENT REFERENCES:	Baxter, Kelly, Incorporated
	Anderson, SC
	Continental Chair Company
	Hickory, NC
	Hickory International
	Hickory, NC
LENGTH OF TYPICAL ASSIGNMENT:	6–8 months
BRANCH OFFICE(S):	None

NAME:	Seidman, Friant, Levine Limited
ADDRESS:	888 7th Avenue, Suite 1604
	New York, NY 10106
TELEPHONE:	212-586-0752
FAX:	212-757-2024
PRINCIPAL(S):	Samuel Seidman
	Ray Friant
	Paul Levine
NUMBER OF YEARS IN BUSINESS:	2
INDUSTRIES SPECIALIZED IN:	Manufacturing
MINIMUM CLIENT SIZE:	$10 million
MAXIMUM CLIENT SIZE:	$200 million
FEE STRUCTURE:	Flat
SUCCESS BONUS:	Yes
EQUITY PARTICIPATION:	Yes
CLIENT REFERENCES:	J. D. Sky Corporation
	Greencastle, PA
	United Container Corporation
	Philadelphia, PA
	Tennessee Chemical
	Copperhill, TN
LENGTH OF TYPICAL ASSIGNMENT:	1 year
BRANCH OFFICE(S):	None

NAME:	The Shepherd's Group, Inc.
ADDRESS:	P.O. Box 345
	Oldwick, NJ 08858-0345
TELEPHONE:	201-785-3350
FAX:	201-730-6267
PRINCIPAL(S):	Charles Figlio, Managing Director
NUMBER OF YEARS IN BUSINESS:	11
INDUSTRIES SPECIALIZED IN:	Industrial
	High-tech
	Services
	Financial services
MINIMUM CLIENT SIZE:	$5 million
MAXIMUM CLIENT SIZE:	$100 million
FEE STRUCTURE:	Hourly or project
SUCCESS BONUS:	Ad hoc basis
EQUITY PARTICIPATION:	Ad hoc basis
CLIENT REFERENCES:	Confidential
LENGTH OF TYPICAL ASSIGNMENT:	Interim Management: 4 months to 1 year
	Diagnostic and plan: 10–12 weeks
BRANCH OFFICE(S):	None

NAME:	Sigoloff & Associates
ADDRESS:	3340 Ocean Park Blvd., Suite 3050
	Santa Monica, CA 90405
TELEPHONE:	213-452-5555
FAX:	213-452-6157
PRINCIPAL(S):	Sanford C. Sigoloff
	Seymour Strasberg
	Peter S. Dealy
	James M. Van Tatenhove
NUMBER OF YEARS IN BUSINESS:	20+
INDUSTRIES SPECIALIZED IN:	Retail
	Real estate
	Others
MINIMUM CLIENT SIZE:	$100 million
MAXIMUM CLIENT SIZE:	No limit
FEE STRUCTURE:	Hourly
SUCCESS BONUS:	Yes
EQUITY PARTICIPATION:	Yes
CLIENT REFERENCES:	Wickes Companies
	Daylin
	Republic
LENGTH OF TYPICAL ASSIGNMENT:	1 year
BRANCH OFFICE(S):	None

NAME:	Alan M. Singer Company
ADDRESS:	800 West Ferry
	Buffalo, NY 14222
TELEPHONE:	716-885-3344
FAX:	716-885-2632
PRINCIPAL(S):	Alan M. Singer
NUMBER OF YEARS	
IN BUSINESS:	19
INDUSTRIES	
SPECIALIZED IN:	Manufacturing (all)
MINIMUM CLIENT SIZE:	$5 million
MAXIMUM CLIENT SIZE:	$150 million
FEE STRUCTURE:	Hourly
SUCCESS BONUS:	Yes
EQUITY PARTICIPATION:	No
CLIENT REFERENCES:	Van Huffel Tube Corporation
	Ohio
	Wilsolite Corporation
	New York
	W & F Manufacturing
	Corporation
	New York
LENGTH OF TYPICAL	
ASSIGNMENT:	4–6 months
BRANCH OFFICE(S):	None

NAME:	Smith Barney, Harris Upham Company, Incorporated
ADDRESS:	1345 Avenue of the Americas New York, NY 10105
TELEPHONE:	212-698-3688
FAX:	212-956-4513
PRINCIPAL(S):	Nicholas J. Sakellariadis Charles J. Lee (San Francisco) Robert C. Martin
NUMBER OF YEARS IN BUSINESS:	5
INDUSTRIES SPECIALIZED IN:	All
MINIMUM CLIENT SIZE:	$400 million
MAXIMUM CLIENT SIZE:	None
FEE STRUCTURE:	Monthly flat fee
SUCCESS BONUS:	Yes
EQUITY PARTICIPATION:	No
CLIENT REFERENCES:	Confidential
LENGTH OF TYPICAL ASSIGNMENT:	Varies
BRANCH OFFICE(S):	350 California Street San Francisco, CA 94104

NAME:	S. Woodrow Sponaugle
ADDRESS:	531 Central Road
	Rye Beach, NH 03871
TELEPHONE:	603-433-2484
FAX:	None
PRINCIPAL(S):	S. Woodrow Sponaugle
NUMBER OF YEARS	
IN BUSINESS:	10
INDUSTRIES	
SPECIALIZED IN:	Services
	Manufacturing
MINIMUM CLIENT SIZE:	$1 million
MAXIMUM CLIENT SIZE:	$25 million
FEE STRUCTURE:	Hourly plus retainer
SUCCESS BONUS:	Yes
EQUITY PARTICIPATION:	Yes
CLIENT REFERENCES:	Confidential
LENGTH OF TYPICAL	
ASSIGNMENT:	One to two years
BRANCH OFFICE(S):	None

NAME:	The Stafford Group
ADDRESS:	835 S. 500 West Stafford Center, Suite 324
	Hebron, IN 46341
TELEPHONE:	219-996-6027
FAX:	219-996-3144
PRINCIPAL(S):	Hansjoerg H. Enderlin
NUMBER OF YEARS IN BUSINESS:	30
INDUSTRIES SPECIALIZED IN:	Hotels
	Restaurants
	Resorts
	Entertainment facilities
	Concessions
MINIMUM CLIENT SIZE:	$1 million
MAXIMUM CLIENT SIZE:	$500 million
FEE STRUCTURE:	Hourly or by day + retainer
SUCCESS BONUS:	Yes
EQUITY PARTICIPATION:	Yes
CLIENT REFERENCES:	Curry Development Chicago, IL
	Ramada Renaissance Springfield, IL
	86th Place Restaurant Merrillville, IN
LENGTH OF TYPICAL ASSIGNMENT:	4 weeks to 1 year
BRANCH OFFICE(S):	None

NAME:	R. F. Stengel & Company, Inc.
ADDRESS:	989 Old Eagle School Road, Suite 811
	Wayne, PA 19087
TELEPHONE:	215-971-9620
FAX:	215-971-9812
PRINCIPAL(S):	Ronald F. Stengel (PA)
	Thomas A. Cawley (PA)
	Frank R. Bodetti (CA)
	William R. Mansfield (CO)
NUMBER OF YEARS IN BUSINESS:	5
INDUSTRIES SPECIALIZED IN:	Manufacturing
	Distribution
	High-tech
	Transportation
MINIMUM CLIENT SIZE:	$50 million
MAXIMUM CLIENT SIZE:	$1+ billion
FEE STRUCTURE:	Hourly or day rate
SUCCESS BONUS:	Sometimes
EQUITY PARTICIPATION:	No
CLIENT REFERENCES:	Storage Technology
	Louisville, CO
	Towle Manufacturing
	Newburyport, MA
	Pryor-Eczel Corporation
	Bensonville, IL
LENGTH OF TYPICAL ASSIGNMENT:	3+ months
BRANCH OFFICE(S):	4939 Kelvin Avenue
	Woodland Hills, CA
	5875 Park Lane Road
	Longmont, CO

NAME:	Jack R. Stone & Associates, Incorporated
ADDRESS:	5950 Berkshire Lane LB 47 Dallas, TX 75225
TELEPHONE:	214-696-4500
FAX:	214-696-6748
PRINCIPAL(S):	Jack R. Stone, Jr. Dennis Ladd Joe Hays
NUMBER OF YEARS IN BUSINESS:	11
INDUSTRIES SPECIALIZED IN:	Manufacturing Service Distribution
MINIMUM CLIENT SIZE:	$3 million
MAXIMUM CLIENT SIZE:	$100 million
FEE STRUCTURE:	Hourly or flat
SUCCESS BONUS:	Yes
EQUITY PARTICIPATION:	No
CLIENT REFERENCES:	Confidential
LENGTH OF TYPICAL ASSIGNMENT:	6 months
BRANCH OFFICE(S):	Northern Bank Building, Suite 1630 200 Capital Avenue Little Rock, AR 72201

NAME:	Strategic Planning and Research Corporation
ADDRESS:	3509 Nancy Court
	Plano, TX 75023-1109
TELEPHONE:	214-241-4491
FAX:	214-241-6735
PRINCIPAL(S):	Dr. John H. Nugent, CPA, CFE
	A. Lavandera
NUMBER OF YEARS IN BUSINESS:	12
INDUSTRIES SPECIALIZED IN:	High-tech
	Manufacturing
	Communications
	Software
MINIMUM CLIENT SIZE:	$1 million
MAXIMUM CLIENT SIZE:	$200 million
FEE STRUCTURE:	Hourly or flat
SUCCESS BONUS:	Sometimes
EQUITY PARTICIPATION:	No
CLIENT REFERENCES:	Datotek, Inc.
	HDS, Inc.
	Iris Corporation
LENGTH OF TYPICAL ASSIGNMENT:	Varies: 3 months to 4 years
BRANCH OFFICE(S):	None

NAME:	Stratford Partners, Incorporated
ADDRESS:	343 West Erie Street, Suite 240
	Chicago, IL 60610
TELEPHONE:	312-943-2998
FAX:	312-943-3035
PRINCIPAL(S):	Jerome P. Frett
	Michael A. Feder
NUMBER OF YEARS IN BUSINESS:	6
INDUSTRIES SPECIALIZED IN:	Leasing
	Transportation
	Retail
MINIMUM CLIENT SIZE:	$10 million
MAXIMUM CLIENT SIZE:	$200 million
FEE STRUCTURE:	Hourly
SUCCESS BONUS:	Yes
EQUITY PARTICIPATION:	No
CLIENT REFERENCES:	North American Car Corporation
	(going concern liquidation)
	Chicago South Shore Railroad
	Looks Furniture Leasing
LENGTH OF TYPICAL ASSIGNMENT:	6–12 months
BRANCH OFFICE(S):	None

NAME:	Sugarman & Company
ADDRESS:	600 Montgomery Street
	San Francisco, CA 94115
TELEPHONE:	415-421-8300
FAX:	415-421-6990
PRINCIPAL(S):	Randy Sugarman
	Judith Bratton
	Ed Barisone
	Alex Frasco
	Greg Bogden
NUMBER OF YEARS IN BUSINESS:	23
INDUSTRIES SPECIALIZED IN:	Manufacturing
	Distribution
	Telecommunication
	Retail
	Lumber
	Health care
MINIMUM CLIENT SIZE:	$3–5 million
MAXIMUM CLIENT SIZE:	$1 billion
FEE STRUCTURE:	Hourly
SUCCESS BONUS:	Varies
EQUITY PARTICIPATION:	No
CLIENT REFERENCES:	General Communications, Inc.
	National Healthcare
	Healthcare Services of America
LENGTH OF TYPICAL ASSIGNMENT:	6 months to 18 months
BRANCH OFFICE(S):	None

NAME:	Sullivan Associates, Incorporated
ADDRESS:	34 Water Street
	Minneapolis, MN 55331
TELEPHONE:	612-474-0901
FAX:	612-474-7059
PRINCIPAL(S):	James W. Sullivan, President
NUMBER OF YEARS	
IN BUSINESS:	15
INDUSTRIES	
SPECIALIZED IN:	Manufacturing
	Distribution
	Retail
	Real estate
MINIMUM CLIENT SIZE:	$5 million
MAXIMUM CLIENT SIZE:	$350 million
FEE STRUCTURE:	Hourly
SUCCESS BONUS:	Yes
EQUITY PARTICIPATION:	No
CLIENT REFERENCES:	K-Tel International
	Twin City Barge
	Durkee-Atwood
LENGTH OF TYPICAL	
ASSIGNMENT:	12–18 months
BRANCH OFFICE(S):	None

NAME:	Texas Corporate Recovery
ADDRESS:	P.O. Box 8142
	Weslaco, TX 78596
TELEPHONE:	512-968-3121
FAX:	512-968-0323
PRINCIPAL(S):	Brian A. Humphreys
NUMBER OF YEARS IN BUSINESS:	5
INDUSTRIES SPECIALIZED IN:	Financial
	Retail
MINIMUM CLIENT SIZE:	$10 million
MAXIMUM CLIENT SIZE:	$100 million
FEE STRUCTURE:	Hourly
SUCCESS BONUS:	No
EQUITY PARTICIPATION:	No
CLIENT REFERENCES:	Confidential
LENGTH OF TYPICAL ASSIGNMENT:	1 year
BRANCH OFFICE(S):	None

NAME:	Triage, Inc.
ADDRESS:	4114 Kottler Drive
	Lafayette Hill, PA 19444
TELEPHONE:	215-233-4344
FAX:	215-233-3977
PRINCIPAL(S):	Diane Freaney
	Carol Mann
NUMBER OF YEARS	
IN BUSINESS:	3
INDUSTRIES	
SPECIALIZED IN:	Family-owned small businesses
	Any industry
MINIMUM CLIENT SIZE:	$1 million
MAXIMUM CLIENT SIZE:	$25 million
FEE STRUCTURE:	Hourly rate
SUCCESS BONUS:	Sometimes on increase in sales and/or profit; never on finding financing
EQUITY PARTICIPATION:	Sometimes
CLIENT REFERENCES:	Confidential
LENGTH OF TYPICAL	
ASSIGNMENT:	3–24 months
BRANCH OFFICE(S):	None

NAME:	Tripp Associates
ADDRESS:	1 Balmorra Road
	Windham, NH 03087
TELEPHONE:	603-886-0074
FAX:	Call first
PRINCIPAL(S):	Alton P. Tripp
NUMBER OF YEARS	
IN BUSINESS:	5
INDUSTRIES	
SPECIALIZED IN:	High-tech
MINIMUM CLIENT SIZE:	$1 million
MAXIMUM CLIENT SIZE:	$100 million
FEE STRUCTURE:	Hourly/monthly
SUCCESS BONUS:	Yes
EQUITY PARTICIPATION:	Yes
CLIENT REFERENCES:	Carlyle Systems
	Positron, Inc.
LENGTH OF TYPICAL	
ASSIGNMENT:	6 months
BRANCH OFFICE(S):	None

NAME:	Turnaround Effect Associates
ADDRESS:	500 One Galleria Tower
	13355 Noel Road
	Dallas, TX 75240
TELEPHONE:	214-307-7061
FAX:	214-380-9493
PRINCIPAL(S):	Thomas E. Acker
NUMBER OF YEARS IN BUSINESS:	5
INDUSTRIES SPECIALIZED IN:	Energy
	Manufacturing
	Real estate
	Health care
	Creditor representation
MINIMUM CLIENT SIZE:	$5 million
MAXIMUM CLIENT SIZE:	$200 million
FEE STRUCTURE:	Hourly or daily
SUCCESS BONUS:	No
EQUITY PARTICIPATION:	No
CLIENT REFERENCES:	Lipshy
	Dallas, TX
	Others confidential
LENGTH OF TYPICAL ASSIGNMENT:	6–12 months
BRANCH OFFICE(S):	None

NAME:	Turnaround Resources, Inc.
ADDRESS:	2413 East Granite Hills Drive
	Sandy, UT 84092
TELEPHONE:	801-942-8616
FAX:	801-571-7521
PRINCIPAL(S):	Peter R. Genereaux
	Bernard Begue
NUMBER OF YEARS	
IN BUSINESS:	2 as a company;
	25 as an individual
INDUSTRIES	
SPECIALIZED IN:	Computer related
	Medical products & services
	Manufacturing
MINIMUM CLIENT SIZE:	$1 million
MAXIMUM CLIENT SIZE:	$200 million
FEE STRUCTURE:	Hourly, daily, or monthly,
	depending on length and stage
	of turnaround
SUCCESS BONUS:	Sometimes
EQUITY PARTICIPATION:	Sometimes
CLIENT REFERENCES:	I. P. Sharp Associates
	Toronto, Canada
	Wicat Systems
	Orem, UT
	DTSS Incorporated
	Hanover, NH
LENGTH OF TYPICAL	
ASSIGNMENT:	Crisis intervention: 1–12 weeks
	Turnaround: 1–2 years
BRANCH OFFICE(S):	None

NAME:	Turnmark Corporation
ADDRESS:	3407 Queensbury Way East
	Colleyville, TX 76034-4861
TELEPHONE:	817-355-9340
FAX:	214-871-1060
PRINCIPAL(S):	William S. Price
NUMBER OF YEARS	
IN BUSINESS:	3
INDUSTRIES	
SPECIALIZED IN:	Manufacturing
	Distribution
	Marketing
	Construction
	Services
MINIMUM CLIENT SIZE:	$1 million
MAXIMUM CLIENT SIZE:	$85 million
FEE STRUCTURE:	Hourly, bi-weekly, and monthly
SUCCESS BONUS:	Sometimes
EQUITY PARTICIPATION:	Not usually
CLIENT REFERENCES:	On request only
LENGTH OF TYPICAL	
ASSIGNMENT:	1–18 months
BRANCH OFFICE(S):	None

NAME:	Tyson, Weisser, Fortune & Associates
ADDRESS:	4830 W. Kennedy Boulevard, Suite 280
	Tampa, FL 33615
TELEPHONE:	813-286-4034
FAX:	813-286-4024
PRINCIPAL(S):	Paul C. Tyson, Chairman
	Ronald N. Weisser, President
NUMBER OF YEARS IN BUSINESS:	5
INDUSTRIES SPECIALIZED IN:	Manufacturing
	Distribution
	Real estate developing
MINIMUM CLIENT SIZE:	$5 million
MAXIMUM CLIENT SIZE:	$50 million
FEE STRUCTURE:	Weekly/monthly retainer with incentives
SUCCESS BONUS:	Yes
EQUITY PARTICIPATION:	Occasionally
CLIENT REFERENCES:	Confidential
LENGTH OF TYPICAL ASSIGNMENT:	6–18 months
BRANCH OFFICE(S):	None

NAME:	Viking Capital Partners
ADDRESS:	5885 Landerbrook Drive
	Cleveland, OH 44124
TELEPHONE:	216-446-9600
FAX:	216-446-0609
PRINCIPAL(S):	Paul L. Gierosky
	Richard S. Adler, Jr.
	Thomas F. Dougherty
NUMBER OF YEARS IN BUSINESS:	4
INDUSTRIES SPECIALIZED IN:	Manufacturing and marketing of industrial and consumer products
MINIMUM CLIENT SIZE:	NR
MAXIMUM CLIENT SIZE:	NR
FEE STRUCTURE:	N.A.
SUCCESS BONUS:	N.A.
EQUITY PARTICIPATION:	Makes equity investments and acquisitions
CLIENT REFERENCES:	NR
LENGTH OF TYPICAL ASSIGNMENT:	Acquires and operates
BRANCH OFFICE(S):	None

NAME:	Walquist & Associates
ADDRESS:	317 S.W. Alder, Suite 900
	Portland, OR 97204
TELEPHONE:	503-225-1111
FAX:	503-226-7058
PRINCIPAL(S):	Ronald L. Walquist
NUMBER OF YEARS	
IN BUSINESS:	6
INDUSTRIES	
SPECIALIZED IN:	Basic manufacturing: plastics,
	wood products, ship repair
	Agriculture
MINIMUM CLIENT SIZE:	$5 million
MAXIMUM CLIENT SIZE:	$500 million
FEE STRUCTURE:	Hourly and bonus
SUCCESS BONUS:	Yes
EQUITY PARTICIPATION:	No
CLIENT REFERENCES:	Grant & Roth Plastics
	1600 N.E. 25th/P.O. Box 585
	Hillsboro, OR 97123-0585
	Power Master, Incorporated
	10401 N.E. Marx
	Portland, OR 97220
	Northwest Marine Iron Works
	5555 North Channel
	Portland, OR 97219
LENGTH OF TYPICAL	
ASSIGNMENT:	6–12 months
BRANCH OFFICE(S):	1011 Western Avenue, Suite 900
	Seattle, WA 98104

NAME:	Westwick Consultants
ADDRESS:	1202-510 West Hastings Street
	Vancouver, British Columbia
	V6B 1L8 Canada
TELEPHONE:	604-681-9776
FAX:	604-683-4497
PRINCIPAL(S):	Roger Mutimer
NUMBER OF YEARS IN BUSINESS:	2
INDUSTRIES SPECIALIZED IN:	Wholesale/retail
MINIMUM CLIENT SIZE:	$2 million
MAXIMUM CLIENT SIZE:	None
FEE STRUCTURE:	Hourly
SUCCESS BONUS:	No
EQUITY PARTICIPATION:	No
CLIENT REFERENCES:	Confidential
LENGTH OF TYPICAL ASSIGNMENT:	1–6 months
BRANCH OFFICE(S):	None

NAME:	Wheeler & Rubin, Incorporated
ADDRESS:	9425 Stenton Avenue
	Philadelphia, PA 19119
TELEPHONE:	215-233-2700
FAX:	215-233-5342
PRINCIPAL(S):	Robert T. Wheeler
	Lee N. Rubin
NUMBER OF YEARS	
IN BUSINESS:	12
INDUSTRIES	
SPECIALIZED IN:	Manufacturing
	High-tech
	Distribution
MINIMUM CLIENT SIZE:	$5 million
MAXIMUM CLIENT SIZE:	$300 million
FEE STRUCTURE:	Hourly or daily
SUCCESS BONUS:	Sometimes
EQUITY PARTICIPATION:	Sometimes
CLIENT REFERENCES:	Roy Weston, Inc.
	Standard Telecommunication
	L.B.L. Group, Inc.
LENGTH OF TYPICAL	
ASSIGNMENT:	6 months
BRANCH OFFICE(S):	None

NAME:	Wilson Phelps Group
ADDRESS:	256 La Cienega Boulevard
	Beverly Hills, CA 90211
TELEPHONE:	213-474-6873
FAX:	213-938-4971
PRINCIPAL(S):	Ted Phelps
	Minda Wilson
NUMBER OF YEARS	
IN BUSINESS:	15
INDUSTRIES	
SPECIALIZED IN:	Manufacturing
	Trucking
	Electronics
MINIMUM CLIENT SIZE:	$5 million
MAXIMUM CLIENT SIZE:	$250 million
FEE STRUCTURE:	Hourly
SUCCESS BONUS:	Seldom
EQUITY PARTICIPATION:	May consider
CLIENT REFERENCES:	Confidential
LENGTH OF TYPICAL	
ASSIGNMENT:	NR
BRANCH OFFICE(S):	317 W. 105 Street
	New York, NY 10025
	212-666-5750

NAME:	Yocum Consulting Associates, Inc.
ADDRESS:	131 17th Street Toledo, OH 43624
TELEPHONE:	419-255-2712
FAX:	419-241-9308
PRINCIPAL(S):	Frederick L. (Rick) Yocum William B. Ball, Jr. Charles A. Stocking Lawrence T. Guyette
NUMBER OF YEARS **IN BUSINESS:**	3
INDUSTRIES **SPECIALIZED IN:**	Automotive Toys & hobbies Metal working Micro computer (distribution) Specialized equipment Engineering services
MINIMUM CLIENT SIZE:	Start-up
MAXIMUM CLIENT SIZE:	$50 million
FEE STRUCTURE:	Hourly
SUCCESS BONUS:	No
EQUITY PARTICIPATION:	Yes
CLIENT REFERENCES:	Confidential
LENGTH OF TYPICAL **ASSIGNMENT:**	Initial effort: 3–6 months Follow-up: 6–18 months
BRANCH OFFICE(S):	None

NAME:	The Zimmerman Company
ADDRESS:	14860 Lloyds Drive
	Minnetonka, MN 55345
TELEPHONE:	612-935-0678
FAX:	Call first
PRINCIPAL(S):	Frederick M. Zimmerman, Ph.D.
NUMBER OF YEARS	
IN BUSINESS:	8
INDUSTRIES	
SPECIALIZED IN:	Manufacturing
MINIMUM CLIENT SIZE:	$2 million
MAXIMUM CLIENT SIZE:	NR
FEE STRUCTURE:	Varies
SUCCESS BONUS:	No
EQUITY PARTICIPATION:	No
CLIENT REFERENCES:	NR
LENGTH OF TYPICAL	
ASSIGNMENT:	More than 6 months
BRANCH OFFICE(S):	None

NAME:	Zolfo, Cooper & Company
ADDRESS:	342 Madison Avenue
	New York, NY 10173
TELEPHONE:	212-818-9150
FAX:	212-599-0675
PRINCIPAL(S):	Frank Zolfo
	Stephen F. Cooper
	Michael E. France
NUMBER OF YEARS	
IN BUSINESS:	8
INDUSTRIES	
SPECIALIZED IN:	All
MINIMUM CLIENT SIZE:	$25 million
MAXIMUM CLIENT SIZE:	No maximum
FEE STRUCTURE:	Hourly
SUCCESS BONUS:	No
EQUITY PARTICIPATION:	No
CLIENT REFERENCES:	Confidential
LENGTH OF TYPICAL	
ASSIGNMENT:	3-month workout to a 4-year
	bankruptcy
BRANCH OFFICE(S):	None

Directory of Debtor-Advocate Bankruptcy Lawyers

INDEX OF DEBTOR-ADVOCATE BANKRUPTCY LAWYERS

Codes for Industries Specialization:

A:	Agriculture & equine	Leg.:	Legal services
B:	Banking, finance	L:	Lodging
C:	Construction	M:	Manufacturing
Cl.:	Clothing	Mr.:	Marine
CR:	Computer-related	Mktg.:	Marketing
D:	Distribution	NR:	Not reported
DC:	Defense contractors	P:	Publishing
Diver.:	Middle market	Pr.:	Printing companies
E:	Electronics	Prj.:	Capital projects
En.:	Energy	R:	Retail
Eng.:	Engineering	RE:	Real estate
Ent.:	Entertainment	S:	Service
F:	Food services	T:	Transportation
HC:	Health care	Tel.:	Telecommunications
HF:	Home furnishings	Tim.:	Timber and logging
HT:	High-tech	U:	Utilities
Hosp.:	Hospitality	UD:	Urban development
I:	Insurance	VC:	Venture capital-backed

Minimum Client Size:

Under $5 million:	Sm.
$5 million to $50 million:	Med.
$50 million and over:	Lg.

Name	Headquarters	Industries Specialization	Min. Size
Ackerman (Neil H.),P.C., Law Offices of	Hempstead, NY	NR	NR
Adelman, Lavine, Gold and Levin	Philadelphia, PA	All	All
Adkins, Frank M.	New Orleans, LA	Mr,C,RE,M, HC,U	Med.
Alston & Bird	Atlanta, GA	RE,U,B,M,Hosp.	Med.
Altick & Corwin	Dayton, OH	M,C,R,RE	Sm.
Angel & Frankel	New York, NY	All	Sm.
Angel & Neistat	Los Angeles, CA	All	Sm.
Arent, Fox, Kintner, Plotkin & Kahn	Washington, DC	RE,C	Med.
Armstrong, McCullen & Philpott, P.C.	Eugene, OR	Tel.,Timb.,A	Sm.
Bacon, Wilson, Ratner, Cohen, Salvage, et al.	Springfield, MA	M,D,C,Other	Sm.
Baker & McKenzie	San Francisco, CA	En.,T,RE	Med.
Barr & Rosenbaum	Spring Valley, NY	HF,M,RE,E	Sm.
Bason, George Francis, Jr.	Washington, DC	NR	Sm.
Beck (James H.), Attorney at Law	Canfield, OH	Leg.	NR
Berman, DeLeve, Kuchan & Chapman	Kansas City, MO	M,T,L	Sm.
Bernstein, McLean, Stark & Hinson	Memphis, TN	RE,C,Tim.	Sm.
Bieber (Raymond S.), Esq.	Honolulu, HI	All	Sm.
Blankenship (Albert L., Jr.), Attorney	Tucson, AZ	C,RE	Sm.
Bressert, Stephen G.	Honesdale, PA	C,L	Sm.
Brown, Rudnick, Freed & Gesmer	Boston, MA	CR,RE,T,F	Sm.
Brown, Todd & Heyburn	Louisville, KY	M,A,D	NR
Buchalter, Nemer, Fields & Younger	Los Angeles, CA	CR,I,En.	Med.
Buchanan & Ingersoll, P.C.	Pittsburgh, PA	B,M,R	Lg.
Bunch & Brock	Lexington, KY	M,R,Eng.	Sm.
Busch & Cole, P.A.	Sarasota, FL	C,F,M,Ent., Hospt.,RE	Sm.
Caldwell, Cannon-Ryan & Riffee	Charleston, WV	Commercial	Sm.
Cavalier & Associates	Houston, TX	RE,T,R,Hosp., M,Ent.,VC	Sm.

Name	Headquarters	Industries Specialization	Min. Size
Chandler & Wax, P.C.	Beaverton, OR	A,T,CR	Sm.
Christianson (Cabot), Law Offices of	Anchorage, AK	En.,F,R,M	NR
Christoffel & Elliott, P.A.	St. Paul, MN	RE,R,D	Sm.
Ciardi, Fishbone & DiDonato	Philadelphia, PA	M,RE,C, Education	Sm.
Cox & Rodnick	Austin, TX	RE	Sm.
Cox & Smith, Inc.	San Antonio, TX	RE,M,B,R	Sm.
Crawford, Crowe & Bainbridge, P.A.	Tulsa, OK	M,En.	NR
Cummings and Pantaleo	Los Angeles, CA	B, Antitrust	Sm.
Danning, Gill, Gould, Diamond & Spector	Los Angeles, CA	Diversified	Sm.
Davis, Polk & Wardwell	New York, NY	M,R,B	Lg.
Diepenbrock, Wulff, Plant & Hannegan	Sacramento, CA	A,Tim.,F,RE, R,En.,B	Sm.
Docter & Docter	Washington, DC	RE,CR,R,M, S	Sm.
Duane, Morris & Heckscher	Philadelphia, PA	Diversified	NR
Dudek (Frisch), Ltd.	Milwaukee, WI	B,C,I,M,D, Leg.,Pr.,RE	Sm.
Eikenburg & Stiles	Houston, TX	RE,T,HC	NR
Elsaesser, Jarzabek & Buchanan, Chtd.	Sandpoint, ID	Tim.,RE,R	Sm.
Espy, Collier H., Jr.	Dothan, AL	A,M,T	Sm.
Fredrikson & Byron	Minneapolis, MN	T,M,RE	Sm.
French, Randal, J.	Boise, ID	All	Sm.
Fuller & Henry	Toledo, OH	B,M,D,R	Sm.
Gallagher (Geri H.), Attorney at Law	Norristown, PA	Diversified	Sm.
Gallagher, Casados & Mann, P.C.	Albuquerque, NM	Diversified	Sm.
Gendel, Raskoff, Shapiro & Quittner	Los Angeles, CA	All	Sm.
Gilbert & Colvin, Attorneys at Law	Fort Worth, TX	Varied	Sm.
Ginnings, Birkelbach, Keith & Delgado, P.C.	El Paso, TX	En.,M,B	Sm.
Goodwin & Goodwin	Charleston, WV	R,En.,M	Sm.
Gordon, Silberman, Wiggins & Childs, P.C.	Birmingham, AL	M,R	Sm.

Name	Headquarters	Industries Specialization	Min. Size
Grace, Locke & Hebdon	Austin, TX	RE,M, Franchising	Sm.
Green, Ning, Lilly & Jones	Honolulu, HI	M,D,R	Sm.
Gross, Goodman & Associates	Cleveland, OH	D,R,M	Sm.
Gullett, Sanford, Robinson & Martin	Nashville, TN	F,L,RE	Sm.
Guy, Lammert & Towne	Akron, OH	R,RE	Sm.
Hafer, Day & Wilson, P.A.	Raleigh, NC	All	All
Hale and Dorr	Boston, MA	RE,M,R	Sm.
Hatch & Leslie	Seattle, WA	M,RE,HC	Sm.
Hirschler, Fleischer, Weinberg, Cox & Allen	Richmond, VA	RE, B, R	Med.
Holleb & Coff	Chicago, IL	All	Sm.
Holleran & Warsco	Fort Wayne, IN	C,HC,M	Med.
Honigman Miller Schwartz & Cohn	Detroit,MI	Automotive	Sm.
Hughes (Scott H.), Law Offices of	Council Bluffs, IA	A	Sm.
Hutchins & Wheeler	Boston, MA	M,HT,CR, Hosp.,F	Sm.
Israel & Israel	Oklahoma City, OK	F, En.	Med.
Jackson (Barry W.), Law Offices of	Fairbanks, AK	Hosp.,RE,L,A,R	Sm.
Jacobs & Crumplar, P.A.	Wilmington, DE	All	All
Jacobsen & Levy, P.A.	Albuquerque, NM	RE,Partnerships	Sm.
Johnson & Gibbs	Dallas, TX	B,C,Cl,En.,I, RE,S,T	Sm.
Jones, Day, Reavis & Pogue	Cincinnati, OH	R,M,RE	All
Jones, Obenchain, Ford, Parkow & Lewis	South Bend, IN	A,M,R,Others	Sm.
Juntunen (Michael E.), Attorney	Grand Forks, ND	A	Sm.
Jurgens & King, P.C.	Santa Fe, NM	R,F,Automotive	Sm.
Kelley Drye & Warren	New York, NY	All	Sm.
Kilpatrick & Cody	Atlanta, GA	T,RE,B,M	Sm.
Komyatte & Freeland, P.C.	Highland, IN	A,M,R,UD	Sm.
Kreis, Enderle, Callander & Hudgins, P.C.	Kalamazoo, MI	M,RE,Tim.	Sm.
Latham & Watkins	Los Angeles, CA	All	Sm.

Name	Headquarters	Industries Specialization	Min. Size
Levine & Eisenberg	Los Angeles, CA	Ent., RE, All	Sm.
Lewis & Brooks	Palo Alto, CA	CR,RE	Sm.
Lewis, Ciccarello & Friedberg	Charleston, WV	NR	Sm.
Lindquist & Vennum	Minneapolis, MN	M,Mktg.,T, Ent.,R	Sm.
Little, Metzger & Lamz, PLC	Metairie, LA	C	Sm.
Lobel, Winthrop & Broker	Irvine, CA	B,Eng.,CR,DC, E,F,HC,Cl, RE	Med.
Long, Tuminello, Besso, Seligman & Quinlan	Bay Shore, NY	R,M,S	Sm.
Mallery, Stern & Halperin	Los Angeles, CA	All	Sm.
Manier, Herod, Hollabaugh & Smith	Nashville, TN	RE,A,Ent.	Sm.
Marshall (H. Gayle), PLC	Lake Charles, LA	NR	NR
Martin (Brett W.), Esq.	Edgewater, CO	A	Sm.
McCarthy & Burke	Washington, DC	C,DC,RE	Sm.
McDowell, Rice and Smith	Kansas City, KS	T,RE,A	Sm.
McGavic & Boyd, P.C.	Eugene, OR	A,Tim.	Sm.
McWhorter, Cobb and Johnson	Lubbock, TX	A,B,En.,F,M, Mktg.,RE	Sm.
Merrill, Stone & Parks	Swainsboro, GA	A,R,M	Sm.
Meyer, Hendricks, Victor, Osborn & Maledon	Phoenix, AZ	Hosp.,RE	Sm.
Minter, Joseph and Thornhill	Austin, TX	RE,R	Sm.
Murphy, Weir & Butler	San Francisco, CA	R,M,RE,B, HT	Med.
Mushkin & Associates	Las Vegas, NV	C,R	NR
Musselman (Robert M.) & Associates	Charlottesville, VA	F	Sm.
Neal (Larry), P.C.	Vancouver, WA	T,B	Sm.
Neeser and Darval Law Office	Willmar, MN	A	Sm.
Neiman, Neiman, Stone & Spellman, P.C.	Des Moines, IA	A,B,C,Cl.,D, HC,M,R,L	Sm.
Nichols, Cafrey, Hill, Evans & Murrelle	Greensboro, NC	B,C,I,RE,S,T	Sm.
Noack (Harold Q., Jr.), Attorney at Law	Boise, ID	A,C,Ent.	Sm.

Name	Headquarters	Industries Specialization	Min. Size
O'Connor, Cavanagh, Anderson, Westover, Killingsworth & Bashears	Tucson, AZ	RE	Sm.
Oliver & Paxinos, P.C.	Billings, MT	Hosp.	Sm.
Pachulski, Stang & Ziehl, P.C.	Los Angeles, CA	Ent., HC,RE	Sm.
Parnell, Crum & Anderson, P.A.	Montgomery, AL	M,T,A,R	Sm.
Peebles, C. David	Ft. Wayne, IN	RE,A,HC	Sm.
Perkins Coie	Seattle, WA	Diversified	Sm.
Petillon & Davidoff	Los Angeles, CA	Hosp.,RE,M	Sm.
Price, Brett L., Law Offices of	Bakersfield, CA	A,En.,RE	Sm.
Prickett, Jones, Elliott, Kristol & Schnee	Wilmington, DE	A,B,C,HC,HF,I, M,Mr.,R,RE,S	Sm.
Redden (Michael)	Portland, OR	Ent.,F,D	Med.
Richards, Spears, Kibbe & Orbe	New York, NY	B,HT	Med.
Robertson, Williams, Ingram & Overbey	Knoxville, TN	M,B,S	Sm.
Robinson, Diamant, Brill & Klausner	Los Angeles, CA	M,RE,HT,Ent,C	Sm.
Romans, Thomas J.	Hackensack, NJ	Diversified	Sm.
Sable, Makoroff, Libenson	Pittsburgh, PA	M,R,All	Sm.
Sacks, Tierney, Kasen & Kerrick, P.A.	Phoenix, AZ	RE, Hosp., M,C	Sm.
Santen & Hughes	Cincinnati, OH	Diversified	Sm.
Schantz, Schatzman & Aaronson, P.A.	Miami, FL	M,R,RE	Sm.
Schwartz, Cooper, Kolb & Gaynor	Chicago, IL	All	All
Seyfarth, Shaw, Fairweather & Geraldson	Chicago, IL	M,T,DC	All
Shefferly & Silverman	Southfield, MI	B	Sm.
Sheinfeld, Maley & Kay, P.C.	Houston, TX	T,R,M,Tel.,RE	All
Silver & Voit	Mobile, AL	A,B,D,Ent.,HC, L,M,T,Tim.	Sm.
Simon (Marilyn), Esqs.	New York, NY	Cl.,R,M,C,RE	Med.
Skadden, Arps, Slate, Meegher & Flom	New York, NY	R,T,M,RE	Sm.
Smith, Carter, Rose, Finley & Hofmann	San Angelo, TX	All, A	Sm.

Name	Headquarters	Industries Specialization	Min. Size
Stearns, Weaver, Miller	Tampa, FL	T, Hosp.	NR
Steffes & MacMurdo	Baton Rouge, LA	RE,C,En.	Sm.
Steinhilben, Swanson, Marles, Curtis, Marone & Wolk	Oshkosh, WI	RE,R,T, Tanneries	Sm.
Stoel, Rives, Boley, Jones& Grey	Portland, OR	A,B,C,CR,E, HC,HT,L,R, RE,Tim.,U	Med.
Stroock & Stroock & Lavan	New York, NY	Diversified	Med.
Stutman, Treister & Glatt	Los Angeles, CA	R,M,HC,Tel., RE,B	Med.
Thomas, Andrew D.	Evansville, IN	A,Rest.	Sm.
Thorne, Grodnik & Ransel	Elkhart, IN	Mobile homes, HC	NR
Timberlake, H. Kenan	Huntsville, AL	Diversified	Sm.
Tompkins & McMaster	Columbia, SC	Diversified	Sm.
Towbin & Zazove, Ltd.	Chicago, IL	M,R,RE,C,HC, S,Pr.,Cl	Sm.
Watkins, Bates, Carey & McHugh	Toledo, OH	M,RE,D	All
Weil, Gotshal & Manges	New York, NY	Diversified	Sm.
Weinstein (John Haas), Ltd.	Opelousas, LA	En.,A,T	Sm.
Wendel, Rosen, Black, Dean & Levitan	Oakland, CA	Diversified	Sm.
Werner, Lindgren & Johnson	New London, WI	Chapter 12	Sm.
Wickwire (Gavin), P.C.	Vienna, VA	B,C	NR
Wise & Cole, P.A.	Charleston, SC	RE	Sm.
Wolf, Block, Schorr and Solis-Cohen	Philadelphia, PA	R,HC,Toxic torts,M,F	Med.
Wolfson & Shepard, Attorneys at Law	Flemington, NJ	RE,B,P,M,T	Sm.
Wood (Walter F.), Law Offices of	Tucson, AZ	Diversified	NR
Wright, Lindsett & Jennings	Little Rock, AR	A,T,RE	Sm.
Wyman, Bantzer, Kuchel & Silbert	Los Angeles, CA	B,RE,M,Ent., HC	Sm.
Zeisler & Zeisler, P.C.	Bridgeport, CT	All	Sm.
Zuckerman, Spaeder, Goldstein, Taylor & Kolker	Washington, DC	RE,Pr.,R,C, En.,Hosp.,HT, Auto.,Ent.	Sm.

NAME:	Law Offices of Neil H. Ackerman, P.C.
ADDRESS:	215 Hilton Avenue Hempstead, NY 11550
TELEPHONE:	516-564-8322
FAX:	516-538-2079
NUMBER OF LAWYERS IN BANKRUPTCY WORK:	1
NUMBER OF YEARS IN THIS SPECIALIZATION:	9
INDUSTRIES SPECIALIZED IN:	NR
MINIMUM CLIENT SIZE:	NR
MAXIMUM CLIENT SIZE:	NR
PERCENTAGE DEBTOR ADVOCACY:	50%
CLIENT REFERENCES:	NR
LENGTH OF TYPICAL ASSIGNMENT:	12–24 months
CONTACT PERSON(S):	Neil H. Ackerman
BRANCH OFFICE(S):	None

NAME:	Adelman, Lavine, Gold and Levin
ADDRESS:	1900 Two Penn Center Plaza
	Philadelphia, PA 19102-1799
TELEPHONE:	215-557-7922
FAX:	215-557-7922
NUMBER OF LAWYERS IN BANKRUPTCY WORK:	18
NUMBER OF YEARS IN SPECIALIZATION:	45
INDUSTRIES SPECIALIZED IN:	All
MINIMUM CLIENT SIZE:	No Minimum
MAXIMUM CLIENT SIZE:	No Maximum
PERCENTAGE DEBTOR ADVOCACY:	60%
CLIENT REFERENCES:	Confidential
LENGTH OF TYPICAL ASSIGNMENT:	Each situation is unique
CONTACT PERSON(S):	Lewis M. Gold
	Robert M. Levin
	Gary M., Schildhorn
	Myron A. Bloom
	Gary D. Bressler
	Steven D. Usdin
	Kevin W. Walsh
	Gary L. Stein
	Debbie S. Buchwald
	Raymond M. Lemisch
	Robert M. Bovarnick
	Douglas N. Candeub
	Tammi J. Lipsky
	Kathleen E. Torbitt
	William H. Karp
BRANCH OFFICE(S):	None

NAME:	Frank M. Adkins, A Professional Corporation
ADDRESS:	650 Poyorus Street New Orleans, LA 70130
TELEPHONE:	504-568-1888
FAX:	504-522-0949
NUMBER OF LAWYERS IN BANKRUPTCY WORK:	NR
NUMBER OF YEARS IN THIS SPECIALIZATION:	15
INDUSTRIES SPECIALIZED IN:	Marine Construction Real estate Manufacturing Hospital/health care Utilities
MINIMUM CLIENT SIZE:	$10 million
MAXIMUM CLIENT SIZE:	$100 million
PERCENTAGE DEBTOR ADVOCACY:	NR
CLIENT REFERENCES:	Triumph LOR, Inc. Clover Construction Co. Montelepre Extended Care, Inc.
LENGTH OF TYPICAL ASSIGNMENT:	18 months
CONTACT PERSON(S):	Frank M. Adkins
BRANCH OFFICE(S):	None

NAME:	Alston & Bird
ADDRESS:	1201 W. Peachtree Street
	Atlanta, GA 30909-3424
TELEPHONE:	404-881-7000
FAX:	404-881-7777
NUMBER OF LAWYERS IN BANKRUPTCY WORK:	4
NUMBER OF YEARS IN THIS SPECIALIZATION:	20+
INDUSTRIES SPECIALIZED IN:	Real estate
	Utilities
	Financial institutions
	Manufacturing
	Lodging
MINIMUM CLIENT SIZE:	$5 million
MAXIMUM CLIENT SIZE:	No maximum
PERCENTAGE DEBTOR ADVOCACY:	50%
CLIENT REFERENCES:	Bajun Electric Cooperative, Inc.
	Baton Rouge, LA
	Great American Management & Investment, Inc.
	Atlanta, GA
LENGTH OF TYPICAL ASSIGNMENT:	24 months
CONTACT PERSON(S):	Neal Batson
	David Butler
	Kit Weitnauer
	Grant Stein
BRANCH OFFICE(S):	700 Thirteenth Street, N.W., Suite 350
	Washington, DC 20005-3960
	202-508-3300

NAME:	Altick & Corwin
ADDRESS:	900 Talbott Tower
	Dayton, OH 45402
TELEPHONE:	513-223-1201
FAX:	513-223-5100
NUMBER OF LAWYERS IN BANKRUPTCY WORK:	1
NUMBER OF YEARS IN THIS SPECIALIZATION:	20
INDUSTRIES SPECIALIZED IN:	Manufacturing
	Construction
	Retail
	Real estate
MINIMUM CLIENT SIZE:	$500,000
MAXIMUM CLIENT SIZE:	$50 million
PERCENTAGE DEBTOR ADVOCACY:	65%
CLIENT REFERENCES:	Hughes Bechtol, Inc.
	6060 Milord
	Dayton, OH 45414
	Polycel, Inc.
	290 Spruce Street
	Columbus, OH 43215
	Cardinal Partner Corporation jointly administered with Cardinal Industries, Inc.
	2255 Kimberly Parkway East
	Columbus, OH 43272
LENGTH OF TYPICAL ASSIGNMENT:	18 to 48 months
CONTACT PERSON(S):	Thomas R. Noland
BRANCH OFFICE(S):	Cincinnati, OH

NAME:	Angel & Frankel, P.C.
ADDRESS:	366 Madison Avenue
	New York, NY 10017
TELEPHONE:	212-286-0100
FAX:	212-286-0783
NUMBER OF LAWYERS IN BANKRUPTCY WORK:	11
NUMBER OF YEARS IN THIS SPECIALIZATION:	Over 25
INDUSTRIES SPECIALIZED IN:	All
MINIMUM CLIENT SIZE:	No minimum
MAXIMUM CLIENT SIZE:	No maximum
CLIENT REFERENCES:	The Lionel Corporation
	Philadelphia, PA.
	Polybac Corporation
	Allentown, PA
	Wedtech Corporation
	New York, NY
	NorthStar Contracting Corp.
	New Rochelle, NY
LENGTH OF TYPICAL ASSIGNMENT:	18–24 months
CONTACT PERSON(S):	Joshua J. Angel
	Bruce Frankel
	John H. Drucker
	Laurence May
BRANCH OFFICE(S):	None

NAME:	Angel & Neistat
ADDRESS:	17th Floor
	888 South Figueroa Street
	Los Angeles, CA 90017
TELEPHONE:	213-689-4500
FAX:	213-689-4651
NUMBER OF LAWYERS IN BANKRUPTCY WORK:	8
NUMBER OF YEARS IN THIS SPECIALIZATION:	16
INDUSTRIES SPECIALIZED IN:	Diversified
MINIMUM CLIENT SIZE:	$500,000
MAXIMUM CLIENT SIZE:	$50 million+
PERCENTAGE DEBTOR ADVOCACY:	65%
CLIENT REFERENCES:	Macco Constructors, Inc.
	14409 Paramount Boulevard
	Paramount, CA 90723
	Great Western Bank
	9301 Corbin Avenue
	Northridge, CA 91328-1010
	Dow Chemical
	c/o Gittler & Wexler
	1888 Century Park East,
	Suite 1520
	Los Angeles, CA 90067
LENGTH OF TYPICAL ASSIGNMENT:	1 to 2 years
CONTACT PERSON(S):	Douglas M. Neistat
	William T. Mayo (San Fran.)
BRANCH OFFICE(S):	San Francisco, CA

NAME:	Arent, Fox, Kintner, Plotkin, & Kahn
ADDRESS:	1060 Connecticut Ave., NW Washington, DC 20036-5339
TELEPHONE:	202-857-6000
FAX:	202-857-6395
NUMBER OF LAWYERS IN BANKRUPTCY WORK:	12
NUMBER OF YEARS IN THIS SPECIALIZATION:	20
INDUSTRIES SPECIALIZED IN:	Real estate Construction
MINIMUM CLIENT SIZE:	$10 million
MAXIMUM CLIENT SIZE:	No maximum
PERCENTAGE DEBTOR ADVOCACY:	50%
CLIENT REFERENCES:	Provided upon request
LENGTH OF TYPICAL ASSIGNMENT:	6 to 18 months
CONTACT PERSON(S):	Roger Frankel
BRANCH OFFICE(S):	7475 Wisconsin Ave. Bethesda, MD 20814-3413 301-657-4800
	8000 Towers Crescent Dr. Vienna, VA 22152-2733 703-847-5800

NAME:	Armstrong, McCullen & Philpott, P.C.
ADDRESS:	1740 Green Acres Road Eugene, OR 97401-1753
TELEPHONE:	503-686-9165
FAX:	503-686-2945
NUMBER OF LAWYERS IN BANKRUPTCY WORK:	3
NUMBER OF YEARS IN THIS SPECIALIZATION:	17
INDUSTRIES SPECIALIZED IN:	Radio stations Fishing Logging
MINIMUM CLIENT SIZE:	$50,000
MAXIMUM CLIENT SIZE:	$1,300,000 and up
PERCENTAGE DEBTOR ADVOCACY:	50%
CLIENT REFERENCES:	Confidential
LENGTH OF TYPICAL ASSIGNMENT:	24 to 36 months
CONTACT PERSON(S):	Owen B. McCullen James B. Caher Barbara K. Bower
BRANCH OFFICE(S):	None

NAME:	Bacon, Wilson, Ratner, Cohen, Salvage, et al.
ADDRESS:	95 State Street Springfield, MA 01103
TELEPHONE:	413-781-0560
FAX:	413-739-7740
NUMBER OF LAWYERS IN BANKRUPTCY WORK:	36
NUMBER OF YEARS IN THIS SPECIALIZATION:	95
INDUSTRIES SPECIALIZED IN:	Manufacturing Distribution Retail Other
MINIMUM CLIENT SIZE:	All
MAXIMUM CLIENT SIZE:	All
PERCENTAGE DEBTOR ADVOCACY:	65%
CLIENT REFERENCES:	Savage Arms, Inc. Bank of New England Arnold Print Works, Inc.
LENGTH OF TYPICAL ASSIGNMENT:	6 to 12 months
CONTACT PERSON(S):	Michael B. Katz Paul R. Salvage Leonard Gold James Krunisek
BRANCH OFFICE(S):	None

NAME:	Baker & McKenzie
ADDRESS:	2 Embarcadero Center, 24th Floor
	San Francisco, CA 94111
TELEPHONE:	415-576-3000
FAX:	415-576-3099
NUMBER OF LAWYERS IN BANKRUPTCY WORK:	Numerous
NUMBER OF YEARS IN THIS SPECIALIZATION:	12
INDUSTRIES SPECIALIZED IN:	Oil and gas
	Energy
	Real estate
	Freight forwarding
MINIMUM CLIENT SIZE:	$10 million
MAXIMUM CLIENT SIZE:	$1 billion
PERCENTAGE DEBTOR ADVOCACY:	50%
CLIENT REFERENCES:	Four Winds Forwarding
	Portland, OR
	Nucorp Energy, Inc.
	San Diego, CA
	Doerring Group
	c/o Thomas F. Lennon
	San Diego, CA
LENGTH OF TYPICAL ASSIGNMENT:	24 to 60 months (or more)
CONTACT PERSON(S):	Donald R. Joseph
BRANCH OFFICE(S):	Chicago
	New York
	Los Angeles
	Dallas
	Miami
	Palo Alto
	San Diego

NAME:	Barr & Rosenbaum
ADDRESS:	664 South Main Street
	Spring Valley, NY 10977
TELEPHONE:	914-352-4080
FAX:	914-352-6777
NUMBER OF LAWYERS IN BANKRUPTCY WORK:	2
NUMBER OF YEARS IN THIS SPECIALIZATION:	25
INDUSTRIES SPECIALIZED IN:	Avionics
	Furniture
	Real estate
	Manufacturing
MINIMUM CLIENT SIZE:	$1 million
MAXIMUM CLIENT SIZE:	$25 million
PERCENTAGE DEBTOR ADVOCACY:	65%
CLIENT REFERENCES:	Emergency Beacon Corp.
	Bronx Beer
	Chestnut Grove Nursery
LENGTH OF TYPICAL ASSIGNMENT:	18 months
CONTACT PERSON(S):	Harvey S. Barr
	Elizabeth A. Haas
BRANCH OFFICE(S):	25 West 39th Street
	New York, NY 10018
	212-868-4090
	4 Cromwell Place
	White Plains, NY 10601
	914-997-7707
	16850 Island Park Road, S.W.
	Fort Myers, FL 33905
	813-433-7777

NAME:	George Francis Bason, Jr.
ADDRESS:	1025 Thomas Jefferson Street, NW, Suite 500 East Washington, DC 20007
TELEPHONE:	202-337-4224
FAX:	202-342-5446
NUMBER OF LAWYERS IN BANKRUPTCY WORK:	1
NUMBER OF YEARS IN THIS SPECIALIZATION:	Over 30 years
INDUSTRIES SPECIALIZED IN:	NR
MINIMUM CLIENT SIZE:	No minimum
MAXIMUM CLIENT SIZE:	No limit
PERCENTAGE DEBTOR ADVOCACY:	25%
CLIENT REFERENCES:	NR
LENGTH OF TYPICAL ASSIGNMENT:	12–18 months
CONTACT PERSON(S):	George Francis Bason, Jr.
BRANCH OFFICE(S):	None

NAME:	James H. Beck, Attorney at Law
ADDRESS:	Olde Courthouse Building
	Canfield, OH 44406
TELEPHONE:	216-533-2601
FAX:	216-533-1180
NUMBER OF LAWYERS IN BANKRUPTCY WORK:	1
NUMBER OF YEARS IN THIS SPECIALIZATION:	32
INDUSTRIES SPECIALIZED IN:	Legal services
MINIMUM CLIENT SIZE:	N.A.
MAXIMUM CLIENT SIZE:	N.A.
PERCENTAGE OF DEBTOR ADVOCACY:	50%
CLIENT REFERENCES:	NR
LENGTH OF TYPICAL ASSIGNMENT:	27 months
CONTACT PERSON(S):	James H. Beck, Esq.
BRANCH OFFICE(S):	None

NAME:	Berman, DeLeve, Kuchan & Chapman
ADDRESS:	1006 Grand Avenue, Suite 1600 Kansas City, MO 64106
TELEPHONE:	816-471-5900
FAX:	816-842-9955
NUMBER OF LAWYERS IN BANKRUPTCY WORK:	3
NUMBER OF YEARS IN THIS SPECIALIZATION:	59
INDUSTRIES SPECIALIZED IN:	Manufacturing Freight transport Hotel & lodging
MINIMUM CLIENT SIZE:	$500,000
MAXIMUM CLIENT SIZE:	$250 million
PERCENTAGE DEBTOR ADVOCACY:	33%
CLIENT REFERENCES:	NR
LENGTH OF TYPICAL ASSIGNMENT:	24–36 months
CONTACT PERSON(S):	Gene A. DeLeve Ronald S. Weiss Jerald S. Enslein
BRANCH OFFICE(S):	8575 West 110th Street, Suite 102 Overland Park, KS 66210

NAME:	Bernstein, McLean, Stark & Hinson
ADDRESS:	1255 Lynnfield Road, Suite 273 Memphis, TN 38119
TELEPHONE:	901-682-6631
FAX:	901-682-6658
NUMBER OF LAWYERS IN BANKRUPTCY WORK:	1
NUMBER OF YEARS IN THIS SPECIALIZATION:	10
INDUSTRIES SPECIALIZED IN:	Real estate Construction Lumber
MINIMUM CLIENT SIZE:	No minimum
MAXIMUM CLIENT SIZE:	No maximum
PERCENTAGE DEBTOR ADVOCACY:	50%
CLIENT REFERENCES:	NR
LENGTH OF TYPICAL ASSIGNMENT:	12 to 18 months
CONTACT PERSON(S):	Thomas Lee Hinson
BRANCH OFFICE(S):	None

NAME:	Raymond S. Bieber, Esq.
ADDRESS:	707 Richards Street, #200
	Honolulu, HI 96813
TELEPHONE:	808-524-7575
FAX:	None
NUMBER OF LAWYERS IN BANKRUPTCY WORK:	1
NUMBER OF YEARS IN THIS SPECIALIZATION:	30
INDUSTRIES SPECIALIZED IN:	All
MINIMUM CLIENT SIZE:	$1 million
MAXIMUM CLIENT SIZE:	No maximum
PERCENTAGE DEBTOR ADVOCACY:	50%
CLIENT REFERENCES:	NR
LENGTH OF TYPICAL ASSIGNMENT:	24 months
CONTACT PERSON(S):	Raymond S. Bieber, Esq.
BRANCH OFFICE(S):	None

NAME:	Albert L. Blankenship, Jr., Attorney
ADDRESS:	2912 North Tucson Boulevard Tucson, AZ 85716
TELEPHONE:	602-881-2300
FAX:	Call first
NUMBER OF LAWYERS IN BANKRUPTCY WORK:	1
NUMBER OF YEARS IN THIS SPECIALIZATION:	16
INDUSTRIES SPECIALIZED IN:	Construction and real estate development
MINIMUM CLIENT SIZE:	$500,000
MAXIMUM CLIENT SIZE:	None
PERCENTAGE DEBTOR ADVOCACY:	50%
CLIENT REFERENCES:	NR
LENGTH OF TYPICAL ASSIGNMENT:	Varies
CONTACT PERSON(S):	Albert L. Blankenship, Jr.
BRANCH OFFICE(S):	None

NAME:	Stephen G. Bressert
ADDRESS:	606 Church Street
	Honesdale, PA 18431
TELEPHONE:	717-253-5953
FAX:	717-253-2926
NUMBER OF LAWYERS IN BANKRUPTCY WORK:	3
NUMBER OF YEARS IN THIS SPECIALIZATION:	30
INDUSTRIES SPECIALIZED IN:	Construction
	Lodging
	Resort
MINIMUM CLIENT SIZE:	$1 million
MAXIMUM CLIENT SIZE:	$75 million
PERCENTAGE DEBTOR ADVOCACY:	50%
CLIENT REFERENCES:	Wayne Crushed Stone
	Eddy Leon Chocolate
	Fowler Floor & Wall
LENGTH OF TYPICAL ASSIGNMENT:	12 months
CONTACT PERSON(S):	Stephen G. Bressert
	Lorna Shaffer
	Jeffrey S. Treat
BRANCH OFFICE(S):	None

NAME:	Brown, Rudnick, Freed & Gesmer
ADDRESS:	One Financial Center Boston, MA 02111
TELEPHONE:	617-330-9000
FAX:	617-438-3278
NUMBER OF LAWYERS IN BANKRUPTCY WORK:	3
NUMBER OF YEARS IN THIS SPECIALIZATION:	50
INDUSTRIES SPECIALIZED IN:	Computer companies Real estate Restaurants Transportation companies
MINIMUM CLIENT SIZE:	$1 million
MAXIMUM CLIENT SIZE:	N.A.
PERCENTAGE DEBTOR ADVOCACY:	43%
CLIENT REFERENCES:	NR
LENGTH OF TYPICAL ASSIGNMENT:	1–2 years
CONTACT PERSON(S):	Joseph Ryan Steven Levine William Baldiga
BRANCH OFFICE(S):	30 Kennedy Plaza Providence, RI 02903

NAME:	Brown, Todd & Heyburn
ADDRESS:	1600 Citizens Plaza
	Louisville, KY 40202
TELEPHONE:	502-589-5400
FAX:	502-581-1087
	502-589-6475
NUMBER OF LAWYERS IN BANKRUPTCY WORK:	2
NUMBER OF YEARS IN THIS SPECIALIZATION:	12
INDUSTRIES SPECIALIZED IN:	Equine
	Manufacturing
	Wholesale distribution
MINIMUM CLIENT SIZE:	N.A.
MAXIMUM CLIENT SIZE:	N.A.
PERCENTAGE DEBTOR ADVOCACY:	32%
CLIENT REFERENCES:	NR
LENGTH OF TYPICAL ASSIGNMENT:	18 months
CONTACT PERSON(S):	Charles R. Keeton
	Helen Lucier
BRANCH OFFICE(S):	2700 Lexington Financial Center
	Lexington, KY 40507-1749
	400 Pearl Street, Suite 204
	Elsby East
	New Albany, IN 47150-0558

NAME:	Buchalter, Nemer, Fields & Younger
ADDRESS:	700 South Flower Street, Suite 700 Los Angeles, CA 90017-4183
TELEPHONE:	213-626-6700
FAX:	213-623-3999
NUMBER OF LAWYERS IN BANKRUPTCY WORK:	4
NUMBER OF YEARS IN THIS SPECIALIZATION:	8; 12; 18; 11
INDUSTRIES SPECIALIZED IN:	Oil & gas Insurance Computer
MINIMUM CLIENT SIZE:	$5 million
MAXIMUM CLIENT SIZE:	N.A.
PERCENTAGE DEBTOR ADVOCACY:	35–60%
CLIENT REFERENCES:	NR
LENGTH OF TYPICAL ASSIGNMENT:	18–36 months
CONTACT PERSON(S):	Stephen F. Biegenzahn Pamela Webster Theodor Albert Robert Izmirian
BRANCH OFFICE(S):	660 Newport Center Drive, Suite 1400 Newport, CA
	333 Market Street, 29th Floor San Francisco, CA
	50 West San Francisco Street, 7th Floor San Jose, CA 95113-2413

NAME:	Buchanan & Ingersoll, P.C.
ADDRESS:	5800 USX Tower
	600 Grant Street
	Pittsburgh, PA 15219
TELEPHONE:	412-562-8800
FAX:	412-562-1041
NUMBER OF LAWYERS IN BANKRUPTCY WORK:	3
NUMBER OF YEARS IN THIS SPECIALIZATION:	15
INDUSTRIES SPECIALIZED IN:	Creditor counsel for banks
	Steel
	Retail
	Consumer
MINIMUM CLIENT SIZE:	$250 million
MAXIMUM CLIENT SIZE:	No limit
PERCENTAGE DEBTOR ADVOCACY:	50%
CLIENT REFERENCES:	NR
LENGTH OF TYPICAL ASSIGNMENT:	Varies
CONTACT PERSON(S):	M. Bruce McCullough
	Gary Phillip Nelson
	George H. Cass
BRANCH OFFICE(S):	1101 Market Street,
	Suite 1450
	Philadelphia, PA 19107
	Mary Sachs Building
	208 N. Third Street, Suite 300
	Harrisburg, PA 17101
	1600 M Street NW, 7th Floor
	Washington, DC 20036

NAME:	Bunch & Brock
ADDRESS:	P.O. Box 2086
	Lexington, KY 40594
TELEPHONE:	606-254-5522
FAX:	606-233-1434
NUMBER OF LAWYERS IN BANKRUPTCY WORK:	4
NUMBER OF YEARS IN THIS SPECIALIZATION:	26; 25; 6; 1
INDUSTRIES SPECIALIZED IN:	Coal mining
	Manufacturing
	Retail
MINIMUM CLIENT SIZE:	$250,000
MAXIMUM CLIENT SIZE:	$60 million
PERCENTAGE DEBTOR ADVOCACY:	60%
CLIENT REFERENCES:	NR
LENGTH OF TYPICAL ASSIGNMENT:	2 years
CONTACT PERSON(S):	W. Thomas Bunch
	Dan D. Brock, Jr.
	Gail M. Bunch
	W. Thomas Bunch II
BRANCH OFFICE(S):	None

NAME:	Busch & Cole, P.A.
ADDRESS:	1605 Main Street,
	Suite 604
	Sarasota, FL 34236
TELEPHONE:	813-365-4055
FAX:	813-365-4219
NUMBER OF LAWYERS IN BANKRUPTCY WORK:	2
NUMBER OF YEARS IN THIS SPECIALIZATION:	13
INDUSTRIES SPECIALIZED IN:	Construction
	Food services
	Manufacturing
	Entertainment
	Hospitality
	Real estate
MINIMUM CLIENT SIZE:	$400,000
MAXIMUM CLIENT SIZE:	$8 million
PERCENTAGE DEBTOR ADVOCACY	60%
CLIENT REFERENCES:	NR
LENGTH OF TYPICAL ASSIGNMENT:	2 years
CONTACT PERSON(S):	R. John Cole, II
BRANCH OFFICE(S):	None

NAME:	Caldwell, Cannon-Ryan & Riffee
ADDRESS:	P.O. Box 4347
	3818 MacCorkle Avenue SE, Suite 101
	Charleston, WV 25364
TELEPHONE:	304-925-2100
FAX:	304-925-2193
NUMBER OF LAWYERS IN BANKRUPTCY WORK:	5
NUMBER OF YEARS IN THIS SPECIALIZATION:	14
INDUSTRIES SPECIALIZED IN:	Commercial
MINIMUM CLIENT SIZE:	$500,000
MAXIMUM CLIENT SIZE:	$20 million
PERCENTAGE DEBTOR ADVOCACY:	70%
CLIENT REFERENCES:	NR
LENGTH OF TYPICAL ASSIGNMENT:	18 months
CONTACT PERSON(S):	Joseph W. Caldwell
	Susan Cannon-Ryan
	Charles A. Riffee
	Mary Jane Pickens
	Shari L. McCommack
BRANCH OFFICE(S):	None

NAME:	Cavalier & Associates
ADDRESS:	6220 Texas Commerce Tower
	Houston, TX 77002
TELEPHONE:	713-228-1171
FAX:	713-228-8741
NUMBER OF LAWYERS	
IN BANKRUPTCY WORK:	1
NUMBER OF YEARS	
IN THIS SPECIALIZATION:	8
INDUSTRIES	
SPECIALIZED IN:	Real estate
	Transportation
	Retail
	Hospitality
	Manufacturing
	Entertainment
	Venture capital-backed
MINIMUM CLIENT SIZE:	No minimum
MAXIMUM CLIENT SIZE:	No maximum
PERCENTAGE DEBTOR	
ADVOCACY:	75%
CLIENT REFERENCES:	NR
LENGTH OF TYPICAL	
ASSIGNMENT:	9 to 12 months
CONTACT PERSON(S):	Craig H. Cavalier
BRANCH OFFICE(S):	None

NAME:	Chandler & Wax, P.C.
ADDRESS:	9400 SW Beaverton Highway, Suite 170
	Beaverton, OR 97005
TELEPHONE:	503-297-9330
FAX:	503-297-9332
NUMBER OF LAWYERS IN BANKRUPTCY WORK:	1
NUMBER OF YEARS IN THIS SPECIALIZATION:	9+
INDUSTRIES SPECIALIZED IN:	Agriculture
	Trucking
	Computers
MINIMUM CLIENT SIZE:	No set minimum
MAXIMUM CLIENT SIZE:	No set maximum
PERCENTAGE DEBTOR ADVOCACY:	95%
CLIENT REFERENCES:	NR
LENGTH OF TYPICAL ASSIGNMENT:	10–20 months
CONTACT PERSON(S):	Jon A. Chandler
BRANCH OFFICE(S):	None

NAME:	Law Offices of Cabot Christianson
ADDRESS:	Suite 302
	911 W. 8th Street
	Anchorage, AK 99501
TELEPHONE:	907-258-6016
FAX:	907-258-2026
NUMBER OF LAWYERS IN BANKRUPTCY WORK:	1
NUMBER OF YEARS IN THIS SPECIALIZATION:	10
INDUSTRIES SPECIALIZED IN:	Native Alaska corporations
	Oil and gas
	Retail
	Restaurants
	Heavy equipment
MINIMUM CLIENT SIZE:	NR
MAXIMUM CLIENT SIZE:	NR
PERCENTAGE DEBTOR ADVOCACY:	60%
CLIENT REFERENCES:	Haida Corporation
	Haideburg, CA
	GSL Oilfield Service Co.
	Austin, TX
	Tope Equipment Co.
	Anchorage, AK
LENGTH OF TYPICAL ASSIGNMENT:	2 years
CONTACT PERSON(S):	Cabot Christianson
BRANCH OFFICE(S):	None

NAME:	Christoffel & Elliott, P.A.
ADDRESS:	386 North Wabasha Street, Suite 805
	St. Paul, MN 55102
TELEPHONE:	612-224-0244
FAX:	612-224-0550
NUMBER OF LAWYERS IN BANKRUPTCY WORK:	2
NUMBER OF YEARS IN THIS SPECIALIZATION:	Gendler—6 years
	Elliott—9 years
INDUSTRIES SPECIALIZED IN:	Real estate
	Retail
	Wholesale
MINIMUM CLIENT SIZE:	No minimum
MAXIMUM CLIENT SIZE:	No limit
PERCENTAGE DEBTOR ADVOCACY:	80%
CLIENT REFERENCES:	NR
LENGTH OF TYPICAL ASSIGNMENT:	1–2 years
CONTACT PERSON(S):	Gordon I. Gendler
	Christopher A. Elliott
BRANCH OFFICE(S):	None

NAME:	Ciardi, Fishbone & DiDonato
ADDRESS:	1900 Spruce Street
	Philadelphia, PA 19103
TELEPHONE:	215-546-4370
FAX:	215-985-4175
NUMBER OF LAWYERS IN BANKRUPTCY WORK:	3
NUMBER OF YEARS IN THIS SPECIALIZATION:	13
INDUSTRIES SPECIALIZED IN:	Manufacturing
	Real estate
	Construction
	Vocational schools
MINIMUM CLIENT SIZE:	$2 million
MAXIMUM CLIENT SIZE:	$30 million
PERCENTAGE DEBTOR ADVOCACY:	55%
CLIENT REFERENCES:	Streamlight, Inc.
	Norristown, PA
	PTC Educational Services, Inc.
	Philadelphia, PA
LENGTH OF TYPICAL ASSIGNMENT:	12 to 24 months
CONTACT PERSON(S):	Edward J. DiDonato
	David S. Fishbone
	Albert A. Ciardi
BRANCH OFFICE(S):	1125 Atlantic Ave.,
	Suite 716
	Atlantic City, NJ 08401

NAME:	Cox & Rodnick
ADDRESS:	507 West 7th Street
	Austin, TX 78701
TELEPHONE:	512-477-2226
FAX:	512-477-2126
NUMBER OF LAWYERS IN BANKRUPTCY WORK:	1
NUMBER OF YEARS IN THIS SPECIALIZATION:	NR
INDUSTRIES SPECIALIZED IN:	Real estate partnerships with tax problems
MINIMUM CLIENT SIZE:	$1 million
MAXIMUM CLIENT SIZE:	No limit
PERCENTAGE DEBTOR ADVOCACY:	50%
CLIENT REFERENCES:	NR
LENGTH OF TYPICAL ASSIGNMENT:	1 year
CONTACT PERSON(S):	Conde Thompson Cox
BRANCH OFFICE(S):	Atlanta, GA

NAME:	Cox & Smith, Incorporated
ADDRESS:	2000 NBC Bank Plaza
	112 E. Pecan Street
	San Antonio, TX 78205
TELEPHONE:	512-554-5500
FAX:	512-226-8395
NUMBER OF LAWYERS IN BANKRUPTCY WORK:	3
NUMBER OF YEARS IN THIS SPECIALIZATION:	12
INDUSTRIES SPECIALIZED IN:	Real estate
	Manufacturing
	Financial institutions
	Retail
MINIMUM CLIENT SIZE:	All
MAXIMUM CLIENT SIZE:	All
PERCENTAGE DEBTOR ADVOCACY:	50%
CLIENT REFERENCES:	Lutheran General Hospital
	American Carting Corp.
	National Bancshares of Texas
LENGTH OF TYPICAL ASSIGNMENT:	16 months
CONTACT PERSON(S):	William H. Lemon, III
	R. Glen Ayers
	Jack Balzerson (Dallas)
BRANCH OFFICE(S):	Walnut Glen Tower
	8144 Walnut Hill Lane
	Dallas, TX
	214-368-4700

NAME:	Crawford, Crowe & Bainbridge, P.A.
ADDRESS:	1714 First National Building Tulsa, OK 74103
TELEPHONE:	918-587-1128
FAX:	918-587-3975
NUMBER OF LAWYERS IN BANKRUPTCY WORK:	2
NUMBER OF YEARS IN THIS SPECIALIZATION:	40–15
INDUSTRIES SPECIALIZED IN:	Manufacturing Oil & gas
MINIMUM CLIENT SIZE:	No minimum
MAXIMUM CLIENT SIZE:	No maximum
PERCENTAGE DEBTOR ADVOCACY:	50%
CLIENT REFERENCES:	NR
LENGTH OF TYPICAL ASSIGNMENT:	18 months to 4 years
CONTACT PERSON(S):	B. Hayden Crawford Robert L. Bainbridge
BRANCH OFFICE(S):	None

NAME:	Cummings and Pantaleo
ADDRESS:	10880 Wilshire Blvd., Suite 2016 Los Angeles, CA 90024
TELEPHONE:	213-475-9232
FAX:	213-474-6824
NUMBER OF LAWYERS IN BANKRUPTCY WORK:	1
NUMBER OF YEARS IN THIS SPECIALIZATION:	10
INDUSTRIES SPECIALIZED IN:	Banking and finance Antitrust-related situations Workout arrangements
MINIMUM CLIENT SIZE:	$500,000
MAXIMUM CLIENT SIZE:	None
PERCENTAGE DEBTOR ADVOCACY:	80%
CLIENT REFERENCES:	Confidential
LENGTH OF TYPICAL ASSIGNMENT:	18 months
CONTACT PERSON(S):	T. J. Pantaleo
BRANCH OFFICE(S):	None

NAME:	Danning, Gill, Gould, Diamond & Spector
ADDRESS:	1800 Century Park East, 7th Floor
	Los Angeles, CA 90067
TELEPHONE:	213-277-0077
FAX:	213-277-5735
NUMBER OF LAWYERS IN BANKRUPTCY WORK:	10
NUMBER OF YEARS IN THIS SPECIALIZATION:	35
INDUSTRIES SPECIALIZED IN:	All
MINIMUM CLIENT SIZE:	No minimum
MAXIMUM CLIENT SIZE:	No limit
PERCENTAGE DEBTOR ADVOCACY:	70%
CLIENT REFERENCES:	NR
LENGTH OF TYPICAL ASSIGNMENT:	18–24 months
CONTACT PERSON(S):	Curtis B. Danning
	David A. Gill
	David Gould
	Richard K. Diamond
	Steven M. Spector
	Howard Kollitz
	David R. Weinstein
	John J. Bingham
	Paul A. Beck
	Steven E. Smith
BRANCH OFFICE(S):	Orange County, CA

NAME:	Davis, Polk & Wardwell
ADDRESS:	One Chase Manhattan Plaza
	New York, NY 10005
TELEPHONE:	212-530-4092
FAX:	212-530-4800
NUMBER OF LAWYERS IN BANKRUPTCY WORK:	5
NUMBER OF YEARS IN THIS SPECIALIZATION:	Over 25
INDUSTRIES SPECIALIZED IN:	Manufacturing
	Retail
	Financial services sectors
MINIMUM CLIENT SIZE:	$150 million
MAXIMUM CLIENT SIZE:	No limit
PERCENTAGE DEBTOR ADVOCACY:	50%
CLIENT REFERENCES:	NR
LENGTH OF TYPICAL ASSIGNMENT:	Varies with size and complexity
CONTACT PERSON(S):	Donald S. Bernstein
	Stephen H. Case
	Lowell G. Harriss
	Karen E. Wagner
	Laureen F. Bedell
BRANCH OFFICE(S):	None

NAME:	Diepenbrock, Wulff, Plant & Hannegan
ADDRESS:	300 Capitol Mall, Suite 1700 P.O. Box 3034 Sacramento, CA 95812-3034
TELEPHONE:	916-444-3910
FAX:	916-446-1696
NUMBER OF LAWYERS IN BANKRUPTCY WORK:	4
NUMBER OF YEARS IN THIS SPECIALIZATION:	35 (Collectively)
INDUSTRIES SPECIALIZED IN:	Agriculture Forest products Food processing Real estate Retail Oil & gas Securities Public pension funds Government agencies
MINIMUM CLIENT SIZE:	$3 million
MAXIMUM CLIENT SIZE:	$56 billion (Cal PERS)
PERCENTAGE DEBTOR ADVOCACY:	50%
CLIENT REFERENCES:	California Public Employees Retirement System Lincoln Plaza 400 "P" Street Sacramento, CA 94229-2707
	Harwood Products #1 Main Street Branscomb, CA 95417
	Mt. Eden Vineyards 6001 Power Inn Road Sacramento, CA 95824
LENGTH OF TYPICAL ASSIGNMENT:	12 to 18 months

CONTACT PERSON(S):   Steven H. Felderstein
                                Michael S. McManus
                                Jane Dickson McKeag
                                Whitney Rimee
BRANCH OFFICE(S):   None

NAME:	Docter & Docter, P.C.
ADDRESS:	1325 G Street NW, Suite 700
	Washington, DC 20005
TELEPHONE:	202-628-6800
FAX:	202-628-5445
NUMBER OF LAWYERS IN BANKRUPTCY WORK:	5
NUMBER OF YEARS IN THIS SPECIALIZATION:	87
INDUSTRIES SPECIALIZED IN:	Real estate
	Computers
	Retailing
	General service businesses
	Light manufacturing
MINIMUM CLIENT SIZE:	$1 million
MAXIMUM CLIENT SIZE:	$30 million
PERCENTAGE DEBTOR ADVOCACY:	70%
CLIENT REFERENCES:	NR
LENGTH OF TYPICAL ASSIGNMENT:	9 months to 3 years
CONTACT PERSON(S):	Charles A. Docter
	Marcia K. Docter
	Ira C. Wolper
	David E. Lynn
	Loren I. Chumey
BRANCH OFFICE(S):	10400 Connecticut Avenue, Suite 513
	Kensington, MD 20895
	1513 King Street
	Alexandria, VA 22314

NAME:	Duane, Morris & Heckscher
ADDRESS:	1500 One Franklin Plaza
	Philadelphia, PA 19102
TELEPHONE:	215-854-6300
FAX:	215-854-6446 or -6337
NUMBER OF LAWYERS IN BANKRUPTCY WORK:	7
NUMBER OF YEARS IN THIS SPECIALIZATION:	20
INDUSTRIES SPECIALIZED IN:	Diversified
MINIMUM CLIENT SIZE:	NR
MAXIMUM CLIENT SIZE:	NR
PERCENTAGE DEBTOR ADVOCACY:	30%
CLIENT REFERENCES:	NR
LENGTH OF TYPICAL ASSIGNMENT:	18 to 24 months
CONTACT PERSON(S):	David T. Sykes

BRANCH OFFICE(S):

Commerce Plaza 3, Suite 430
5050 Tilgham Street
Allentown, PA 18104
215-391-1220

3985 Adler Place, Suite 100
Bethlehem, PA 18017
215-868-9968

The Payne Shoemaker Building
240 N. Third Street, 10th Floor
Harrisburg, PA 17108-1003
717-238-8161

Sagemore Corporate Center
8000 Sagemore Drive,
   Suite 8303
Marlton, NJ 08055
609-988-3100

18 W. Airy Street, Suite 406
Norristown, PA 19401
215-275-7098

53 Darby Road
Paoli, PA 19301
215-647-3555

One Franklin Plaza, Suite 1500
Philadelphia, PA 19102
215-854-3400

1201 Market Street, Suite 1500
Wilmington, DE 19801
302-571-5550

NAME:	Frisch Dudek, Ltd.
ADDRESS:	825 N. Jefferson
	Milwaukee, WI 53202
TELEPHONE:	414-273-4000
FAX:	414-273-1189
NUMBER OF LAWYERS IN BANKRUPTCY WORK:	3
NUMBER OF YEARS IN THIS SPECIALIZATION:	10+
INDUSTRIES SPECIALIZED IN:	Banking
	Printing
	Construction
	Real estate
	Insurance
	Manufacturing
	Distribution
	Legal services
MINIMUM CLIENT SIZE:	Under $5 million
MAXIMUM CLIENT SIZE:	Up to $50 million
PERCENTAGE DEBTOR ADVOCACY:	50%
CLIENT REFERENCES:	Confidential
LENGTH OF TYPICAL ASSIGNMENT:	9 to 15 months
CONTACT PERSON(S):	Patrick B. Howell
	Edward J. Prinley
	Curtis A. Paulsen
BRANCH OFFICE(S):	None

NAME:	Eikenburg & Stiles
ADDRESS:	1100 First City National Bank Building
	Houston, TX 77002
TELEPHONE:	713-652-2144
FAX:	713-655-6986
NUMBER OF LAWYERS IN BANKRUPTCY WORK:	2
NUMBER OF YEARS IN THIS SPECIALIZATION:	8
INDUSTRIES SPECIALIZED IN:	Real estate
	Transportation
	Medical
MINIMUM CLIENT SIZE:	NR
MAXIMUM CLIENT SIZE:	NR
PERCENTAGE DEBTOR ADVOCACY:	20%
CLIENT REFERENCES:	NR
LENGTH OF TYPICAL ASSIGNMENT:	12 months
CONTACT PERSON(S):	Mitchell J. Buchman
	Rebecca Leigh
BRANCH OFFICE(S):	None

NAME:	Elsaesser, Jarzabek & Buchanan, Chtd.
ADDRESS:	P.O. Box 1049
	Sandpoint, ID 83864
TELEPHONE:	208-263-8517
FAX:	208-263-0759
NUMBER OF LAWYERS IN BANKRUPTCY WORK:	3
NUMBER OF YEARS IN THIS SPECIALIZATION:	12
INDUSTRIES SPECIALIZED IN:	Lumber manufacturers
	Small retailers
	Real estate developments
MINIMUM CLIENT SIZE:	$250,000
MAXIMUM CLIENT SIZE:	No limit
PERCENTAGE DEBTOR ADVOCACY:	50%
CLIENT REFERENCES:	NR
LENGTH OF TYPICAL ASSIGNMENT:	18 months to 2 years
CONTACT PERSON(S):	Ford Elsaesser
	Barbara Buchanan
	Andrea Siler
BRANCH OFFICE(S):	Rivertown Mall, Suite 204
	Priest River, ID 83856

NAME:	Collier H. Espy, Jr.
ADDRESS:	305 North Oates Street, Suite E
	Dothan, AL 36303
TELEPHONE:	205-793-6288
FAX:	205-793-6603
NUMBER OF LAWYERS IN BANKRUPTCY WORK:	1
NUMBER OF YEARS IN THIS SPECIALIZATION:	12
INDUSTRIES SPECIALIZED IN:	Agriculture
	Food processing
	Manufacturing
	Transportation
MINIMUM CLIENT SIZE:	No minimum
MAXIMUM CLIENT SIZE:	No maximum
PERCENTAGE DEBTOR ADVOCACY:	95%
CLIENT REFERENCES:	Bob's Feed Mills, Inc.
LENGTH OF TYPICAL ASSIGNMENT:	6 to 12 months
CONTACT PERSON(S):	Collier H. Espy, Jr.
BRANCH OFFICE(S):	None

NAME:	Fredrikson & Byron, P.A.
ADDRESS:	1100 International Centre
	Minneapolis, MN 55402
TELEPHONE:	612-347-7000
FAX:	612-347-7077
NUMBER OF LAWYERS	
IN BANKRUPTCY WORK:	4
NUMBER OF YEARS	
IN THIS SPECIALIZATION:	22
INDUSTRIES	
SPECIALIZED IN:	Trucking
	Manufacturing
	Real estate
MINIMUM CLIENT SIZE:	No minimum
MAXIMUM CLIENT SIZE:	No maximum
PERCENTAGE DEBTOR	
ADVOCACY:	60%
CLIENT REFERENCES:	Endotronics, Inc.
	Bridgemans, Inc.
	Tony Downs, Inc.
LENGTH OF TYPICAL	
ASSIGNMENT:	4 to 10 months
CONTACT PERSON(S):	James L. Baillie
	William I. Kampf
	John M. Koneck
BRANCH OFFICE(S):	None

NAME:	Randal J. French
ADDRESS:	816 W. Bannock, Suite 405
	Boise, ID 83701-0328
TELEPHONE:	208-383-0030
FAX:	208-383-0412
NUMBER OF LAWYERS IN BANKRUPTCY WORK:	1
NUMBER OF YEARS IN THIS SPECIALIZATION:	6
INDUSTRIES SPECIALIZED IN:	All
MINIMUM CLIENT SIZE:	$100,000
MAXIMUM CLIENT SIZE:	$10 million
PERCENTAGE DEBTOR ADVOCACY:	70%
CLIENT REFERENCES:	NR
LENGTH OF TYPICAL ASSIGNMENT:	12 Months
CONTACT PERSON(S):	Randal J. French
BRANCH OFFICE(S):	None

NAME:	Fuller & Henry
ADDRESS:	One Seagate, Suite 1700
	Toledo, OH 43603
TELEPHONE:	419-247-2517
FAX:	419-247-2665
NUMBER OF LAWYERS	
IN BANKRUPTCY WORK:	5
NUMBER OF YEARS	
IN THIS SPECIALIZATION:	12
INDUSTRIES	
SPECIALIZED IN:	Banking
	Automobiles
	Glass
	Utilities
	Manufacturing
	Distribution
	Retail
MINIMUM CLIENT SIZE:	No minimum
MAXIMUM CLIENT SIZE:	No maximum
PERCENTAGE DEBTOR	
ADVOCACY:	50%
CLIENT REFERENCES:	General Motors Corporation
	Libbey-Owens Ford Co.
	Toledo Edison Company
LENGTH OF TYPICAL	
ASSIGNMENT:	18 to 36 months
CONTACT PERSON(S):	Thomas S. Zaremba (1)
	Mary Ann Whipple (2)
BRANCH OFFICE(S):	(1) 2790 Huntington Center
	Columbus, OH 43215
	(2) 125 Jefferson Street
	Port Clinton, OH 43452

NAME:	Geri H. Gallagher, Attorney at Law
ADDRESS:	18 West Airy Street Norristown, PA 19401
TELEPHONE:	215-527-0377
FAX:	215-525-2472
NUMBER OF LAWYERS IN BANKRUPTCY WORK:	1
NUMBER OF YEARS IN THIS SPECIALIZATION:	10
INDUSTRIES SPECIALIZED IN:	Diversified
MINIMUM CLIENT SIZE:	No minimum
MAXIMUM CLIENT SIZE:	No maximum
PERCENTAGE DEBTOR ADVOCACY:	65%
CLIENT REFERENCES:	NR
LENGTH OF TYPICAL ASSIGNMENT:	1–2 years
CONTACT PERSON(S):	Geri H. Gallagher
BRANCH OFFICE(S):	None

NAME:	Gallagher, Casados & Mann, P.C.
ADDRESS:	P.O. Box 968
	Albuquerque, NM 87103
TELEPHONE:	505-243-7848
FAX:	505-764-0153
NUMBER OF LAWYERS IN BANKRUPTCY WORK:	1
NUMBER OF YEARS IN THIS SPECIALIZATION:	11
INDUSTRIES SPECIALIZED IN:	Areas not limited
MINIMUM CLIENT SIZE:	Amounts not limited
MAXIMUM CLIENT SIZE:	Amounts not limited
PERCENTAGE DEBTOR ADVOCACY:	60%
CLIENT REFERENCES:	NR
LENGTH OF TYPICAL ASSIGNMENT:	12–18 months
CONTACT PERSON(S):	Nathan H. Mann
BRANCH OFFICE(S):	None

NAME:	Gendel, Raskoff, Shapiro & Quittner
ADDRESS:	801 Century Park East, 6th Floor Los Angeles, CA 90067
TELEPHONE:	213-277-5400
FAX:	213-277-9493
NUMBER OF LAWYERS IN BANKRUPTCY WORK:	18 in bankruptcy, 11 in workouts
NUMBER OF YEARS IN THIS SPECIALIZATION:	50
INDUSTRIES SPECIALIZED IN:	All
MINIMUM CLIENT SIZE:	No minimum
MAXIMUM CLIENT SIZE:	No maximum
PERCENTAGE DEBTOR ADVOCACY:	80%
CLIENT REFERENCES:	Sanford C. Sigoloff & Associates Attn: Sanford C. Sigoloff 213-452-2218
	Sanwa Bank Attn: Melvin O. Reford, Executive Vice President 213-613-2756
	Mitsui Manufacturers Bank Attn: Stephen P. Pastor, Senior Vice President 213-489-8814
LENGTH OF TYPICAL ASSIGNMENT:	NR
CONTACT PERSON(S):	Barney Shapiro
BRANCH OFFICE(S):	None

NAME:	Gilbert & Colvin, Attorneys at Law
ADDRESS:	1035 First Republic Bank Tower
	801 Cherry Street
	Fort Worth, TX 76102-6810
TELEPHONE:	817-336-7883
FAX:	817-336-5316
	817-878-0650
NUMBER OF LAWYERS IN BANKRUPTCY WORK:	3
NUMBER OF YEARS IN THIS SPECIALIZATION:	47; 25; 17
INDUSTRIES SPECIALIZED IN:	Varied
MINIMUM CLIENT SIZE:	$500,000
MAXIMUM CLIENT SIZE:	$50 million
PERCENTAGE DEBTOR ADVOCACY:	60%
CLIENT REFERENCES:	NR
LENGTH OF TYPICAL ASSIGNMENT:	18 months
CONTACT PERSONS(S):	Ben M. Gilbert
	Joseph Colvin
	Burton H. Gilbert
BRANCH OFFICE(S):	None

NAME:	Ginnings, Birkelbach, Keith & Delgado, P.C.
ADDRESS:	416 N. Stanton Street, #700 El Paso, TX 79901
TELEPHONE:	915-532-5929
FAX:	915-532-7073
NUMBER OF LAWYERS IN BANKRUPTCY WORK:	3
NUMBER OF YEARS IN THIS SPECIALIZATION:	Keith 15; Mott 7; Luttrell 6
INDUSTRIES SPECIALIZED IN:	Oil & gas Manufacturing Financial institutions Publicly held companies
MINIMUM CLIENT SIZE:	$100,000 annually
MAXIMUM CLIENT SIZE:	$10 million annually
PERCENTAGE DEBTOR ADVOCACY:	60%
CLIENT REFERENCES:	NR
LENGTH OF TYPICAL ASSIGNMENT:	6–18 months
CONTACT PERSON(S):	Gerald P. Keith H. Christopher Mott Leslie M. Luttrell
BRANCH OFFICE(S):	None

NAME:	Goodwin & Goodwin
ADDRESS:	P.O. Box 2107
	Charleston, WV 25328
TELEPHONE:	304-346-7000
FAX:	304-344-9692
NUMBER OF LAWYERS IN BANKRUPTCY WORK:	3
NUMBER OF YEARS IN THIS SPECIALIZATION:	20
INDUSTRIES SPECIALIZED IN:	Retail
	Coal-related
	Manufacturing
MINIMUM CLIENT SIZE:	$1 million
MAXIMUM CLIENT SIZE:	No limit
PERCENTAGE DEBTOR ADVOCACY:	70%
CLIENT REFERENCES:	NR
LENGTH OF TYPICAL ASSIGNMENT:	3 years
CONTACT PERSON(S):	Thomas R. Goodwin
	Richard E. Rowe
	Susan C. Wittemeier
BRANCH OFFICE(S):	P.O. Box 349
	Ripley, WV 25271
	201 3rd Street
	Towne Square
	Parkersburg, WV 26101
	Commerce National Plaza
	301 E. Main Street
	Lexington, KY 40507

NAME:	Gordon, Silberman, Wiggins & Childs, P.C.
ADDRESS:	1400 SouthTrust Tower Birmingham, AL 35203
TELEPHONE:	205-328-0640
FAX:	205-254-1500
NUMBER OF LAWYERS IN BANKRUPTCY WORK:	2
NUMBER OF YEARS IN THIS SPECIALIZATION:	35
INDUSTRIES SPECIALIZED IN:	Soft goods, both manufacturing and selling
MINIMUM CLIENT SIZE:	None
MAXIMUM CLIENT SIZE:	$150 million
PERCENTAGE DEBTOR ADVOCACY:	25%
CLIENT REFERENCES:	NR
LENGTH OF TYPICAL ASSIGNMENT:	2 years
CONTACT PERSON(S):	Wilbur G. Silberman Harvey L. Wachsman
BRANCH OFFICE(S):	100 Washington Street, Suite 2 Huntsville, AL 35801

NAME:	Grace, Locke & Hebdon
ADDRESS:	100 Congress Avenue, Suite 1001
	Austin, TX 78701-4042
TELEPHONE:	512-478-1200
FAX:	512-478-1276
NUMBER OF LAWYERS IN BANKRUPTCY WORK:	2
NUMBER OF YEARS IN THIS SPECIALIZATION:	18
INDUSTRIES SPECIALIZED IN:	Real estate
	Manufacturing
	Franchised businesses
MINIMUM CLIENT SIZE:	Under $500,000
MAXIMUM CLIENT SIZE:	Large corporations
PERCENTAGE DEBTOR ADVOCACY:	40%
CLIENT REFERENCES:	The Frost National Bank of San Antonio
	The Travelers Insurance Company
	American Rockwood, Inc.
	Seguin State Bank
	Skidmore, Owings and Merrill
LENGTH OF TYPICAL ASSIGNMENT:	18 months
CONTACT PERSON(S):	Jay Hurst, Austin
	Matt Rosenstein, San Antonio
BRANCH OFFICE(S):	2000 Frost Bank Tower
	San Antonio, TX 78205-1497
	512-225-3031

NAME:	Green, Ning, Lilly & Jones
ADDRESS:	707 Richards Street, Suite 700
	Honolulu, HI 96813
TELEPHONE:	808-531-2415
FAX:	808-531-2415
NUMBER OF LAWYERS IN BANKRUPTCY WORK:	2
NUMBER OF YEARS IN THIS SPECIALIZATION:	10
INDUSTRIES SPECIALIZED IN:	Manufacturing
	Distribution
	Retail
MINIMUM CLIENT SIZE:	No minimum
MAXIMUM CLIENT SIZE:	No maximum
PERCENTAGE DEBTOR ADVOCACY:	50%
CLIENT REFERENCES:	NR
LENGTH OF TYPICAL ASSIGNMENT:	12 to 24 months
CONTACT PERSON(S):	Howard R. Green
	Ke-Ching Ning (fluent in Chinese)
BRANCH OFFICE(S):	None

NAME:	Gross, Goodman & Associates
ADDRESS:	Terminal Tower
	50 Public Square, Suite 1326
	Cleveland, OH 44113-2204
TELEPHONE:	216-781-3434
FAX:	216-781-1749
NUMBER OF LAWYERS IN BANKRUPTCY WORK:	1
NUMBER OF YEARS IN THIS SPECIALIZATION:	10
INDUSTRIES SPECIALIZED IN:	Distribution
	Retail
	Apparel manufacturing
MINIMUM CLIENT SIZE:	No minimum
MAXIMUM CLIENT SIZE:	$235 million
PERCENTAGE DEBTOR ADVOCACY:	100%
CLIENT REFERENCES:	Bobbie Brooks, Inc.
LENGTH OF TYPICAL ASSIGNMENT:	18 months
CONTACT PERSON(S):	Gerald Kurland
BRANCH OFFICE(S):	None

NAME:	Gullett, Sanford, Robinson & Martin
ADDRESS:	P.O. Box 2757
	230 Fourth Avenue North, 3rd Floor
	Nashville, TN 37219-0757
TELEPHONE:	615-244-4994
FAX:	615-242-8219
NUMBER OF LAWYERS IN BANKRUPTCY WORK:	6
NUMBER OF YEARS IN THIS SPECIALIZATION:	16
INDUSTRIES SPECIALIZED IN:	Food services
	Lodging
	Real estate
MINIMUM CLIENT SIZE:	No minimum
MAXIMUM CLIENT SIZE:	No maximum
PERCENTAGE DEBTOR ADVOCACY:	70%
CLIENT REFERENCES:	Po Folks, Inc.
	Attn: John Scott, President
	P.O. Box 17406
	Nashville, TN 37217
	Southern Hospitality Corporation
	Attn: Henry R. Hillenmeyer, President
	P.O. Box 48
	Nashville, TN 37202
LENGTH OF TYPICAL ASSIGNMENT:	One year
CONTACT PERSON(S):	G. Rhea Bucy
BRANCH OFFICE(S):	None

NAME:	Guy, Lammert & Towne
ADDRESS:	2210 First National Tower
	Akron, OH 44308-1449
TELEPHONE:	216-535-2151
FAX:	216-535-9048
NUMBER OF LAWYERS IN BANKRUPTCY WORK:	3
NUMBER OF YEARS IN THIS SPECIALIZATION:	20
INDUSTRIES SPECIALIZED IN:	Retail
	Real estate
MINIMUM CLIENT SIZE:	$2 million
MAXIMUM CLIENT SIZE:	$25 million
PERCENTAGE DEBTOR ADVOCACY:	60%
CLIENT REFERENCES:	NR
LENGTH OF TYPICAL ASSIGNMENT:	3 years
CONTACT PERSON(S):	John J. Guy
	Thomas E. Lammert
	E. Jane Bell
BRANCH OFFICE(S):	P.O. Box 6426
	Canton, OH 44706-0426
	216-452-1818

NAME:	Hafer, Day & Wilson, P.A.
ADDRESS:	4600 Marriott Drive, Suite 400
	Raleigh, NC 31447
TELEPHONE:	919-787-4111
FAX:	919-783-8893
NUMBER OF LAWYERS IN BANKRUPTCY WORK:	2
NUMBER OF YEARS IN THIS SPECIALIZATION:	10+
INDUSTRIES SPECIALIZED IN:	All
MINIMUM CLIENT SIZE:	No minimum
MAXIMUM CLIENT SIZE:	No maximum
PERCENTAGE DEBTOR ADVOCACY:	50%
CLIENT REFERENCES:	Confidential
LENGTH OF TYPICAL ASSIGNMENT:	6 weeks
CONTACT PERSON(S):	Richard C. McElroy III
BRANCH OFFICE(S):	None

NAME:	Hale and Dorr
ADDRESS:	60 State Street
	Boston, MA 02109
TELEPHONE:	617-742-9100
FAX:	617-742-9108
NUMBER OF LAWYERS	
IN BANKRUPTCY WORK:	12
NUMBER OF YEARS	
IN THIS SPECIALIZATION:	30
INDUSTRIES	
SPECIALIZED IN:	Real estate
	Manufacturing
	Retail
MINIMUM CLIENT SIZE:	No minimum
MAXIMUM CLIENT SIZE:	No limit
PERCENTAGE DEBTOR	
ADVOCACY:	60%
CLIENT REFERENCES:	NR
LENGTH OF TYPICAL	
ASSIGNMENT:	1 year
CONTACT PERSON(S):	Paul P. Daley
	C. Hall Swaim
	Mark N. Polebaum
	John D. Sigel
	Raymond L. Miolla
	Albert A. Notini
	Fredric J. Bendremer
	Steven E. Boyce
	Laura Coyne
	Joseph P. Craven
	Paul G. Igoe
	Elizabeth M. Leonard
BRANCH OFFICE(S):	1455 Pennsylvania Avenue NW
	Washington, DC 20004
	1155 Elm Street
	Manchester, NH 03101

NAME:	Hatch & Leslie
ADDRESS:	701 5th Avenue, Suite 2700
	Seattle, WA 98104
TELEPHONE:	206-622-0090
FAX:	206-386-5464
NUMBER OF LAWYERS IN BANKRUPTCY WORK:	5
NUMBER OF YEARS IN THIS SPECIALIZATION:	40+
INDUSTRIES SPECIALIZED IN:	Manufacturing
	Real estate
	Medical
	Professionals
MINIMUM CLIENT SIZE:	No minimum
MAXIMUM CLIENT SIZE:	No limit
PERCENTAGE DEBTOR ADVOCACY:	50%
CLIENT REFERENCES:	NR
LENGTH OF TYPICAL ASSIGNMENT:	10 months to 2 years
CONTACT PERSON(S):	Jack J. Cullen
	Willard Hatch
	Dillon E. Jackson
	Craig Sternberg
	John Rizzardi
BRANCH OFFICE(S):	None

NAME:	Hirschler, Fleischer, Weinberg, Cox & Allen
ADDRESS:	P.O. Box 1Q 629 East Main St. Richmond, VA 23202
TELEPHONE:	804-771-9531
FAX:	804-644-0957
NUMBER OF LAWYERS IN BANKRUPTCY WORK:	5
NUMBER OF YEARS IN THIS SPECIALIZATION:	20
INDUSTRIES SPECIALIZED IN:	Real estate Banking and finance Retail
MINIMUM CLIENT SIZE:	$1 million
MAXIMUM CLIENT SIZE:	$500 million
PERCENTAGE DEBTOR ADVOCACY:	85%
CLIENT REFERENCES:	Retail chains and stores in the states of VA, MD, DC, and NC Real estate developers in the states of VA, MD, DC, and NC Names will be furnished only on request and with the permission of the clients
LENGTH OF TYPICAL ASSIGNMENT:	6 months to 2 years
CONTACT PERSON(S):	Allan S. Buffenstein
BRANCH OFFICE(S):	817 Air Park Road, Suite 1 Ashland, VA 23005 804-771-9570 Fax: 804-798-6415

NAME:	Holleb & Coff
ADDRESS:	55 East Monroe Street, Suite 4100 Chicago, IL 60613
TELEPHONE:	312–807-4600
FAX:	312-807-3971
NUMBER OF LAWYERS IN BANKRUPTCY WORK:	9
NUMBER OF YEARS IN THIS SPECIALIZATION:	30
INDUSTRIES SPECIALIZED IN:	All
MINIMUM CLIENT SIZE:	No minimum
MAXIMUM CLIENT SIZE:	No maximum
PERCENTAGE DEBTOR ADVOCACY:	40%
CLIENT REFERENCES:	Available upon request
LENGTH OF TYPICAL ASSIGNMENT:	6 to 18 months
CONTACT PERSON(S):	Keith J. Shapiro Christopher J. Horvay L. Judson Todhunter Joseph L. Matz
BRANCH OFFICE(S):	None

NAME:	Holleran & Warsco
ADDRESS:	927 South Harrison Street, P.O. Box 11587 Fort Wayne, IN 46859
TELEPHONE:	219-423-2537
FAX:	219-424-0051
NUMBER OF LAWYERS IN BANKRUPTCY WORK:	2
NUMBER OF YEARS IN THIS SPECIALIZATION:	10
INDUSTRIES SPECIALIZED IN:	Construction Health care Manufacturing
MINIMUM CLIENT SIZE:	$5 million
MAXIMUM CLIENT SIZE:	$100 million
PERCENTAGE DEBTOR ADVOCACY:	70%
CLIENT REFERENCES:	NR
LENGTH OF TYPICAL ASSIGNMENT:	3 years
CONTACT PERSON(S):	Mark A. Warsco James T. Young
BRANCH OFFICE(S):	None

NAME:	Honigman Miller Schwartz & Cohn
ADDRESS:	2290 First National Building Detroit, MI 48226
TELEPHONE:	313-256-7800
FAX:	313-962-0176
NUMBER OF LAWYERS IN BANKRUPTCY WORK:	4
NUMBER OF YEARS IN THIS SPECIALIZATION:	20+
INDUSTRIES SPECIALIZED IN:	Automotive
MINIMUM CLIENT SIZE:	No minimum
MAXIMUM CLIENT SIZE:	No limit
PERCENTAGE DEBTOR ADVOCACY:	25%
CLIENT REFERENCES:	NR
LENGTH OF TYPICAL ASSIGNMENT:	Varies with assignment
CONTACT PERSON(S):	Robert B. Weiss Sheldon S. Toll Steven G. Howell Donald F. Baty, Jr.
BRANCH OFFICE(S):	3100 First Interstate Bank Plaza Houston, TX 77002
	15260 Ventura Blvd., Suite 820 Sherman Oaks, CA 91403
	One Harbour Place, Suite 350 Tampa, FL 33602
	222 Lakeview Avenue, Suite 800 West Palm Beach, FL 33401

NAME:	Law Offices of Scott H. Hughes
ADDRESS:	403 First Federal Savings
	& Loan Building
	Council Bluffs, IA 51503
TELEPHONE:	712-328-0058
FAX:	712-328-0246
NUMBER OF LAWYERS	
IN BANKRUPTCY WORK:	1
NUMBER OF YEARS	
IN THIS SPECIALIZATION:	6
INDUSTRIES	
SPECIALIZED IN:	Agriculture
MINIMUM CLIENT SIZE:	No minimum
MAXIMUM CLIENT SIZE:	$1 billion
PERCENTAGE DEBTOR	
ADVOCACY:	75%
CLIENT REFERENCES:	NR
LENGTH OF TYPICAL	
ASSIGNMENT:	Varies
CONTACT PERSON(S):	Scott H. Hughes
BRANCH OFFICE(S):	None

NAME:	Hutchins & Wheeler
ADDRESS:	101 Federal Street
	Boston, MA 02110
TELEPHONE:	617-951-6600
FAX:	617-951-1295
NUMBER OF LAWYERS IN BANKRUPTCY WORK:	1
NUMBER OF YEARS IN THIS SPECIALIZATION:	14
INDUSTRIES SPECIALIZED IN:	Manufacturing
	High-tech
	Computer-related
	Food
	Restaurants
MINIMUM CLIENT SIZE:	No minimum
MAXIMUM CLIENT SIZE:	No maximum
PERCENTAGE DEBTOR ADVOCACY:	50%
CLIENT REFERENCES:	Computer Devices, Inc.
	Linnell Circle
	Nutting Lake, MA
	Ridgewood Nursing Home
	Attleboro, MA
	Ultimate Gifts, Inc.
	Danvers, MA
LENGTH OF TYPICAL ASSIGNMENT:	18 months
CONTACT PERSON(S):	Mark N. Berman
BRANCH OFFICE(S):	159 Town Hall Square
	Falmouth, MA 02540

NAME:	Israel & Israel
ADDRESS:	911 NW 57th St.
	Oklahoma City, OK 73118
TELEPHONE:	405-843-1911
FAX:	405-848-2463
NUMBER OF LAWYERS IN BANKRUPTCY WORK:	3
NUMBER OF YEARS IN THIS SPECIALIZATION:	15+
INDUSTRIES SPECIALIZED IN:	Food related
	Oil and gas
MINIMUM CLIENT SIZE:	$5 million
MAXIMUM CLIENT SIZE:	$20 million
PERCENTAGE DEBTOR ADVOCACY:	75%
CLIENT REFERENCES:	NR
LENGTH OF TYPICAL ASSIGNMENT:	18 months
CONTACT PERSON(S):	Jay G. Israel
BRANCH OFFICE(S):	None

NAME:	Law Offices of Barry W. Jackson
ADDRESS:	527 Fourth Avenue
	Fairbanks, AK 99701
TELEPHONE:	907-456-7791
FAX:	907-456-8005
NUMBER OF LAWYERS IN BANKRUPTCY WORK:	1
NUMBER OF YEARS IN THIS SPECIALIZATION:	18
INDUSTRIES SPECIALIZED IN:	Hotels
	Real estate
	Agriculture
	Retail
	Not-for-profit companies
	Resorts
	Mining
MINIMUM CLIENT SIZE:	No minimum
MAXIMUM CLIENT SIZE:	$100 million
PERCENTAGE DEBTOR ADVOCACY:	35%
CLIENT REFERENCES:	Kawerak, Inc.
	P.O. Box 505
	Nome, AK 99762
	F.A.L.C.C. dba Yakutat Lodge
	P.O. Box 287
	Yakutat, AK 99689
	McCauley's Reprographics, Inc.
	721 Gaffney Road
	Fairbanks, AK 99701
LENGTH OF TYPICAL ASSIGNMENT:	Varies per client
CONTACT PERSON(S):	Barry W. Jackson
BRANCH OFFICE(S):	3105A Lakeshore Drive, Suite 102
	Anchorage, AK 99503
	907-248-3278

NAME:	Jacobs & Crumplar, P.A.
ADDRESS:	2 East 7th Street
	Wilmington, DE 19899
TELEPHONE:	302-656-5445
FAX:	302-656-5875
NUMBER OF LAWYERS IN BANKRUPTCY WORK:	2
NUMBER OF YEARS IN THIS SPECIALIZATION:	12
INDUSTRIES SPECIALIZED IN:	All
MINIMUM CLIENT SIZE:	No minimum
MAXIMUM CLIENT SIZE:	No maximum
PERCENTAGE DEBTOR ADVOCACY:	90%
CLIENT REFERENCES:	Confidential
LENGTH OF TYPICAL ASSIGNMENT:	2 years
CONTACT PERSON(S):	Gloria Jones
	Robert Jacobs
BRANCH OFFICE(S):	None

NAME:	Jacobsen & Levy, P.A.
ADDRESS:	1110 Pennsylvania NE
	Albuquerque, NM 87110
TELEPHONE:	505-268-6707
FAX:	505-268-6629
NUMBER OF LAWYERS	
IN BANKRUPTCY WORK:	2
NUMBER OF YEARS	
IN THIS SPECIALIZATION:	14
INDUSTRIES	
SPECIALIZED IN:	Real estate
	General partnerships
MINIMUM CLIENT SIZE:	No minimum
MAXIMUM CLIENT SIZE:	No limit
PERCENTAGE DEBTOR	
ADVOCACY:	35%
CLIENT REFERENCES:	San Marcos Plaza, Ltd.
	Albuquerque, NM
	Vawtpower Inc.
	Albuquerque, NM
LENGTH OF TYPICAL	
ASSIGNMENT:	At least 2 years on average
CONTACT PERSON(S):	James C. Jacobsen
	Kathryn Levy
BRANCH OFFICE(S):	None

NAME: Johnson & Gibbs
ADDRESS: 900 Jackson Street
                                      Dallas, TX 75202-4499
TELEPHONE: 214-977-9517
FAX: 214-977-9004
NUMBER OF LAWYERS
IN BANKRUPTCY WORK: 14
NUMBER OF YEARS
IN THIS SPECIALIZATION: 22
INDUSTRIES
SPECIALIZED IN: Banking
                                      Construction
                                      Clothing
                                      Energy
                                      Insurance
                                      Real estate
                                      Service
                                      Transportation
MINIMUM CLIENT SIZE: $1 million
MAXIMUM CLIENT SIZE: $1 billion +
PERCENTAGE DEBTOR
ADVOCACY: 50%

CLIENT REFERENCES:

Republic Health Corporation
Attn: James H. Johnson,
    General Counsel
15303 Dallas Parkway,
    Suite 1400
Dallas, TX 75248

RCP Investments, Inc.
f/k/a Estes Homes
1010 N. Finance Center Drive,
    Suite 100
Tucson, AZ 85710
Attn: William Estes, Jr.

Lewis H. Sandler
Southwest Realty, Ltd.
5949 Sherry Lane, Suite 1435
Dallas, TX 75225

Anterra Realty
(Murray Property Group)
5520 LBJ Freeway, Suite 300
Dallas, TX 75240

**LENGTH OF TYPICAL
ASSIGNMENT:**

Six months to two years

CONTACT PERSON(S):

Mark MacDonald
Dan Artz

BRANCH OFFICE(S):

100 Congress Avenue,
    Suite 1400
Austin, TX 78701

1200 First City Tower
1001 Fannin Street
Houston, TX 77002-6778

1001 Pennsylvania Avenue, N.W.,
    Suite 745
Washington, D.C. 20004

NAME: Jones, Day, Reavis & Pogue
ADDRESS: 7 West Seventh Street
                                   Cincinnati, OH 45202
TELEPHONE: 513-579-7384
FAX: 513-579-7839
NUMBER OF LAWYERS
IN BANKRUPTCY WORK: 45
NUMBER OF YEARS
IN THIS SPECIALIZATION: 10+
INDUSTRIES
SPECIALIZED IN: Retail
                                   Manufacturing
                                   Real estate
                                   Resort management
MINIMUM CLIENT SIZE: No minimum
MAXIMUM CLIENT SIZE: No maximum (currently
                                      representing a client with
                                      $10 billion of debt)
PERCENTAGE DEBTOR
ADVOCACY: 70%

CLIENT REFERENCES:	Federated Department Stores, Inc. Allied Stores Corporation 7 West Seventh Street Cincinnati, OH 45202 513-579-7000 Dennis J. Broderick Vice President and General Counsel
	Cardinal Industries, Inc. 2255 Kimberly Parkway Columbus, OH 43232 614-755-5907 Jay Alix, Trustee
	Fairfield Communities, Inc. 2800 Cantrell Road Little Rock, AR 72202 501-664-6000 Marcel J. Dumeny
	Kendavis Holding Company 106 West Sixth Street Ft. Worth, TX 76101 817-335-5101 Joseph B. Freeman
LENGTH OF TYPICAL ASSIGNMENT:	18 months to 2 years
CONTACT PERSON(S):	(see below)
BRANCH OFFICE(S):	3300 First Atlanta Tower 2 Peachtree Street Atlanta, GA 30383-3101 404-521-3939 Christopher Carson
	301 Congress Avenue, Suite 1200 Austin, TX 78701 512-477-3939 Mina A. Clark
	225 West Washington Chicago, IL 60606 312-782-3939 David S. Kurtz

North Point
901 Lakeside Avenue
Cleveland, OH 44114
216-586-3939
David G. Heiman

1900 Huntington Center
41 South High Street
Columbus, OH 43215
614-469-3939
H. Theodore Meyer

2300 Trammell Crow Center
2001 Ross Avenue
Dallas, TX 75201
214-220-3939
Henry L. Gompf

355 South Grand Avenue,
 Suite 3000
Los Angeles, CA 90071
213-625-3939
William G. Wilson

599 Lexington Avenue
New York, NY 10022
212-326-3939
Marc S. Kirschner

One Mellon Bank Center,
 31st Floor
500 Grant Street
Pittsburgh, PA 15219
412-391-3939
Paul M. Pohl

Metropolitan Square
1450 G Street, N.W.
Washington, D.C. 20005-2088
202-879-3939
David C. Roseman

NAME:	Michael E. Juntunen, Attorney
ADDRESS:	218 S. 3rd Street, P.O. Box 1663 Grand Forks, ND 58206-1663
TELEPHONE:	701-746-9335
FAX:	701-775-5317 (call first)
NUMBER OF LAWYERS IN BANKRUPTCY WORK:	1
NUMBER OF YEARS IN THIS SPECIALIZATION:	7
INDUSTRIES SPECIALIZED IN:	Agriculture Agribusiness related
MINIMUM CLIENT SIZE:	$150,000
MAXIMUM CLIENT SIZE:	$5 million
PERCENTAGE DEBTOR ADVOCACY:	60%
CLIENT REFERENCES:	NR
LENGTH OF TYPICAL ASSIGNMENT:	18–24 months
CONTACT PERSON(S):	Michael E. Juntunen
BRANCH OFFICE(S):	None

NAME:	Jurgens & King, P.C.
ADDRESS:	411 Paseo de Peralta
	Santa Fe, NM 87501
TELEPHONE:	505-988-1858
FAX:	505-984-1754
NUMBER OF LAWYERS	
IN BANKRUPTCY WORK:	2
NUMBER OF YEARS	
IN THIS SPECIALIZATION:	7
INDUSTRIES	
SPECIALIZED IN:	Automotive
	Restaurants
	Real estate
MINIMUM CLIENT SIZE:	No minimum
MAXIMUM CLIENT SIZE:	No maximum
PERCENTAGE DEBTOR	
ADVOCACY:	60%
CLIENT REFERENCES:	NR
LENGTH OF TYPICAL	
ASSIGNMENT:	24+ months
CONTACT PERSON(S):	Leslie C. King, III
	James R. Jurgens
BRANCH OFFICE(S):	None

NAME:	Kelley Drye & Warren
ADDRESS:	101 Park Avenue
	New York, NY 10178
TELEPHONE:	212-808-7800
FAX:	212-808-7897
NUMBER OF LAWYERS IN BANKRUPTCY WORK:	20
NUMBER OF YEARS IN THIS SPECIALIZATION:	20+
INDUSTRIES SPECIALIZED IN:	All
MINIMUM CLIENT SIZE:	No minimum
MAXIMUM CLIENT SIZE:	No maximum
PERCENTAGE DEBTOR ADVOCACY:	50%
CLIENT REFERENCES:	NR
LENGTH OF TYPICAL ASSIGNMENT:	6 months
CONTACT PERSON(S):	Sandra Mayerson
BRANCH OFFICE(S):	Los Angeles, CA
	Washington, DC
	Miami, FL
	Stamford, CT
	Parsippany, NJ
	Brussels
	Tokyo

NAME:	Kilpatrick & Cody
ADDRESS:	Suite 3100
	100 Peachtree Street
	Atlanta, GA 30303
TELEPHONE:	404-572-6500
FAX:	404-572-6555
NUMBER OF LAWYERS IN BANKRUPTCY WORK:	6
NUMBER OF YEARS IN THIS SPECIALIZATION:	20
INDUSTRIES SPECIALIZED IN:	Airlines
	Real estate (development and syndication)
	Finance
	Carpet manufacturing
MINIMUM CLIENT SIZE:	All
MAXIMUM CLIENT SIZE:	All
PERCENTAGE DEBTOR ADVOCACY:	50%
CLIENT REFERENCES:	Hilton Head Corporation
	c/o Charles E. Fraser
	Marion Corporation Equity Committee
	c/o Skylink America, Inc.
	International Horizons, Inc.
	Original Appalachian Artworks, Inc., licensor to Coleco Industries, Inc.
LENGTH OF TYPICAL ASSIGNMENT:	30 months
CONTACT PERSON(S):	Dennis S. Meir
	Alfred S. Lurey
	Joel B. Piassick
	Duncan A. Roush
	Deborah B. Zink
	Steven Kratsch

BRANCH OFFICE(S):   Suite 500
                                    2501 M Street, N.W.
                                    Washington, DC 20037

                                    68 Pall Mall
                                    London SW1 Y5ES
                                    U.K.

NAME:	Komyatte & Freeland, P.C.
ADDRESS:	9650 Gordon Drive
	Highland, IN 46322
TELEPHONE:	219-924-9820
FAX:	None
NUMBER OF LAWYERS IN BANKRUPTCY WORK:	1
NUMBER OF YEARS IN THIS SPECIALIZATION:	19
INDUSTRIES SPECIALIZED IN:	Agriculture
	Clothing
	Manufacturing
	Retail
	Urban development
MINIMUM CLIENT SIZE:	All
MAXIMUM CLIENT SIZE:	All
PERCENTAGE DEBTOR ADVOCACY:	80%
CLIENT REFERENCES:	A-Pest Control
	9119 Indiana Place
	Merrillville, IN
	Parkway Mechanical
	509 W. 84th Street
	Merrillville, IN
	Ray Kindig
	Route 1, Box 120
	Brook, IN
LENGTH OF TYPICAL ASSIGNMENT:	18 to 36 months
CONTACT PERSON(S):	Daniel L. Freeland
BRANCH OFFICE(S):	None

NAME:	Kreis, Enderle, Callander & Hudgins, P.C.
ADDRESS:	800 Comerica Building Kalamazoo, MI 49007
TELEPHONE:	616-382-3784
FAX:	616-382-2083
NUMBER OF LAWYERS IN BANKRUPTCY WORK:	1
NUMBER OF YEARS IN THIS SPECIALIZATION:	10
INDUSTRIES SPECIALIZED IN:	Paper manufacturing Chemical manufacturing Real estate development Syndication workouts
MINIMUM CLIENT SIZE:	No minimum
MAXIMUM CLIENT SIZE:	No limit
PERCENTAGE DEBTOR ADVOCACY:	90%
CLIENT REFERENCES:	NR
LENGTH OF TYPICAL ASSIGNMENT:	1 year
CONTACT PERSON(S):	Robert B. Borsos
BRANCH OFFICE(S):	None

NAME:	Latham & Watkins
ADDRESS:	633 West 5th Street
	Los Angeles, CA 90071
TELEPHONE:	213-485-1234
FAX:	213-891-8713
NUMBER OF LAWYERS IN BANKRUPTCY WORK:	3
NUMBER OF YEARS IN THIS SPECIALIZATION:	20
INDUSTRIES SPECIALIZED IN:	All
MINIMUM CLIENT SIZE:	None
MAXIMUM CLIENT SIZE:	None
PERCENTAGE DEBTOR ADVOCACY:	20%
CLIENT REFERENCES:	NR
LENGTH OF TYPICAL ASSIGNMENT:	3 months to 6 years
CONTACT PERSON(S):	Robert J. Rosenberg
	Michael S. Lurey
	Ronald Hanson
BRANCH OFFICE(S):	885 3rd Avenue
	New York, NY 10022
	233 South Wacker Drive
	Chicago, IL 60606
	San Diego
	Washington, D.C.
	San Francisco
	Orange County
	London

NAME:	Levine & Eisenberg
ADDRESS:	1900 Avenue of the Stars, Suite 1440 Los Angeles, CA 90067
TELEPHONE:	213-551-0010
FAX:	213-551-3059
NUMBER OF LAWYERS IN BANKRUPTCY WORK:	19
NUMBER OF YEARS IN THIS SPECIALIZATION:	18
INDUSTRIES SPECIALIZED IN:	Entertainment Real estate All others
MINIMUM CLIENT SIZE:	$1 million
MAXIMUM CLIENT SIZE:	No maximum
PERCENTAGE DEBTOR ADVOCACY:	100%
CLIENT REFERENCES:	DeLaurentis Entertainment Group Triad America Aca Joe, Inc.
LENGTH OF TYPICAL ASSIGNMENT:	18 months
CONTACT PERSON(S):	Joseph A. Eisenberg
BRANCH OFFICE(S):	None

NAME:	Lewis & Brooks
ADDRESS:	505 Hamilton Avenue, Suite 300
	Palo Alto, CA 94301
TELEPHONE:	415-327-8785
FAX:	415-326-5343
NUMBER OF LAWYERS IN BANKRUPTCY WORK:	2
NUMBER OF YEARS IN THIS SPECIALIZATION:	14
INDUSTRIES SPECIALIZED IN:	Computers
	Software
	Real estate
MINIMUM CLIENT SIZE:	$1 million
MAXIMUM CLIENT SIZE:	No maximum
PERCENTAGE DEBTOR ADVOCACY:	90%
CLIENT REFERENCES:	Margaux, Inc.
	Aurora Systems, Inc.
LENGTH OF TYPICAL ASSIGNMENT:	6 months
CONTACT PERSON(S):	Lincoln A. Brooks
	William C. Lewis
BRANCH OFFICE(S):	None

NAME:	Lewis, Ciccarello & Friedberg
ADDRESS:	P.O. Box 1746
	One Valley Square, Suite 700
	Charleston, WV 25301
	(or 25326 for Box)
TELEPHONE:	304-345-2000
FAX:	304-343-7999
NUMBER OF LAWYERS IN BANKRUPTCY WORK:	3
NUMBER OF YEARS IN THIS SPECIALIZATION:	20; 12; 10
INDUSTRIES SPECIALIZED IN:	All
MINIMUM CLIENT SIZE:	None
MAXIMUM CLIENT SIZE:	None
PERCENTAGE DEBTOR ADVOCACY:	60%
CLIENT REFERENCES:	NR
LENGTH OF TYPICAL ASSIGNMENT:	18 months
CONTACT PERSON(S):	Paul M. Friedberg
	John A. Rollins
	Frances W. McCoy
BRANCH OFFICE(S):	None

NAME:	Lindquist & Vennum
ADDRESS:	4200 IDS Center
	80 South 8th Street
	Minneapolis, MN 55402
TELEPHONE:	612-371-3211
FAX:	612-371-3207
NUMBER OF LAWYERS IN BANKRUPTCY WORK:	7
NUMBER OF YEARS IN THIS SPECIALIZATION:	35
INDUSTRIES SPECIALIZED IN:	Manufacturing
	Advertising
	Direct mail marketing
	Trucking
	Entertainment
	Retail
MINIMUM CLIENT SIZE:	No minimum
MAXIMUM CLIENT SIZE:	No maximum
PERCENTAGE DEBTOR ADVOCACY:	60%
CLIENT REFERENCES:	Arctic Enterprises, Inc.
	a/k/a Minstar, Inc.
	Minneapolis, MN
	K-tel International, Inc.
	Minneapolis, MN
	Brown & Bigelow
	St. Paul, MN
LENGTH OF TYPICAL ASSIGNMENT:	6 months to 2 years
CONTACT PERSON(S):	Rosanne H. Wirth
	Melvin I. Orenstein
	Donald C. Swenson
	John J. Connelly
	Mark R. Johnson
	Robert B. Raschke
	James A. Lodoen

BRANCH OFFICE(S):   West Suburban Office
740 East Lake Street
Wayzata, MN 55391

NAME:	Little, Metzger & Lamz (PLC)
ADDRESS:	3421 North Causeway Boulevard, Suite 700
	Metairie, LA 70002
TELEPHONE:	504-831-2447
FAX:	504-834-7089
NUMBER OF LAWYERS IN BANKRUPTCY WORK:	1
NUMBER OF YEARS IN THIS SPECIALIZATION:	10
INDUSTRIES SPECIALIZED IN:	Construction
MINIMUM CLIENT SIZE:	$1 million
MAXIMUM CLIENT SIZE:	$45 million
PERCENTAGE DEBTOR ADVOCACY:	50%
CLIENT REFERENCES:	NR
LENGTH OF TYPICAL ASSIGNMENT:	2 years
CONTACT PERSON(S):	Gerard G. Metzger
BRANCH OFFICE(S):	None

NAME:	Lobel, Winthrop & Broker
ADDRESS:	19800 MacArthur Blvd., Suite 1100 Irvine, CA 92715
TELEPHONE:	714-476-7400
FAX:	714-476-7444
NUMBER OF LAWYERS IN BANKRUPTCY WORK:	11
NUMBER OF YEARS IN THIS SPECIALIZATION:	20
INDUSTRIES SPECIALIZED IN:	Banking and finance Engineering Computer related Defense contractors Energy Food processing Health care Clothing Real estate
MINIMUM CLIENT SIZE:	$5 million
MAXIMUM CLIENT SIZE:	$100 million
PERCENTAGE DEBTOR ADVOCACY:	80%
CLIENT REFERENCES:	Mavi & Sons McComb Realty Partners Chem-Tech Industries, Inc. Simi Corp. Canyon Lake Property Owners Association
LENGTH OF TYPICAL ASSIGNMENT:	18 months
CONTACT PERSON(S):	William N. Lobel Marc J. Winthrop Jeffrey W. Broker Todd C. Ringstad Robert E. Opera Rebecca Callahan
BRANCH OFFICE(S):	None

NAME:	Long, Tuminello, Besso, Seligman & Quinlan
ADDRESS:	120 Fourth Avenue Bay Shore, NY 11706
TELEPHONE:	516-666-2500
FAX:	516-666-8401
NUMBER OF LAWYERS IN BANKRUPTCY WORK:	2
NUMBER OF YEARS IN THIS SPECIALIZATION:	15
INDUSTRIES SPECIALIZED IN:	Retail Manufacturing Service
MINIMUM CLIENT SIZE:	No minimum
MAXIMUM CLIENT SIZE:	$300,000
PERCENTAGE DEBTOR ADVOCACY:	50%
CLIENT REFERENCES:	NR
LENGTH OF TYPICAL ASSIGNMENT:	18 months to confirmation
CONTACT PERSON(S):	Harold Seligman John Nelson
BRANCH OFFICE(S):	None

NAME:	Mallery, Stern & Halperin
ADDRESS:	11845 W. Olympic Blvd., Suite 1090
	Los Angeles, CA 90064
TELEPHONE:	213-473-5400
FAX:	213-477-1312
NUMBER OF LAWYERS IN BANKRUPTCY WORK:	6
NUMBER OF YEARS IN THIS SPECIALIZATION:	10
INDUSTRIES SPECIALIZED IN:	All
MINIMUM CLIENT SIZE:	$500,000
MAXIMUM CLIENT SIZE:	$5 million and up
PERCENTAGE DEBTOR ADVOCACY:	40%
CLIENT REFERENCE:	Chung Hwa Bank Taipei, Taiwan
	American Intermediaries, Inc.
LENGTH OF TYPICAL ASSIGNMENT:	3 to 9 months
CONTACT PERSON(S):	Ivan W. Halperin
BRANCH OFFICE(S):	Glendale, CA

NAME:	Manier, Herod, Hollabaugh & Smith
ADDRESS:	2200 One Nashville Place 150 Fourth Avenue North Nashville, TN 37219
TELEPHONE:	615-244-0030
FAX:	615-242-4203
NUMBER OF LAWYERS IN BANKRUPTCY WORK:	2
NUMBER OF YEARS IN THIS SPECIALIZATION:	15
INDUSTRIES SPECIALIZED IN:	Real estate Agriculture Music industry and entertainment General Chapter 11 practice
MINIMUM CLIENT SIZE:	No minimum
MAXIMUM CLIENT SIZE:	No maximum
PERCENTAGE DEBTOR ADVOCACY:	50%
CLIENT REFERENCES:	Nashville Symphony Association Midtown Plaza, Ltd. Nashville Union Stockyards, Inc.
LENGTH OF TYPICAL ASSIGNMENT:	6 to 9 months
CONTACT PERSON(S):	C. Kinian Cosner, Jr. B. Gail Reese
BRANCH OFFICE(S):	None

NAME:	H. Gayle Marshall (PLC)
ADDRESS:	910 Ford Street
	Lake Charles, LA 70601
TELEPHONE:	318-433-1414
FAX:	318-433-1414 (Ext. 13)
NUMBER OF LAWYERS IN BANKRUPTCY WORK:	1
NUMBER OF YEARS IN THIS SPECIALIZATION:	18
INDUSTRIES SPECIALIZED IN:	Diversified
MINIMUM CLIENT SIZE:	No minimum
MAXIMUM CLIENT SIZE:	No maximum
PERCENTAGE DEBTOR ADVOCACY:	50%
CLIENT REFERENCES:	NR
LENGTH OF TYPICAL ASSIGNMENT:	1 year
CONTACT PERSON(S):	H. Gayle Marshall
BRANCH OFFICE(S):	None

NAME:	Brett W. Martin, Esq.
ADDRESS:	2014 Lamar Street
	Edgewater, CO 80214
TELEPHONE:	303-237-4109
FAX:	Call first
NUMBER OF LAWYERS	
IN BANKRUPTCY WORK:	1
NUMBER OF YEARS	
IN THIS SPECIALIZATION:	8
INDUSTRIES	
SPECIALIZED IN:	Dairy farms
MINIMUM CLIENT SIZE:	$500,000
MAXIMUM CLIENT SIZE:	$10 million
PERCENTAGE DEBTOR	
ADVOCACY:	50%
CLIENT REFERENCES:	NR
LENGTH OF TYPICAL	
ASSIGNMENT:	18 months
CONTACT PERSON(S):	Brett W. Martin
BRANCH OFFICE(S):	None

NAME:	McCarthy & Burke
ADDRESS:	1220 19th Street, N.W.
	Washington, DC 20036
TELEPHONE:	202-775-0999
FAX:	202-659-3742
NUMBER OF LAWYERS IN BANKRUPTCY WORK:	1
NUMBER OF YEARS IN THIS SPECIALIZATION:	15
INDUSTRIES SPECIALIZED IN:	Construction
	Government contractors
	Real estate
MINIMUM CLIENT SIZE:	$300,000
MAXIMUM CLIENT SIZE:	$70 million
PERCENTAGE DEBTOR ADVOCACY:	70%
CLIENT REFERENCES:	Confidential
LENGTH OF TYPICAL ASSIGNMENT:	14 to 16 months; some shorter
CONTACT PERSON(S):	Philip J. McNutt
BRANCH OFFICE(S):	None

NAME:	McDowell, Rice and Smith
ADDRESS:	600 Security Bank
	Kansas City, KS 66101
TELEPHONE:	913-621-5400
FAX:	913-621-7238
NUMBER OF LAWYERS IN BANKRUPTCY WORK:	3
NUMBER OF YEARS IN THIS SPECIALIZATION:	24
INDUSTRIES SPECIALIZED IN:	Trucking
	Real estate
	Farming
MINIMUM CLIENT SIZE:	$200,000
MAXIMUM CLIENT SIZE:	$100 million
PERCENTAGE DEBTOR ADVOCACY:	50%
CLIENT REFERENCES:	Coleman American Moving Services
	Kroh Brothers, L.P.
	Cherry Creek Shopping Center
LENGTH OF TYPICAL ASSIGNMENT:	1 year
CONTACT PERSON(S):	R. Pete Smith
	Daniel J. Flanagan
	James S. Willis
BRANCH OFFICE(S):	120 W. 12th Street, 8th Floor
	Kansas City, MO 64105-1932
	816-221-5400
	FAX: 816-474-7304

NAME:	McGavic & Boyd, P.C.
ADDRESS:	P.O. Box 10163
	Eugene, OR 97440
TELEPHONE:	503-485-4555
FAX:	503-342-5309
NUMBER OF LAWYERS IN BANKRUPTCY WORK:	3
NUMBER OF YEARS IN THIS SPECIALIZATION:	37
INDUSTRIES SPECIALIZED IN:	Agriculture
	Logging & timber
MINIMUM CLIENT SIZE:	None
MAXIMUM CLIENT SIZE:	None
PERCENTAGE DEBTOR ADVOCACY:	50%
CLIENT REFERENCES:	NR
LENGTH OF TYPICAL ASSIGNMENT:	24 months
CONTACT PERSON(S):	Derrick E. McGavit
	Keith Y. Boyd
	Carolyn G. Wade
BRANCH OFFICE(S):	None

NAME:	McWhorter, Cobb and Johnson
ADDRESS:	1722 Broadway
	Lubbock, TX 78401
TELEPHONE:	806-762-0214
FAX:	806-762-8014
NUMBER OF LAWYERS	
IN BANKRUPTCY WORK:	6
NUMBER OF YEARS	
IN THIS SPECIALIZATION:	10
INDUSTRIES	
SPECIALIZED IN:	Agriculture
	Banking and finance
	Oil and gas
	Food services
	Manufacturing
	Marketing
	Real estate
MINIMUM CLIENT SIZE:	$1.5 million
MAXIMUM CLIENT SIZE:	$50 million
PERCENTAGE DEBTOR	
ADVOCACY:	70%

CLIENT REFERENCES:

Brunken Enterprises, Inc.
P.O. Box 64840
Lubbock, Texas 79464
CONTACT: Calvin C. Brunken

White Farms, Inc.
Box 355
Sutherland, Nebraska 69165
CONTACT: Darrel White

Bentley's Department Store
3118 Slaton Highway
Lubbock, Texas 79404
CONTACT: Tom Beck

Valley Rendering Company
P.O. Box 1849
Clovis, New Mexico 88101
CONTACT: Richard P. Jerome

Russell Farms
P.O. Box 180
Progreso, Texas 78597
CONTACT: Jesse R. Russell

Marble Brothers Partnership
P.O. Box 68
South Plains, Texas 79258
CONTACT: Don H. Marble

LENGTH OF TYPICAL ASSIGNMENT:

1 to 3 years

CONTACT PERSON(S):

David R. Langston
Max R. Tarbox
Joseph F. Postnikoff

BRANCH OFFICE(S):

3520 Executive Center Drive
Travis Building, Suite 165
Austin, Texas 78731

NAME:	Merrill, Stone & Parks
ADDRESS:	P.O. Box 129
	Swainsboro, GA 30401
TELEPHONE:	912-237-7029
FAX:	912-237-9211
NUMBER OF LAWYERS IN BANKRUPTCY WORK:	2
NUMBER OF YEARS IN THIS SPECIALIZATION:	20
INDUSTRIES SPECIALIZED IN:	Farming
	Agriculture related
	Retail
	Small manufacturing
MINIMUM CLIENT SIZE:	No minimum
MAXIMUM CLIENT SIZE:	$6 million
PERCENTAGE DEBTOR ADVOCACY:	60%
CLIENT REFERENCES:	Confidential
LENGTH OF TYPICAL ASSIGNMENT:	1 year
CONTACT PERSON(S):	Charles Brett Merrill
	Jesse C. Stone
BRANCH OFFICE(S):	None

NAME:	Meyer, Hendricks, Victor, Osborn & Maledon
ADDRESS:	2700 North 3rd Street, Suite 4000 Phoenix, AZ 85004
TELEPHONE:	602-263-8700
FAX:	602-266-6751
NUMBER OF LAWYERS IN BANKRUPTCY WORK:	3
NUMBER OF YEARS IN THIS SPECIALIZATION:	30
INDUSTRIES SPECIALIZED IN:	Resorts and real estate
MINIMUM CLIENT SIZE:	$50,000
MAXIMUM CLIENT SIZE:	$100 million
PERCENTAGE DEBTOR ADVOCACY:	30%
CLIENT REFERENCES:	NR
LENGTH OF TYPICAL ASSIGNMENT:	12 months
CONTACT PERSON(S):	Jean K. FitzSimon C. Taylor Ashworth Charles G. Case
BRANCH OFFICE(S):	None

NAME:	Minter, Joseph and Thornhill
ADDRESS:	811 Barton Springs Road, Suite 800 Austin, TX 78704
TELEPHONE:	512-478-1075
FAX:	512-478-5838
NUMBER OF LAWYERS IN BANKRUPTCY WORK:	2
NUMBER OF YEARS IN THIS SPECIALIZATION:	8
INDUSTRIES SPECIALIZED IN:	Real estate Retail sales
MINIMUM CLIENT SIZE:	$100,000
MAXIMUM CLIENT SIZE:	$20 million
PERCENTAGE DEBTOR ADVOCACY:	80%
CLIENT REFERENCES:	Texas Tool and Fastener Wesley Schreiber Dickchut Construction
LENGTH OF TYPICAL ASSIGNMENT:	1 to 2 years
CONTACT PERSON(S):	William C. Davidson
BRANCH OFFICE(S):	None

NAME:	Murphy, Weir & Butler
ADDRESS:	101 California Street, Suite 3900 San Francico, CA 94111
TELEPHONE:	415-398-4700
FAX:	415-412-7879
NUMBER OF LAWYERS IN BANKRUPTCY WORK:	36
NUMBER OF YEARS IN THIS SPECIALIZATION:	16
INDUSTRIES SPECIALIZED IN:	All types of enterprises represented. Areas of recent large case activity include: Retailing Manufacturing Real estate Technology-based industries Financial services
MINIMUM CLIENT SIZE:	$5 million annual sales/investment
MAXIMUM CLIENT SIZE:	More than $1 billion
PERCENTAGE DEBTOR ADVOCACY:	33%

CLIENT REFERENCES: Equitec Financial Group, Inc.
                                      Oakland, CA

                                      Priam Corporation
                                      San Jose, CA

                                      Domain Technology, Inc.
                                      San Jose, CA

                                      Bell National Corporation
                                      San Francisco, CA

                                      U.S. Leisure, Inc.
                                      Incline Village, NV

                                      Williams & Burrows
                                      Belmont, CA

                                      Sunseed Genetics
                                      Hollister, CA

                                      Evans Products
                                      Miami, FL

**LENGTH OF TYPICAL
ASSIGNMENT:**   Length varies
CONTACT PERSON(S):   Patrick A. Murphy
                                      Penn Ayers Butler
                                      Andrea T. Porter

NAME:	Mushkin & Associates
ADDRESS:	930 South Third Street, #300
	Las Vegas, NV 89101
TELEPHONE:	702-386-3999
FAX:	702-388-0617
NUMBER OF LAWYERS	
IN BANKRUPTCY WORK:	2
NUMBER OF YEARS	
IN THIS SPECIALIZATION:	7
INDUSTRIES	
SPECIALIZED IN:	Construction
	Retail
MINIMUM CLIENT SIZE:	N.A.
MAXIMUM CLIENT SIZE:	N.A.
PERCENTAGE DEBTOR	
ADVOCACY:	75%
CLIENT REFERENCES:	
LENGTH OF TYPICAL	
ASSIGNMENT:	72 months, if plan of
	reorganization is confirmed
	and complied with
CONTACT PERSON(S):	Mark C. Hafer
BRANCH OFFICE(S):	None

NAME:	Robert M. Musselman & Associates
ADDRESS:	413 7th Street, N.E. Charlottesville, VA 22901
TELEPHONE:	804-977-4500
FAX:	804-973-2515
NUMBER OF LAWYERS IN BANKRUPTCY WORK:	5
NUMBER OF YEARS IN THIS SPECIALIZATION:	20
INDUSTRIES SPECIALIZED IN:	Restaurants Food services
MINIMUM CLIENT SIZE:	No minimum
MAXIMUM CLIENT SIZE:	$55 million
PERCENTAGE DEBTOR ADVOCACY:	80%
CLIENT REFERENCES:	Kings Supermarkets Finney Mortgage Co. Danville, VA Old Mill Apartments, Ltd. Lynchburg, VA
LENGTH OF TYPICAL ASSIGNMENT:	10 to 24 months
CONTACT PERSON(S):	Robert M. Musselman Douglas E. Little Gail S. Ogle Richard D. Shepherd Daniel G. Bloor
BRANCH OFFICE(S):	None

NAME:	Larry Neal, P.C.
ADDRESS:	800 North Devine Road
	Vancouver, WA 98661
TELEPHONE:	206-694-1286
FAX:	206-694-1748
NUMBER OF LAWYERS IN BANKRUPTCY WORK:	1
NUMBER OF YEARS IN THIS SPECIALIZATION:	8
INDUSTRIES SPECIALIZED IN:	Trucking
	Stock brokerage
MINIMUM CLIENT SIZE:	None
MAXIMUM CLIENT SIZE:	None
PERCENTAGE DEBTOR ADVOCACY:	50%
CLIENT REFERENCES:	NR
LENGTH OF TYPICAL ASSIGNMENT:	9 months
CONTACT PERSON(S):	Larry Neal
BRANCH OFFICE(S):	None

NAME:	Neeser and Darval Law Office
ADDRESS:	1101 South First Street
	Willmar, MN 56201
TELEPHONE:	612-235-1876
FAX:	612-235-1934
NUMBER OF LAWYERS IN BANKRUPTCY WORK:	2
NUMBER OF YEARS IN THIS SPECIALIZATION:	12
INDUSTRIES SPECIALIZED IN:	Agriculture
MINIMUM CLIENT SIZE:	$50,000
MAXIMUM CLIENT SIZE:	$2 million
PERCENTAGE DEBTOR ADVOCACY:	55%
CLIENT REFERENCES:	CJW Farms
	Renville, MN
LENGTH OF TYPICAL ASSIGNMENT:	8 to 10 months
CONTACT PERSON(S):	M. Barry Darval
	Dennis Neeser
BRANCH OFFICE(S):	None

NAME:	Neiman, Neiman, Stone & Spellman, P.C.
ADDRESS:	1119 High Street Des Moines, IA 50308-2674
TELEPHONE:	515-282-8846
FAX:	515-282-9247
NUMBER OF LAWYERS IN BANKRUPTCY WORK:	4
NUMBER OF YEARS IN THIS SPECIALIZATION:	137
INDUSTRIES SPECIALIZED IN:	Agriculture Banking and finance Construction Clothing Distribution Health care Manufacturing Retail Lodging
MINIMUM CLIENT SIZE:	No minimum
MAXIMUM CLIENT SIZE:	No maximum
PERCENTAGE DEBTOR ADVOCACY:	70%
CLIENT REFERENCES:	Requests reference checking with other law firms.
LENGTH OF TYPICAL ASSIGNMENT:	2 years
CONTACT PERSON(S):	John Neiman
BRANCH OFFICE(S):	9 offices

NAME:	Nichols, Cafrey, Hill, Evans & Murrelle
ADDRESS:	1400 Renaissance Plaza Greensboro, NC 27401
TELEPHONE:	919-379-1390
FAX:	919-379-1195
NUMBER OF LAWYERS IN BANKRUPTCY WORK:	3
NUMBER OF YEARS IN THIS SPECIALIZATION:	10
INDUSTRIES SPECIALIZED IN:	Banking and finance Construction Insurance Real estate Services Transportation
MINIMUM CLIENT SIZE:	$500,000
MAXIMUM CLIENT SIZE:	$5 million and above
PERCENTAGE DEBTOR ADVOCACY:	Uncertain
CLIENT REFERENCES:	Mason & Dixon Lines, Inc. Robert W. Patterson, MD, PA
LENGTH OF TYPICAL ASSIGNMENT:	NR
CONTACT PERSON(S):	William L. Stocks Everett B. Saslow, Jr.
BRANCH OFFICE(S):	None

NAME:	Harold Q. Noack, Jr., Attorney at Law
ADDRESS:	345 Bobwhite Court, Suite 110 P.O. Box 875 Boise, ID 83701
TELEPHONE:	208-336-2480
FAX:	208-336-6701
NUMBER OF LAWYERS IN BANKRUPTCY WORK:	1
NUMBER OF YEARS IN THIS SPECIALIZATION:	15
INDUSTRIES SPECIALIZED IN:	Farming Construction Recreational vehicle dealers Movie theaters
MINIMUM CLIENT SIZE:	No limit
MAXIMUM CLIENT SIZE:	No limit
PERCENTAGE DEBTOR ADVOCACY:	70%
CLIENT REFERENCES:	NR
LENGTH OF TYPICAL ASSIGNMENT:	24–36 months
CONTACT PERSON(S):	Harold Q. Noack, Jr.
BRANCH OFFICE(S):	None

NAME:	O'Connor, Cavanagh, Anderson, Westover, Killingsworth & Bashears
ADDRESS:	One South Church Avenue, Suite 2200 Tucson, AZ 85701
TELEPHONE:	602-628-4620
FAX:	602-624-9564
NUMBER OF LAWYERS IN BANKRUPTCY WORK:	1
NUMBER OF YEARS IN THIS SPECIALIZATION:	8
INDUSTRIES SPECIALIZED IN:	Single-asset real estate partnerships
MINIMUM CLIENT SIZE:	Asset values: $1 million
MAXIMUM CLIENT SIZE:	Asset values: $300 million
PERCENTAGE DEBTOR ADVOCACY:	75%
CLIENT REFERENCES:	NR
LENGTH OF TYPICAL ASSIGNMENT:	6–18 months
CONTACT PERSON(S):	Scott Gibson
BRANCH OFFICE(S):	Phoenix, AZ Sun City, AZ

NAME:	Oliver & Paxinos, P.C.
ADDRESS:	P.O. Box 20537
	Billings, MT 59104
TELEPHONE:	406-259-7795
FAX:	406-248-7875
NUMBER OF LAWYERS IN BANKRUPTCY WORK:	1
NUMBER OF YEARS IN THIS SPECIALIZATION:	6
INDUSTRIES SPECIALIZED IN:	Bar & restaurant chains
MINIMUM CLIENT SIZE:	$675,000
MAXIMUM CLIENT SIZE:	$5 million
PERCENTAGE DEBOT ADVOCACY:	70%
CLIENT REFERENCES:	NR
LENGTH OF TYPICAL ASSIGNMENT:	1 year
CONTACT PERSON(S):	Phillip R. Oliver
BRANCH OFFICE(S):	None

NAME:	Pachulski, Stang & Ziehl, P.C.
ADDRESS:	10100 Santa Monica Blvd., Suite 1100 Los Angeles, CA 90067
TELEPHONE:	213-277-6910
FAX:	213-201-0760
NUMBER OF LAWYERS IN BANKRUPTCY WORK:	7
NUMBER OF YEARS IN THIS SPECIALIZATION:	8
INDUSTRIES SPECIALIZED IN:	Entertainment Health care Real estate
MINIMUM CLIENT SIZE:	No minimum
MAXIMUM CLIENT SIZE:	No maximum
PERCENTAGE DEBTOR ADVOCACY:	60%
CLIENT REFERENCES:	NR
LENGTH OF TYPICAL ASSIGNMENT:	18 to 30 months
CONTACT PERSON(S):	Richard Pachulski James Stang Robert Orgel Ira Kharasch Thomsen Young Stanley Goldich Jeremy Richards
BRANCH OFFICE(S):	None

NAME:	Parnell, Crum & Anderson, P.A.
ADDRESS:	641 South Lawrence Street, P.O. Box 2189 Montgomery, AL 36102-2189
TELEPHONE:	205-832-4202
FAX:	205-832-4703
NUMBER OF LAWYERS IN BANKRUPTCY WORK:	2
NUMBER OF YEARS IN THIS SPECIALIZATION:	15
INDUSTRIES SPECIALIZED IN:	Manufacturing Interstate trucking Farming operations Retail sales
MINIMUM CLIENT SIZE:	$250,000
MAXIMUM CLIENT SIZE:	$15 million
PERCENTAGE DEBTOR ADVOCACY:	15%
CLIENT REFERENCES:	NR
LENGTH OF TYPICAL ASSIGNMENT:	10–15 months
CONTACT PERSON(S):	Charles N. Parnell III Judith C. D'Alessandro
BRANCH OFFICE(S):	None

NAME:	C. David Peebles
ADDRESS:	127 W. Berry Street
	Ft. Wayne, IN 46802
TELEPHONE:	219-426-0674
FAX:	219-424-4105
NUMBER OF LAWYERS IN BANKRUPTCY WORK:	1
NUMBER OF YEARS IN THIS SPECIALIZATION:	25+
INDUSTRIES SPECIALIZED IN:	Commercial real estate
	Agriculture
	Nursing Home
MINIMUM CLIENT SIZE:	$500,000
MAXIMUM CLIENT SIZE:	$4,500,000
PERCENTAGE DEBTOR ADVOCACY:	80%
CLIENT REFERENCES:	Confidential
LENGTH OF TYPICAL ASSIGNMENT:	$1\frac{1}{2}$ to 3 years
CONTACT PERSON(S):	C. David Peebles
BRANCH OFFICE(S):	None

NAME:	Perkins Coie
ADDRESS:	1201 Third Avenue, 40th Floor
	Seattle, WA 98101-3099
TELEPHONE:	206-583-8888
FAX:	206-583-8500
NUMBER OF LAWYERS IN BANKRUPTCY WORK:	15
NUMBER OF YEARS IN THIS SPECIALIZATION:	4
INDUSTRIES SPECIALIZED IN:	Diversified
MINIMUM CLIENT SIZE:	No minimum
MAXIMUM CLIENT SIZE:	No limit
PERCENTAGE DEBTOR ADVOCACY:	65%
CLIENT REFERENCES:	NR
LENGTH OF TYPICAL ASSIGNMENT:	Varies
CONTACT PERSON(S):	Kurt Becker
BRANCH OFFICE(S):	None

NAME:	Petillon & Davidoff
ADDRESS:	9841 Airport Boulevard, Suite 1500
	Los Angeles, CA 90045
TELEPHONE:	213-776-1684
FAX:	213-841-1358
NUMBER OF LAWYERS IN BANKRUPTCY WORK:	1
NUMBER OF YEARS IN THIS SPECIALIZATION:	8
INDUSTRIES SPECIALIZED IN:	Restaurants
	Real estate
	Manufacturing
MINIMUM CLIENT SIZE:	$1.5 million
MAXIMUM CLIENT SIZE:	$100 million
PERCENTAGE DEBTOR ADVOCACY:	70%
CLIENT REFERENCES:	NR
LENGTH OF TYPICAL ASSIGNMENT:	4 months to 2 years
CONTACT PERSON(S):	Brian L. Davidoff
BRANCH OFFICE(S):	None

NAME:	Law Offices of Brett L. Price
ADDRESS:	Suite 450
	5201 California Avenue
	Bakersfield, CA 93309
TELEPHONE:	805-323-3400
FAX:	805-323-3957
NUMBER OF LAWYERS IN BANKRUPTCY WORK:	1
NUMBER OF YEARS IN THIS SPECIALIZATION:	6
NDUSTRIES SPECIALIZED IN:	Oil and gas
	Farming
	Commercial and industrial real estate
MINIMUM CLIENT SIZE:	$100,000
MAXIMUM CLIENT SIZE:	$30 million
PERCENTAGE DEBTOR ADVOCACY:	40%
CLIENT REFERENCES:	Confidential
LENGTH OF TYPICAL ASSIGNMENT:	36 to 48 months
CONTACT PERSON(S):	Brett L. Price
BRANCH OFFICE(S):	None

NAME:	Prickett, Jones, Elliott, Kristol & Schnee
ADDRESS:	1310 King Street, P.O. Box 1328 Wilmington, DE 19899
TELEPHONE:	302-888-6500
FAX:	302-888-6549
NUMBER OF LAWYERS IN BANKRUPTCY WORK:	2
NUMBER OF YEARS IN THIS SPECIALIZATION:	13
INDUSTRIES SPECIALIZED IN:	Agriculture Financial institutions Construction Health care Home furnishings Insurance Manufacturing Marine products Retail Real estate Services
MINIMUM CLIENT SIZE:	Under $5 million
MAXIMUM CLIENT SIZE:	Above $50 million
PERCENTAGE DEBTOR ADVOCACY:	70%
CLIENT REFERENCES:	NR
LENGTH OF TYPICAL ASSIGNMENT:	18 to 36 months
CONTACT PERSON(S):	William L. Witham, Jr. Norman L. Pernick
BRANCH OFFICE(S):	26 The Green Dover, DE 19901
	217 W. State Street Kennett Square, PA 19348

NAME:	Michael Redden
ADDRESS:	4370 N.E. Halsey
	Portland, OR 97213
TELEPHONE:	503-284-5118
FAX:	same
NUMBER OF LAWYERS IN BANKRUPTCY WORK:	1
NUMBER OF YEARS IN THIS SPECIALIZATION:	7
INDUSTRIES SPECIALIZED IN:	Entertainment
	Food processing
	Marketing
	Primary emphasis on tax liens in bankruptcy
MINIMUM CLIENT SIZE:	$500,000
MAXIMUM CLIENT SIZE:	$5 million
PERCENTAGE DEBTOR ADVOCACY:	95%
CLIENT REFERENCES:	None available without clients' permission
LENGTH OF TYPICAL ASSIGNMENT:	9 months
CONTACT PERSON(S):	Michael Redden
BRANCH OFFICE(S):	None

NAME:	Richards, Spears, Kibbe & Orbe
ADDRESS:	140 Broadway
	New York, NY 10005
TELEPHONE:	212-514-9000
FAX:	212-514-9510
NUMBER OF LAWYERS IN BANKRUPTCY WORK:	2
NUMBER OF YEARS IN THIS SPECIALIZATION:	7
INDUSTRIES SPECIALIZED IN:	Securities/financial
	High-tech
MINIMUM CLIENT SIZE:	$10 million
MAXIMUM CLIENT SIZE:	$100 million
PERCENTAGE DEBTOR ADVOCACY:	60%
CLIENT REFERENCES:	NR
LENGTH OF TYPICAL ASSIGNMENT:	36 months
CONTACT PERSON(S):	Jonathan Kibbe
	Lee S. Richards
BRANCH OFFICE(S):	None

NAME:	Robertson, Williams, Ingram & Overbey
ADDRESS:	Andrew Johnson Plaza, 14th Floor
	Knoxville, TN 37902
TELEPHONE:	615-522-2717
FAX:	615-522-7929
NUMBER OF LAWYERS IN BANKRUPTCY WORK:	2
NUMBER OF YEARS IN THIS SPECIALIZATION:	9
INDUSTRIES SPECIALIZED IN:	Manufacturing
	Banking and finance
	Service
	Real estate
MINIMUM CLIENT SIZE:	$250,000
MAXIMUM CLIENT SIZE:	$9,500,000
PERCENTAGE DEBTOR ADVOCACY:	55%
CLIENT REFERENCES:	NR
LENGTH OF TYPICAL ASSIGNMENT:	6–8 months
CONTACT PERSON(S):	Thomas Lynn Tarpy
	Jeffrey A. Woods
BRANCH OFFICE(S):	None

NAME:	Robinson, Diamant, Brill & Klausner
ADDRESS:	1888 Century Park East, Suite 1500 Los Angeles, CA 90067
TELEPHONE:	213-277-7400
FAX:	213-277-7584
NUMBER OF LAWYERS IN BANKRUPTCY WORK:	7
NUMBER OF YEARS IN THIS SPECIALIZATION:	24
INDUSTRIES SPECIALIZED IN:	Manufacturing Real estate High technology Entertainment Construction
MINIMUM CLIENT SIZE:	No minimum
MAXIMUM CLIENT SIZE:	No maximum
PERCENTAGE DEBTOR ADVOCACY:	60%
CLIENT REFERENCES:	Tellus Industries, Inc. Continental Forge Chase Revel, Inc., dba *Entrepreneur* magazine
LENGTH OF TYPICAL ASSIGNMENT:	24 months
CONTACT PERSON(S):	Gilbert Robinson Martin J. Brill Edward M. Walkowitz Lawrence A. Diamant Gary G. Klausner Douglas Kappler Philip Gasteler
BRANCH OFFICE(S):	None

NAME:	Thomas J. Romans
ADDRESS:	27 Warren Street
	Hackensack, NJ 07601
TELEPHONE:	201-489-0027
FAX:	201-342-5120
NUMBER OF LAWYERS IN BANKRUPTCY WORK:	1
NUMBER OF YEARS IN THIS SPECIALIZATION:	10+
INDUSTRIES SPECIALIZED IN:	Diversified
MINIMUM CLIENT SIZE:	$250,000
MAXIMUM CLIENT SIZE:	$10 million
PERCENTAGE DEBTOR ADVOCACY:	80%
CLIENT REFERENCES:	NR
LENGTH OF TYPICAL ASSIGNMENT:	Varies
CONTACT PERSON(S):	Thomas J. Romans
BRANCH OFFICE(S):	None

NAME:	Sable, Makoroff & Libenson
ADDRESS:	7th Floor, Frick Building
	Pittsburgh, PA 15219
TELEPHONE:	412-471-4996
FAX:	412-281-2859
NUMBER OF LAWYERS IN BANKRUPTCY WORK:	2
NUMBER OF YEARS IN THIS SPECIALIZATION:	30
INDUSTRIES SPECIALIZED IN:	Representation includes all types of industries, with special emphasis in manufacturing and retail
MINIMUM CLIENT SIZE:	$500,000
MAXIMUM CLIENT SIZE:	Creditors and official committees in billion-dollar companies
PERCENTAGE DEBTOR ADVOCACY:	50%
CLIENT REFERENCES:	National Bank for Cooperatives
	Mid-State Bank
	Allegheny International, Committee of Unsecured Creditors
	Wheeling, Pittsburgh Steel— Creditors Committee
	IBJ Schroeder—Indenture Trustee of Sharon Steel Debt Issue
LENGTH OF TYPICAL ASSIGNMENT:	3 years
CONTACT PERSON(S):	Robert G. Sable, Esq.
	David W. Lampl, Esq.
BRANCH OFFICE(S):	N.A.

NAME:	Sacks, Tierney, Kasen & Kerrick, P.A.
ADDRESS:	Citibank Tower 3300 N. Central Ave., 20th Floor Phoenix, AZ 85012-2576
TELEPHONE:	602-279-4900
FAX:	602-279-2027
NUMBER OF LAWYERS IN BANKRUPTCY WORK:	5
NUMBER OF YEARS IN THIS SPECIALIZATION:	10
INDUSTRIES SPECIALIZED IN:	Real estate Hospitality Manufacturing Construction
MINIMUM CLIENT SIZE:	No minimum
MAXIMUM CLIENT SIZE:	No maximum
PERCENTAGE DEBTOR ADVOCACY:	40%
CLIENT REFERENCES:	NR
LENGTH OF TYPICAL ASSIGNMENT:	18 to 36 months
CONTACT PERSON(S):	Marcia J. Busching Peter W. Sorensen Paul G. Johnson Dale C. Schian Gordon E. Hunt
BRANCH OFFICE(S):	None

NAME:	Santen & Hughes
ADDRESS:	105 East Fourth Street, Suite 1825 Cincinnati, OH 45202
TELEPHONE:	513-721-4450
FAX:	513-721-7644
NUMBER OF LAWYERS IN BANKRUPTCY WORK:	1
NUMBER OF YEARS IN THIS SPECIALIZATION:	10
INDUSTRIES SPECIALIZED IN:	Numerous
MINIMUM CLIENT SIZE:	No limit
MAXIMUM CLIENT SIZE:	No limit
PERCENTAGE DEBTOR ADVOCACY:	50%
CLIENT REFERENCES:	NR
LENGTH OF TYPICAL ASSIGNMENT:	No typical case
CONTACT PERSON(S):	Charles M. Meyer, Esq.
BRANCH OFFICE(S):	None

NAME:	Schantz, Schatzman & Aaronson, P.A.
ADDRESS:	Southeast Financial Center, #3650
	Miami, FL 33131-2394
TELEPHONE:	305-371-3100
FAX:	305-371-2024
NUMBER OF LAWYERS IN BANKRUPTCY WORK:	4
NUMBER OF YEARS IN THIS SPECIALIZATION:	28
INDUSTRIES SPECIALIZED IN:	Manufacturing
	Retail
	Real estate
MINIMUM CLIENT SIZE:	No minimum
MAXIMUM CLIENT SIZE:	No maximum
PERCENTAGE DEBTOR ADVOCACY:	44%
CLIENT REFERENCES:	NR
LENGTH OF TYPICAL ASSIGNMENT:	6 months to 1 year
CONTACT PERSON(S):	Laurence M. Schantz
	Robert S. Schatzman
	Geoffrey S. Aaronson
	Marte V. Singerman
BRANCH OFFICE(S):	None

NAME:	Schwartz, Cooper, Kolb & Gaynor
ADDRESS:	Two First National Plaza Chicago, IL 60603
TELEPHONE:	312-726-0845
FAX:	312-726-0886
NUMBER OF LAWYERS IN BANKRUPTCY WORK:	6
NUMBER OF YEARS IN THIS SPECIALIZATION:	70
INDUSTRIES SPECIALIZED IN:	All
MINIMUM CLIENT SIZE:	No minimum
MAXIMUM CLIENT SIZE:	No maximum
PERCENTAGE DEBTOR ADVOCACY:	60%
CLIENT REFERENCES:	NR
LENGTH OF TYPICAL ASSIGNMENT:	Each situation is unique
CONTACT PERSON(S):	Malcolm M. Gaynor
BRANCH OFFICE(S):	None

NAME:	Seyfarth, Shaw, Fairweather & Geraldson
ADDRESS:	55 East Monroe Street, Suite 4200 Chicago, IL 60603
TELEPHONE:	312-346-8000
FAX:	312-269-8869
NUMBER OF LAWYERS IN BANKRUPTCY WORK:	4
NUMBER OF YEARS IN THIS SPECIALIZATION:	10–20
INDUSTRIES SPECIALIZED IN:	Railroad Defense and aerospace General manufacturing
MINIMUM CLIENT SIZE:	$2 million
MAXIMUM CLIENT SIZE:	$200 million
PERCENTAGE DEBTOR ADVOCACY:	33%
LENGTH OF TYPICAL ASSIGNMENT:	$1-1\frac{1}{2}$ years
CONTACT PERSON(S):	Theodore E. Cornell Cynthia G. Swiger Michael R. Levinson Gus A. Paloian
BRANCH OFFICE(S):	One Century Plaza, Suite 3000 Los Angeles, CA 90067-3067
	767 Third Avenue New York, 10017-2013
	815 Connecticut Avenue, NW Washington, DC 20006-4004
	101 California Street, Suite 2900 San Francisco, CA 94111-5853
	770 L Street, Suite 1150 Sacramento, CA 90814-3323
	Avenue Louise 500, Boite 8 1050 Brussels, Belgium

NAME:	Shefferly & Silverman
ADDRESS:	400 Galleria Officentre, Suite 413
	Southfield, MI 48034
TELEPHONE:	313-352-7650
FAX:	313-352-7656
NUMBER OF LAWYERS IN BANKRUPTCY WORK:	2
NUMBER OF YEARS IN THIS SPECIALIZATION:	12
INDUSTRIES SPECIALIZED IN:	Mortgage Banking
MINIMUM CLIENT SIZE:	$500,000
MAXIMUM CLIENT SIZE:	$120 million
PERCENTAGE DEBTOR ADVOCACY:	50%
CLIENT REFERENCES:	NR
LENGTH OF TYPICAL ASSIGNMENT:	1 year
CONTACT PERSON(S):	Phillip J. Shefferly, Partner
	Geoffrey L. Silverman, Partner
BRANCH OFFICE(S):	None

NAME:	Sheinfeld, Maley & Kay, P.C.
ADDRESS:	3700 First City Tower
	Houston, TX 77002
TELEPHONE:	713-658-8881
FAX:	713-658-9756
NUMBER OF LAWYERS IN BANKRUPTCY WORK:	12
NUMBER OF YEARS IN THIS SPECIALIZATION:	25
INDUSTRIES SPECIALIZED IN:	Airline
	Retail
	Manufacturing
	Communications
	Real estate
MINIMUM CLIENT SIZE:	No minimum
MAXIMUM CLIENT SIZE:	No limit
PERCENTAGE DEBTOR ADVOCACY:	70%
CLIENT REFERENCES:	NR
LENGTH OF TYPICAL ASSIGNMENT:	18 months to 2 years
CONTACT PERSON(S):	Myron M. Sheinfeld
	Henry J. Kaim
	John P. Melko
	T. Glover Roberts
	Barbara J. Houser
	Lenard M. Parkins
	Kyung S. Lee
	Joel P. Kay
	Robert A. DeWitt
	Patrick L. Hughes
	John F. Higgins
	Thomas S. Henderson
BRANCH OFFICE(S):	None

NAME:	Silver & Voit
ADDRESS:	4317-A Midmost Drive
	Mobile, AL 36609-5589
TELEPHONE:	205-343-0800
FAX:	205-343-0862
NUMBER OF LAWYERS IN BANKRUPTCY WORK:	5
NUMBER OF YEARS IN THIS SPECIALIZATION:	25
INDUSTRIES SPECIALIZED IN:	Agriculture
	Banking and finance
	Distribution
	Entertainment
	Health care
	Legal profession
	Manufacturing
	Transportation
	Timber and logging
MINIMUM CLIENT SIZE:	$500,000
MAXIMUM CLIENT SIZE:	$5 million and up
PERCENTAGE DEBTOR ADVOCACY:	40%
CLIENT REFERENCES:	Star Video, Inc.
	Fleet Direct Sales, Inc.
	East Bay Limited Partnership
LENGTH OF TYPICAL ASSIGNMENT:	8 to 14 months
CONTACT PERSON(S):	Irving Silver
	Lawrence B. Voit
BRANCH OFFICE(S):	None

NAME:	Marilyn Simon, Esqs.
ADDRESS:	200 Park Avenue South
	New York, NY 10003-1503
TELEPHONE:	212-529-4400
FAX:	212-529-4823
NUMBER OF LAWYERS IN BANKRUPTCY WORK:	2
NUMBER OF YEARS IN THIS SPECIALIZATION:	16
INDUSTRIES SPECIALIZED IN:	Textile
	Retail
	Manufacturing
	Construction
	Real estate
MINIMUM CLIENT SIZE:	$5 million
MAXIMUM CLIENT SIZE:	$100 million
PERCENTAGE DEBTOR ADVOCACY:	55%
CLIENT REFERENCES:	NR
LENGTH OF TYPICAL ASSIGNMENT:	12–18 months
CONTACT PERSON(S):	Marilyn Simon
	Ira Herman
BRANCH OFFICE(S):	None

NAME:	Skadden, Arps, Slate, Meegher & Flom
ADDRESS:	919 Third Avenue New York, NY 10022-9931
TELEPHONE:	212-735-2850
FAX:	212-735-2000
NUMBER OF LAWYERS IN BANKRUPTCY WORK:	4
NUMBER OF YEARS IN THIS SPECIALIZATION:	22
INDUSTRIES SPECIALIZED IN:	Retail Airlines Steel Real estate
MINIMUM CLIENT SIZE:	No minimum
MAXIMUM CLIENT SIZE:	No limit
PERCENTAGE DEBTOR ADVOCACY:	10%
CLIENT REFERENCES:	NR
LENGTH OF TYPICAL ASSIGNMENT:	1–2 years
CONTACT PERSON(S):	Michael L. Cook Alesia Ranney-Marinelli Kayalyn A. Marafloti John Wm. Butler, Jr.
BRANCH OFFICE(S):	Los Angeles Washington Boston Wilmington Chicago

NAME:	Smith, Carter, Rose, Finley & Hofmann
ADDRESS:	222 West Harris Avenue, P.O. Box 2540 San Angelo, TX 76902-2540
TELEPHONE:	915-653-6721
FAX:	915-653-9580
NUMBER OF LAWYERS IN BANKRUPTCY WORK:	3
NUMBER OF YEARS IN THIS SPECIALIZATION:	10
INDUSTRIES SPECIALIZED IN:	All, including farms and ranches in Chapter 12
MINIMUM CLIENT SIZE:	Less than $1,000,000
MAXIMUM CLIENT SIZE:	More than $10 million
PERCENTAGE DEBTOR ADVOCACY:	45%
CLIENT REFERENCES:	Willconstruct, Inc. Ozona, TX
	Parkway Apartments Brady, TX
	Gator Pump, Inc. Brownwood, TX
	James R. Duncan San Angelo, TX
	Hal E. Nolke Merzon, TX
LENGTH OF TYPICAL ASSIGNMENT:	1 to 2 years
CONTACT PERSON(S):	Barry W. Sheridan Samuel S. Allen Dana A. Ehrlich
BRANCH OFFICE(S):	None

NAME:	Stearns, Weaver, Miller
ADDRESS:	One Tampa City Center, 33rd Floor
	Tampa, FL 33602
TELEPHONE:	813-223-4800
FAX:	813-222-5089
NUMBER OF LAWYERS IN BANKRUPTCY WORK:	3
NUMBER OF YEARS IN THIS SPECIALIZATION:	15+
INDUSTRIES SPECIALIZED IN:	Airlines
	Shipping
	Hotels
	Real estate development
	Distribution
	Marine
MINIMUM CLIENT SIZE:	No minimum
MAXIMUM CLIENT SIZE:	No maximum
PERCENTAGE DEBTOR ADVOCACY:	70%
CLIENT REFERENCES:	Phoenix Ventures, Inc. a/k/a Air Florida
	1717 Main Street
	Dallas, TX 75201
	Murray Industries, Inc.
	702 Sarasota Quay
	Sarasota, FL
LENGTH OF TYPICAL ASSIGNMENT:	18 to 30 months
CONTACT PERSON(S):	John K. Olson
	Robert A. Mark
	Harold D. Moorefield
BRANCH OFFICE(S):	150 W. Flagler St.
	Miami, FL 33130

NAME:	Steffes & MacMurdo
ADDRESS:	10311 Jefferson Highway, A-2
	Baton Rouge, LA 70809
TELEPHONE:	504-291-5857
FAX:	504-291-1971
NUMBER OF LAWYERS IN BANKRUPTCY WORK:	5
NUMBER OF YEARS IN THIS SPECIALIZATION:	13
INDUSTRIES SPECIALIZED IN:	Real estate (developed & undeveloped)
	Construction
	Oil & gas related
MINIMUM CLIENT SIZE:	$200,000/Year
MAXIMUM CLIENT SIZE:	$20 million/Year
PERCENTAGE DEBTOR ADVOCACY:	34%
CLIENT REFERENCES:	NR
LENGTH OF TYPICAL ASSIGNMENT:	1 year
CONTACT PERSON(S):	William F. Steffes
BRANCH OFFICE(S):	None

NAME:	Steinhilben, Swanson, Marles, Curtis, Marone & Wolk
ADDRESS:	P.O. Box 617
	Oshkosh, WI 54902
TELEPHONE:	414-235-6690
FAX:	414-426-5530
NUMBER OF LAWYERS IN BANKRUPTCY WORK:	2
NUMBER OF YEARS IN THIS SPECIALIZATION:	Swanson 8; Wolk 6
INDUSTRIES SPECIALIZED IN:	Apartment complexes
	Shopping centers
	Tanneries
	Trucking
MINIMUM CLIENT SIZE:	$100,000
MAXIMUM CLIENT SIZE:	$2–5 million
PERCENTAGE DEBTOR ADVOCACY:	60%
CLIENT REFERENCES:	NR
LENGTH OF TYPICAL ASSIGNMENT:	1–2 years
CONTACT PERSON(S):	Paul G. Swanson
	Christine Wolk
BRANCH OFFICE(S):	None

NAME:	Stoel, Rives, Boley, Jones & Grey
ADDRESS:	900 SW Fifth Avenue, Suite 2300 Portland, OR 97204-1268
TELEPHONE:	503-224-3380
FAX:	503-220-2480
NUMBER OF LAWYERS **IN BANKRUPTCY WORK:**	5
NUMBER OF YEARS **IN THIS SPECIALIZATION:**	25
INDUSTRIES **SPECIALIZED IN:**	Agriculture Banking and finance Construction Computer-related Middle market Electronics Health care High-tech Lodging Retail Real estate Timber & logging Utilities
MINIMUM CLIENT SIZE:	$5 million
MAXIMUM CLIENT SIZE:	$50 million
PERCENTAGE DEBTOR **ADVOCACY:**	70%
CLIENT REFERENCES:	NR
LENGTH OF TYPICAL **ASSIGNMENT:**	9 months
CONTACT PERSON(S):	William M. McAllister Richard C. Josephson Peter L. Slinn Mark H. Peterman Bradford Anderson

BRANCH OFFICE(S):

One Union Square
600 University, 36th Floor
Seattle, WA 98101-3197
206-624-0900
Fax: 206-386-7500

Suite 202
2043 Woodland Pkwy
St. Louis, MO 63146
314-569-4300

Suite 725
Seafirst Financial Center
805 Broadway
Vancouver, WA 98660-3213
206-699-5900

NAME:	Stroock & Stroock & Lavan
ADDRESS:	Seven Hanover Square
	New York, NY 10004
TELEPHONE:	212-806-5400
FAX:	212-806-6006
NUMBER OF LAWYERS IN BANKRUPTCY WORK:	11
NUMBER OF YEARS IN THIS SPECIALIZATION:	Over 60 years
INDUSTRIES SPECIALIZED IN:	All sectors, including real estate, steel, manufacturing, retail, and financial services
MINIMUM CLIENT SIZE:	$10 million
MAXIMUM CLIENT SIZE:	No upper limit
PERCENTAGE DEBTOR ADVOCACY:	30%
CLIENT REFERENCES:	Southmark Corporation
	1601 LBJ Freeway,
	Suite 800
	Dallas, TX 75234
	Coleco Industries
	80 Darling Drive
	Avon, CT 06001
	Western Union
	One Lake Street
	Upper Saddle River, NJ 07458
LENGTH OF TYPICAL ASSIGNMENT:	1 to 2 years

CONTACT PERSON(S):   *New York*

Andrew DeNatale   (212) 806-5442
Daniel H. Golden   (212) 806-5423
Jack Gross   (212) 806-5444
Lawrence Handelsman   (212) 806-5426
Fred Hodara   (212) 806-5642
Robin Keller   (212) 806-5424
Lewis Kruger   (212) 806-5430
Mark Speiser   (212) 806-5437

Miami
Scott L. Baena   (305) 789-9320

Los Angeles
Ronald L. Leibow   (213) 556-5817
Thomas B. Walper   (213) 556-5813

BRANCH OFFICE(S):   2029 Century Park East,
                             Floors 16 and 18
                          Los Angeles, CA 90067

                          1150 Seventeenth St., N.W.,
                             Suite 600
                          Washington, DC 20036

NAME:	Stutman, Treister, & Glatt
ADDRESS:	3699 Wilshire Blvd.,
	Suite 900
	Los Angeles, CA 90010
TELEPHONE:	213-251-5100
FAX:	213-251-5288
NUMBER OF LAWYERS IN BANKRUPTCY WORK:	29
NUMBER OF YEARS IN THIS SPECIALIZATION:	40
INDUSTRIES SPECIALIZED IN:	Retailing
	Manufacturing
	Hospitality
	Telecommunications
	Real estate
	Banking and finance
	Others
MINIMUM CLIENT SIZE:	$10 million
MAXIMUM CLIENT SIZE:	$10 billion +
PERCENTAGE DEBTOR ADVOCACY:	75%

CLIENT REFERENCES:

workouts:
Mattel Inc.
Los Angeles

Tiger International
New York

Petro-Lewis, Inc.
Denver

Ideal Basic, Inc.
Denver

Chapter 11's:
Campeau Corp.
Cincinnati

The Wickes Companies
Los Angeles

Public Services Co, of
  New Hampshire
Manchester

**LENGTH OF TYPICAL
ASSIGNMENT:**   18 to 24 months

CONTACT PERSON(S):   Bruce M. Spector
Herman Glatt
Kenneth N. Klee
Jeffrey Krause

BRANCH OFFICE(S):   None

NAME:	Andrew D. Thomas
ADDRESS:	2906 First Ave.
	Evansville, IN 47710
TELEPHONE:	812-422-2222
FAX:	None
NUMBER OF LAWYERS IN BANKRUPTCY WORK:	1
NUMBER OF YEARS IN THIS SPECIALIZATION:	10
INDUSTRIES SPECIALIZED IN:	Agriculture
	Restaurants
MINIMUM CLIENT SIZE:	$150,000
MAXIMUM CLIENT SIZE:	$14 million
PERCENTAGE DEBTOR ADVOCACY:	50%
CLIENT REFERENCES:	Pride Enterprises, Inc.
	G & M Mechanical
	Erectors, Inc.
LENGTH OF TYPICAL ASSIGNMENT:	24 Months
CONTACT PERSON(S):	Andrew D. Thomas
BRANCH OFFICE(S):	None

NAME:	Thorne, Grodnik & Ransel
ADDRESS:	228 West High Street
	Elkhart, IN 46516
TELEPHONE:	219-294-7473
FAX:	219-294-5390
NUMBER OF LAWYERS	
IN BANKRUPTCY WORK:	6
NUMBER OF YEARS	
IN THIS SPECIALIZATION:	20
INDUSTRIES	
SPECIALIZED IN:	Mobile homes
	Recreational vehicles
	Health care
MINIMUM CLIENT SIZE:	NR
MAXIMUM CLIENT SIZE:	NR
PERCENTAGE DEBTOR	
ADVOCACY:	30%
CLIENT REFERENCES:	Leisuretime Products
LENGTH OF TYPICAL	
ASSIGNMENT:	18 months
CONTACT PERSON(S):	William A. Thorne
	J. Richard Ransel
	James R. Byron
	Glenn L. Duncan
	Steven L. Hostetler
	J. A. Whitmer
BRANCH OFFICE(S):	P.O. Box 1210
	Mishawaka, IN 46544

NAME:	H. Kenan Timberlake
ADDRESS:	106 South Side Square
	Huntsville, AL 35801
TELEPHONE:	205-539-3496
FAX:	None
NUMBER OF LAWYERS	
IN BANKRUPTCY WORK:	1
NUMBER OF YEARS	
IN THIS SPECIALIZATION:	20
INDUSTRIES	
SPECIALIZED IN:	Diversified
MINIMUM CLIENT SIZE:	No minimum
MAXIMUM CLIENT SIZE:	No limit
PERCENTAGE DEBTOR	
ADVOCACY:	30%
CLIENT REFERENCES:	NR
LENGTH OF TYPICAL	
ASSIGNMENT:	5 years
CONTACT PERSON(S):	H. Kenan Timberlake
BRANCH OFFICE(S):	None

NAME:	Tompkins and McMaster
ADDRESS:	The Palmetto Building,
	4th Floor
	Columbia, SC 29202
TELEPHONE:	803-799-4499
FAX:	803-252-2240
NUMBER OF LAWYERS	
IN BANKRUPTCY WORK:	1
NUMBER OF YEARS	
IN THIS SPECIALIZATION:	5
INDUSTRIES	
SPECIALIZED IN:	Diversified
MINIMUM CLIENT SIZE:	$100,000
MAXIMUM CLIENT SIZE:	$20 billion
PERCENTAGE DEBTOR	
ADVOCACY:	50%
CLIENT REFERENCES:	NR
LENGTH OF TYPICAL	
ASSIGNMENT:	NR
CONTACT PERSON(S):	B. Lindsay Crawford, III
BRANCH OFFICE(S):	None

NAME:	Towbin & Zazove, Ltd.
ADDRESS:	20 South Clark Street, Suite 2210 Chicago, IL 60603
TELEPHONE:	312-621-1900
FAX:	312-621-0839
NUMBER OF LAWYERS IN BANKRUPTCY WORK:	4
NUMBER OF YEARS IN THIS SPECIALIZATION:	10
INDUSTRIES SPECIALIZED IN:	Manufacturing Retail Printing Real estate Construction Hotel Health care Clothing service
MINIMUM CLIENT SIZE:	No minimum
MAXIMUM CLIENT SIZE:	No maximum
PERCENTAGE DEBTOR ADVOCACY:	65%
CLIENT REFERENCES:	FJW Industries, Inc. Chicago, IL Pelron Company Chicago, IL Unichem Company Chicago, IL
LENGTH OF TYPICAL ASSIGNMENT:	30 months
CONTACT PERSON(S):	Steven B. Towbin Daniel A. Zazove Stephen T. Bobo Michael J. Golde
BRANCH OFFICE(S):	None

NAME:	Watkins, Bates, Carey & McHugh
ADDRESS:	1200 National Bank Building
	Toledo, OH 43604-1157
TELEPHONE:	419-241-2100
FAX:	419-241-1960
NUMBER OF LAWYERS IN BANKRUPTCY WORK:	3
NUMBER OF YEARS IN THIS SPECIALIZATION:	11
INDUSTRIES SPECIALIZED IN:	Steel
	Real estate
MINIMUM CLIENT SIZE:	No minimum
MAXIMUM CLIENT SIZE:	No maximum
PERCENTAGE DEBTOR ADVOCACY:	80%
CLIENT REFERENCES:	Systems Associates, Inc.
	500 Lehman Avenue
	Bowling Green, OH 43402
	Ohio Citizens Bank
	405 Madison Ave.
	Toledo, OH 43603-1688
	Johnson Honda
	1605 N. Monroe St.
	Monroe, MI 48161
LENGTH OF TYPICAL ASSIGNMENT:	2 years
CONTACT PERSON(S):	John M. Carey
BRANCH OFFICE(S):	None

NAME:	Weil, Gotshal & Manges
ADDRESS:	767 Fifth Avenue
	New York, NY 10153
TELEPHONE:	212-310-8500
FAX:	212-310-8007
NUMBER OF LAWYERS IN BANKRUPTCY WORK:	13
NUMBER OF YEARS IN THIS SPECIALIZATION:	30
INDUSTRIES SPECIALIZED IN:	All industries
MINIMUM CLIENT SIZE:	No minimum
MAXIMUM CLIENT SIZE:	No limit
PERCENTAGE DEBTOR ADVOCACY:	65%
CLIENT REFERENCES:	NR
LENGTH OF TYPICAL ASSIGNMENT:	Large and complex, 2–4 years
CONTACT PERSON(S):	Harvey R. Miller
	Alan B. Miller
	Bruce R. Zirinsky
	Richard P. Krasnow
BRANCH OFFICE(S):	1615 L Street NW
	Washington, DC 20036
	901 Main Street
	Dallas, TX 75202
	700 Louisiana
	Houston, TX 77002
	701 Brickell Avenue
	Miami, FL 33131

NAME:	John Haas Weinstein, Ltd.
ADDRESS:	410 South Union Street, P.O. Box 8 Opelousas, LA 70570
TELEPHONE:	318-948-4700
FAX:	318-948-4172
NUMBER OF LAWYERS IN BANKRUPTCY WORK:	1
NUMBER OF YEARS IN THIS SPECIALIZATION:	15
INDUSTRIES SPECIALIZED IN:	Oil & gas Agricultural Aviation
MINIMUM CLIENT SIZE:	$1 million
MAXIMUM CLIENT SIZE:	No limit
PERCENTAGE DEBTOR ADVOCACY:	50%
CLIENT REFERENCES:	NR
LENGTH OF TYPICAL ASSIGNMENT:	12–18 months
CONTACT PERSON(S):	John Weinstein
BRANCH OFFICE(S):	Baton Rouge, LA

NAME:	Wendel, Rosen, Black, Dean & Levitan
ADDRESS:	1221 Broadway, 20th Floor Oakland, CA 94705
TELEPHONE:	415-834-6600
FAX:	415-834-1928
NUMBER OF LAWYERS IN BANKRUPTCY WORK:	1
NUMBER OF YEARS IN THIS SPECIALIZATION:	21
INDUSTRIES SPECIALIZED IN:	Diversified
MINIMUM CLIENT SIZE:	$500,000
MAXIMUM CLIENT SIZE:	$50 million
PERCENTAGE DEBTOR ADVOCACY:	60%
CLIENT REFERENCES:	NR
LENGTH OF TYPICAL ASSIGNMENT:	4 months to 5 years
CONTACT PERSON(S):	Michael D. Cooper
BRANCH OFFICE(S):	None

NAME:	Werner, Lindgren & Johnson
ADDRESS:	P.O. Box 305
	New London, WI 54961
TELEPHONE:	414-982-7200
FAX:	414-982-7215
NUMBER OF LAWYERS IN BANKRUPTCY WORK:	2
NUMBER OF YEARS IN THIS SPECIALIZATION:	Michael G. Trewin 5
	James S. Lindgren 15
INDUSTRIES SPECIALIZED IN:	Chapter 12 bankruptcy
MINIMUM CLIENT SIZE:	$1 million
MAXIMUM CLIENT SIZE:	$5 million
PERCENTAGE DEBTOR ADVOCACY:	80%
CLIENT REFERENCES:	NR
LENGTH OF TYPICAL ASSIGNMENT:	5 years
CONTACT PERSON(S):	Michael G. Trewin
	James S. Lindgren
BRANCH OFFICE(S):	None

NAME:	Gavin Wickwire, P.C.
ADDRESS:	8230 Boone Blvd.,
	Suite 400
	Vienna, VA 22182
TELEPHONE:	703-790-8750
FAX:	703-448-1767
NUMBER OF LAWYERS	
IN BANKRUPTCY WORK:	3
NUMBER OF YEARS	
IN THIS SPECIALIZATION:	20
INDUSTRIES	
SPECIALIZED IN:	Banking
	Construction
MINIMUM CLIENT SIZE:	NR
MAXIMUM CLIENT SIZE:	NR
PERCENTAGE DEBTOR	
ADVOCACY:	70%
CLIENT REFERENCES:	NR
LENGTH OF TYPICAL	
ASSIGNMENT:	6 months to 1 year
CONTACT PERSON(S):	Patrick J. Kierney
	Christopher L. Rogan
	Mary Ann Ingberg
	Stanley M. Salus
	(Washington, DC)
BRANCH OFFICE(S):	Two Lafayette Center,
	Suite 450
	1133 21st Street, N.W.
	Washington, DC 20036-3302
	National Guardian Life Bldg.,
	Suite 300
	2 East Gilman Street
	Madison, WI 53703-1683

NAME:	Wise & Cole, P.A.
ADDRESS:	151 Meeting Street, Suite 200
	Charleston, SC 29401
TELEPHONE:	803-577-7032
FAX:	803-722-4794
NUMBER OF LAWYERS IN BANKRUPTCY WORK:	3
NUMBER OF YEARS IN THIS SPECIALIZATION:	3–5
INDUSTRIES SPECIALIZED IN:	Real estate
	Business reorganizations
MINIMUM CLIENT SIZE:	$1 million
MAXIMUM CLIENT SIZE:	$15 million
PERCENTAGE DEBTOR ADVOCACY:	60%
CLIENT REFERENCES:	NR
LENGTH OF TYPICAL ASSIGNMENT:	18 months
CONTACT PERSON(S):	W. Andrew Gowder, Jr.
	Gregg Meyers
	Steven Steinert
BRANCH OFFICE(S):	None

NAME:	Wolf, Block, Schorr and Solis-Cohen
ADDRESS:	Twelfth Floor, Pack Building Philadelphia, PA 19102-2678
TELEPHONE:	215-977-2000
FAX:	215-977-2334
NUMBER OF LAWYERS IN BANKRUPTCY WORK:	12
NUMBER OF YEARS IN THIS SPECIALIZATION:	29
INDUSTRIES SPECIALIZED IN:	Retail Health care Toxic torts Manufacturing Food services
MINIMUM CLIENT SIZE:	$5 million
MAXIMUM CLIENT SIZE:	No maximum
PERCENTAGE DEBTOR ADVOCACY:	60%
CLIENT REFERENCES:	Miller & Rhoads, Inc. Coston, Inc. Puzco, Inc. Franklin Computer, Inc.
LENGTH OF TYPICAL ASSIGNMENT:	1 year
CONTACT PERSON(S):	Marvin Krasny
BRANCH OFFICE(S):	Great Valley, PA

NAME:	Wolfson & Shepard, Attorneys at Law
ADDRESS:	1 Capner Street Flemington, NJ 08822
TELEPHONE:	201-782-9333
FAX:	201-782-3818
NUMBER OF LAWYERS IN BANKRUPTCY WORK:	1
NUMBER OF YEARS IN THIS SPECIALIZATION:	14
INDUSTRIES SPECIALIZED IN:	Real estate development Banking—lending Publishing Manufacturing Trucking
MINIMUM CLIENT SIZE:	$200,000
MAXIMUM CLIENT SIZE:	$5 million
PERCENTAGE DEBTOR ADVOCACY:	50%
CLIENT REFERENCES:	NR
LENGTH OF TYPICAL ASSIGNMENT:	12–24 months
CONTACT PERSON(S):	William S. Wolfson, Esq.
BRANCH OFFICE(S):	3 Elm Street Morristown, NJ

NAME:	Law Offices of Walter F. Wood
ADDRESS:	450 West Paseo Redondo, Suite 204
	Tucson, AZ 85701
TELEPHONE:	602-884-9191
FAX:	602-791-9181
NUMBER OF LAWYERS IN BANKRUPTCY WORK:	1
NUMBER OF YEARS IN THIS SPECIALIZATION:	13
INDUSTRIES SPECIALIZED IN:	Diversified
MINIMUM CLIENT SIZE:	NR
MAXIMUM CLIENT SIZE:	NR
PERCENTAGE DEBTOR ADVOCACY:	80%
CLIENT REFERENCES:	NR
LENGTH OF TYPICAL ASSIGNMENT:	24–30 months
CONTACT PERSON(S):	Walter F. Wood
BRANCH OFFICE(S):	None

NAME:	Wright, Lindsett & Jennings
ADDRESS:	2200 Worthen Bank Bldg.
	Little Rock, AR 72201
TELEPHONE:	501-371-0808
FAX:	501-376-9442
NUMBER OF LAWYERS IN BANKRUPTCY WORK:	8
NUMBER OF YEARS IN THIS SPECIALIZATION:	20+
INDUSTRIES SPECIALIZED IN:	Farming
	Trucking
	Apartment complexes
	Motels and hotels
	Real estate development
MINIMUM CLIENT SIZE:	$500,000
MAXIMUM CLIENT SIZE:	$5 million +
PERCENTAGE DEBTOR ADVOCACY:	30%
CLIENT REFERENCES:	NR
LENGTH OF TYPICAL ASSIGNMENT:	12 to 24 months
CONTACT PERSON(S):	Isaac Scott, Jr.
	David M. Powell
	Charles T. Coleman
	J. William Spivey
	James Glover
BRANCH OFFICE(S):	None

NAME:	Wyman, Bantzer, Kuchel & Silbert
ADDRESS:	15th Floor Two Century Plaza 2049 Century Park East Los Angeles, CA 90067
NUMBER OF LAWYERS IN BANKRUPTCY WORK:	9
NUMBER OF YEARS IN THIS SPECIALIZATION:	15
INDUSTRIES SPECIALIZED IN:	Financial institutions Real estate Manufacturing Entertainment Hospitality
MINIMUM CLIENT SIZE:	No minimum
MAXIMUM CLIENT SIZE:	No maximum
CLIENT REFERENCES:	The Wickes Companies (Examiner) THC Financial Corp. (Trustee in Ch. 11) Manda Financial Corp. (Trustee in Ch. 11) American Continental Corp. Gibraltar Financial Corp.
LENGTH OF TYPICAL ASSIGNMENT:	6 months to 10 years
CONTACT PERSON(S):	James J. Feder
BRANCH OFFICE(S):	Washington, DC Irvine, CA

NAME:	Zeisler & Zeisler, P.C.
ADDRESS:	558 Clinton Ave.
	Bridgeport, CT 06605
TELEPHONE:	203-368-4234
FAX:	203-367-9678
NUMBER OF LAWYERS IN BANKRUPTCY WORK:	7
NUMBER OF YEARS IN THIS SPECIALIZATION:	25
INDUSTRIES SPECIALIZED IN:	All
MINIMUM CLIENT SIZE:	Less than $1 million
MAXIMUM CLIENT SIZE:	Unlimited
PERCENTAGE DEBTOR ADVOCACY:	70%
CLIENT REFERENCES:	E & F Construction Co.
	Bridgeport, CT
	Thatcher Glass Co.
	New York, NY
	Gateway Bank
	Norwalk, CT
	Hitchcock Chair Co.
	Riverton, CT
LENGTH OF TYPICAL ASSIGNMENT:	1 to 2 years
CONTACT PERSON(S):	Richard Zeisler
	James Verillo
	Craig Lifland
	James Berman
BRANCH OFFICE(S):	None

NAME:	Zuckerman, Spaeder, Goldstein, Taylor & Kolker
ADDRESS:	1201 Connecticut Avenue, NW Suite 600 Washington, DC 20036
TELEPHONE:	202-778-1800
FAX:	202-822-8106
NUMBER OF LAWYERS IN BANKRUPTCY WORK:	4
NUMBER OF YEARS IN THIS SPECIALIZATION:	20+
INDUSTRIES SPECIALIZED IN:	Real estate Printing companies Retail Construction Oil and gas Resort properties High-tech Automobile sales Broadcasting
MINIMUM CLIENT SIZE:	$1 million
MAXIMUM CLIENT SIZE:	$100 million +
PERCENTAGE DEBTOR ADVOCACY	80%
CLIENT REFERENCES:	Confidential
LENGTH OF TYPICAL ASSIGNMENT:	1 to 3 years
CONTACT PERSON(S):	Bruce Goldstein Nelson Craig Cohen Janet Melburger Judith Sturtz Karp
BRANCH OFFICE(S):	300 East Lombard Street Baltimore, MD 21202 201 South Biscayne Blvd., Suite 900 Miami, FL 33131